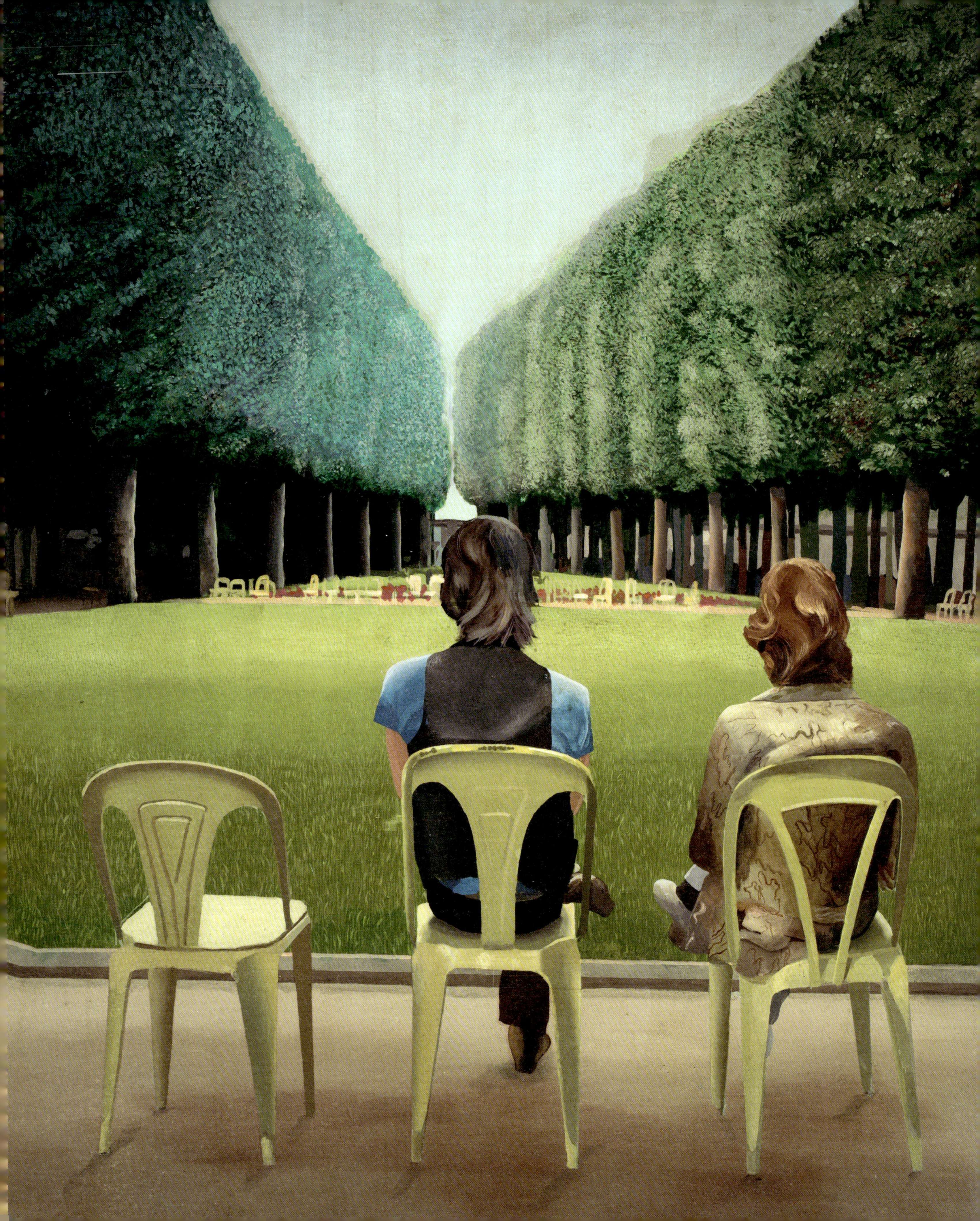

Edited by
Martin Gayford,
Martin Kemp
and Jane Munro

HOCKNEY'S EYE

THE ART AND TECHNOLOGY OF DEPICTION

THE FITZWILLIAM MUSEUM, UNIVERSITY OF CAMBRIDGE
AND THE HEONG GALLERY IN ASSOCIATION WITH
PAUL HOLBERTON PUBLISHING

First published in 2022 to accompany the exhibition

HOCKNEY'S EYE THE ART AND TECHNOLOGY OF DEPICTION

The Fitzwilliam Museum, Cambridge, 15 March – 29 August 2022
The Heong Gallery, Cambridge, 15 March – 29 August 2022
Teylers Museum, Haarlem, 24 September 2022 – 30 January 2023

ISBN 978 1 913645 12 0

British Library Cataloguing in Publication Data

A catalogue record for this book is available from the British Library

Produced by
Paul Holberton Publishing
89 Borough High Street
London SE1 1NL
paulholberton.com

Designed by Laura Parker

Printing by e-Graphic Srl, Verona

Front cover: fig. 11, detail
Frontispiece: fig. 22, detail
Back cover: fig. 49, detail

Note to reader

The figure numbers for exhibited works are followed by either **F**, for those at the Fitzwilliam Museum, or **H**, for those at the Heong Gallery.

CONTENTS

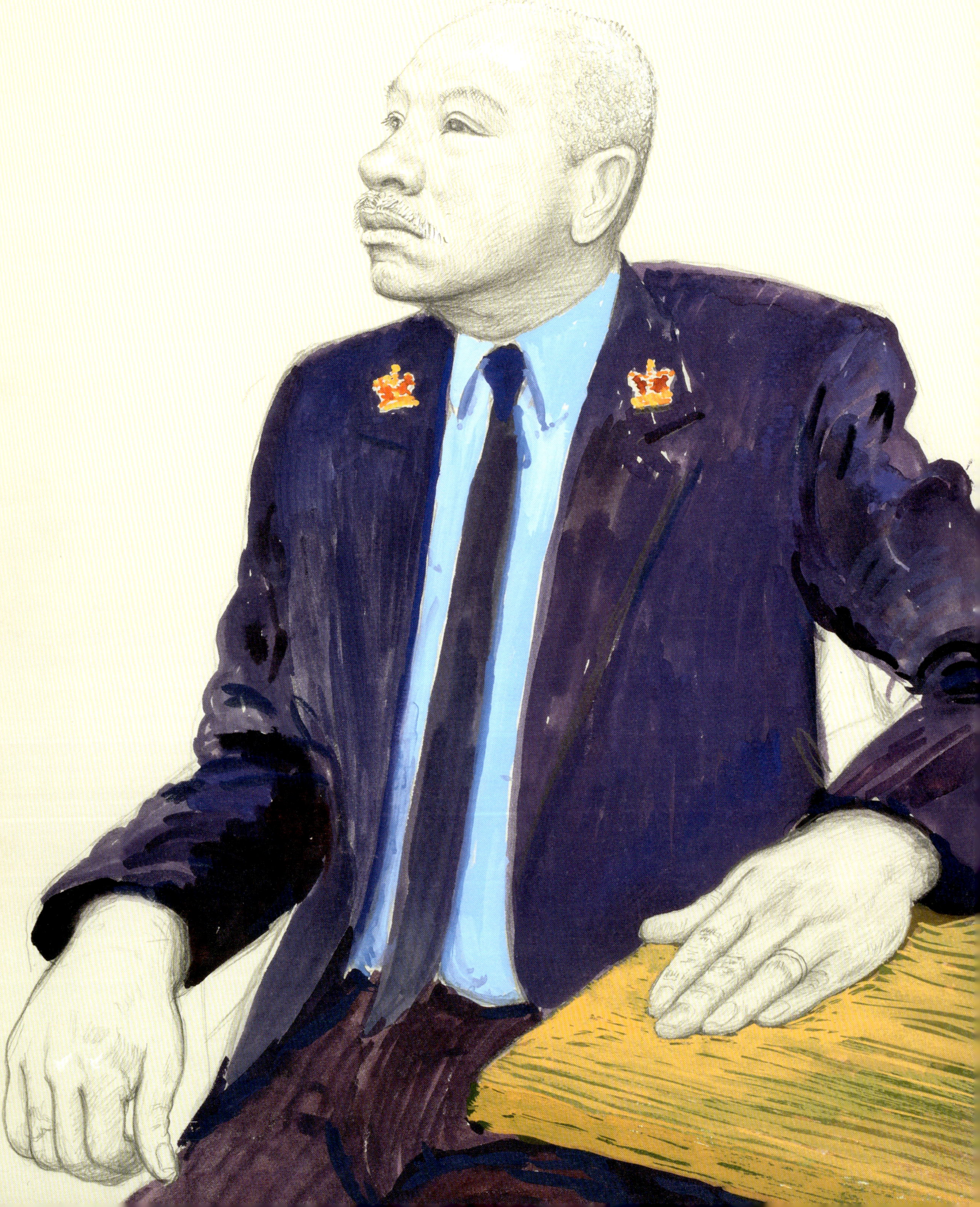

Foreword

David Hockney is perhaps the most intellectually restless of contemporary painters. In both his understanding of the art of the past and his use of cameras, digital drawing, the iPad, and digital film, he is exploring a tradition of creative experiment with optical devices that, he argues, predates Canaletto's use of the camera obscura or Ingres's camera lucida, going right back to the birth of Renaissance naturalism in the fifteenth century. *Hockney's Eye* ponders the ways the artist brings together hand, eye and optical instruments, experimentation that depends as much on his close looking at the some of the greatest painters in the Western tradition as on his embrace of new visual technologies.

By emulating and critiquing artists like Fra Angelico or Hobbema, and by experimenting with optical objects and digital know-how, Hockney's art has challenged the way we see the world. Relaxing the borders between the art, science and technology, Hockney can always be relied upon for a new perspective on the world around us, one based on the rewards of deep looking, by both artist and viewer.

One of the great virtues of a Cambridge College is the way it can bring together outstanding talents from different academic fields to share their different ways of seeing and understanding the world. Out of one such conversation at Downing, between Martin Kemp, distinguished art historian and Honorary Fellow, and Susan Lintott, Director of The Heong Gallery, came the idea of developing an exhibition focusing on Hockney's lifelong experiments in the pictorial ordering of space and, more broadly, his representations of the seen world. From this initial idea grew a partnership with The Fitzwilliam Museum, which brought on board Martin's co-curators, eminent writer and critic Martin Gayford and the Fitzwilliam's own Jane Munro. Their conversations with each other, and with David Hockney, have resulted in a joint exhibition, and publication, of which both institutions are very proud. We hope that this quality of open-ended discussion – a balance between art historical investigation of some of Hockney's key areas of interest and analysis of his own responsive experiments – is everywhere apparent. We are delighted that an edition of the exhibition will travel to the Teyler's Museum, Haarlem, one of the oldest museums in the Netherlands, founded in 1784 as a centre for contemporary art and science: there could be no more fitting venue for this ambitiously cross-disciplinary venture. We pay tribute to its brilliant and long-standing director, Marjan Scharloo.

We are hugely grateful to all three curators and to every member of our teams who have worked so tirelessly on this project. We have been overwhelmed by the generosity of both institutional and private lenders, and we should not fail to express our gratitude in particular to the David Hockney Foundation, David Thomson, the Ross Foundation, David Dawson and the Duke and Duchess of Devonshire. We are grateful too for the support of the exhibition's funders, in particular the Rothschild Foundation, the Heong Gallery 1717 Patrons and the Fitzwilliam Museum Development Trust and its benefactors. Above all, we would like to thank David Hockney himself. We could not have done this without him.

There was a time when the Cambridge Tripos policed disciplinary borders less rigorously than it does now (allowing, for example, Martin Kemp to switch from Natural Sciences to History of Art in the 1960s). This project demonstrates that the phenomena of seeing and experiencing are germane to both science and art. We hope more such easing of borders, in Cambridge and far beyond, will, quite soon, enable further cross-pollination of ideas and innovation to help us all look differently at the world we inhabit.

Alan Bookbinder, Master of Downing College
Luke Syson, Director and Marlay Curator, The Fitzwilliam Museum

Acknowledgements

This exciting collaborative venture would not have been possible without the generous support of our exhibition funders: The Fitzwilliam Museum Development Trust; Rothschild Foundation; The Heong Gallery 1717 Patrons; Alwyn Heong; Chris Bartram; Endurance Estates and MPM Properties; Lucy Gordon Ptashne and Mark Ptashne; Mark Green; Mervyn and Jill Parry; Simon Wood.

The Fitzwilliam Museum would also like to thank the following for their vital contribution to its exhibitions programme: University of Cambridge; Arts Council England; UKRI (UK Research and Innovation) through the HEMG (Higher Education Museums, Galleries and Collections) Fund.

This exhibition has been made possible as a result of the Government Indemnity Scheme. The Fitzwilliam Museum would like to thank HM Government for providing Government Indemnity and the Department for Digital, Culture, Media and Sport and Arts Council England for arranging the indemnity.

The curators, Fitzwilliam Museum and Downing College would like to record their profound gratitude to the private collectors, museums, libraries and foundations who have so generously lent to the exhibition: The Arts Council Collection, Southbank Centre, London; The Bodleian Libraries, University of Oxford; Chatsworth House Trust, Devonshire Collection; Estate of the late Mrs Elizabeth Corob and Boodle Hatfield LLP; David Dawson; David Hockney, Inc., Los Angeles; History of Science Museum, University of Oxford; David Hockney Foundation; The National Gallery, London; National Maritime Museum, Greenwich, London; Ross Foundation; Royal Collection Trust; Science Group Museum; Sotheby's; Tate; David Thomson; Victoria and Albert Museum, London; Whipple Museum of the History of Science, University of Cambridge; The Wordsworth Trust, Dove Cottage, Grasmere.

At Downing, Susan Lintott, Director of the Heong Gallery, and Prerona Prasad have been key to the project from its initiation, contributing invaluable ideas and support. They have made the collaboration an enormous pleasure. Susan and Prerona would like to thank The Heong Gallery Advisory Board, The Heong Gallery Management Committee, Rob Beardwell, Barry Everitt, Jo Finnie Jones, Mike Haddock, Catherine Middleton, and Martin Kemp for his advice and guidance and his support of The Heong Gallery.

Martin Kemp thanks Judith (Judd) Flogdell for her unstinting support.

Colleagues at the Fitzwilliam Museum have responded with enthusiasm and imagination to an exhibition which in effect amounts to a museum 'take-over'. Rebecca Virag has embraced with gusto the multi-faceted role of project curator with patience, efficiency and good humour. She, and we, have benefited throughout from Lynda Clark's expertise and fine eye for detail. Richard Carpenter, David Evans, Erica Emond, Karen Livingstone, Harry Metcalf and Ellie Saggers have steered the complex project to its impressive physical conclusion in the Fitzwilliam's galleries.

Warmest thanks also to: Claire Alfrey; Andrew Bowker; Kate Carreno; Edward Cheese; Jo Dillon; Len Dunne; Ian Hardwick; Liz Irvine; Michael Jones; John Lancaster; Nyl Fall; Richard Farleigh; Tracy Harding; Jane Ison; Olivia Lewis; Ruth Mcphee; Kate Noble; Daniel Pett; Suzanne Reynolds; Emma Shaw; Neal Spencer; Miranda Stearn; Victoria Sutcliffe; Kerry Wallis; Philip Wheeler.

As ever, Luke Syson's insights have been invaluable in shaping the project.

We have benefited from the advice and guidance of many individuals. Particular thanks to: Silke Ackermann; Maria Balshaw; Albany Bell; Lucy Blaxland; Helen Copping; Jeff Cowton; Richard Dark; Edith Devaney; Tom Eddison; Kevin Fewster; Gabriele Finaldi; Jenny Foot; David Franklin; Ciara Gallagher; Jean-Pierre Gonçalves de Lima; Peter Goulds; Julie Green; Felix Hale; Joanne Hoareau; Melanie Howard; Tristram Hunt; Shannan Kelly; Tim Knox; Steven Kruse; Nadine Loach; Josh Nall; Richard Ovenden; Steph Parmee; Wendy Phillips; Lizzie Powell; Lauren Porter; Jo Quinton-Tulloch; Philip Steadman; Liba Taub; Molly Tillett; Rebecca Turner; Sara van der Linde; Terry van Druten; Jonathan Wilkinson; Liz Wilkinson; Tony Willett.

We are grateful to Holmes Studio for an exhibition design as thoughtful as it is joyous.

Paul Holberton, Laura Parker and the team at Paul Holberton Publishing have been agile and inspired collaborators in the production of this elegant book.

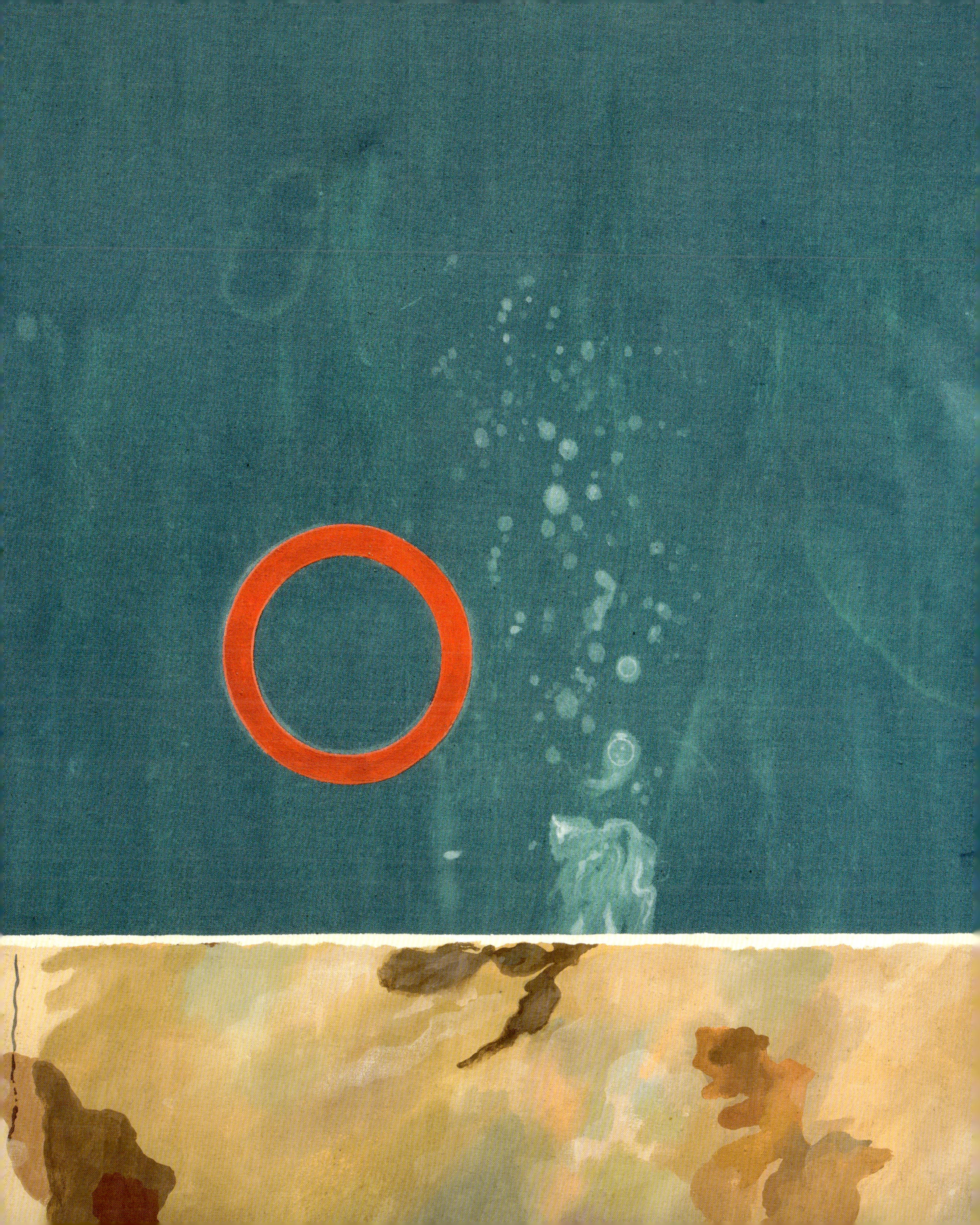

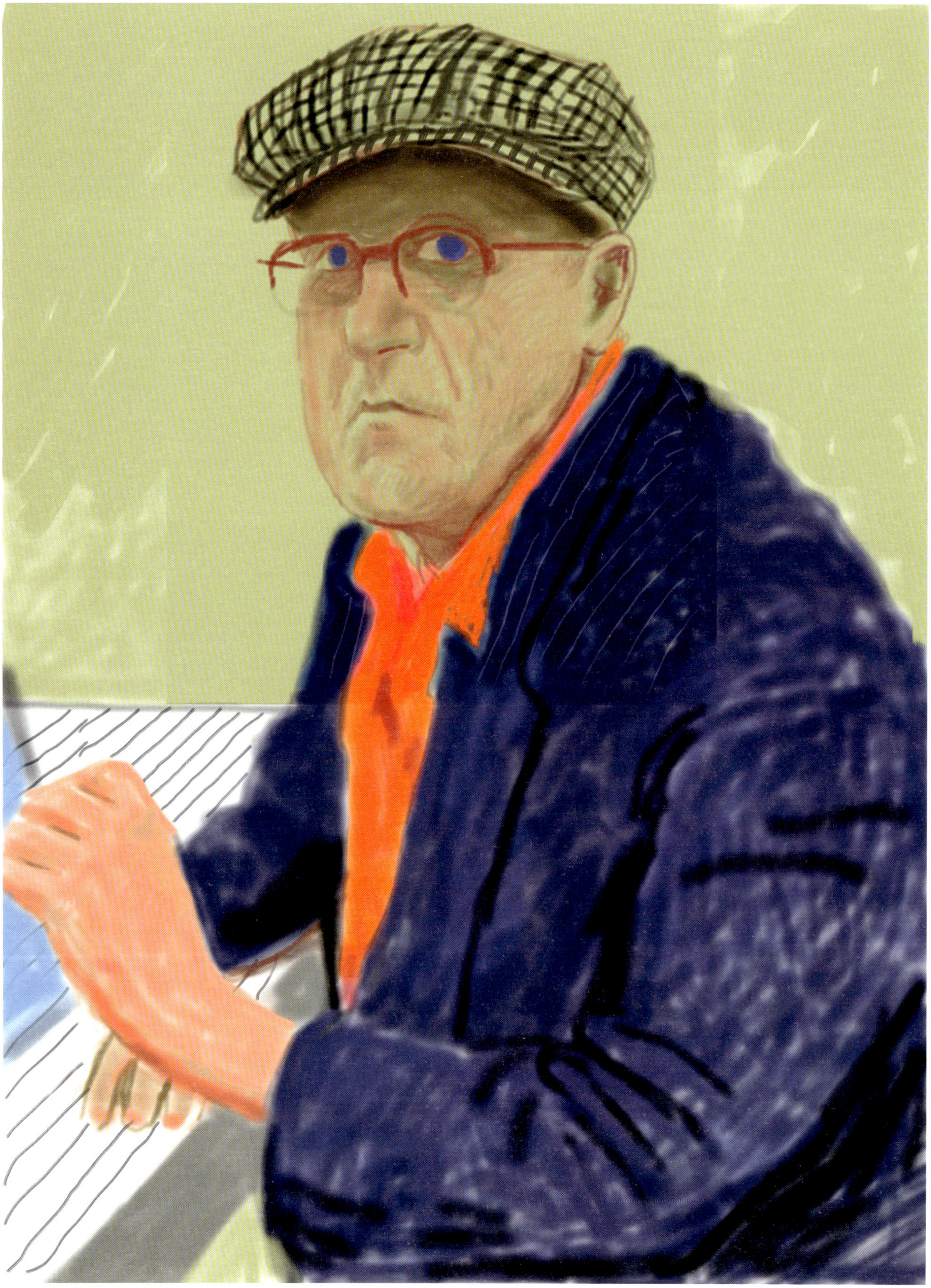

Martin Gayford, Martin Kemp and Jane Munro

Introduction: the 'Hockney thesis'

The immediate catalyst for the Cambridge exhibition *Hockney's Eye* and this accompanying book has been the presence of the Heong Gallery at Downing College, a radiant exhibition space created five years ago by the architects Caruso St John from a ramshackle outbuilding that once served as stables. The product of the catalysis has been an ever-expanding project with the Fitzwilliam Museum, with its world-class collection of paintings and drawings – appropriately enough given Hockney's avid consumption of pictorial art from all periods and places.

The more general catalyst is of course the art of Hockney himself. He has claim to be the best-known and best-loved painter in the world. A constant preoccupation over the course of his long career has been to explore how we see the world around us and how these acts of seeing can be expressed in painting and drawing, both now and throughout history. This investigation has involved radical questioning of the conventions of linear perspective and the related technology of photography. He has conducted a sustained dialogue between what he calls "eyeballing" – scrutinizing the seen thing with direct and unaided intensity – and more system-based and machine-made forms of representation. His most prominent entry into the public and historical debate came with his experimental exploration of two of the optical systems of imitation – the camera obscura and camera lucida – culminating in his now famous book, *Secret Knowledge* (2001), in which he aspired to re-cast the history of Western naturalistic art.

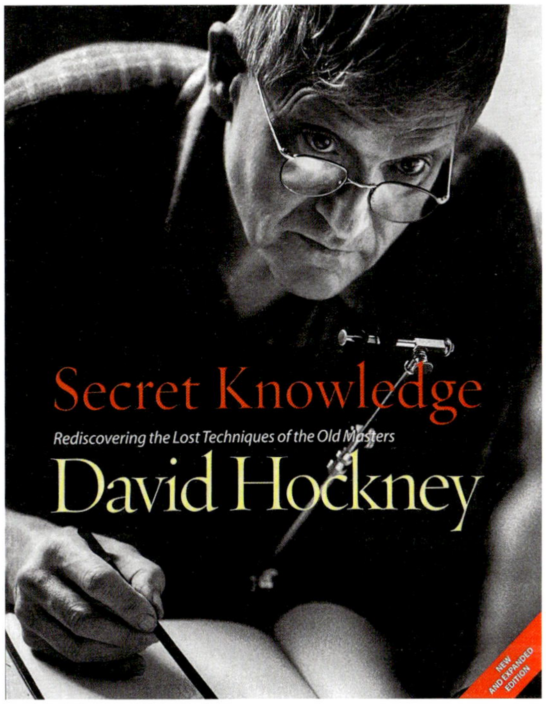

The scope of *Secret Knowledge* shapes our present agenda, which not only embraces artistic representations but also the actual optical devices to which artists have resorted in their ambition to capture the appearance of nature on two-dimensional surfaces. Hockney's claims that optical devices were used comprehensively by artists from the Renaissance onwards have proved to be highly controversial. He is in effect saying that we (and art historians in particular) have missed the procedure that lay behind half a millennium

1 | F David Hockney, *Self Portrait II, 14th March 2012*, iPad drawing. Collection of the artist

2 Front cover, David Hockney, *Secret Knowledge. Rediscovering the Lost Techniques of the Old Masters*, Thames & Hudson, London (2001), edn 2002

of naturalism in Western art. In this scheme, photography was not so much a new invention in the 1830s as a natural continuation of earlier instrumental imitation. Generally speaking, the public reception of what we may call the 'Hockney thesis' was more favourable than the reaction of the academic world. The public at large is more receptive to the idea that experts have missed the point than the experts are to entertain the idea that they might have done so.

Our present endeavour is not to prove or falsify the 'Hockney thesis' but to look at art that was almost certainly accomplished with the aid of optical devices, to examine Hockney's creative experiments with such devices and to his explore how his personal visions of space, light and colour stand in opposition to the 'photographic' image, with its one-eyed viewpoint and the fixed geometry of perspective. He is asking us, what is real? Does a virtuoso demonstration of perspectival illusion or a vivid photograph correspond to the way we really see? He protests that photography will never replace painting, "because it is not real enough". 'Real' in this sense does not refer to a precise optical match but to the experiential process of the painter devouring what his mobile eyes see, his expressing this experience by making marks on surfaces, followed by the willing reception of these marks by different viewers. Hockney prodigiously admires the masters of naturalistic illusion at the same time as saying they were wrong to think theirs was the only kind of visual truth.

We are not overtly taking sides in the noisy historical debate, but gathering together visual experiences addressed by the 'Hockney thesis', exploring how they enrich our own looking, just as they have nourished Hockney's own vibrant practice. Visitors and readers can reach their own conclusions.

The context of the exhibition in a great and diverse university sets the tone. Seeing, knowing and representing are vital issues across a wide variety of disciplines, ranging from philosophy to anatomy. Hockney's own procedures range from the ancient business of marking flat surfaces with coloured pigments to dynamic videos and computer vision. The challenges he proposes impinge on more sciences and technologies than we can directly include or even enumerate. The whole project is an open invitation to embark with him on his journey of creative looking, to ask questions and to play with ideas – rather than being presented with a fixed series of curatorial assertions.

The 'Hockney thesis' rests upon decades of experiments with technologies and strategies of depicting space in a way that is instantly recognizable, as art and as landscape, portraiture, still life, or whatever the subject matter. Throughout the diverse visual approaches and subjects, the personal voice of Hockney somehow continues to be immediately discernible. In the Heong Gallery exhibition we chart the artist's approaches to capturing space and visual reality from the 1960s to the present day, through representative works in multiple media, from drawing and painting to photographic collage and digital painting. In the Heong, we are presented with a compact conspectus of his sustained visual quests across the whole range of his long and prolific career. In conjunction with the comparative historical works in the Fitzwilliam, the development of the 'thesis' can be perceived through Hockney's own œuvre and though his incessant dialogue with admired predecessors.

At the Fitzwilliam, we explore Hockney's ideas in historical perspective, drawing substantially on the Museum's superlative collections. We juxtapose Hockney's own camera lucida portraits with landscape and portrait drawings made using newly invented optical aids. The users included a series of nineteenth-century artists of the distinction of Thomas Girtin, Paul Sandby and Cornelius Varley, as well as ruefully rank amateurs like the scientist Henry Talbot. They allow us to consider Hockney in the tradition of great artist-innovators who were eager to use new technologies to help them see, and depict, the world differently.

Then there is Ingres, the trigger for the 'Hockney thesis'. While Lucian Freud felt that looking at the French master's superb portrait drawings was like "gazing across a barrier at something unreachable",[1] Hockney sought to decrypt Ingres's technical brilliance by his own experiments. His extraordinary series of portraits of warders at the National Gallery, London is at once an interrogation of, and a direct homage, to Ingres; bringing their work in dialogue as we do here only highlights Hockney's own conclusion that no amount of technological intervention can replace artistic virtuosity.

Elsewhere, Hockney's work navigates and insinuates its way throughout the Fitzwilliam's picture galleries in telling interventions that invite us to think again about modes of seeing and representing. Bright-burning *Tygers* from the 1960s, inspired by the poetry of William Blake, meet playful 'Tygers' (leopards, actually), painted in 1776 by George Stubbs, animal painter *extraordinaire*. The unflinching directness of William Hogarth's portraits of his jowelly contemporaries finds echo in Hockney's own, unforgiving, series of iPad self-portraits (figs. 1, 3–10), as it does in a recent self-portrait from a group of works begun in late 2021 (fig. 11). Like other such sequences by Hockney, these are defined by technique and time. They are all executed quickly and broadly so the marks of the artist's brush are clearly visible. Hockney quotes a Chinese proverb – to paint three elements are required, 'the hand, the eye, and the heart. Two won't do.'

Another early work, *Shame*, allusively heightens the predicament of the desperate woman in Alfred Elmore's *On the Brink* (1865), as she stares woefully into space, about to lose something even more precious than her wager in the gambling room.

"Landscape," according to Hockney, is "a spatial thrill." But it is not one that relies on the rigours of Renaissance perspective, which for Hockney was formulated by architects (Brunelleschi and Alberti). Consequently, "its rules are all about buildings; you don't notice the perspective so much in trees and vegetation"[2] The natural world makes its own perspectival sense. In *Huggate, St Mary's Church Spire* space recedes over the rolling late summer fields into the distant horizon, punctuated by the church spire; billowing clouds recall the wide-open skies of seventeenth-century Dutch landscape and marine painters, but especially the airy skyscapes of John Constable, for whom the sky was famously "the chief organ of sentiment".

A potent influence on Hockney throughout his career, Monet's paintings act as a form of historic prism though which to understand Hockney's own. "Monet has made us see a bit more clearly," Hockney has said; his pictures "can make us see things that we might not notice without them."[3] With its crocheted canopy of white blossom, violet shadows and interwoven brushstrokes of reds, pinks and blues, Monet's *Springtime* conveys a vibrant truth about the flowering orchard at his home in Giverny that would be impossible in a more conventionally naturalistic palette. Perhaps taking his cue from Monet, the iPad paintings Hockney made of his own Normandy surroundings exploit the instantaneity of a different medium, the iPad app, to record springtime relentlessly unfolding: each artist creates a sense of freshness and renewal that we both see and feel.

The present book is not a record of the exhibition as such, although all the works in the two shows are illustrated, with the exception of some of the many iPad drawings and paintings. The essays present a series of riffs on his seeing and showing. His ever-questing temperament has never allowed him to settle into a repetitious rut, whatever the popularity and success of the mode he was favouring at the time.

After a broad-ranging review of the key issues, we explore the idiosyncrasies of standard linear perspective, which was handled by artists from the Renaissance onwards with greater freedom and awareness of its shortcomings than is often allowed. The natural and contrived motifs in the major loan of Meindert Hobbema's famed *Avenue*, depicted in plunging perspective, are set beside Hockney's radical re-envisioning of the spatial zones beside the road that leads to the Dutch town of Middelharnis.

Following his close scrutiny of portrait drawings by J.-A.-D. Ingres, Hockney's conclusion that the Neoclassical painter availed himself of the camera lucida guided the creation of his series of large drawn portraits of individual warders in the National Gallery. The kinds of optical device that Hockney exploited to such good effect are looked at

LEFT TO RIGHT

3 | F David Hockney, *Self Portrait, 9th March 2012*, iPad drawing. Collection of the artist

4 | F David Hockney, *Self Portrait, 10th March 2012*, iPad drawing. Collection of the artist

5 | F David Hockney, *Self Portrait I, 13th March 2012*, iPad drawing. Collection of the artist

6 | F David Hockney, *Self Portrait I, 16th March 2012*, iPad drawing. Collection of the artist

7 | F David Hockney, *Self Portrait III, 20th March 2012*, iPad drawing. Collection of the artist

8 | F David Hockney, *Self Portrait I, 25th March 2012*, iPad drawing. Collection of the artist

9 | F David Hockney, *Self Portrait IV, 25th March 2012*, iPad drawing. Collection of the artist

10 | F David Hockney, *Self Portrait, 19th April 2012*, iPad drawing. Collection of the artist

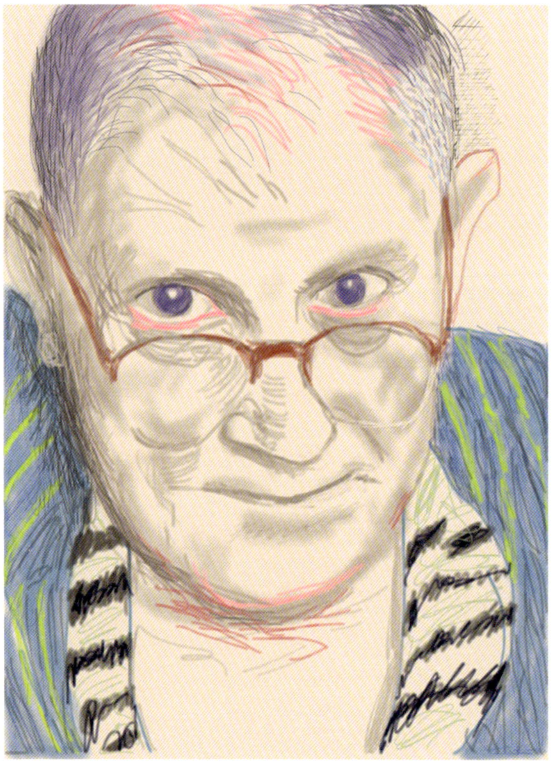

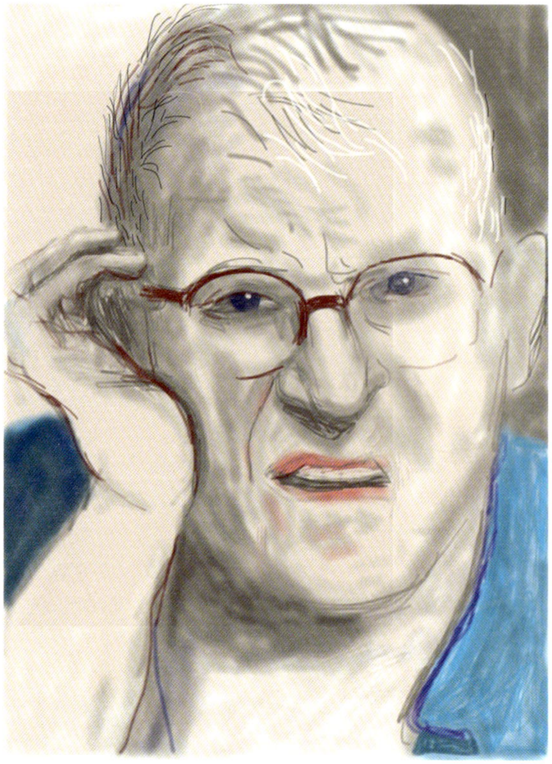

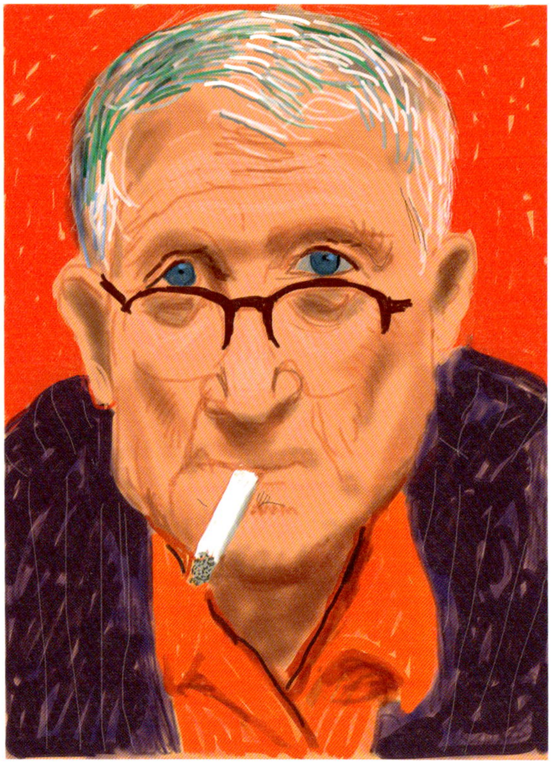

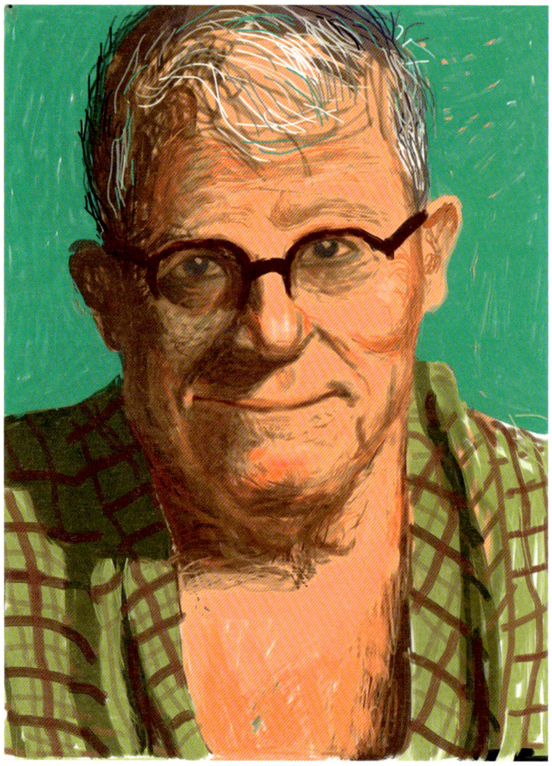

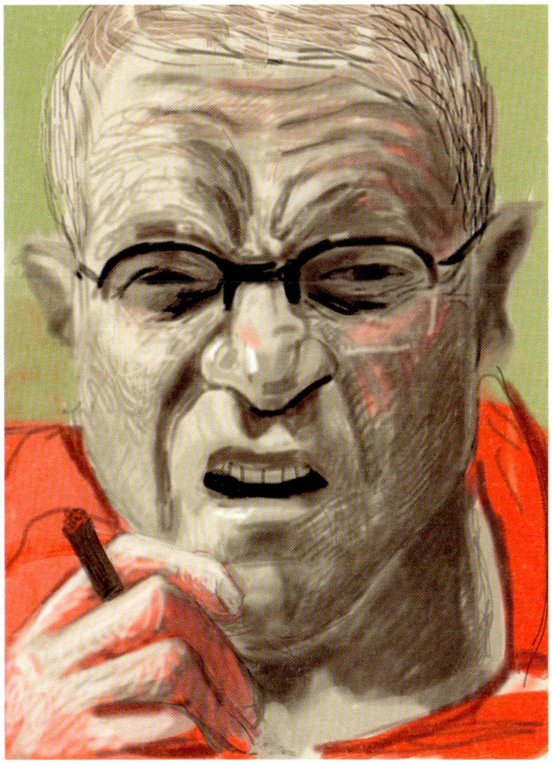
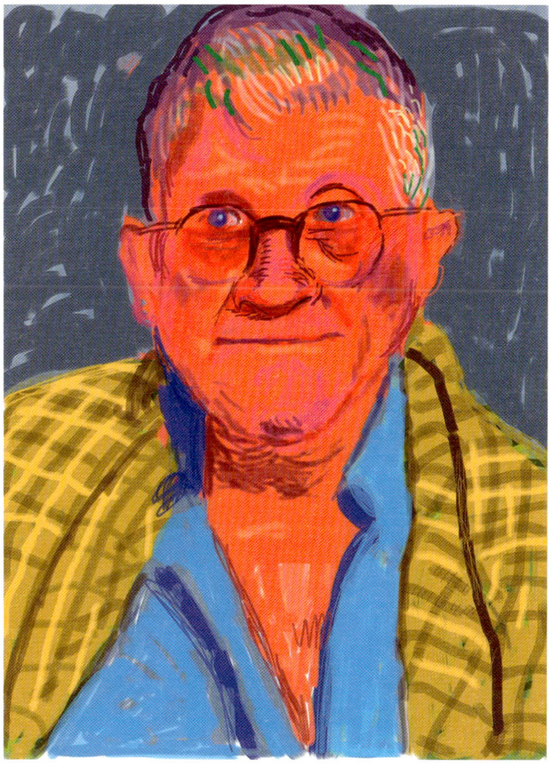
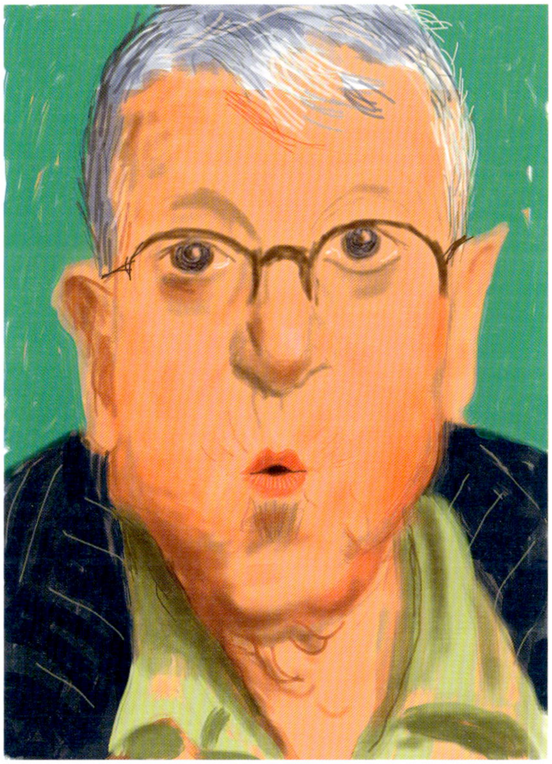
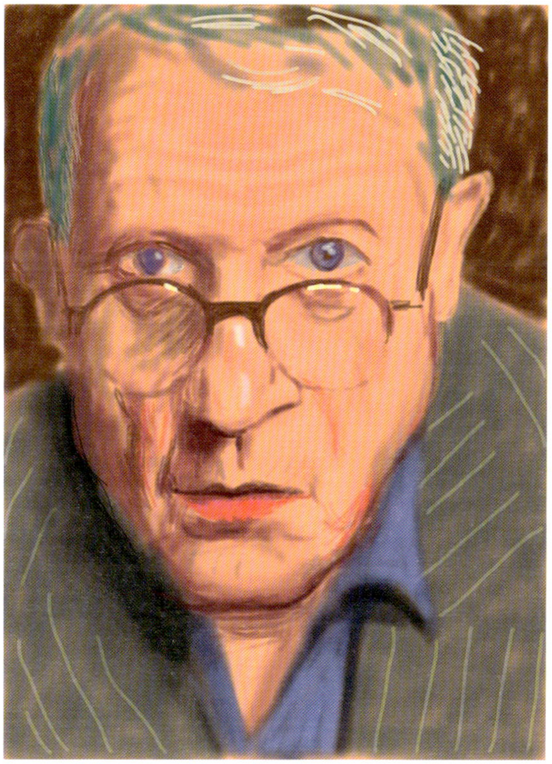

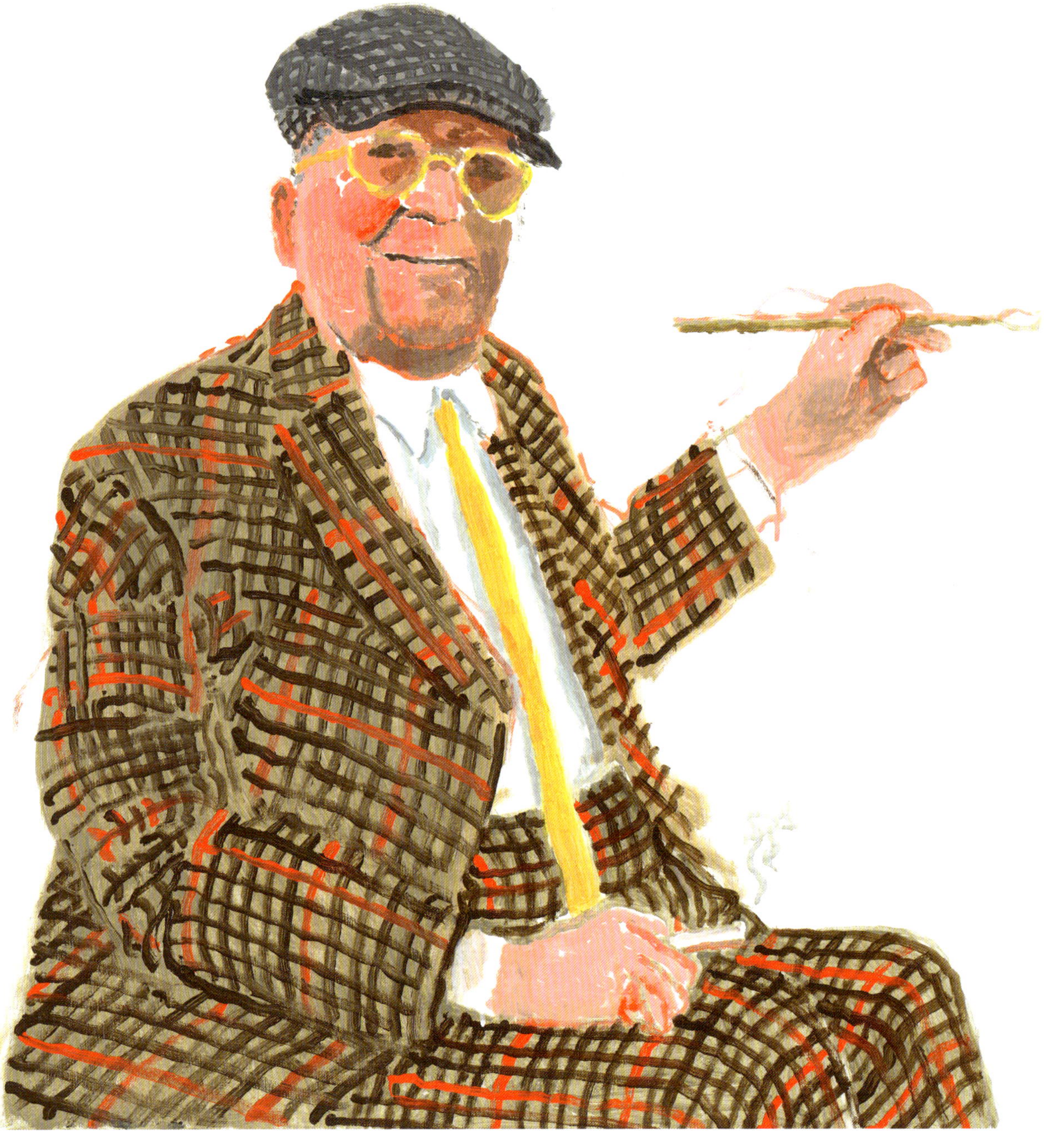

11 | F David Hockney,
Self Portait, 22nd November 2021, acrylic on canvas,
91.4 x 76.2 cm. Collection of the artist

in their own right in their historical contexts, presenting clear evidence of the way they served topographical artists, notably Canaletto, the great painter of *vedute* (views) in Venice. Far from being regarded as 'cheating', the use of the latest visual technologies by landscapists, professional and amateur, was a matter of pride. As Hockney has pointed out, if the user has no skill in drawing, the results would be "melancholy to behold", to quote William Henry Fox Talbot,[4] whose artistic humiliation in the face of the accomplishments of his sister and wife precipitated his quest to 'fix' the camera images in what became known as photographs.

The huge advances in brain sciences in the last few decades can be brought into productive dialogue with Hockney's more instinctive experiments. The extraordinary complexities of how we see and make sense of what we are seeing, not least in relation to expectation and context, are instinctively explored by Hockney in a diverse and sustained way. As he comes to abandon orthodox linear perspective, a variety of other spatial clues come in play. These include dynamic motifs and vivid colour acting in space and time. Hockney's recent dialogues with the distinguished scientist of visual perception and the brain Sir Colin Blakemore have centred on the way we use rapid perceptual shots to assemble coherent space as we move through it and as objects move in space. Hockney and Blakemore share a quest for the means by which we see space that goes far beyond perspective and the photograph.

Finally the latest scientific analysis and computer vision techniques are applied to the brilliant predella panels of *The Annunciation* and *The Miracle of St Zenobius* in the Fitzwilliam, painted by Domenico Veneziano in early Renaissance Florence. We see how modern techniques of analysis and spatial reconstruction can elucidate the highly ordered courtyard and garden in the *Annunciation* and the more varied perspectival array in the street scene of the *Miracle*. We know that one of Hockney's first artistic loves was a reproduction of Fra Angelico's comparable *Annunciation* hanging on a wall in his school in Bradford. Decades later, he painted his own version in "reverse perspective".

From Renaissance Florence, via Bradford, we journey with Hockney though twentieth-century concepts of space, computer-made images, modern neuro-science and electronic analyses of Florentine art .... We come in a satisfying circle.

Notes

1 Robert Hughes, 'On Lucian Freud', *The New York Review*, 13 August 1987. **2** Martin Gayford in conversation with David Hockney. **3** Hockney and Gayford 2016, 82. **4** Talbot 1844.

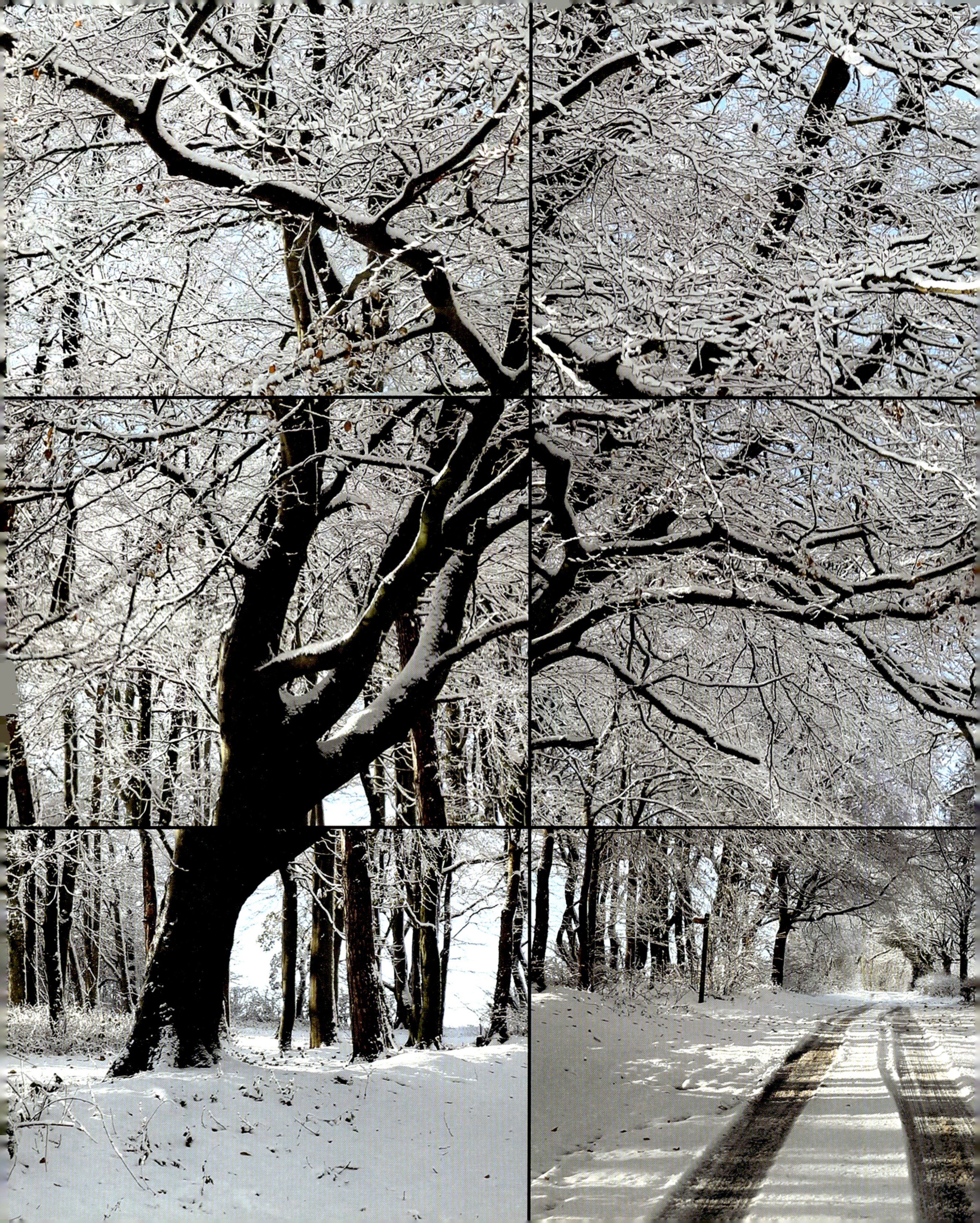

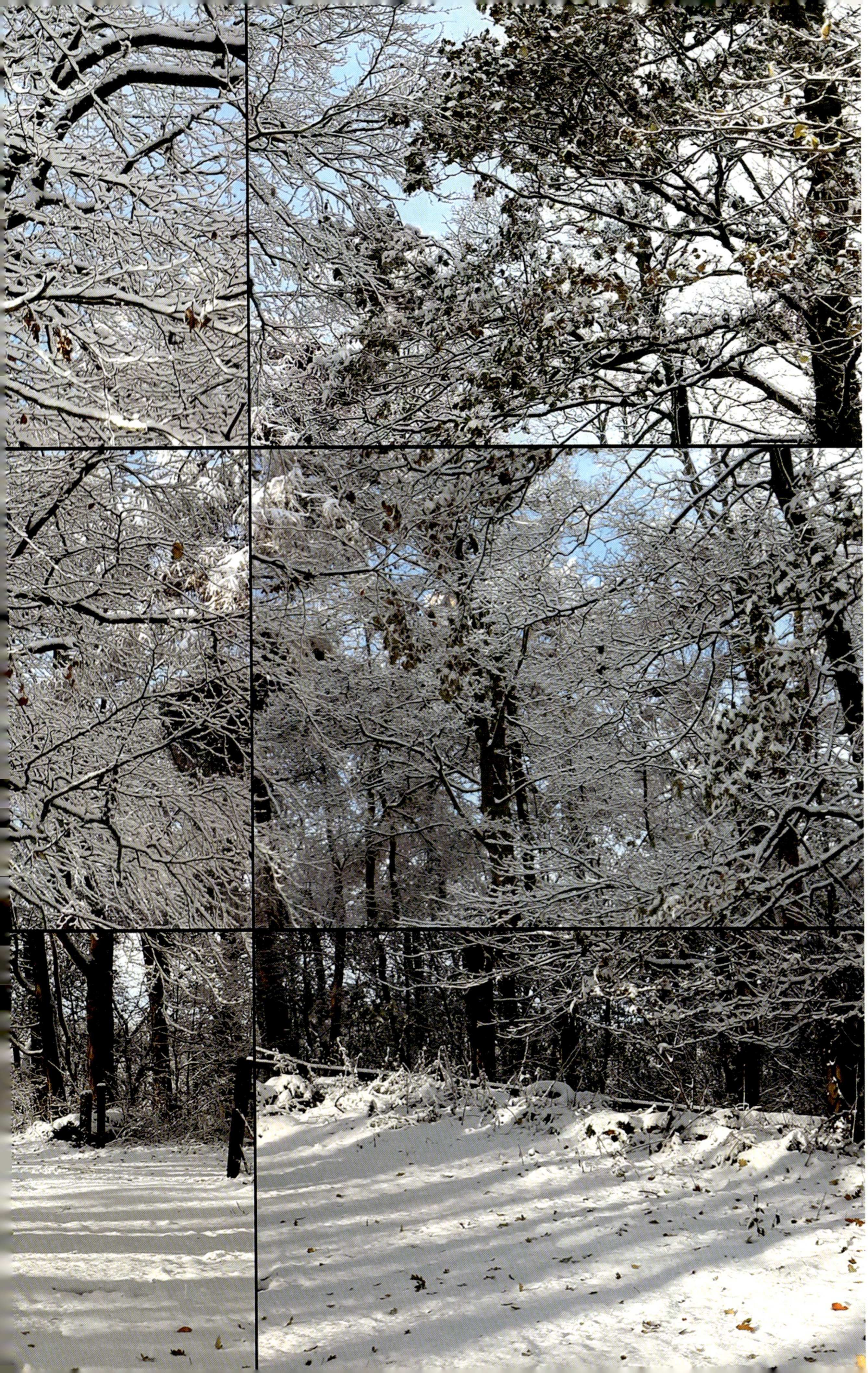

JOURNEYS INTO SPACE

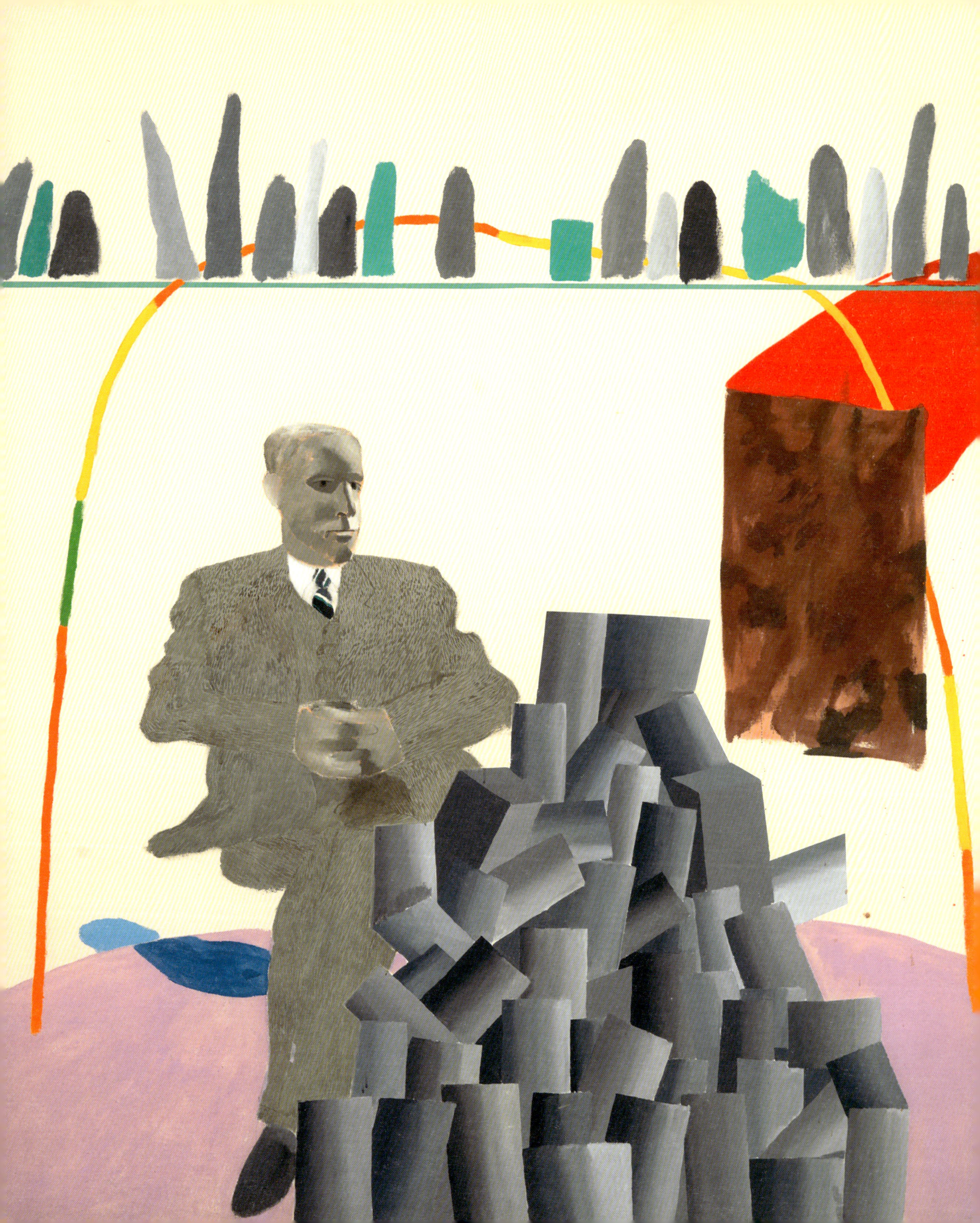

Martin Gayford

David Hockney: space explorer

David Hockney's extraordinary career can be viewed from many vantage points. He might be considered as an artist working within a British, Yorkshire, American or these days even a French tradition. A critic might analyse his work from a modernist, post-modernist or traditionalist perspective. All these angles of vision are valid, but none is self-evidently superior to the others. Each reveals different aspects of his life and art: it emphasizes certain traits and details but omits or minimizes others.

In that respect, these varied critical and historical sketches of Hockney are like all pictures. All are different, some may be more informative than others, but none is 'correct' (Hockney observes that there is no such thing as a correct perspective, just differing ways of depicting the bewildering flux of reality.)

Rather than considering Hockney in terms of style, movement or historical 'period', this exhibition takes a novel angle. It proposes that his numerous metamorphoses in medium, technique and manner are all connected by the quest to depict the three dimensions of the real world on the flat plane of a picture not 'correctly' but more vividly, in a manner closer to our experience. This is a problem with which Hockney has been grappling since his student days, and his attempts to solve it, more than style or even subject, are what gives unity to his vast output.

Consider four works by Hockney as dissimilar (at least to a casual viewer) as *Portrait Surrounded by Artistic Devices* (1965, fig. 19), *Le Parc des Sources, Vichy* (1970, fig. 22), *Woldgate Woods, Winter* (2010, fig. 29) and *Viewers Looking at a Ready-made with Skull and Mirrors* (2018, fig. 46). Chronologically, these are spread over half a century; nothing links them in terms of style. The traditional categories of art history – is it Impressionist, Romantic or Baroque? – are no help here. The most a critic might venture is that they are all representational (and that's not entirely true of *Portrait Surrounded by Artistic Devices*).

True, there is a clarity about all four, a visual snap which grabs the viewer's attention from across a room: but this is not a matter of style or idiom, more a question of creative sensibility. Hockney loves clarity, both in words and pictures. "It's very, very clear" is one of his highest accolades.

Nor is there any consistency in medium between this quartet of Hockney works. The first two are paintings, though very unlike in immediate effect, one verging on abstraction, the other apparently 'naturalistic' (to use a contentious term). In contrast, *Woldgate Woods* consists of digital videos, synchronized and presented on nine screens. while *Viewers Looking at a Ready-made* is a 'digital drawing', made with the aid of a state-of-the-art camera and computer imaging.

When he saw the first retrospective of his own work, shown at the Whitechapel Art Gallery in 1970, Hockney himself was struck by "how protean" his work was (and that was only the product of a decade's rapid evolution). But conversely, when he saw his pictures gathered together, he also noted: "I began to see for the first time the way things worked, the way my mind was working".[1]

That is the hidden relationship between those four remarkable, and remarkably diverse, masterpieces. They all demonstrate how his mind has been working for over six decades. So here is one perspective in which Hockney's art can be seen – to use a term not usually applied to his pictures – as *conceptual*. That is, it is to do with ideas, but not with thoughts borrowed from philosophy or political doctrines. Instead they attempt to solve the conundrum: how do you paint, draw, film or photograph something so it is convincingly positioned in space?

This preoccupation places Hockney in another wider and longer vista, connecting him not only with his contemporaries and predecessors in the European tradition, but also with artists in distant times and places:

A lot of my early paintings are just isometric: that means they have no single vanishing point. I always thought it was better. That was an intuitive feeling, but I was well aware that isometric perspective was Japanese and Chinese.

Hockney's relationship with the works of past centuries is considered (from many vantage-points) in the juxtapositions and displays at the Fitzwilliam Museum. These investigate for the first time some of the evidence for one of Hockney's most striking claims – that there was widespread use of the camera by artists before the public announcement of the advent of photography in 1839. As Hockney puts it: "The normal view of photography is that it was an immaculate conception: it came from nowhere. The truth is that photography is the child of painting."

One of his most radical contentions is that all types of picture (two dimensional representations of the 3D world) share certain problems, and hence, in a sense, a common history. He therefore groups paintings, drawings and prints together with photographs, film and computer games in one new category – 'picture'. Hence the title of the book *A History of Pictures*.

At the Fitzwilliam, works made by Hockney using one of the optical tools in use in the early nineteenth century, the camera lucida, are juxtaposed with others definitely or arguably created by eighteenth- or early nineteenth-century artists using that device, and also the camera obscura and Cornelius Varley's Graphic Telescope.

Hockney's attempt to reconfigure art history is not a pastime or chance interest: it flows naturally from the development of his work – and from thinking about how it was done. His complaint against many conventional accounts of the art of the past is that they show little curiosity about the practical nitty-gritty of creating a picture. An artist, Hockney protests, wants to know *how* things were made – hence his own pre-occupation with the tools of his trade.

This has led him to take a close interest in the gadgets and equipment used by painters in the past. Almost all pictures, he has remarked, are and always have been made with the use of tools (a brush is a tool). Every such implement offers particular possibilities, but also has corresponding limitations. For example, you make a lino cut with gouges and knifes, so you don't make fine lines, "it would be too niggly". But take an etching plate and needle, "and it's about fine lines".

Similarly, Hockney noted that many painters since 1839 (himself included) have used photography as a tool. This led him to wonder what uses earlier artists found for cameras and lenses *before* 1839, when they both existed and were easily available (although a chemical method for fixing an image did not).

To Hockney's list of Far Eastern 'isometric' models, one could add 'Egyptian'. Among his earliest masterpieces, painted when he was still a student at the Royal College of Art, was *A Grand Procession of Dignitaries in the Semi-Egyptian Style* (1961, fig. 12). It is, he explains, 'semi-Egyptian' because the figures are presented in a frieze processing along the rectangle of the picture, rather than set in space receding into it.

However, although the central figure has a somewhat Pharaoh-like look, Hockney's work is not entirely in the ancient Egyptian manner. As the witty and erudite title written on the picture (one of Hockney's earliest exercises in explanatory naming) insists, the painting is only *semi*-Egyptian. He assumed, he explained, that "there must have been rules for Egyptian painting because it lasted so long". The young Hockney, by adding elements derived from gestural abstraction and the *art brut* of Jean Dubuffet, together with others of his own devising, obviously was not following the rules in the way a painter in the time of Ramesses II might have done.

Clearly, at this stage he already understood that that the making of paintings, drawings and other images is a process which follows rules. Furthermore, he had worked out that there are

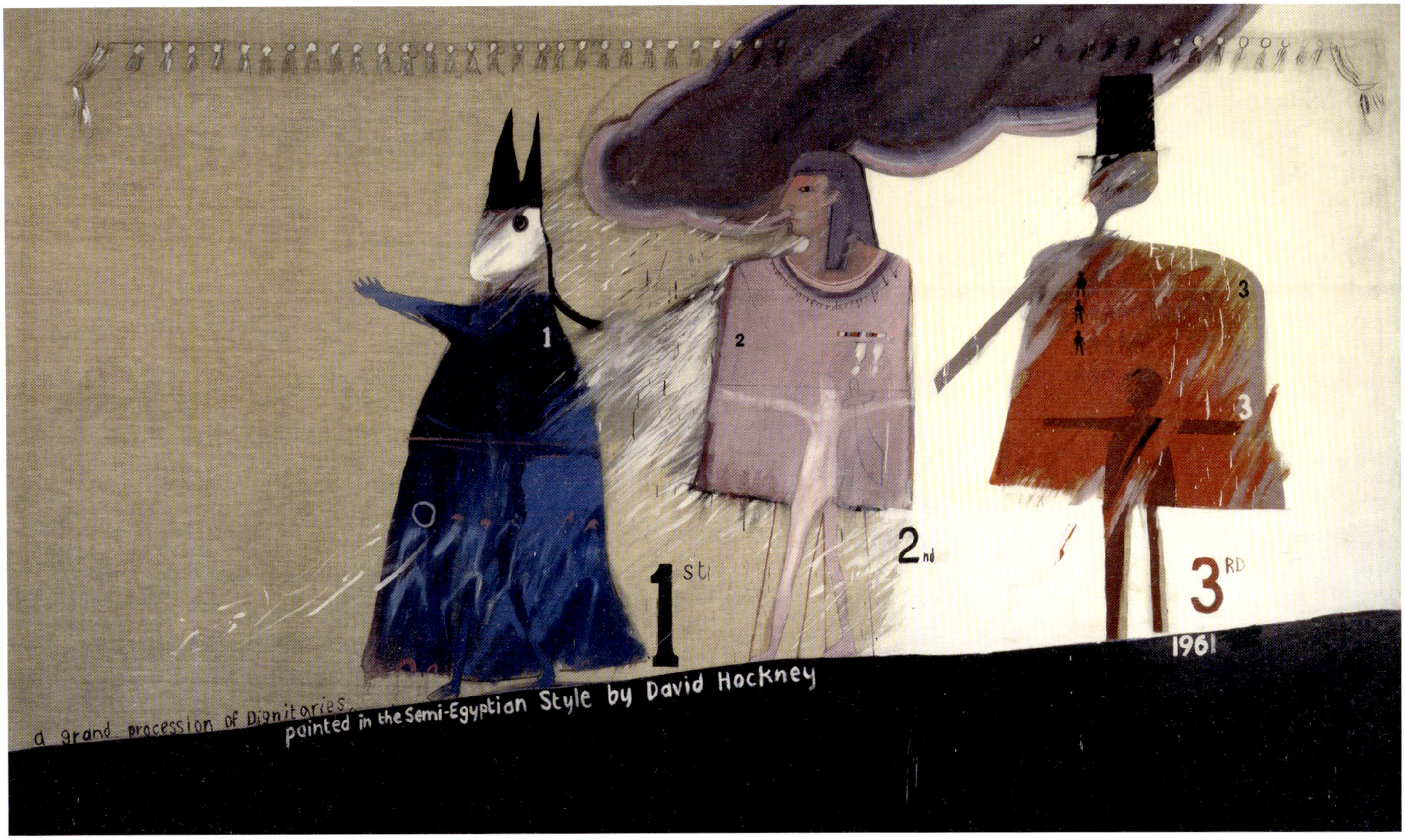

12 David Hockney, *A Grand Procession of Dignitaries in the Semi-Egyptian Style*, 1961, oil on canvas, 213.4 x 365.8 cm. Private collection

various competing sets of such formulae, none of which is more 'correct' than any of the others. Lastly, Hockney had grasped that an artist did not have to follow any of these protocols rigidly. You could change these conventions or mix and match between different systems (as he had done by mixing ancient Egyptian and post-war Parisian in his procession of dignitaries).

Thus his painting *Arizona* (1964, fig. 13) is a fantasy of the south-western USA (location of many a cowboy film) assembled from a mesa-like stack resembling a slice taken out of a colour-field painting by a then fashionable exponent of it such as Morris Louis, together with a winding road and some cottonwool clouds in an idiom suggesting a children's book. To these, in the lower part of the canvas, he has added a fairly naturalistic head of a native American, what looks like a geological specimen (or perhaps a modernist sculpture) on a plinth and in the middle a strange object like a megalithic standing stone, painted in an almost pointillist idiom. Somehow, these all cohere into a witty and beautiful whole.

So, at the beginning of Hockney's lifelong exploration of ways of depicting the world, we find him acting on the insight which he formulated much later: "The wonderful thing about visual space is that you can just *invent* it".

Perhaps the young Hockney was able to reflect on the entire course of art from ancient Egypt up to the 1960s, in this droll, detached manner, because of his training. Like many of his contemporaries at British art schools, he had been inducted into the methods handed down from the Italian Renaissance, then a little later into those of early twentieth-century Paris and contemporary New York.

The first part of this education was as significant as the second. As a mature artist Hockney was profoundly affected by Matisse and Picasso, but also by Piero della Francesca and Fra Angelico. The last-named was perhaps the first notable artist whose work Hockney ever saw (see fig. 141).

"There was a reproduction of his *Annunciation* in the top corridor at Bradford Grammar

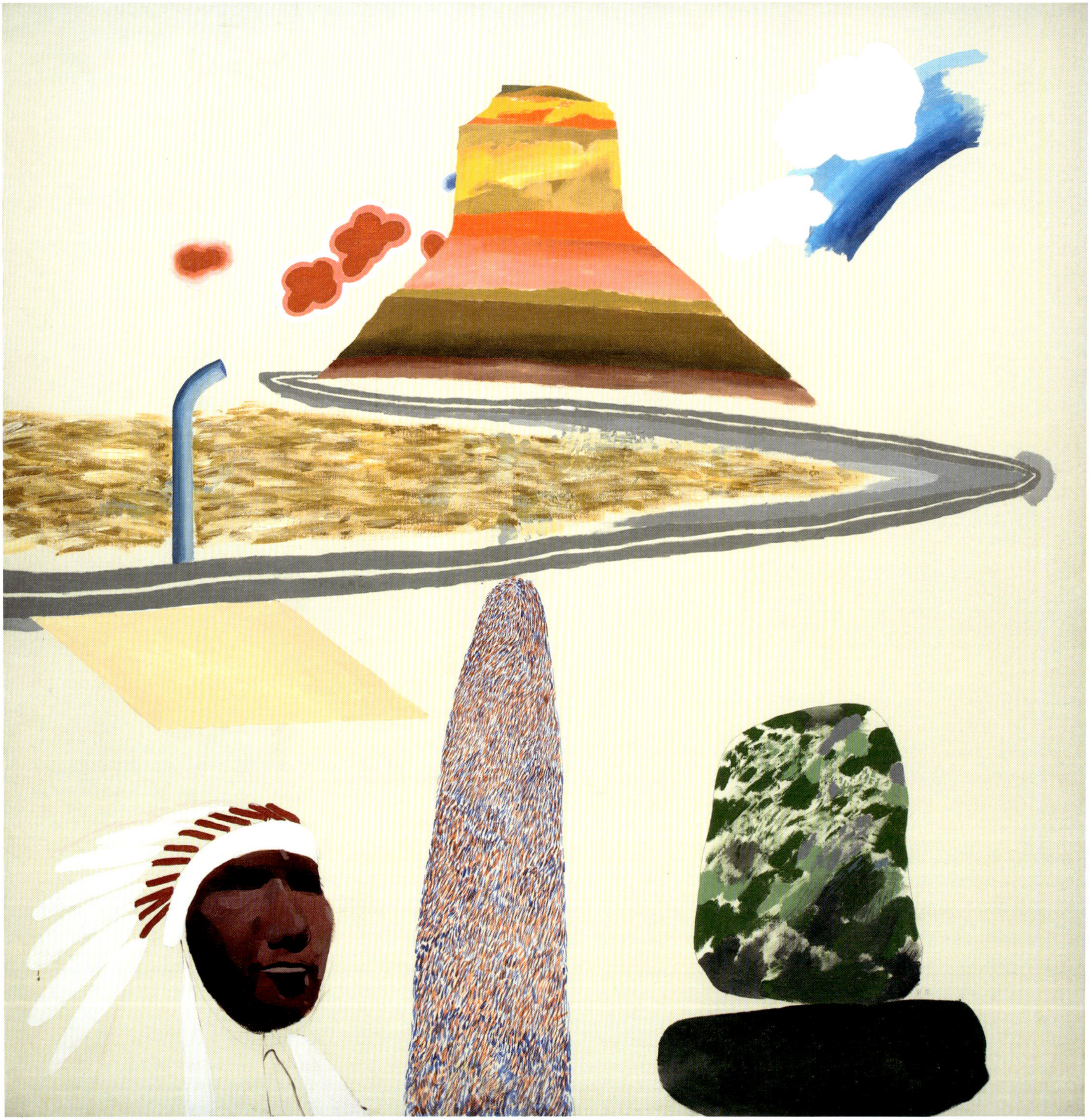

13 | H David Hockney,
Arizona, 1964, acrylic
on canvas, 153 x 153 cm.
Private collection

school, so when I was an eleven-year-old I was looking at it. I've always loved it." The fact that this was hanging there was in itself a result of the nineteenth-century British cult of the Quattrocento (Hockney was not the only artist of his generation to be affected by the bright colour and tender fall of light in Piero and Fra Angelico; Euan Uglow is another example).

At Bradford School of Art between 1953 and 1957 Hockney learnt to draw with a virtuoso facility in a manner that had been handed down via nineteenth- and earlier twentieth-century intermediaries such as Henry Tonks at the Slade, ultimately derived from such predecessors as Michelangelo, Raphael and Leonardo. As soon as he arrived at the Royal College of Art, Hockney's remarkable abilities were noticed by his contemporaries RB Kitaj and Frank Bowling.

Kitaj actually bought one of the drawings of a skeleton (a stock aid to anatomical teaching) that Hockney made in his first weeks at the RCA (fig. 14). "I'd been to art school in New York and in Vienna," Kitaj recalled, "and had quite a lot of experience, and I'd never seen such a beautiful drawing." Picasso famously boasted that he could draw like Raphael by the age of twelve; the evidence is that Hockney, having started rather later, could also do so by the time he was 22.

At the Royal College, Hockney moved rapidly from an idiom which would have been comprehensible to Raphael to a form of abstraction which was related to the work of older British artists such as Alan Davie (he summed up this short phase as "Alan Davie cum Jackson Pollock cum Roger Hilton"). This, however, didn't seem right for him: "I used to think, 'How do you push this? It can't go anywhere. Even Jackson Pollock's painting is a dead end'."

At this point, Kitaj suggested that, since the young Hockney was full of ideas and beliefs, he should try inserting those into his pictures. He did, and from that point, Hockney the artist we know began to emerge. The result was the kind of painting we see in, for example, *Tyger Painting No. 2* or *Shame* (both 1960, figs. 16 and 17) in which the shallow space of Abstract Expressionism, created by paint marks rather than any variety of perspective, is invaded by concrete objects and also words ('Tyger', from the William Blake poem of the same title, was among the first).

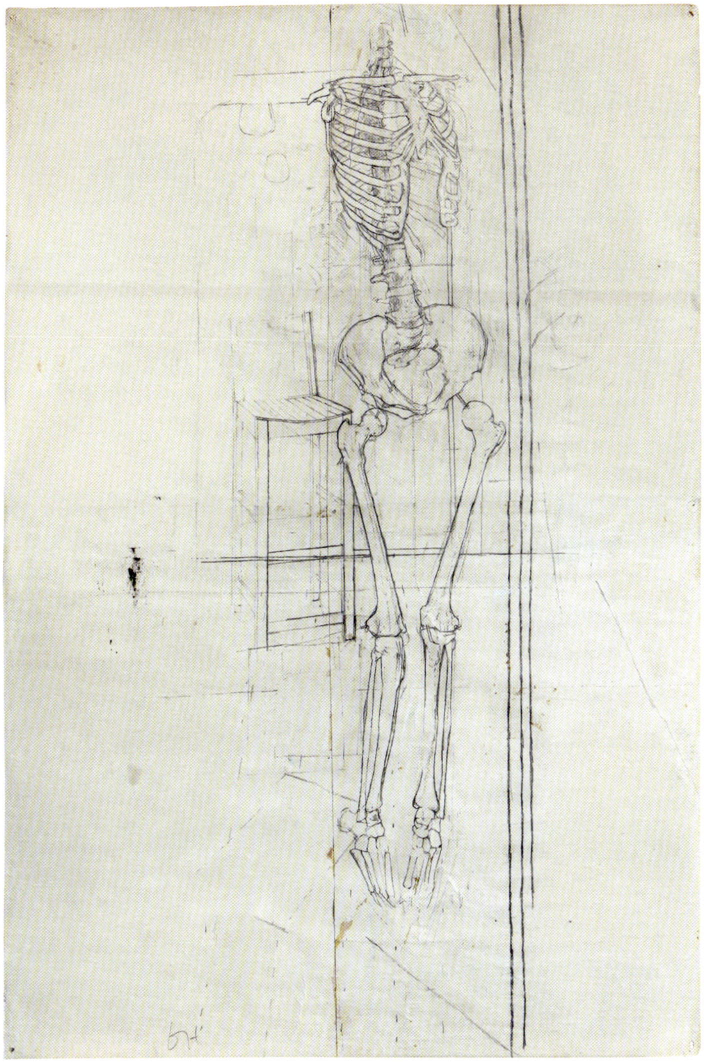

14 | H David Hockney, *Skeleton Study II, Royal College of Art*, 1959, pencil on paper, 104 x 71 cm. Private collection

"When you put a word on a painting," Hockney explained, "it has a similar effect in a way to a figure; it's a little bit of human thing that you immediately read; it's not just paint."[2] This remark, by the way, is why he defined the perceptual world as "*at least* 4D": apart from the space and time represented in every picture, there were also "human things" such as memories, emotions and associations which affect our experience of what we see.

In *A Man Thinking* (1962–63; fig. 18) with typical directness Hockney used the cartoonist's convention of the 'thinks' balloon to suggest what is happening inside this imaginary figure's head (perhaps happy thoughts about the year of 1962).

From painting words on his abstractions, Hockney quite quickly moved to depicting people

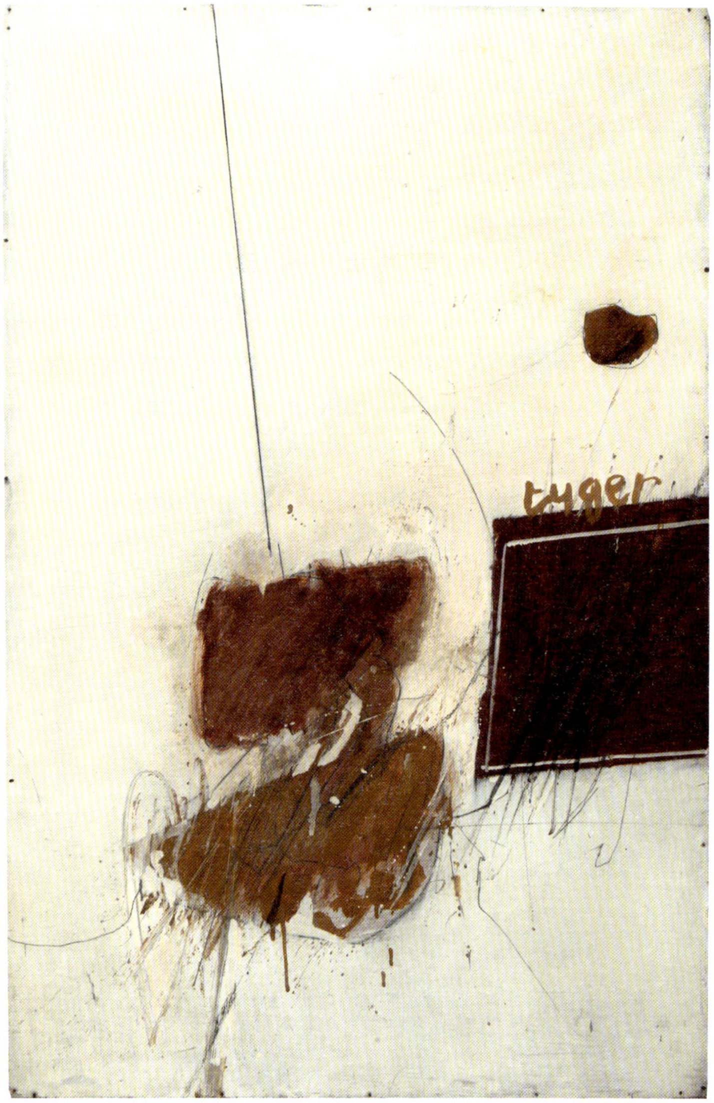

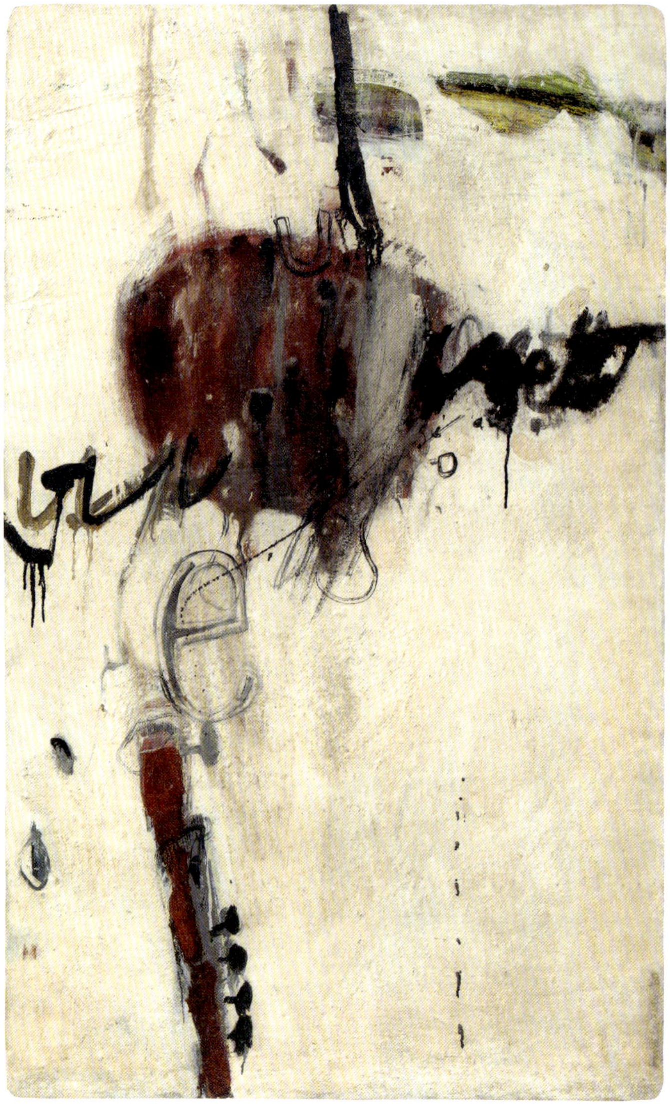

15 | F David Hockney, *Tyger*, 1960, oil and pencil on board, 76.2 x 50.8 cm Private collection

16 | F David Hockney, *Tyger Painting No. 2*, 1960, oil on board, 102 x 63.5 cm. Private collection

and things. In the polarized art world of the time, this was a defiant move. He had come out as that unfashionable thing, a figurative artist. Joe Tilson remembers Harry Fischer of the powerful Marlborough Fine Art gallery being shown some of Hockney's works by Paul Kasmin (later Hockney's dealer but then a junior employee at the Marlborough). "Victorian gimmicks, Mr Kasmin, we don't show that!" But Hockney persisted.

A year after *Arizona*, Hockney produced *Portrait Surrounded by Artistic Devices* (1965, fig. 19), which is at once a witty, beautiful painting in its own right and an art historical manifesto in visual terms. At its centre, Hockney noted, is a figure based on a drawing of his father, Kenneth. The "artistic devices" which surround him were "images and elements of my own and other artist's work and ideas of the time".

It's not hard to list at least some of these. The curved purple zone on which the portrait figure is seated looks rather like the *mise-en-scène* of a Francis Bacon picture. But the 'space-frame' in which Bacon trapped his human and animal subjects has been replaced by a multi-coloured arch. This is not much more than a line, but it is positioned in pictorial space by two other elements. At the right its rainbow-line is overlapped by a curved red and brown object that looks as if it might be a component from a welded and painted steel sculpture by Anthony Caro (who shared the same dealer as Hockney, Kasmin). At the top, there is a sort of curtain, or at

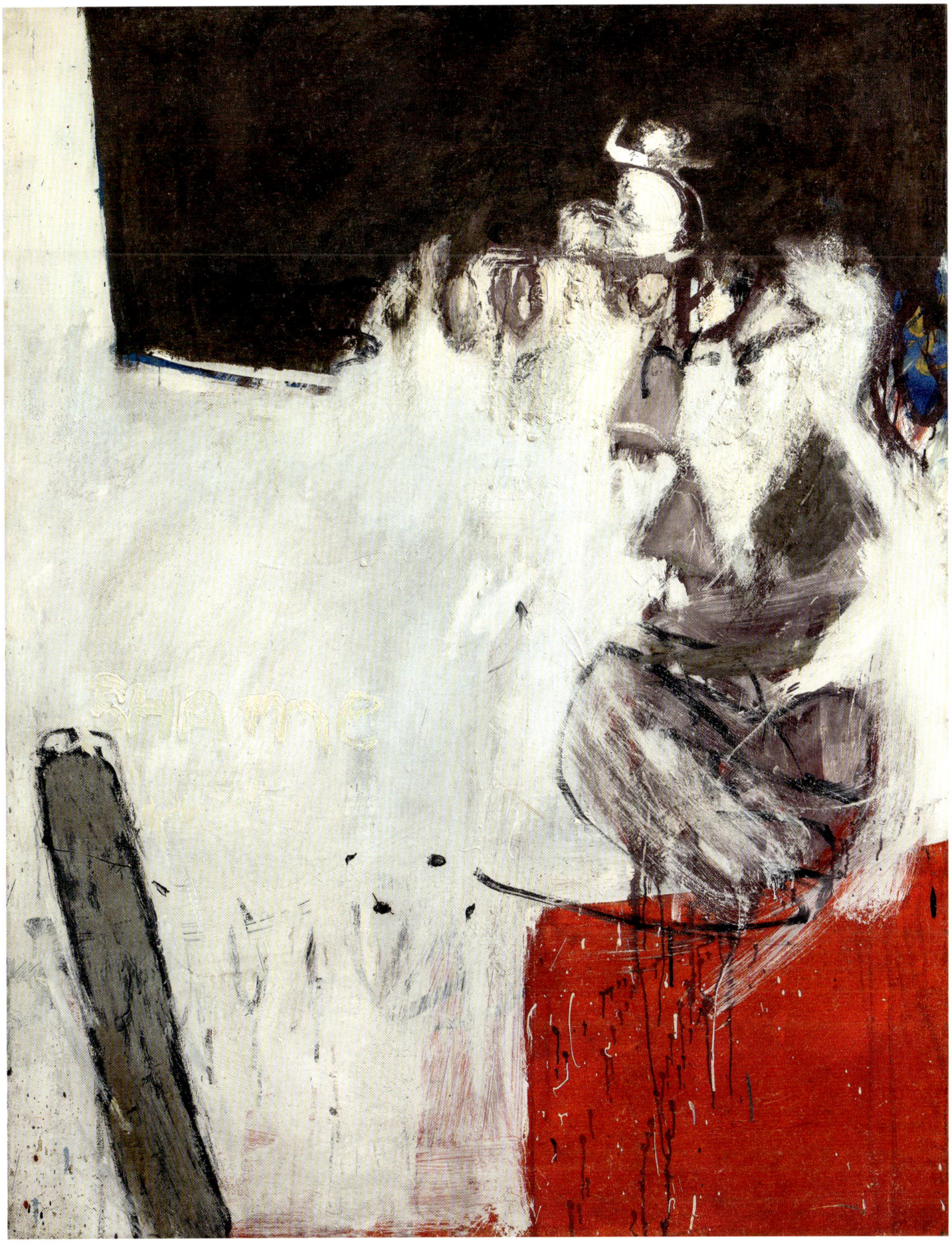

17 | F David Hockney, *Shame*,
1960, oil on board, 127 x 102 cm.
Private collection

1962

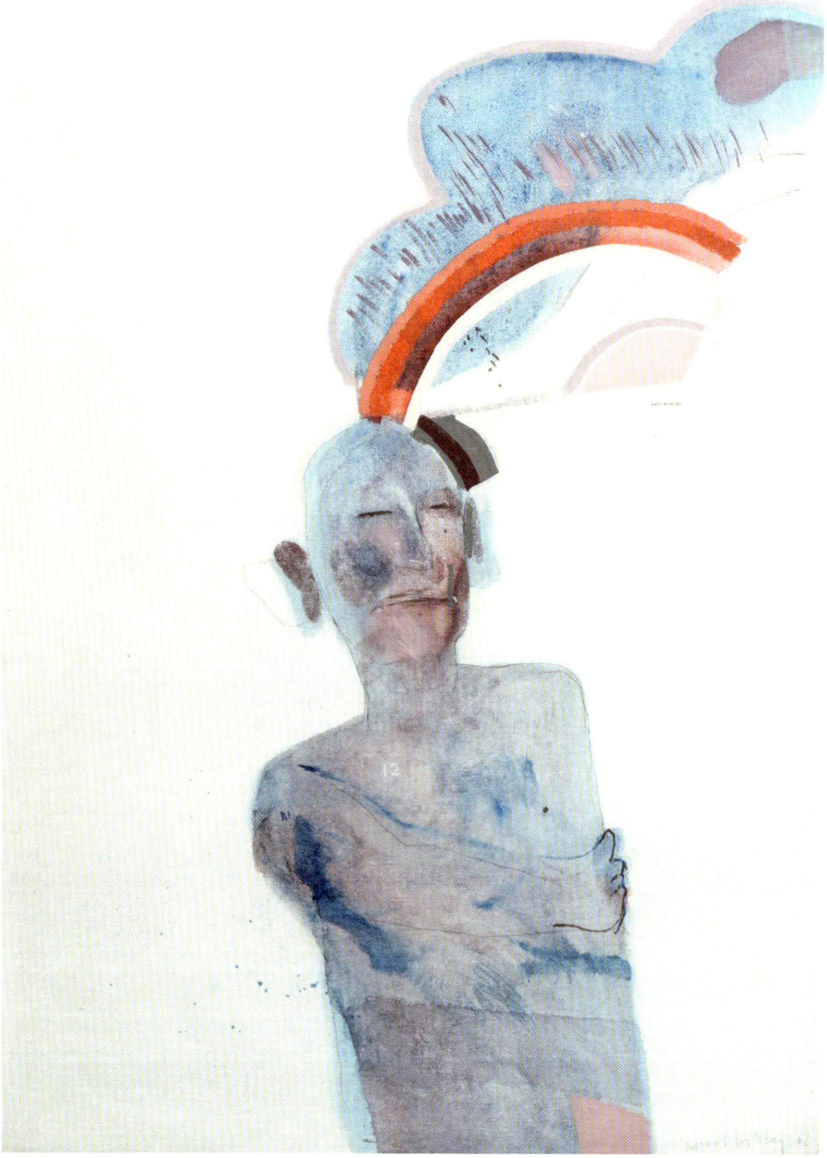

18 | F David Hockney,
A Man Thinking, 1962–63,
oil on canvas, 91 x 63 cm.
Private collection

least pelmet, made up of grey and turquoise brush strokes which look as if they might have escaped from a colour-field work by, say, Morris Louis.

This was not the first time that Hockney included this motif; in fact the first vestigial curtain was at the top of *A Grand Procession of Dignitaries.* It was an indication of Hockney's sense that there was a close relationship between the pictures and the stage, and that in a sense all paintings were theatrical.

In the foreground is a pile of cylinders, which are perhaps a reference to Cézanne's assertion that a figure was "just a cone, a cylinder and a sphere". Hockney was convinced that "a figure is really more than that". But the cylinders themselves are making a further point. They are created from patches of grey pigment by deploying the devices of light and shade plus highlights and reflected light, which have been part of the battery of naturalistic artists since the days of the ancient Greeks.

In that way, the grey oblongs are endowed with a powerful, indeed irresistible, sense of three-dimensionality. You can't help feeling that they seem more solid and rounded than the figure behind. What's more, Hockney casually shows us how the trick is done – that all this is simply a visual device. Nonetheless, he remains an astonishingly skilful exponent of these skills – described by E.H. Gombrich in a celebrated essay, 'The Heritage of Apelles'. It was apparently Apelles of Kos and his Greek contemporaries in the fourth century BC who first used what in Latin was called *splendor* – the highlight. Together with reflected light and shadow these are still among the most important ways in which a naturalistic painter can evoke a sense of surface and volume, that is, can make metal gleam, silk shimmer and an object seem, like those cylinders in Hockney's picture, solid and tangible.

Hockney gave many displays of this virtuosity in the still-life drawings he made on an iPad in 2010, in which varied forms, surfaces and textures are endlessly evoked by deft use of line, touch, chiaroscuro and reflections (fig. 20). Even so he remains conscious that they are still "visual devices".

He often points out that shadows are optional: in a way you can choose to notice them – or not. "You can ignore shadows when you are drawing, as the earlier ancient Greeks did, for example. I can if I draw with just a line; you can choose not to put them in." Many highly sophisticated visual cultures, the Chinese and Japanese for example, barely use light and shade at all.

As time went on he came to connect their prominence in European art to optical instruments. The camera, in other words, made us shadow-conscious. He had not yet reached this conclusion in 1971, yet as his painting *Beach Umbrella* demonstrates he was already intrigued

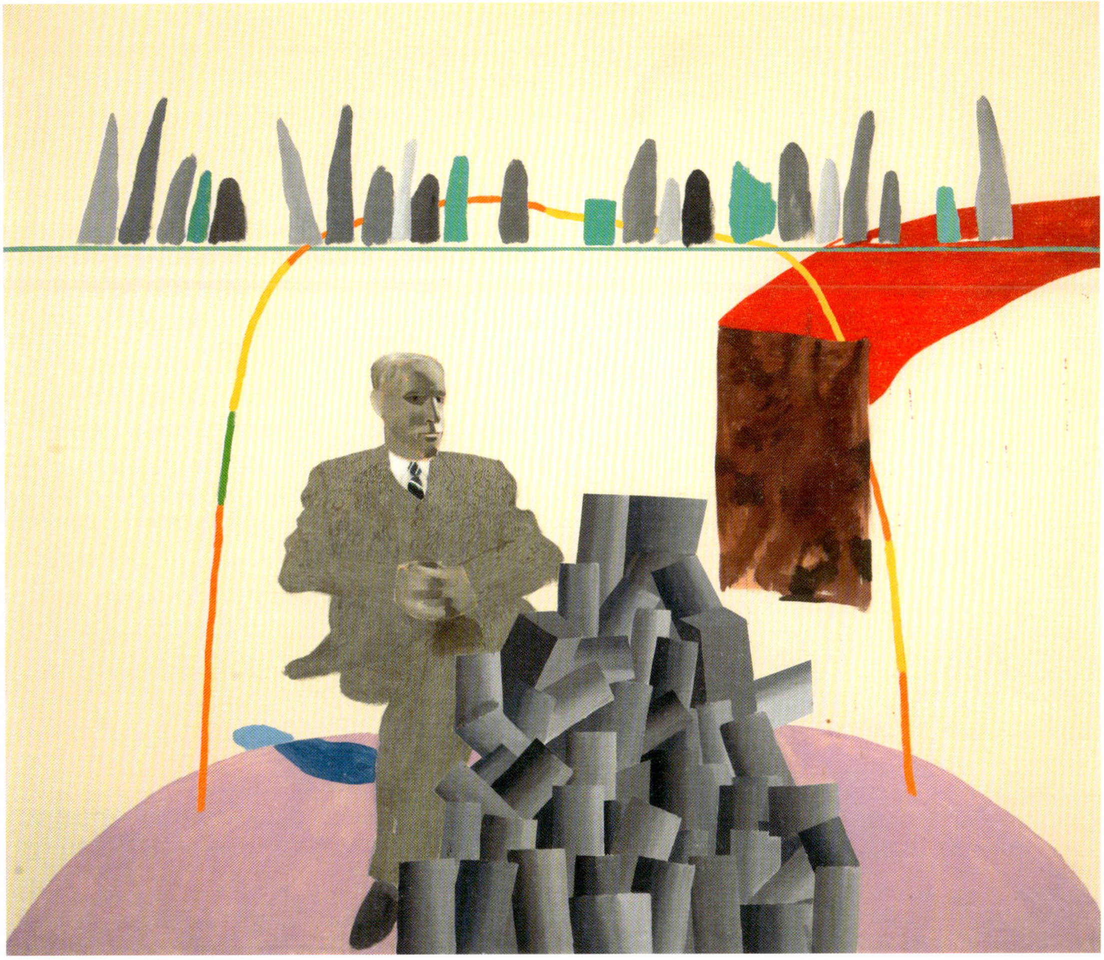

19 | H David Hockney, *Portrait Surrounded by Artistic Devices,* 1965, acrylic on canvas, 152.4 x 182.9 cm. Arts Council Collection, Southbank Centre, London, AC 823

by the possibilitiies and paradoxes presented by shadows (fig. 21). Rather than the brightly coloured umbrella itelf, it is the distorted shadow it casts on the beach which creates the visual drama of the painting – and the space. This picture is in a way a portrait of a shadow.

As he carried on working and thinking Hockney came up against a form of visual representation which many people claimed to be not just another set of pictorial rules, but something much more than that – the objective truth. This was, of course, the photograph. By the late 1960s Hockney had become a keen photographer and used his camera as an alternative to his sketchbook and drawing equipment for making preparatory studies. He notes, however, "I always knew that you couldn't draw from [photographs] very well, because you couldn't see and feel volume in the way you can in life".

Some of his work of around this date has a strongly photographic air – though that's often accompanied by an equally powerful sense of fifteenth-century Italy. That's true of *Le Parc des Sources, Vichy* (1970, fig. 22) and the *Portrait of Sir David Webster* (1971, see fig. 117). The precise profile and hieratic air of the latter make the retiring General Administrator of the Royal Opera House seem like a Renaissance ruler such as Federico da Montefeltro as painted by Piero.

Le Parc des Sources is arranged in the manner of a performance, with the row of seats for spectators in the foreground. The spectacle that they are viewing is a display of perspectival recession (rather as the receding forest is the real subject of Uccello's *Hunt in the Forest* of c. 1465–70, fig. 24). The twist in the Hockney is that the audience is admiring a piece of horticultural legerdemain (in other words a visual device). Although we seem to be looking at an avenue,

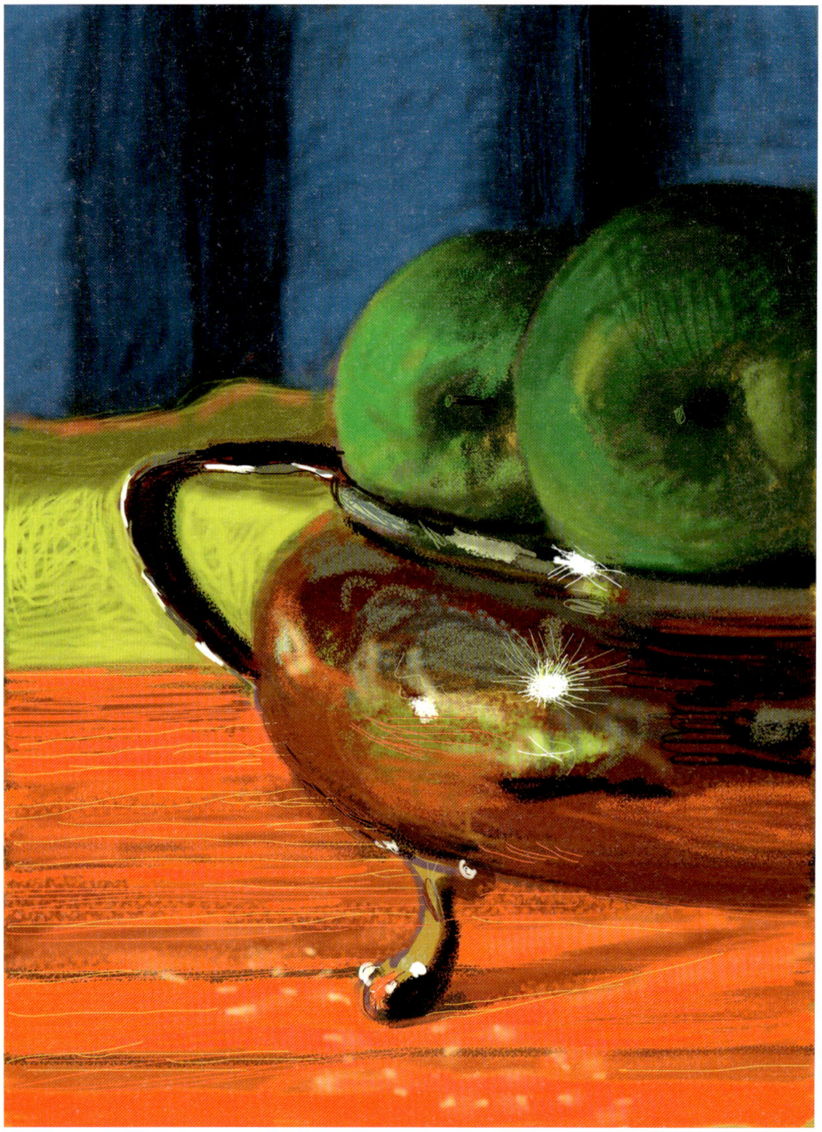

20 | H David Hockney, *24th February 2011*, iPad drawing. Collection of the artist

diminishing as it disappears into the distance, in reality it is a triangular lawn in a park skilfully arranged to give this illusion.

Hockney's paintings of the late 1960s and early 1970s are among his best-known (and loved). Nonetheless, he oppressed by a sense that he was being directed by a force with which he did not altogether sympathize.

"There was something wrong with what I was doing – I've called it 'obsessive naturalism' – but then I didn't know what it was." It took a while for him to realise that the problem was photography – not as a technique *per se*, for he did and does continue to use it, but as the final arbiter of visual reality. "Most people feel that the world looks like the photograph". Slowly, Hockney came to disagree. "I've always assumed that the photograph is nearly right, but that little bit it misses by, makes it miss by a mile. This is what I grope at."

A photograph, Hockney reasoned, does not and cannot correspond to experience. A picture projected by a lens "will only have one perspective". In this respect it resembled the linear perspective promulgated by Brunelleschi, which, as Philip Steadman has pointed out, is a mathematical algorithm; a similar rule of optics applied when a lens was used to take a picture. But Hockney felt that, far from being the acme of verisimilitude, it was actually utterly dissimilar from the human experience of seeing.

When a human being is looking at a scene the questions are: What do I see first? What do I see second? What do I see third? A photograph sees it all at once – in one click of the lens from a single point of view – but we don't. And it's the fact that it takes us time to see it that makes the space.

This has implications for all explorers of pictorial space.

Hockney argued the space we perceive is not really a single, fixed Renaissance box, with lines receding like tram rails towards a distant vanishing-point. It is much more fluid. "The eye moves all the time. When my eye moves in one direction, the perspective goes that way. So it's constantly changing."

In the early 1980s, he set about finding a way to use a camera to make a picture which would not have the faults he diagnosed in conventional photography. Firstly he did this by making works out of multiple polaroid photographs taken sequentially.

These were arguably truer to our experience in that we do not perceive a spectacle such as a young man splashing about in a pool as a single, frozen instant. Our perceptions are in constant flux, but we interpret them – process them, you might say – in terms of what we know: what happened before, what may well come next. The eye, as Hockney has frequently said, is connected to the mind.

From the composite polaroids, he moved on to make photographic collages (or "joiners"), made up of hundreds of individual photographs pieced

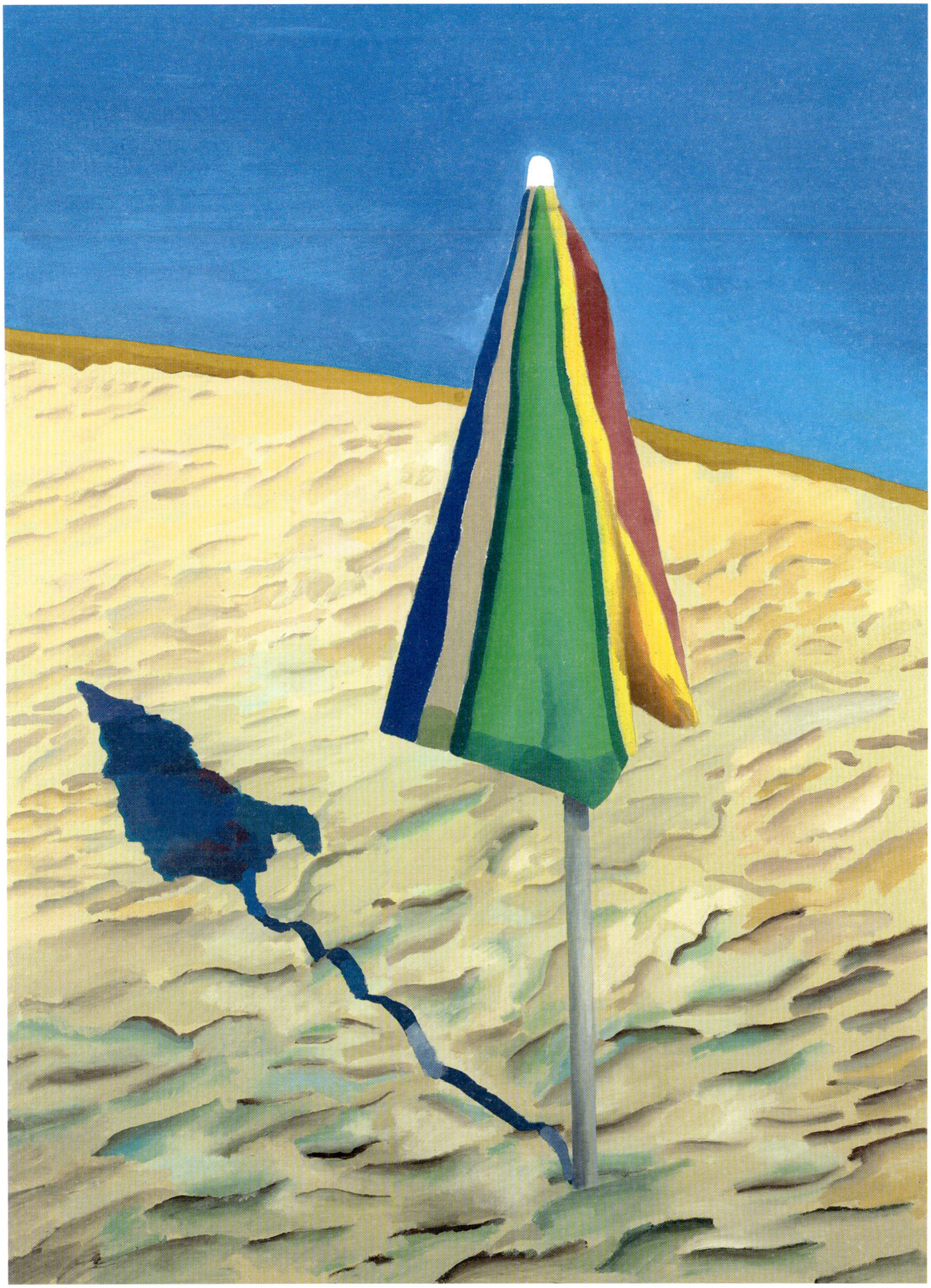

21 | F David Hockney,
Beach Umbrella, 1971, acrylic
on canvas, 121.9 x 90.8 cm.
Private collection

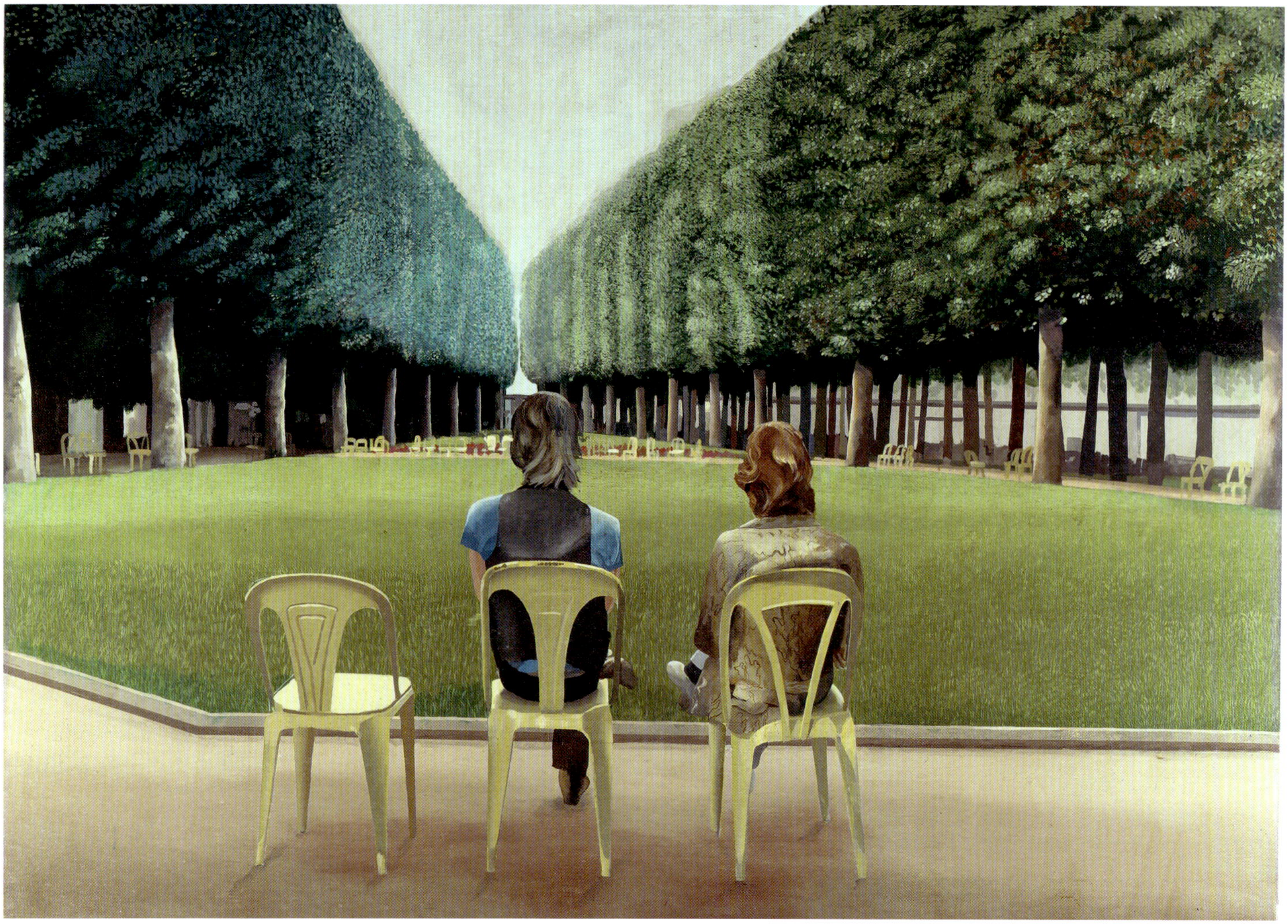

22 | F David Hockney,
Le Parc des Sources, Vichy,
1970, acrylic on canvas,
213.8 x 306.8 cm.
Private collection

23 Hockney, Ossie Clark
and Mo McDermott in the
Parc des Sources, Vichy,
1970. Photograph taken
by George Lawson

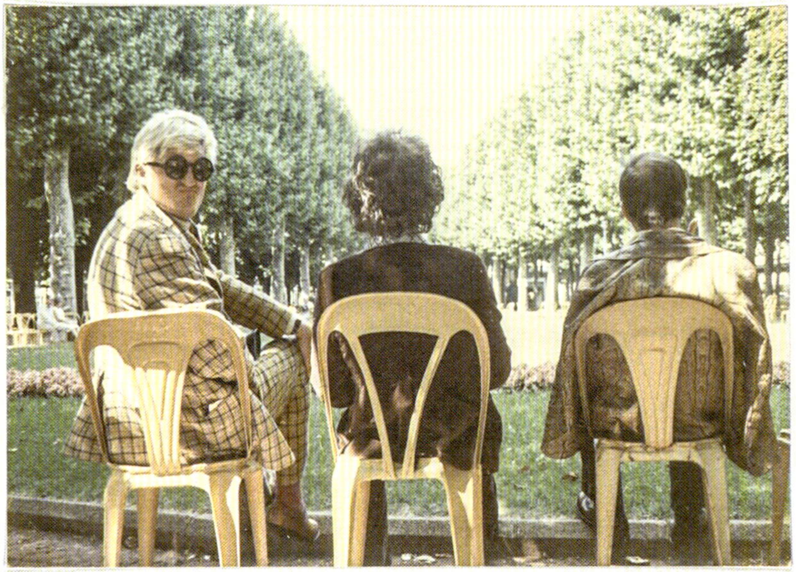

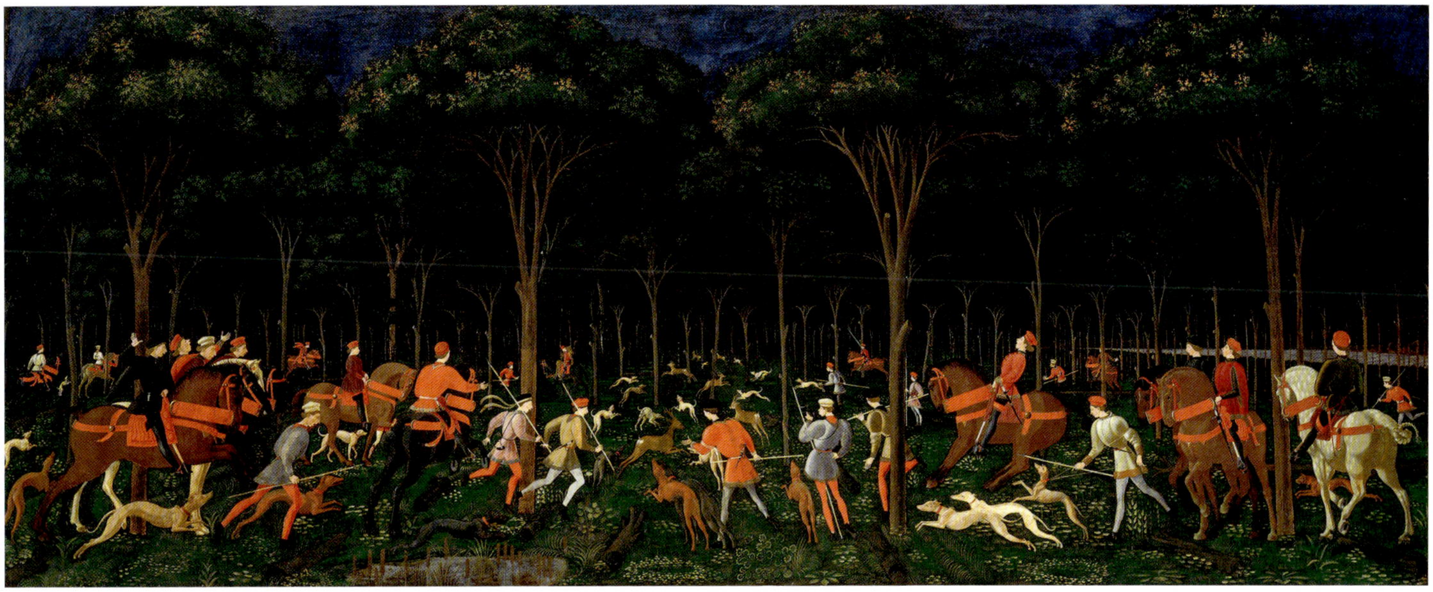

to together to form a single image. Examples such as *Walking in the Zen Garden* (1983, fig. 25) or *The Scrabble Game* (1983, fig. 27) resemble photographs that have been somehow shattered or fragmented.

I began looking at photography from various points of view. They said perspective was built into the camera. But my experiments showed that when you put two or three photographs together, you can alter perspective. The first picture I made where I felt I had done that was in Japan, where I photographed Walking in the Zen Garden at the Ryoanji Temple, Kyoto, Feb. 1983.

Of course, that celebrated arrangement of raked gravel and carefully positioned rocks, a masterpiece of Japanese art, is actually oblong in plan. That is not, however, how it would look in any picture made using single-point perspective – nor in any single photographic shot, in which the garden would appear as a trapezoid or triangle. Hockney made it rectangular in his picture by moving around himself and taking shots from differing positions. "I was very excited when I did that," he recalled: "I felt I had made a photograph without Western perspective".

Hockney connects his photographic collages of the 1980s with his concurrent discovery of Chinese art. So you could think of these works as a critique of traditional Western ways of depicting space. In Far Eastern paintings, he realised, there was no fixed vanishing point but instead the vantage-point of the viewer constantly shifted (he termed this the principle of 'moving focus'). His photo-works took him to Chinese scrolls. But another way of thinking about it is as a profound reconsideration of the roots of European modernist painting.

E.H. Gombrich hailed Hockney's 'joiners' as the first application of cubism to photography, and indeed these works, like many of his paintings and drawings of the 1980s, were partly the result of Hockney's meditation on the cubism of Picasso and Braque.

"Cubism is now treated like a style, pigeon-holed and that's it." But what Picasso and Braque had achieved was not, Hockney believed, a passing idiom – perhaps a steppingstone on the path to abstraction – but a revolution in the way the world was depicted. "Cubism was an attack on the perspective that had been known and used for five hundred years. It was the first big, big change since the Renaissance."

The principle on which the 'joiners' were created was that instead of everything being seen from a single point of view, each object – and often every distinct aspect of an item – was looked at from a different distance and angle, and generally from very close to. For that reason Hockney always took a ladder with him. Thus, in *Pearblossom Hwy.*, "The markings on the road

24 Uccello (Paolo di Dono), *Hunt in the Forest*, c. 1465–70, tempera and oil, with traces of gold, on panel, 73.3 x 177 cm. Ashmolean, Oxford, WA1850.31

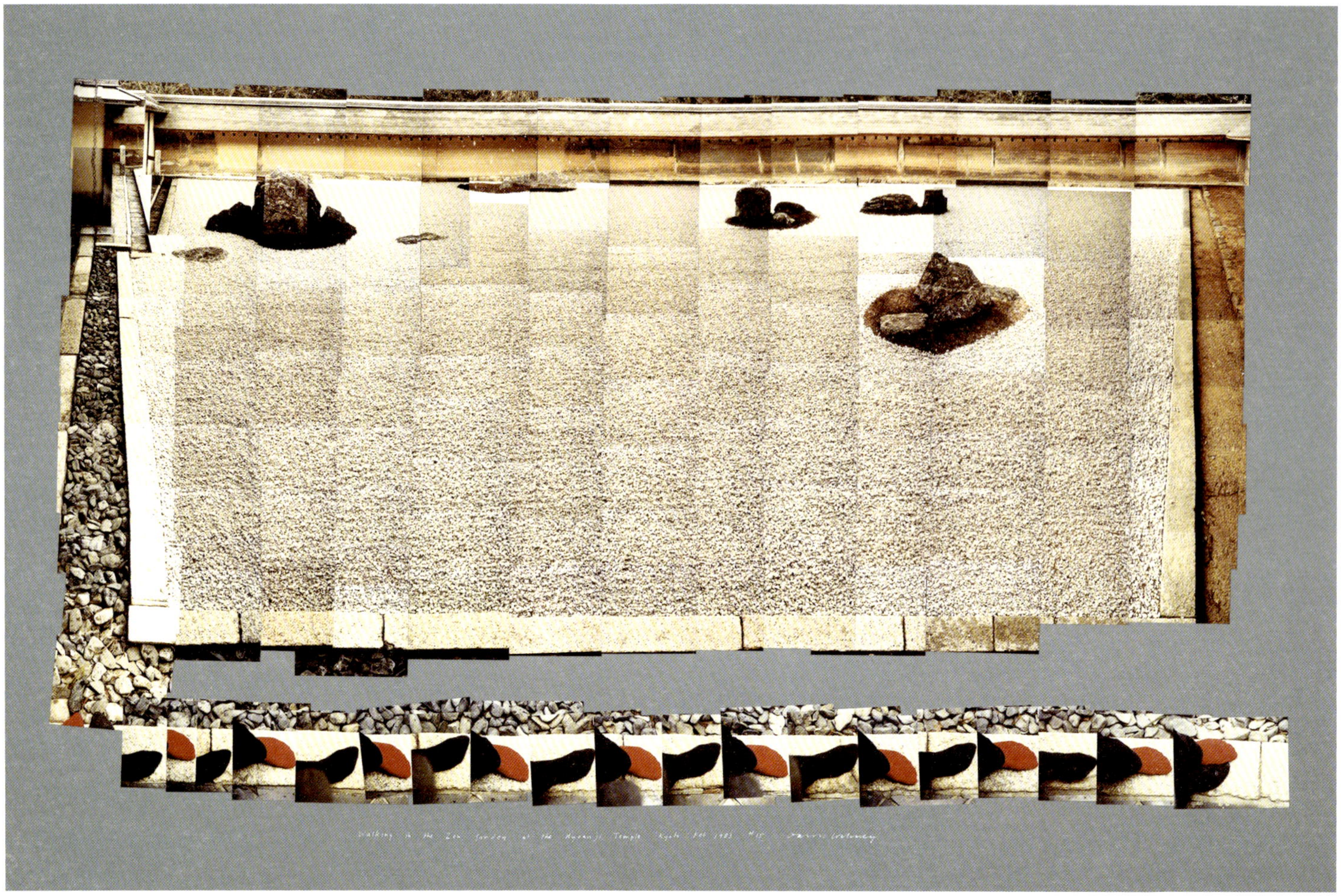

25 | H David Hockney, *Walking in the Zen Garden at the Ryoanji Temple, Kyoto, February 1983*, photographic collage, edition 15 of 20, 101.6 x 158.8 cm. Collection of the artist

were done from a ladder, you had to be up above them looking straight down" (fig. 26). For a week he worked from about 9 to 11 each morning, so the sun was in the same position, then as soon as the days shots were processed, he set about the delicate and difficult task of piecing them together:

We took a room in a motel in Palmdale. We'd have the photographs processed there, then next day I'd pick them up then I'd be gluing quite a few down to see what to do next. When I'd done that, I could decide, 'Well, now I'll do it this way next, from that point, and so on. It was a very, very elaborate work'. I realised with 850 photographs making it up, that was going to happen. Any little variation will lead to others.

A photographic collage such as *The Scrabble Game* (1983, fig. 27) has a considerable amount in common with a cubist work by Picasso or Braque from around 1912. Like many of those its subject is effectively a table-top, the objects on it and a few figures around it, all of them fragmented because they are seen from differing positions and also over an extended period of time.

Hockney's ultimate conclusion was that what he was doing, relating one object to another in pictorial space, was a form of *drawing*. He was not using charcoal or a pen but it was drawing, nonetheless. For similar reasons Hockney classifies a series of works made in 2018 with a digital camera as "photographic drawings". These are made with sophisticated twenty-first-century software and digital cameras, but the result still requires innumerable subjective decisions about where to place one thing relative to another in space.

The act of drawing is fundamental to Hockney's art and to his life as well. He once confessed,

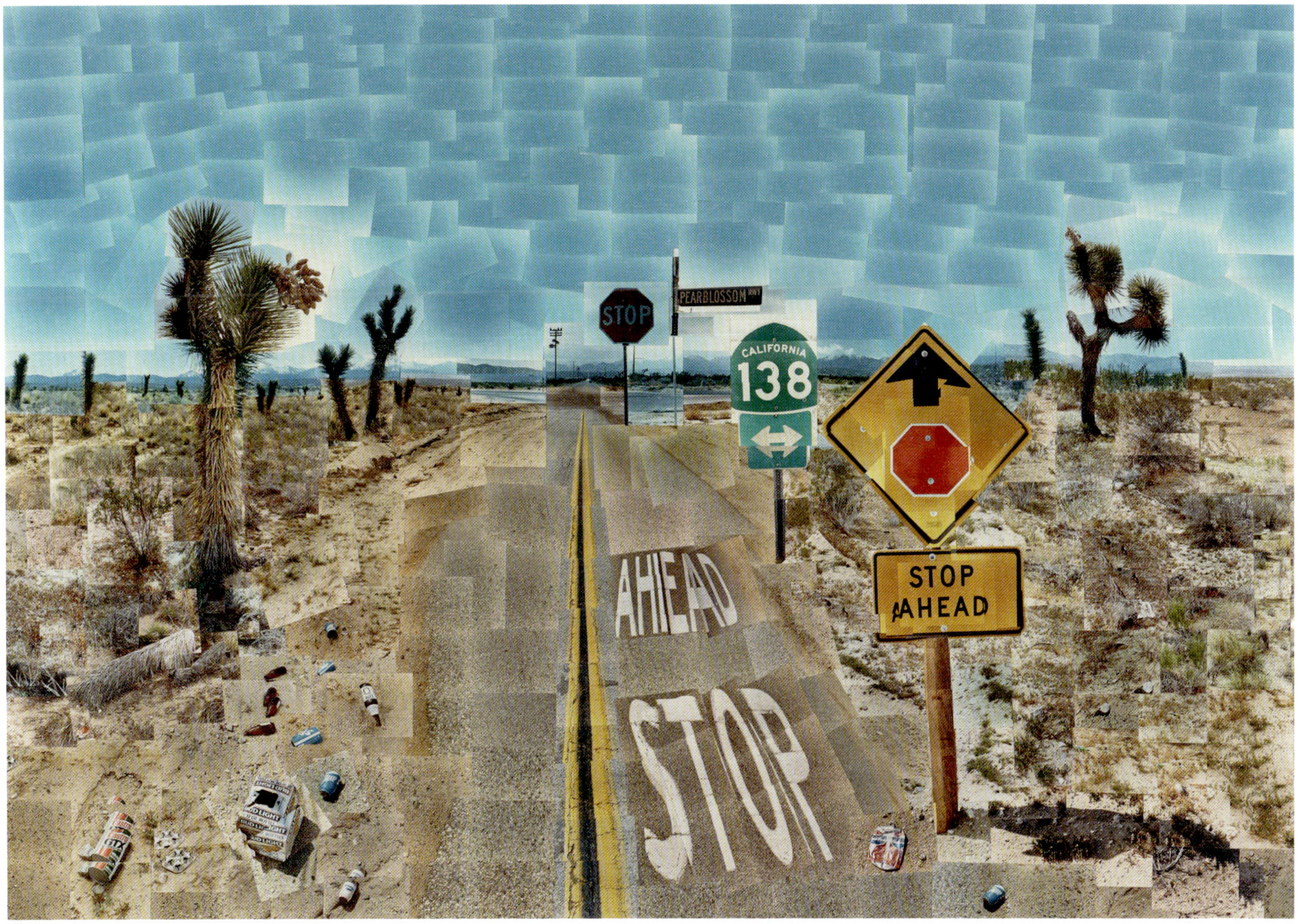

"I draw all the time" – then added, "Wasn't it Degas who said, 'I'm just a man who likes to draw'? That's me, I'm just a man who likes to draw." However, he also relishes variety and therefore enjoys making different *kinds* of lines. Throughout his career he has moved from medium to medium, exploring both traditional ways of making a mark on paper such as charcoal, pencil, coloured crayon, and a variety of differing pens and inks, plus printing-making media including etching and lithography in many modes, both colour and monochrome. Hockney has also approached a series of sometimes unexpected devices with the question in mind, 'How could this be a tool for drawing?'

Among these devices was the camera, which, as we have seen, Hockney concluded he was using to make an unusual type of drawing. In the 1980s he also repurposed the fax and colour photocopier, both then novel hi-tech pieces of office equipment, to make a remarkable series of prints. Around the same time he experimented with computer drawing, but found the technology too slow ("It drove me mad. I'd have finished but the drawing would still be being done.").

At the end of 2008, however, he found that the hardware and software had speeded up enough for him to use. At this point he made a series of digital drawings of which *Matelot Kevin Druez 1*, (2009, fig. 28) is one. Hockney drew these on a graphics tablet, and the result was printed out by an ink-jet printer. At the time he explained what he was doing:

What you are really doing is drawing in a printing machine. You don't look at your hand, you look at the screen. Then I print it out, see what it's looking like, see what colours you get. So you actually use the colours that the printing machine makes. Using this medium means you miss some things – you miss texture – but you gain a lot.

26 David Hockney, *Pearblossom Hwy., 11 – 18th April 1986, (Second Version)*, photographic collage, 181.6 x 271.8 cm. The J. Paul Getty Museum, Los Angeles, 97.XM.39

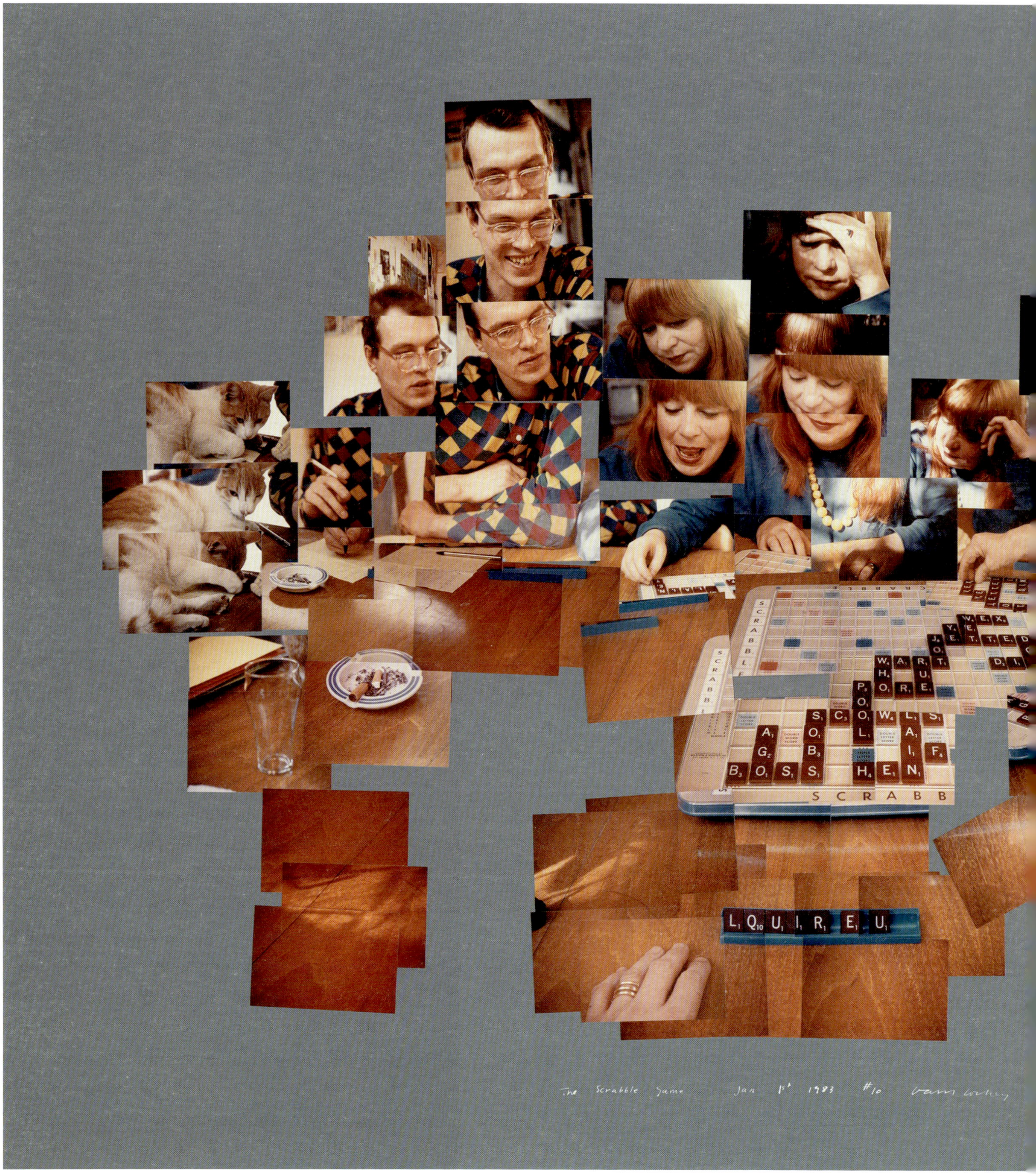
The Scrabble Game Jan 1st 1983 #10
LQUIREU

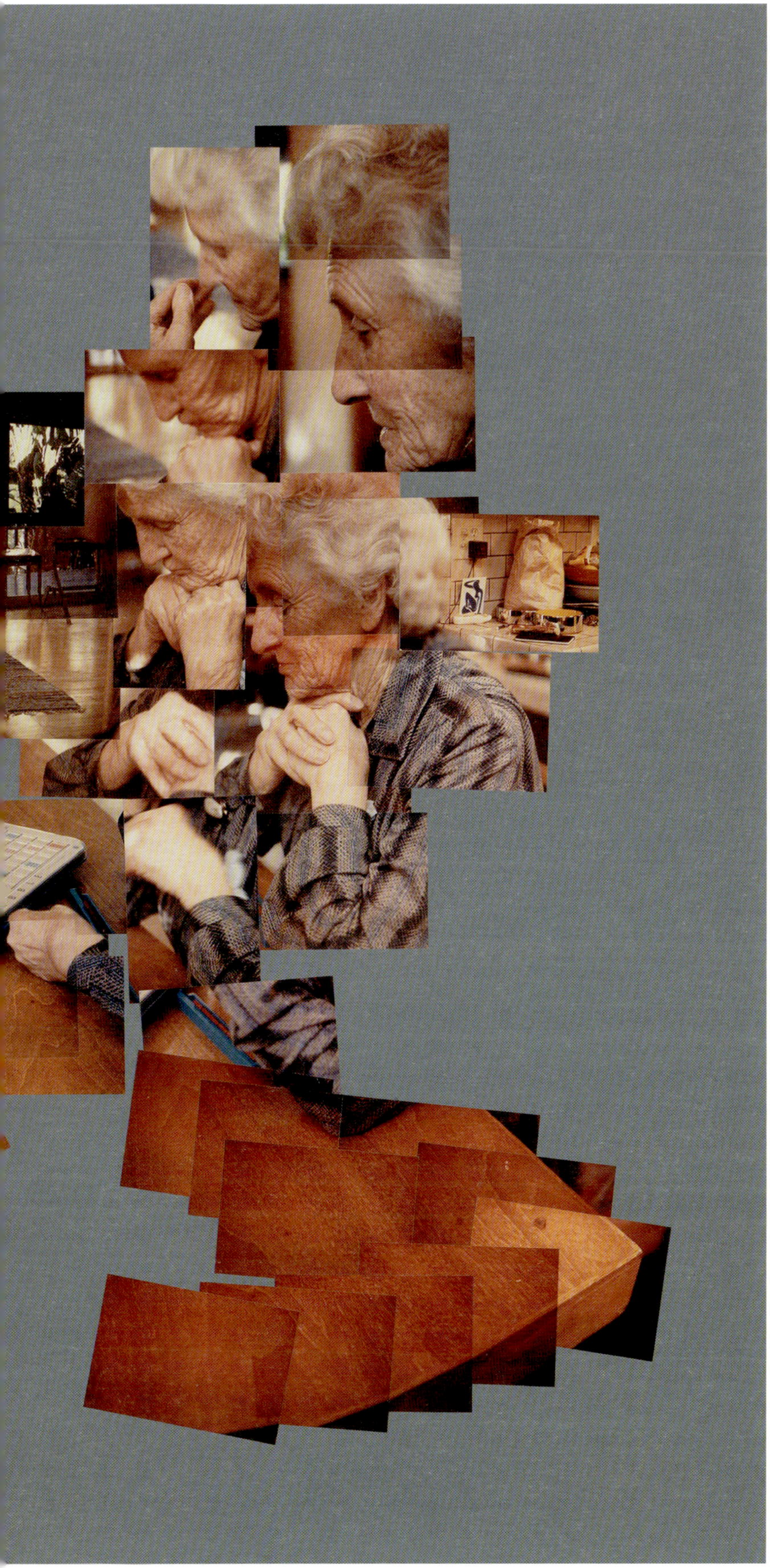

27 | H David Hockney,
The Scrabble Game, January 1st 1983, photographic collage, edition 10 of 20, 99 x 147.3 cm.
Collection of the artist

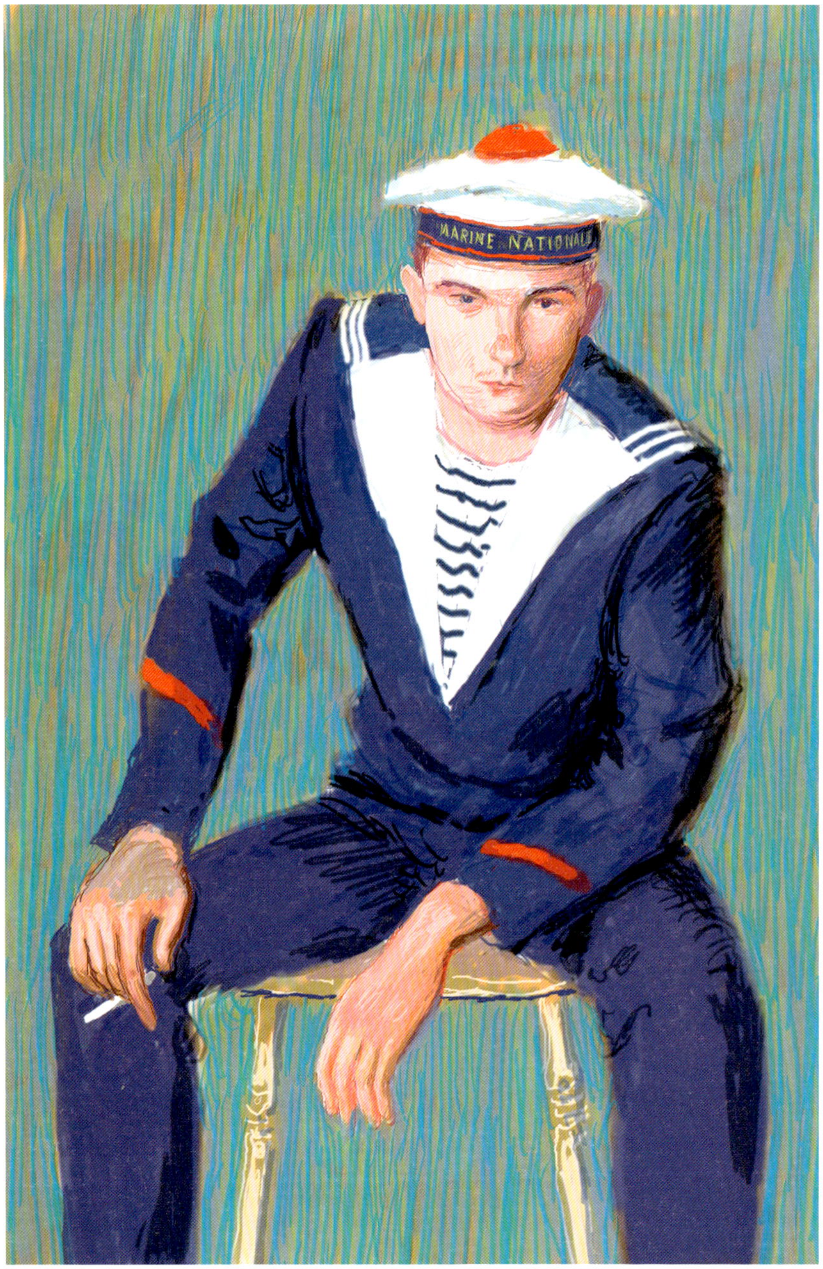

28 | H David Hockney,
Matelot Kevin Druez 1, 2009,
inkjet printed computer drawing on paper, edition 20 of 30, 124.5 x 85 cm.
Private collection

A similar calculus of gain and loss applies in Hockney's view to every medium. "Media are about how you make marks, or don't make them. In linocuts, for example, everything has to be bold. You don't make tiny, thin lines in a linocut, it would be too niggly. But get an etching plate, and it's about fine lines."

This has been his philosophy over the past decade as he has employed a series of brand-new tools – the iPhone and the iPad, using first his finger then a stylus, with different editions of the Brushes app, and for works such as *Viewers Looking at a Ready-made with Skull and Mirrors*, made in 2018, a complex amalgam of digital photograph, imaging and virtual collage.

In every case, the technique has characteristic advantages and disadvantages – the point of the exercise from Hockney's point of view being to play to each one's strengths. But they are all ways of depicting the visible world around us. That is what drawing and its twin discipline painting both are. This, in Hockney's view, is an enterprise that has, quite literally, fundamental dimensions.

"Painting is an art of time and space or so it seems to me. A big thing in drawing is being able to put a figure in space – and you make space through time." The fact that a photograph was an instantaneous image, recording only the usually tiny amount of time that the shutter was open, was another problem with camera-made images as far as Hockney was concerned. He believes that our experience of the world is indissolubly connected with the passage of time. First we see one thing, then another, and relate the two together. His 'joiners' illustrated that truth: they were not the product of a single shutter-click, but of hundreds spread over many hours – then pieced together.

In a photograph it's the same time on every part of the surface. That's not true in a painting; it's not true even in a painting made from a photograph. That makes a considerable difference. It's why you can't look at a photograph for too long. In the end, it is just a fraction of a second, so you don't see the subject in layers.

Every picture, Hockney contends, contains a certain amount of time. Some take hours to make, some years. But a single photograph may comprise only a small fraction of a second. This

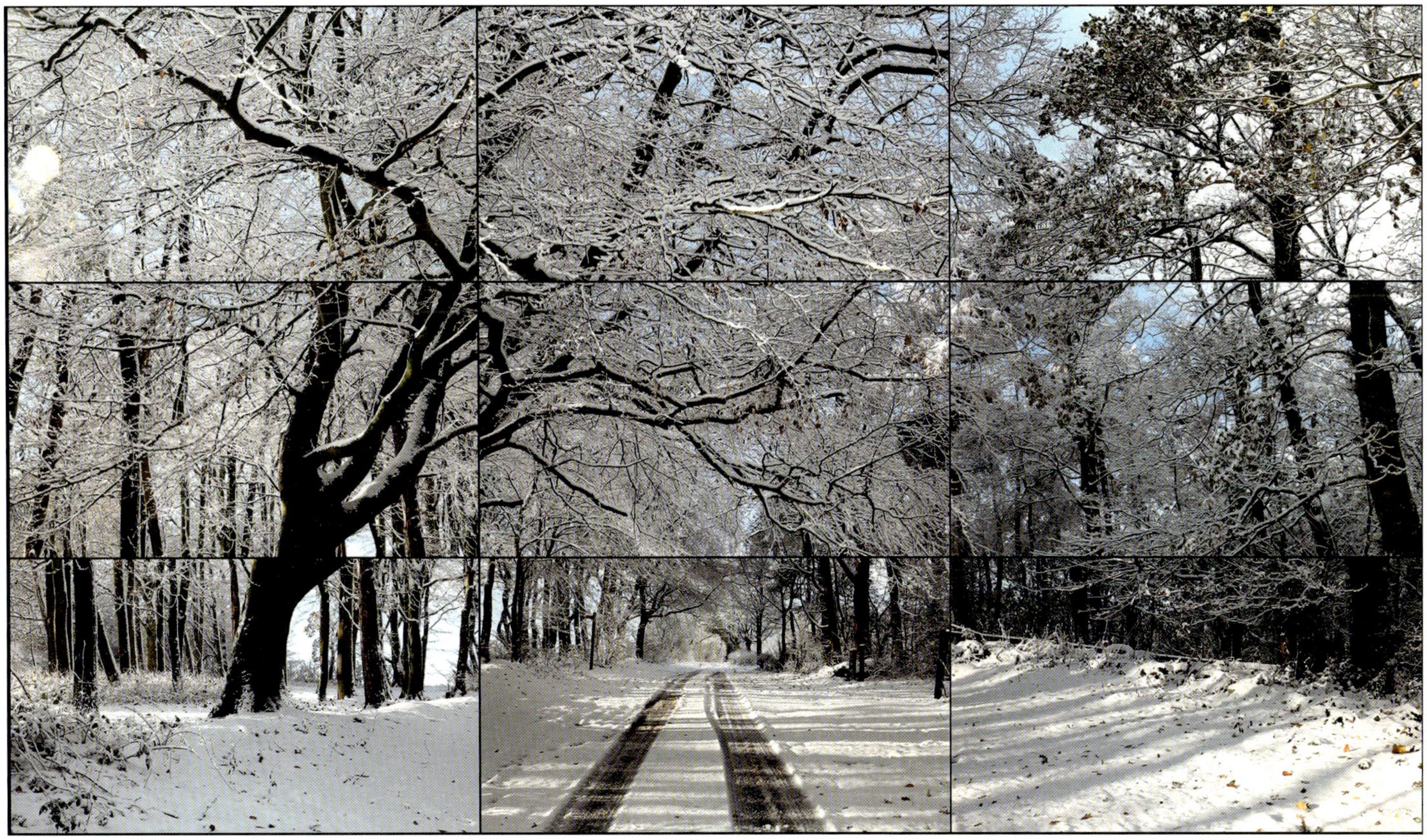

is why although photographs in his view are good at registering the surfaces of objects, especially when seen shallow relief, they are much less able to handle landscape. This last involves long vistas, the sky, the horizon. It is essentially, as he puts it, "a *spatial* thrill".

Among Hockney's most extraordinary inventions of recent years were filmed landscapes, such as *Woldgate Woods, Winter 2010.* These contain multiple photographic images in the manner of the 'joiners', but also time – not just, like a scene in a film, the seconds or minutes the action lasted. Hockney's multi-screen films of around 2010 incorporate time *within* the overall image because (a point not always appreciated) there are temporal intervals of perhaps a second or two between the sequences on each screen.

If you were in that car, driving along Woldgate, in reality your eyes would be moving, registering different aspects of the passing trees and undergrowth from ever-changing angles and at slightly different moments. So does *Woldgate Woods, Winter* (fig. 29). In a way it is a highly traditional work – a snow scene, one from a set of the seasons which goes back to Pieter Bruegel the Elder, and further to the late Middle Ages. In another way it is – as we have just seen – unprecedented. The combination is typical of Hockney. To go back to the distinctions with which we began, he is both a traditional artist and a highly contemporary one. He uses the newest of techniques to explore the oldest of problems, confident that "there's always another way to do it".

He has demonstrated that that is true of portraiture and landscape, genres long declared dead by critics and theorists of art, which he has nonetheless triumphantly revived. The same holds for the art (or science) of picturing space, for history of art and indeed for Hockney himself. It is always possible to see them from a different point of view, in a fresh perspective.

29 | F David Hockney, *Woldgate Woods, Winter 2010*, 2010–11, 9 digital videos synchronized and presented on 9 monitors to comprise a single artwork, duration: 49:00. Collection of the artist

Notes

Unless otherwise stated all quotation are from the author's conversations with David Hockney, 1995–2021. **1** Hockney 1977, p. 203. **2** Ibid., p. 41.

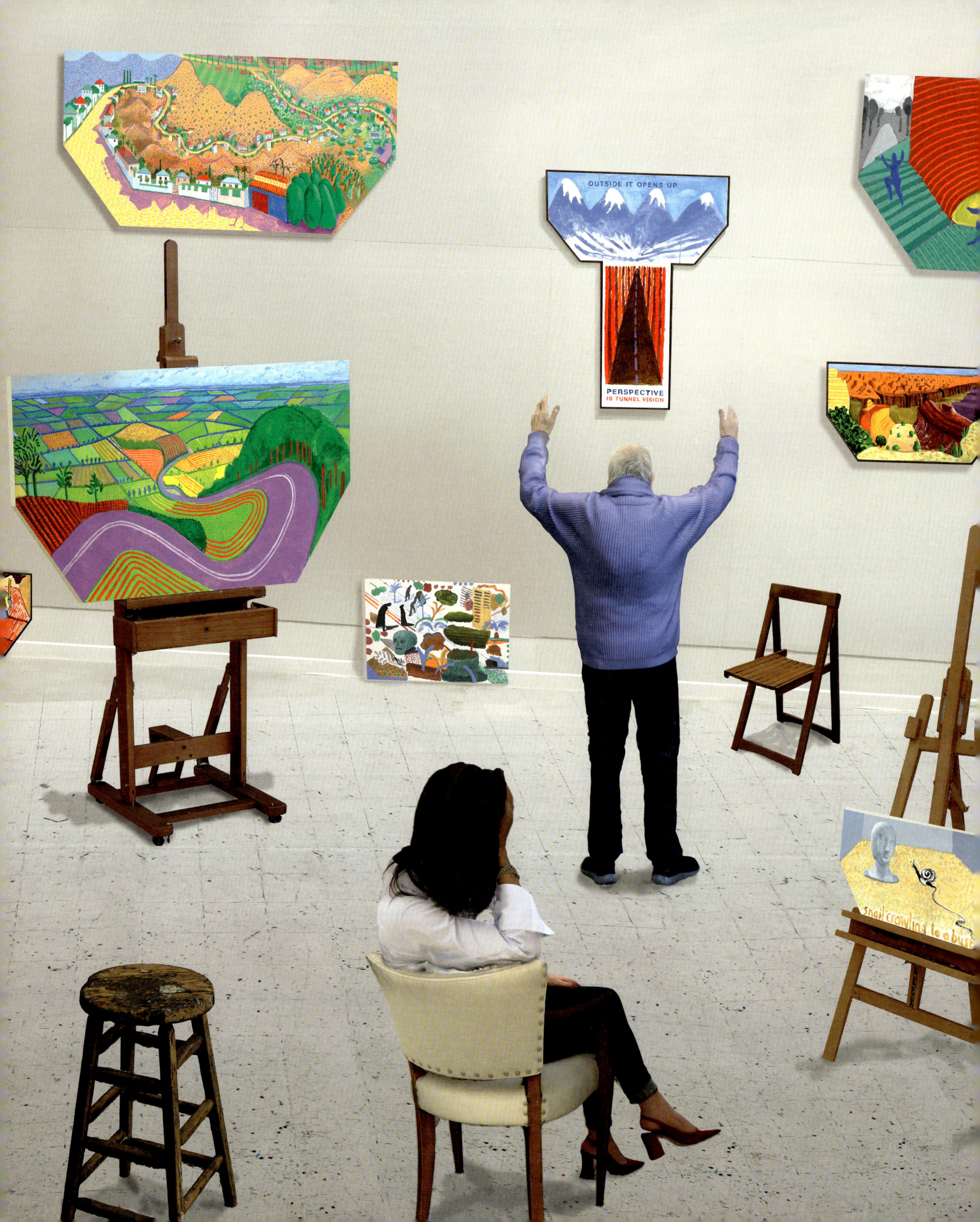
OUTSIDE IT OPENS UP
PERSPECTIVE
IS TUNNEL VISION

Martin Kemp

Seeing through perspective

Perspective was very important to artists. Invented and perfected in fifteenth-century Italy, its foundations in geometrical optics endowed the painter with a 'theory' or 'science' with which to promote the status of painting as a 'Liberal Art' alongside music, which claimed to be founded on mathematical harmonies. Perspective presented a formula for the systematic rendering of solid forms in geometrical spaces under the embrace of directional light. It aspired to represent nature accurately as seen by a viewer from a predetermined viewpoint. When the architect Filippo Brunelleschi contrived his optically generated 'portraits' of the Florentine Baptistery and Palazzo Vecchio, and when Leon Battista Alberti in his seminal little book, *On Painting,* outlined how to depict space according to a consistent optical formula, the Renaissance ambition to imitate nature seemed to have taken a measured and measurable leap forward.[1]

The perspectival revolution spawned a series of treatises, beginning with Alberti in 1435/36. Instructional books of increasing complexity and dogmatism proliferated in the era of art academies from the mid sixteenth century onwards, outlining techniques for laying out optical spaces with objects orientated in any given way. The illustrated example comes from an English edition of the popular and much-translated *La perspective pratique* by the French mathematician Jean Dubreuil, first published in 1642, with a three-volume edition in 1679 (fig. 30).[2] It showed how objects orientated at any angle to the spectator could be characterized on a receding floor according to geometrical optics, each with its own vanishing point along the shared horizon line. This spatial square-dance of

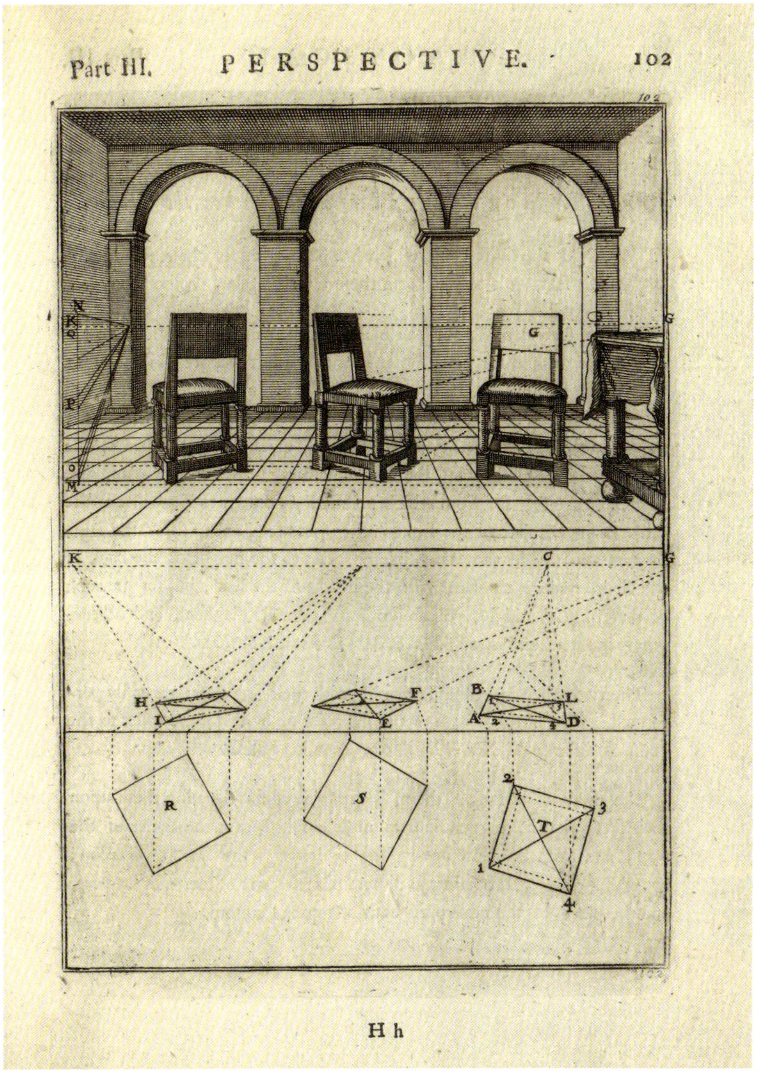

30 'Three Chairs at Different Angles in a Tiled Loggia', from Jean Dubreuil, *The Practice of Perspective: Or, An Easy Method of Representing Natural Objects According to the Rules of Art*, London, 4th edition, 1765, Part III, p. 102

chairs and other items of furniture is shared with the computer-generated interiors of Hockney's California studio (fig. 44).

So far so good. But the story is by no means as neat as this. For most practitioners, perspective was a working tool that delivered convincing results when used in a pragmatic manner, without following the rules slavishly. We can imagine that trainee artists groaned when faced with elaborate geometrical constructions, while most mature painters used perspectival constructions only in as far as it served their functional needs in the variety of pictorial tasks that they took on. Even Dubreuil later admitted in a book on fortifications that "neither I or my like have enough patience to bind ourselves to these rules" in every case.[3] The number of paintings in which perspectival constructions were elaborately and comprehensively realised as their prime feature is unexpectedly small – if much discussed. We think most notably of Piero della Francesca in the fifteenth century, and Dutch seventeenth-century painters of domestic and church interiors. With Vermeer and other Dutch painters, we also enter the realm of the camera obscura, the pre-photographic box equipped with a lens, and the 'dark chamber' on a larger walk-in scale.[4] It is this strain of instrumental devices that we witness with Canaletto (see figs. 88, 91, 93–95) and his successor 'view-painters' (see fig. 96).

Many of the subjects favoured in the sixteenth and eighteenth centuries, including landscapes, seascapes and portraits, did not necessarily involve linear perspective. There may well be a sense of the changing scale of figures and objects at various depths into the space of the picture, in which perspective is implicit, but the constructions were judged 'by eye' rather than calculated. Hobbema's powerfully perspectival *Avenue at Middelharnis* (fig. 49) and the drawings for Simon de Vlieger's seascapes (fig. 53) are exceptions rather than the rule amongst outdoor paintings.

A rough count of paintings in the Fitzwilliam Museum from 1400 to 1800 yields the following numbers: 237 in which there is no obvious use of perspective; 469 in which perspective is implicit; 33 in which perspectival motifs are readily apparent; 18 in which perspective plays a dominant and determining role.[5] Expressed in percentages: no perspective 31.3%; implicit perspective 62%; perspectival motifs 4.4%; dominant perspective 2.3%. It would be surprising if any rounded collections of international old masters in European and American galleries would depart significantly from these figures, even though the Fitzwilliam contains an unusually large number of flower paintings.

Even in cases where geometrical perspective was applied certain problems of an optical nature presented themselves. One anomaly was recognized by the most meticulous Renaissance advocate of geometrical perspective, Piero della Francesca. He pointed out that if our angle of vision exceeds 90°, a square (say a tile on a pavement) would be portrayed as deeper than it is wide.[6] The strange things that can happen with a wide-angle view are vividly demonstrated by Paolo Uccello's off-centre perspective in his small panel of *The Jew's Attempt to Destroy the Host*.[7]

An extreme example of the bizarre optical results of very wide-angle views is Daniel Vosmaer's painting of Delft viewed though an imaginary loggia (fig. 31). The vanishing point is located at the left margin of the canvas. Given the very tiny angles between successive diagonals though the rows of square tiles, Vosmaer has unsurprisingly lost a degree of control over the geometrical construction, with the result that some of the rows of tiles appear to be gently curved. Even viewing the painting from a viewpoint at the extreme left does not rectify the geometrical deviations, though the overall optical effect becomes very striking. The effect from a normal viewing point in front of the picture is rather Hockney-ish.

Other key problems were identified by Leonardo da Vinci in his unpublished writings and were to appear in printed treatises over the course of succeeding centuries. They centred on wide-angle vision, in which "all the depicted objects will look monstrous" at their wider extremes.[8] If we look at a wide wall running across our field of vision, the wall will be further away at its extreme ends and should seem less high at the ends than in the middle. If we look at a colonnade oriented in the same way, the spaces between the columns will seem to become narrower at wider angles. Also, as the columns are placed towards the lateral ends of the colonnade, moving further from our eye, we should see more of their circumference. We

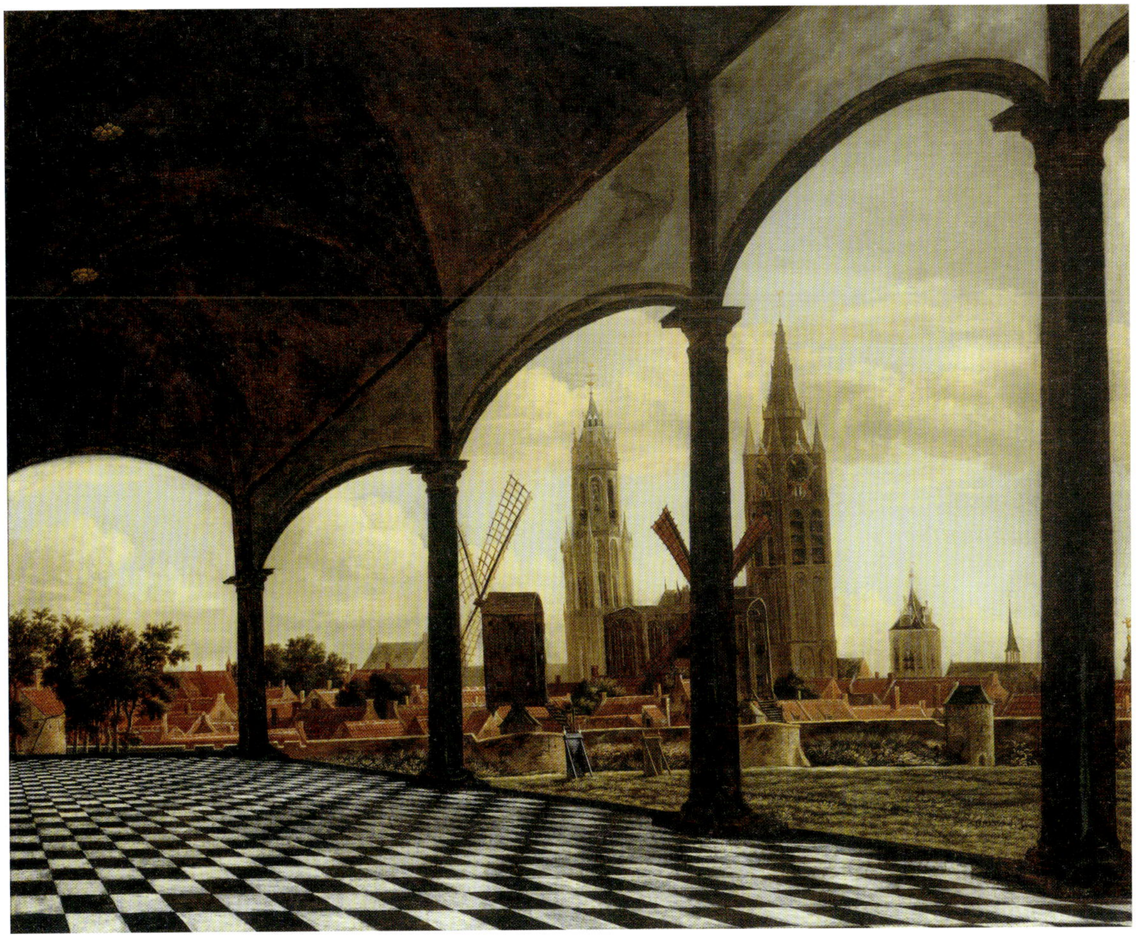

31 Danile Vosmaer, *A View of Delft Through an Imaginary Loggia*, 1663, oil on canvas, 91 x 113 cm. Museum Princenhof, Delft, B 1-36

may also mention that a sphere set off-centre in a picture should undergo elliptical distortion if the geometry were to be rigidly applied. In practice, painters almost never attempted to replicate such effects. They settled for walls with straight lines at the top and bottom, for columns of identical dimension across the picture surface and for spheres with circular perimeters regardless of position. These 'look right' pictorially and function for us as spectators.

A rare example that follows the optical geometry of foreshortened spheres (or rather a half-sphere mounted on a cylinder) is Jan van der Heyden's view of the new town hall in Amsterdam (fig. 32). The dome and its drum are asymmetrically distorted. The agent who delivered the painting to the Medici Grand Duke Cosimo III explained that it should be viewed through a fixed "instrument of iron which is attached to the frame". Viewed from the authorized point at its right margin as a kind of peep-show, the dome's perspective functioned perfectly. Earlier versions by Jan and very similar views by Gerrit Berckheyde (fig. 33), are designed for free-style viewing and render the dome conventionally. For the eccentric dome Jan must have made a complex geometrical projection or used a camera - probably the latter. It is likely that both Jan and Gerrit regularly used a camera tracing as the basis for their popular views taken from stock viewing positions.

Jan's viewing experiment raises the perennial problem of one-eyed vision from a fixed viewpoint. Drawing a human foetus in a womb with great sculptural conviction, Leonardo squeezed in a note to the effect that "a picture seen with one eye will not demonstrate such relief as when it is seen with both eyes".[9] The rigid fixing of the monocular viewpoint also causes potential problems for a mobile viewer, since the spatial illusion within the

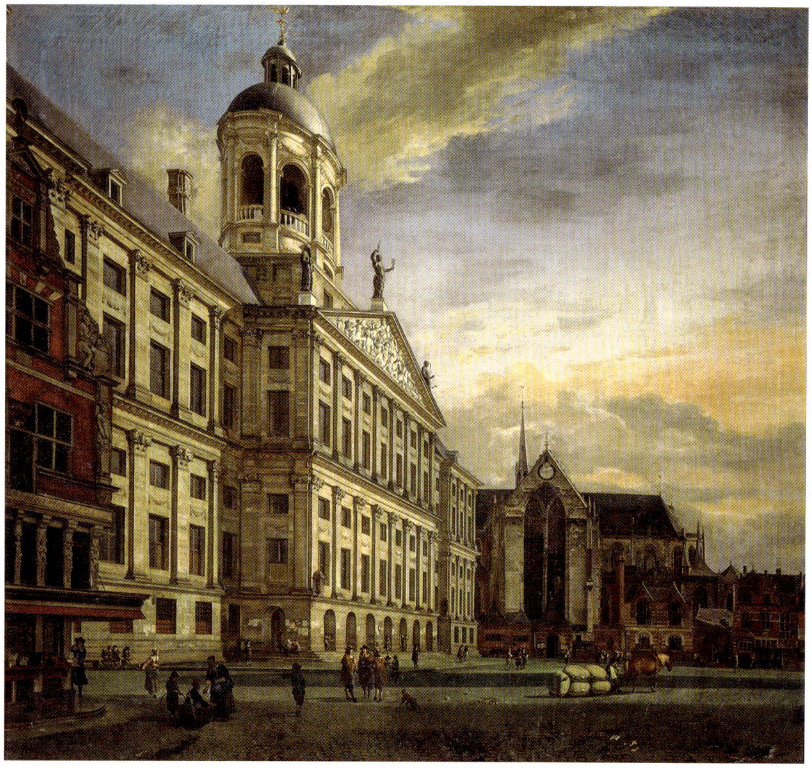

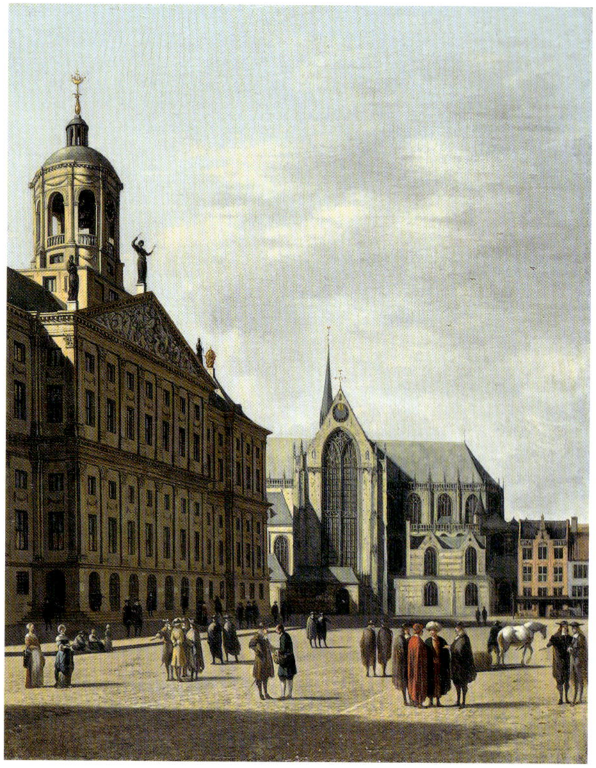

32 Jan van der Heyden, *Amsterdam, Dam Square with the Town Hall and the Nieuwe Kerk*, 1667, oil on canvas, 85 x 92 cmGalleria degli Uffizi, Florence, 1890: 1211

33 Gerrit Adriaensz Berckheyde, *The Town Hall of Amsterdam*, c. 1674, oil on panel, 40.3 x 32.3 cm. Fitzwilliam Museum, No. 44

picture will only work perfectly from the stipulated viewpoint. In practice the illusion retains a surprising degree of robustness from less than ideal viewpoints, and canny artists minimized the problem by disguising the relationship between real and painted spaces. For example, in his *Last Supper*, Leonardo floated the coffered ceiling ambiguously in space rather than anchoring it visually to the walls and vault of the refectory. Furthermore, the viewpoint for Leonardo's mural is high above that of any spectator, however tall, contradicting his written advice that subjects should always be portrayed as if at the right height for the spectator.

The sum total of these problems with orthodox perspective led Leonardo to separate the internally consistent geometry of "artificial perspective" from the way we actually see things according to "natural perspective". There is no overt parade of 'artificial perspective' in his works after 1500. Leonardo proves to be an unexpected ally for David Hockney – not least in Hockney's more emphatic rejection of the tyranny of the monocular viewpoint in the 1960s.

As Martin Gayford shows, no painter since Pablo Picasso has mounted a more inventive, impulsive, varied and exciting assault on standard techniques of spatial representation than David Hockney. His great and much-loved double portraits of the late 1960s and early 1970s, exemplified by *Mr and Mrs Clark with Percy* (1970–71) and *George Lawson and Wayne Sleep* (1972–75, fig. 118), breathed a cool frontal geometry and perspectival devices worthy of Piero della Francesca, whom he studied avidly. A California drawing from 1966 is both flatly linear and strongly perspectival – even if it is not governed by a precise vanishing-point (fig. 34). In his *California Bank* (fig. 35) he exploits a flat, almost abstract composition in which depth is established through our awareness of the relative scale of schematic trees, shrubs and the high-rise building. Geometrical flatness becomes the dominant motif some years later in *Rubber Ring Floating in a Swimming Pool* (fig. 36), which serves as a virtually abstract composition because the pool, its tiled edge and the ring are viewed from a static, monocular viewpoint.

However, in keeping with his perpetual desire to refresh the means and ends of his art, Hockney began to feel that "there was

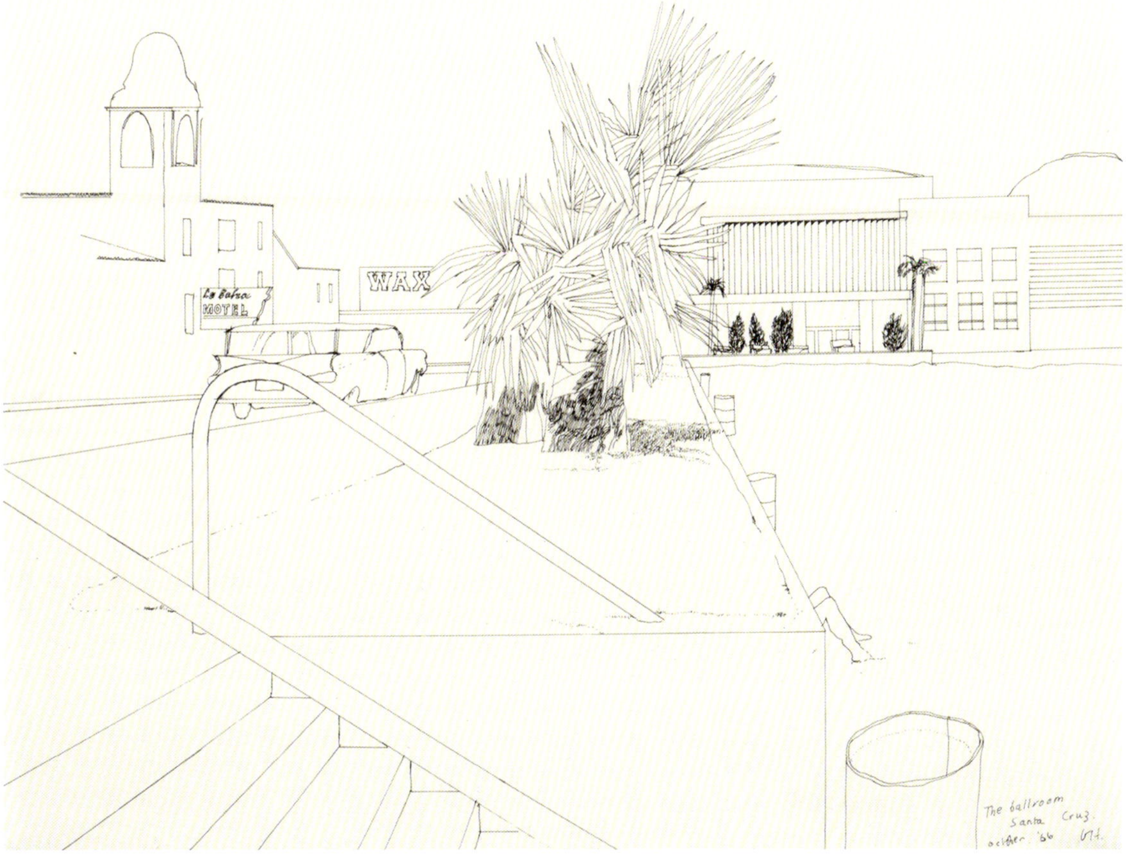

34 | F David Hockney, *The Ballroom, Santa Cruz,* 1966, pen and ink on paper, 24.8 x 31 cm. Private collection

something wrong with what I was doing – I've called it 'obsessive naturalism' – but then I didn't know what it was. Photography was causing it."[10] He decided that he needed to move away from his existing kind of cool naturalism with its monocular viewpoint. As he has said, 'Any photograph ... will only have one perspective. In real life when you are looking at ten people in a room there are a thousand. Because the moment the eye moves, it changes. That's what real life is. The eye moves all the time."[11]

His anti-perspectival move brought with it an emphasis on the limitations of photography as an analogue of how we actually see objects and spaces. Straightforward photography of the kind with which we are most familiar, not least via our mobile phones, ossifies the monocular viewpoint because that is how the optics of a camera works. It is worth noting that the standard space in computer graphics, with its x, y and z axes, is essentially the same as that constructed by Alberti. Indeed, Antonio Criminisi's pioneering technique of single-view metrology can be used to reconstruct automatically the actual spaces in perspectival paintings.[12]

This is not to say that photographic media and computer vision have offered no potential for Hockney. As we have seen, he has (amongst other things) exploited multiple viewing angles in his 'joiners' (figs. 25, 26), and collaged mobile views from multiple video cameras to compile compound scenes (figs. 44 and 46). And, as we will see, he has also recently made substantial use of computers to render objects at complex angles in large spaces.

Looking in the broadest way at the phase of perspectival naturalism from the Renaissance to the nineteenth century – and embracing the practice of photography – Hockney developed great overarching claims about the history of art over the centuries. These claims were broadcast in his book *Secret Knowledge. Rediscovering*

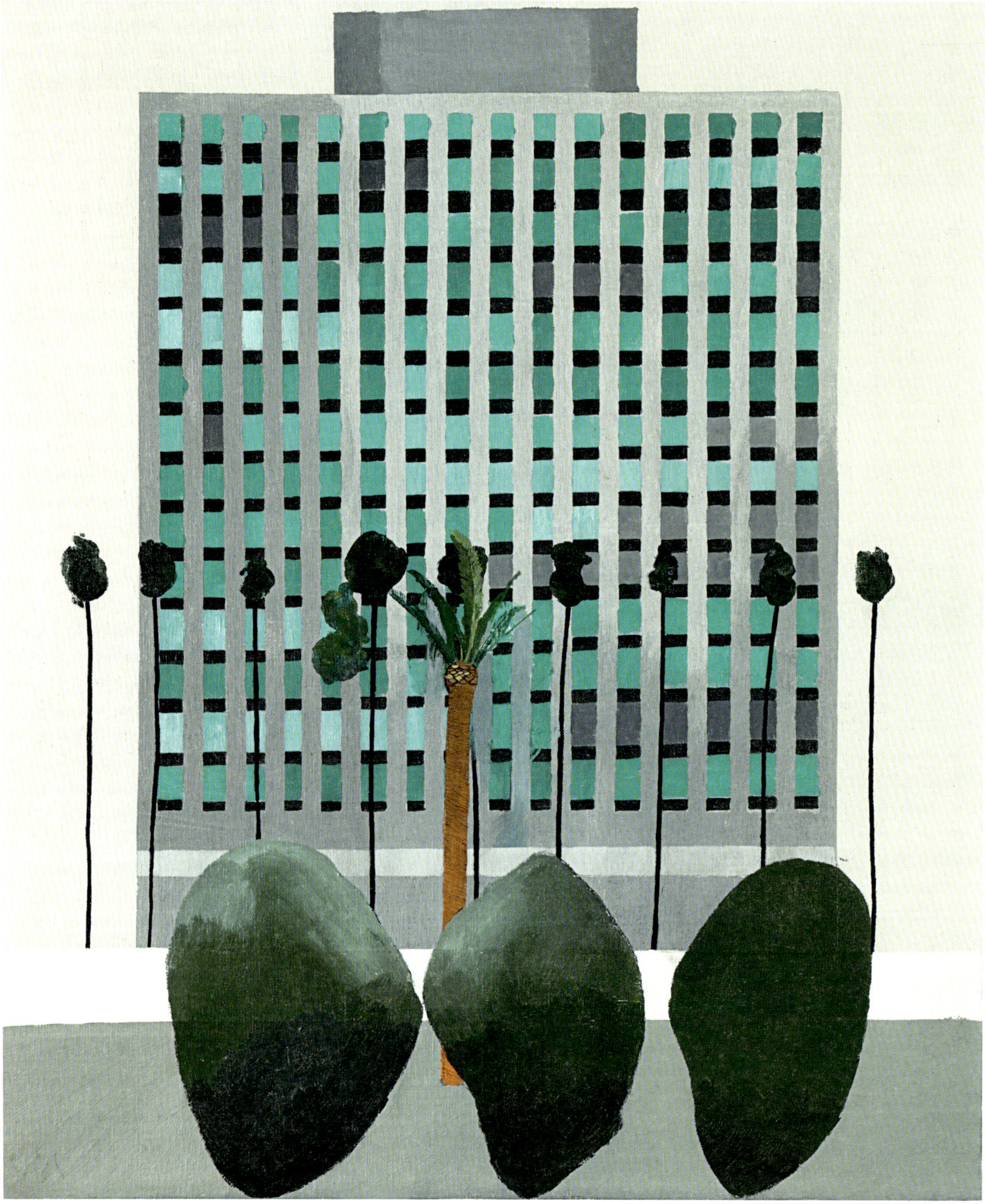

35 | F David Hockney,
California Bank, 1964,
acrylic on canvas, 76.2
x 63.5 cm. Private collection

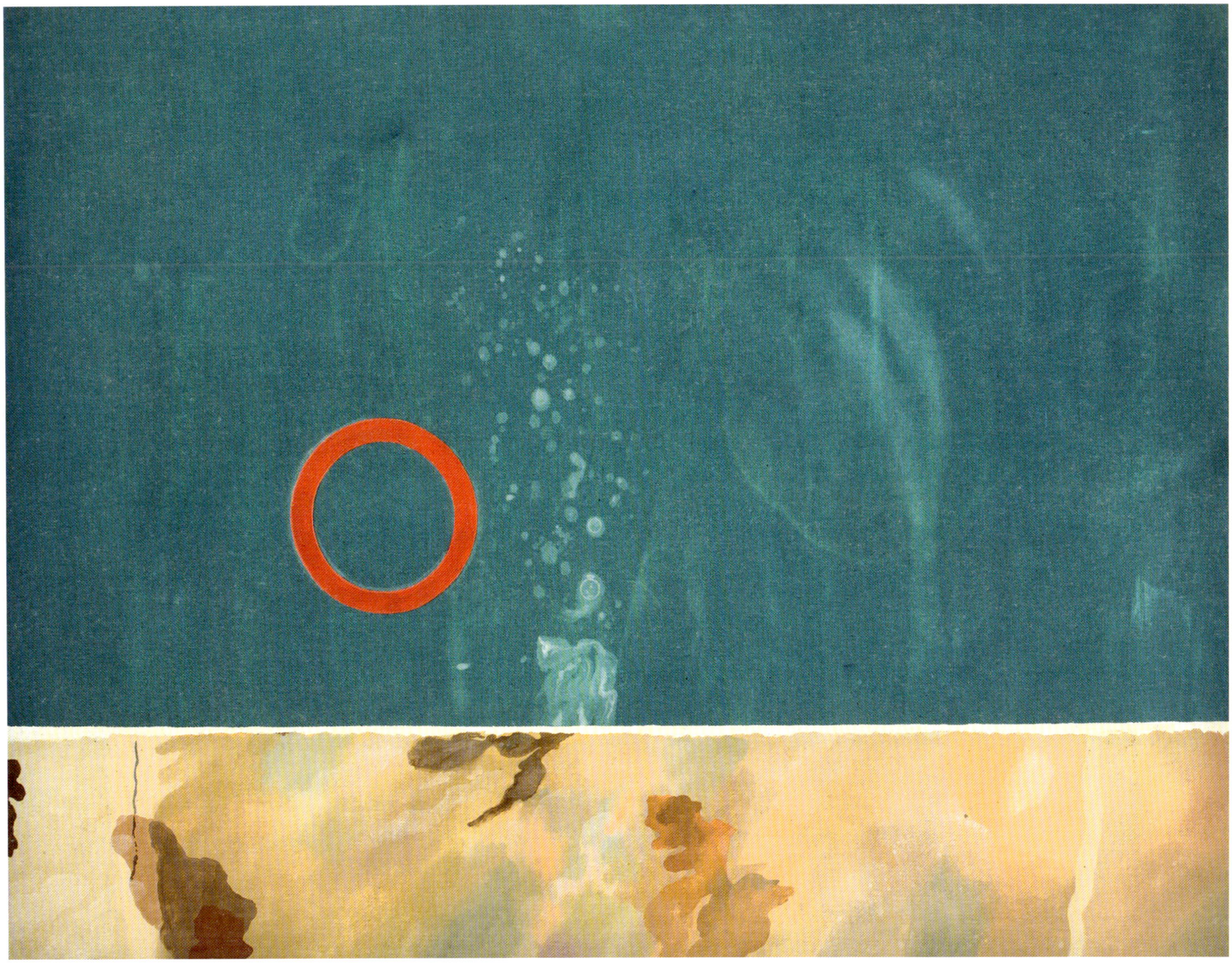

the Lost Techniques of the Old Masters in 2001, which received extensive attention in the media. It "rewrites the story of how Western artists made the great drawings and paintings of the last six centuries and in doing so blows the lid off the art establishment .... What he has discovered is that artists ... have used lenses and mirrors to project color images ... on to flat surfaces, and then traced those projected scenes with life-like precision on to canvas or paper."[13] This method did not just apply to the familiar suspects such as Vermeer, but to very large numbers of paintings that achieved high levels of 'photographic' realism. In effect art historians were being told that they had missed the central means that enabled painters to make things look notably 'real'. To say that the claims were controversial is an understatement. It is not comfortable for historians to be told that during their years' looking at their favoured artists they have failed to address the central procedure with which they achieved their ends.

The story began in 1999, when Hockney looked at an exhibition of portraits by J.-A.-D. Ingres in the National Gallery in London, as discussed below by Jane Munro.[14] Hockney decided that the visual evidence indicated that the French master had used a camera lucida as a convenient way to make drawn likenesses of posh visitors to Rome (figs. 103–09). From there, he surveyed a

36 | H David Hockney, *Rubber Ring Floating in a Swimming Pool*, 1971, acrylic on canvas, 91.4 x 122 cm. Private collection

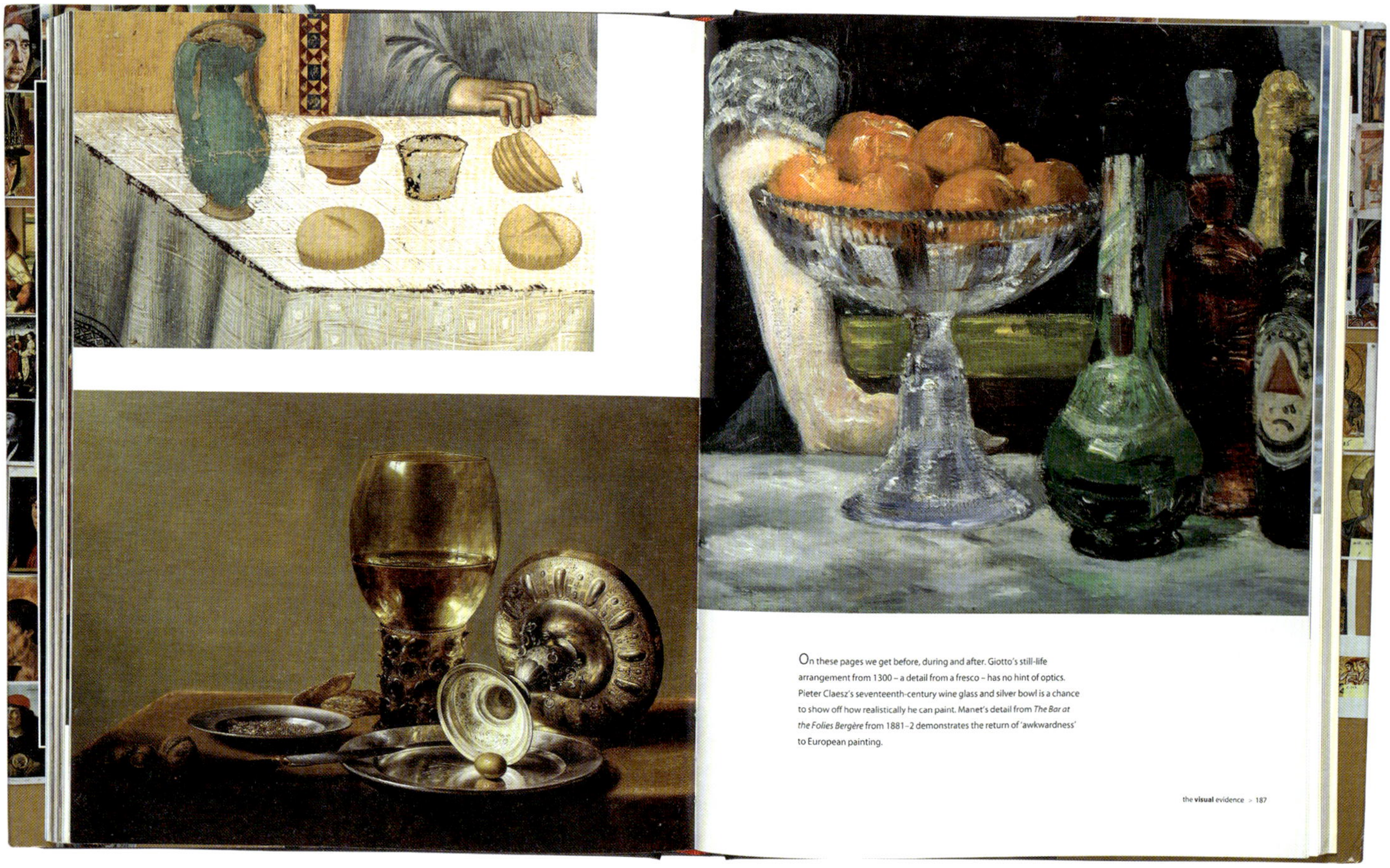

37 Pages 186–87 from David Hockney, *Secret Knowledge*, showing a detail of *The Death of the Knight of Celano* in the Upper Church of San Francesco, Assisi (painter unknown), a still life by Pieter Claesz, Berlin, Staatliche Museen, Berlin, and detail of Éduoard Manet, *Bar at the Folies Bergère*, The Courtauld Gallery, London

wide spread of paintings from the Renaissance to the twentieth century for signs that, rather than relying upon straightforward 'eyeballing' (free vision in the normal way), large numbers involved the use of optical devices to achieve naturalism. In the carefully orchestrated pages of the book, he offered an eloquent series of visual contrasts. For example, details of three still lifes from the fourteenth, seventeenth and nineteenth centuries show a progression from a naïve but effective evocation of objects on a squared tablecloth (not unlike some of Hockney's iPad sketches of table-top still lifes), through a virtuoso piece of naturalistic painting by Pieter Claesz to an 'eyeballed' array of vessels and fruits from Manet's *Bar at the Folies Bergère* (fig. 37), which moved beyond the 'photographic' manner in a way that compares closely with Hockney's iPad drawings (fig. 38).

Hockney realised this great historical sweep in an extraordinary panorama of reproductions pinned to the walls of his large studios (fig. 39). Whether the viewer believes that the prime determinant for this 'visual shape' in the history of Western art is the use of optical devices, the sense of grand progression towards and beyond naturalism is compelling.

For Hockney, the dominance of a certain kind of realistic image is more than a stylistic matter. He sees the command of naturalism as a very powerful social and political tool.

The great tyrants – Hitler, Stalin and Mao – … all demand lens-based pictures and use them to consolidate their power. It is also the period of the world's bloodiest conflicts, way beyond anything previously known. Are these things connected? Certainly, control of the media was essential for the slaughter.[15]

I would extend this prescription to the naturalistic image more generally rather than limiting it to those using lenses.[16] One of the points of skill in naturalistic representation is that its virtuosi can portray the false as convincingly as the real. This observation gains fresh potency in our world of visual lying on the internet. Over the ages, the Church rediscovered the power of the realistic image, although from diametrically opposed points of view in its Catholic and Reformed versions. Rulers and national institutions used naturalistic portrayals to broadcast the 'reality' – factual or fictional – of their persons, glories and accomplishments.

In his quest to analyse the role of optical devices, Hockney performed his own 'experimental proofs' to show how the devices might be exploited. He constructed a room-sized camera obscura with a lens in his London studio, exploring how it might operate with various kinds of subject, above all to create portraits (and copy 3D casts of heads) and still lifes. He also used a concave mirror as a projection device. The visual quality of the projected images, upside down and tonally consolidated in a way peculiar to such projections, matched Dutch paintings particularly well. The inversion of the images could be used positively – to help translate the image of a particular detail, say a nose, into coloured patches of colour, light and shade on a flat surface.

Above all, Hockney undertook an extensive series of camera lucida portraits to achieve rapid likenesses in the manner of Ingres (figs. 97–102). Drawing on his 'experiments', Hockney stressed three important features of the optical processes. The first is that drawing an image convincingly in a 'camera' requires considerable graphic skill of the kind that Henry Talbot conspicuously lacked (fig. 84). The second is that an expression of the kind that a sitter cannot hold for long could be rapidly captured. The third is that an optical device does not dictate how and when it is deployed in the making of a drawing or painting. With the camera lucida portraits, Hockney used the device briefly to establish the basic configuration of the sitter's face (not least the intervals between features), while the details were added by eye. In a painting that uses a camera obscura, the projected image can be used in a wide variety of ways at various stages in the generation of the image.

This is not the place to undertake a comprehensive analysis of the 'Hockney thesis' as it has been called. In keeping with the debate

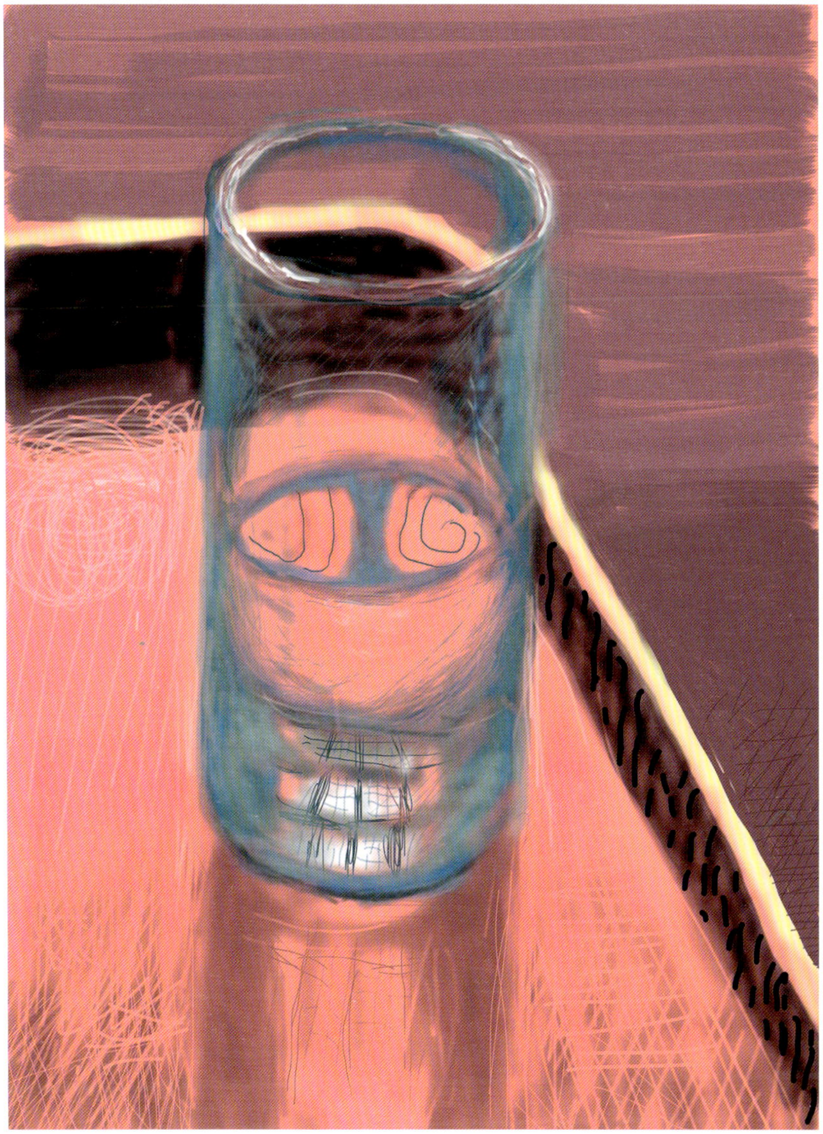

38 | H David Hockney, *10th August 2010*, iPad drawing. Collection of the artist

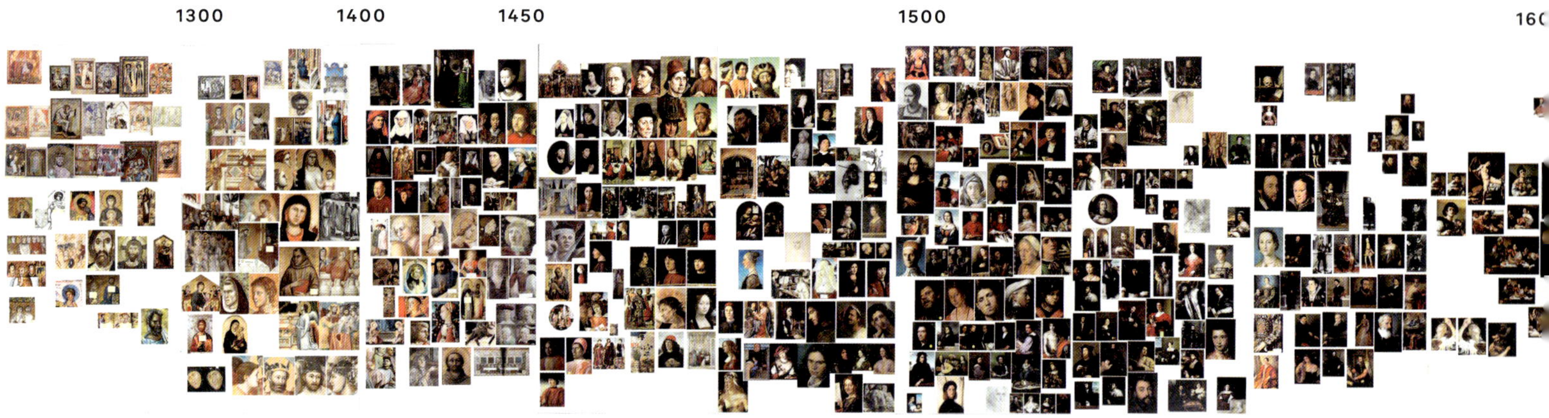

39a,b David Hockney, *The Great Wall*, 2000, colour laser copies on 18 panels, 2.44 x 1.22 m each, 2.44 x 21.95 m. overall. Collection of the David Hockney Foundation

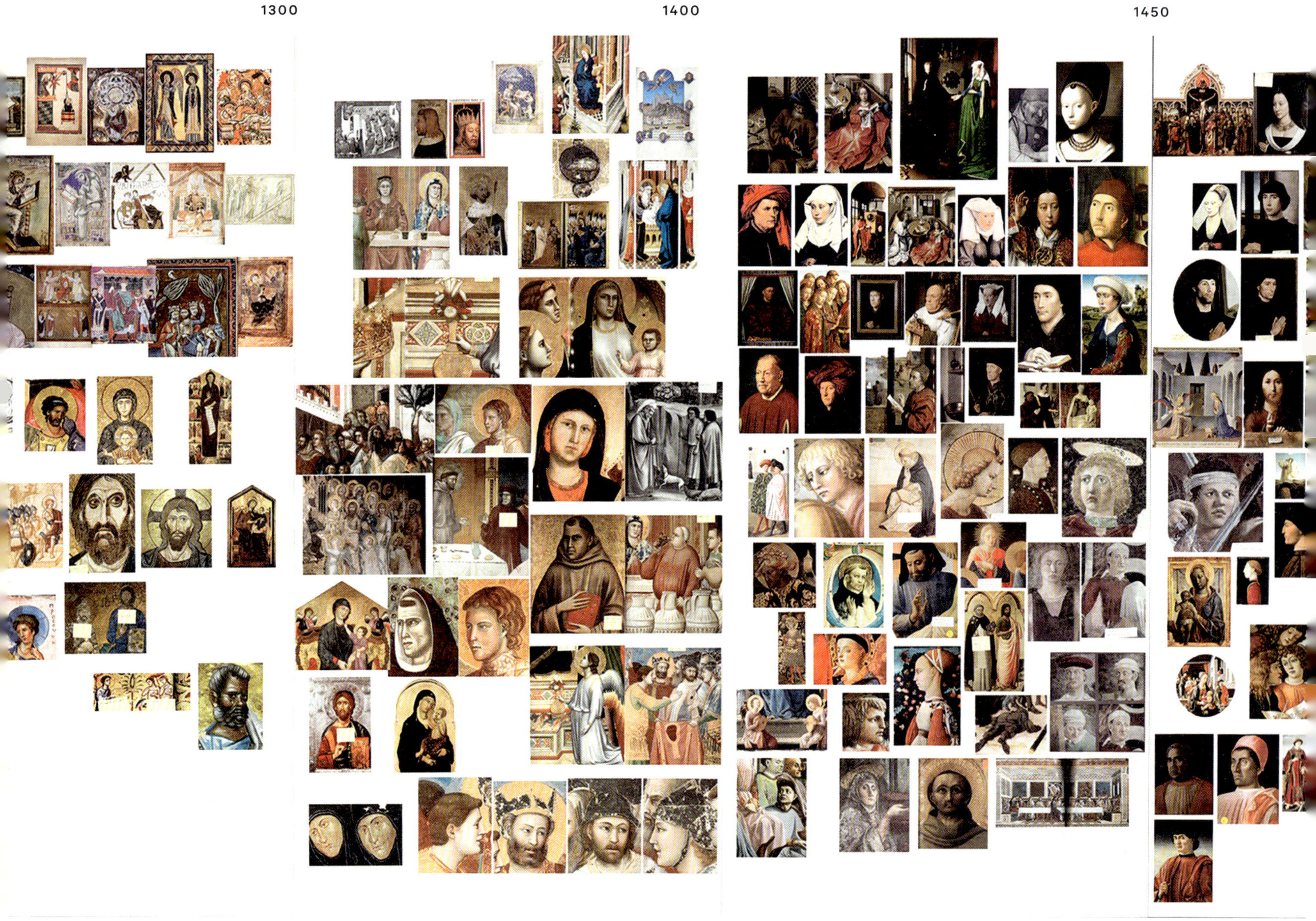

1650

1839

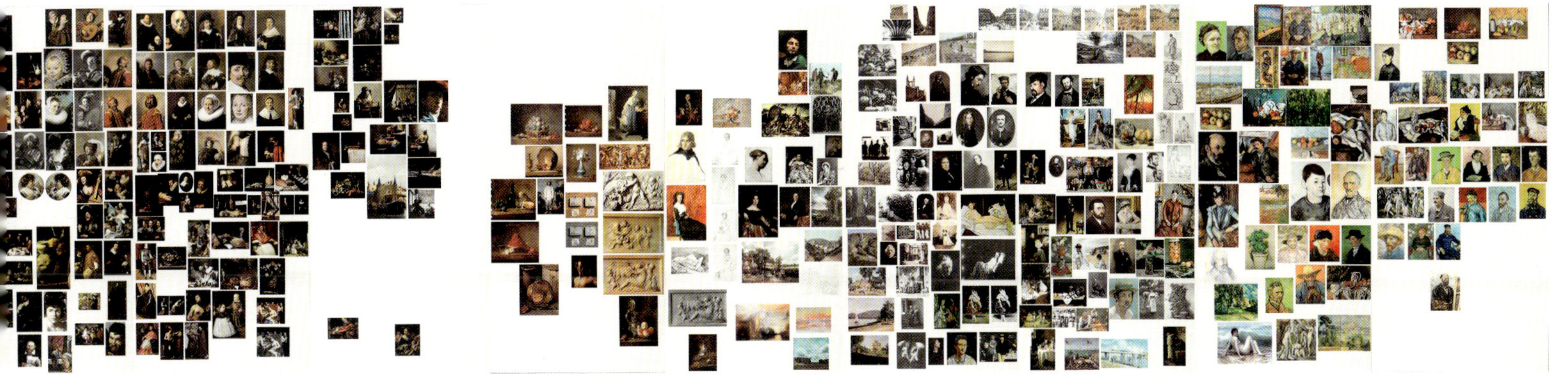

1500

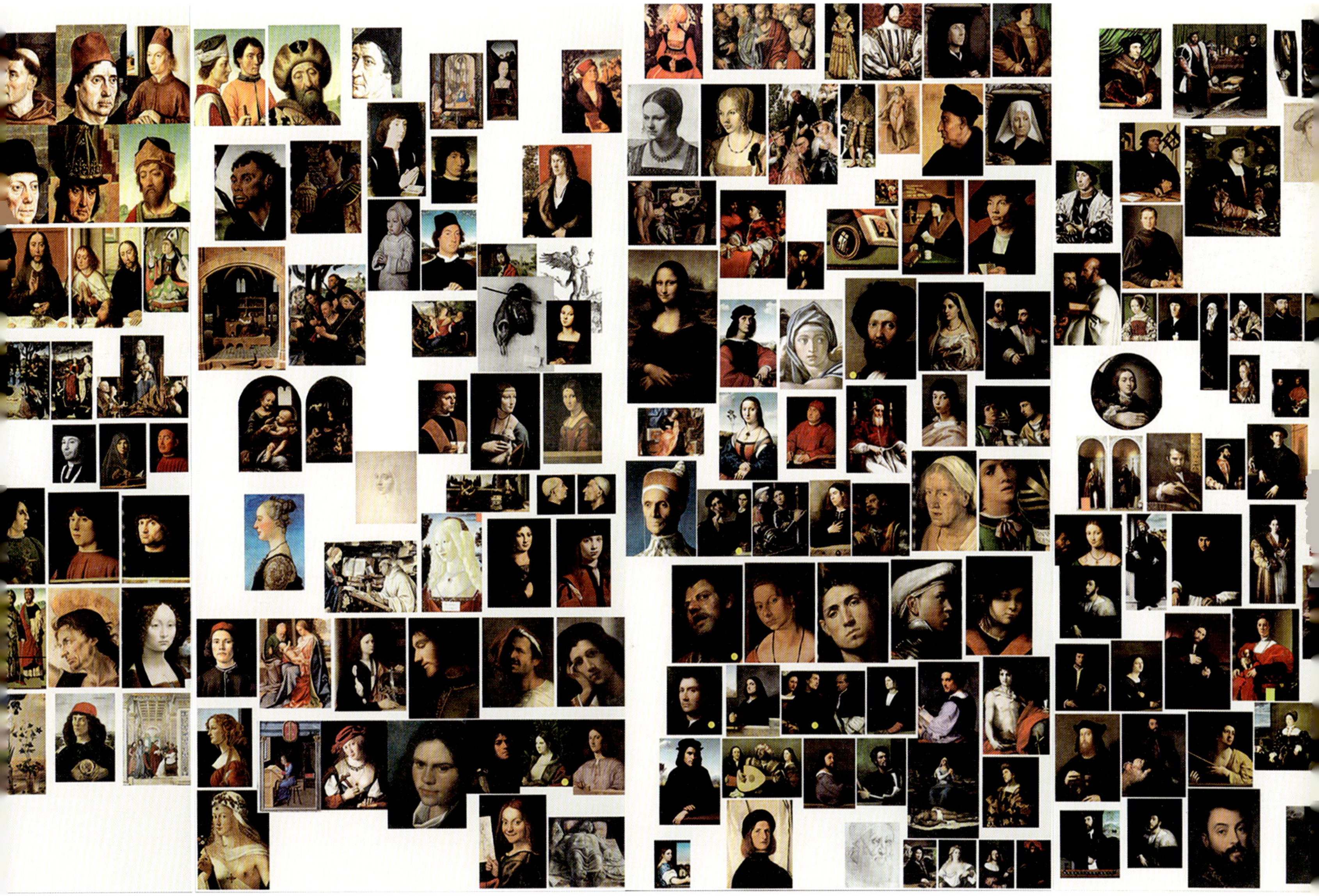

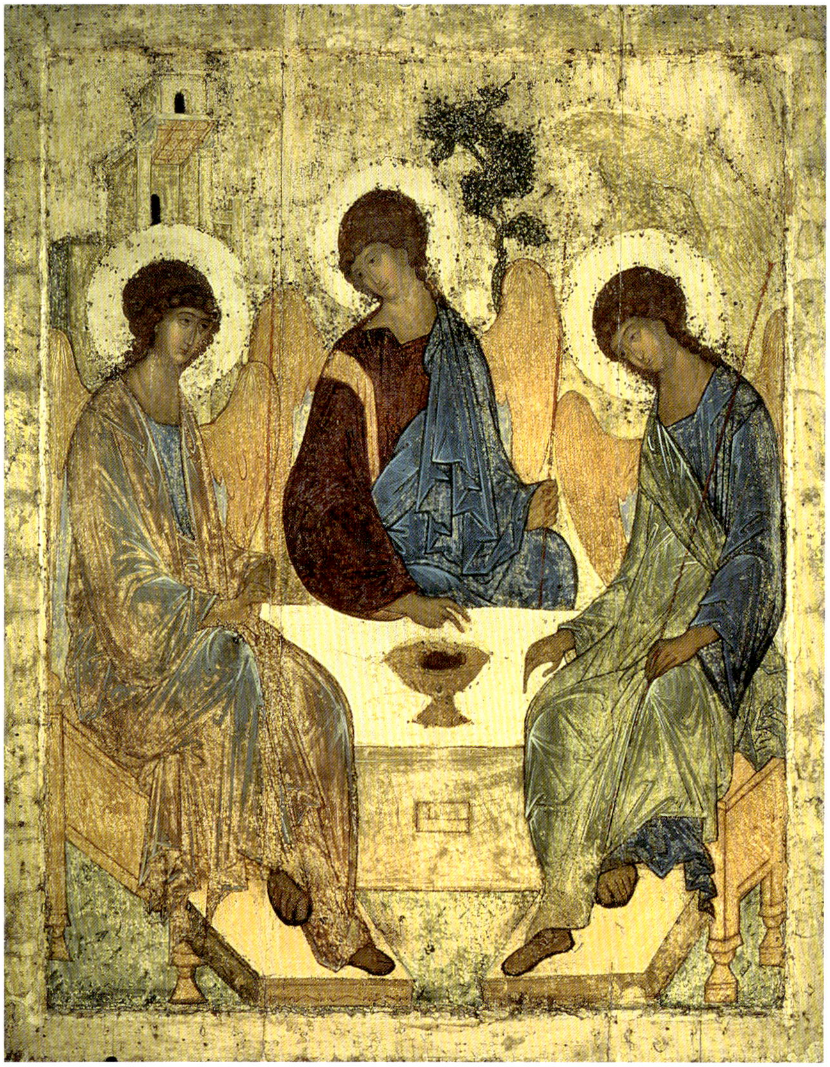

40 Andrei Rublev, *The Trinity*, 1411 or 1425–27, tempera, 142 × 114 cm. Tretyakov Gallery, Moscow

I conducted with the artist in a series of faxed letters – many published in the book – I continue to believe that optical devices were used more extensively than most art historians have been prepared to acknowledge but not as extensively as Hockney wishes.

As always, Hockney moved on. He had achieved what he wanted, artistically and historically. There followed a series of large watercolour portraits undertaken in washes with pure 'eyeballing' and no linear drawing. As Martin Gayford shows, varied modes of probing how space might be represented and how marks on a flat surface might evoke seen phenomena were subsequently explored with astonishing fertility. Here, given my concern with historical perspectives, I intend to highlight one extreme example of Hockney's dismissal of the vanishing point. This concerns what has become known as 'reverse perspective'.

The term has come to refer to the way that forms and space have been (and are) characterized in in Greek, Eastern and Russian Orthodox icons. A superb example is Andrei Rublev's *Trinity*, representing the figures of God, Christ and Holy Spirit in the guise of three angelic visitors to Abraham and Sarah, as recounted in Genesis (fig. 40). It was probably painted in the 1420s, at about the same time as Masaccio's perspectival *Trinity with Donors*, with its insistent vanishing point. Far from portraying the sides of rectangular forms as converging towards a single point, Rublev portrays the lateral sides of the platform and the angels' chairs as diverging into the distance. In the light of Renaissance perspective, the depiction of space looks 'primitive' and devoid of naturalistic conviction – however well the image traditionally serves its devotional function.

A transformation in the way such spatial motifs were interpreted was effected by Russian writers in the early twentieth century. Far from being viewed as an old and obsolete technique, the spatial effects were regarded as precociously 'modern', as anticipations of the revolution wrought by Picasso and his fellow Cubists. The leading advocate of this view was Pavel Florensky, a priest, theologian and extraordinary polymath, executed under Stalin's regime in 1937.[17] The key text was a lecture on reverse perspective delivered by Florensky in 1920. It was only published in Russian in 1976 and in English in 2002.

Florensky mounted a sustained assault on standard linear perspective on a variety of geometrical and optical grounds, including non-Euclidian geometry, modern physics and saccadic eye movements. His target was to prove that space in traditional icon painting is truer to actual seeing, consistent with modern notions of space, and akin to the latest pictorial techniques such as cubism.

All this is vigorous and challenging, but it is not tenable historically. The 'reverse perspective' of icons is not an *optical* technique at all.[18] It does not envisage the spectator as an eye-witness to some kind of visual reality. It was not 'reversing' whatever perspectival system prevailed in ancient Roman naturalistic painting (not least in stage scenery), which was theologically, historically and geographically remote. Early Byzantine icons, from which Eastern Orthodox art is descended, deliberately portray subjects, above all holy figures, as *outside* earthly time and space. There is no sense in which the spectator is an eyewitness to what was happening in real time and space. In part, this otherworldly character was to protect devotional images from iconoclasm. The closer the holy figures might come to our appearance the more visually mundane they would become and the more vulnerable to the biblical proscription of 'graven images'. The Virgin was the Queen of Heaven, beyond the stars, not a local woman. Rublov's *Trinity* is a vision seen in visionary terms, not a time-based narrative as a slice of reality.

What has this by-way in art history got to do with Hockney? He was introduced to Florensky's lecture by a member of his entourage, Jean-Pierre Gonçalves de Lima (known as J-P), who sensed it would resonate with the shaped canvases with which Hockney was then experimenting and that it would chime with his denunciation of conventional perspective. The results are described in a handsome exhibition book with folding plates of 2018, *Something New in Painting (and Photography) [and even Printing]*.[19] The text is by Laurence Weschler, an important author and long-term staff writer at *The New Yorker*, who has consistently and effectively supported Hockney's visual quests.

The alternative of 'reverse perspective' was explored by Hockney in a series of pictorial fields that dispensed with the normal rectangular boundaries. The unconventional shapes initiated a dynamic viewing experience in concert with the anti-perspectival and brilliantly coloured spaces they contained. At the centre of the experiments were visual dialogues with two classic paintings, Fra Angelico's *Annunciation* at the top of the stairs in the monastery of San Marco in Florence (fig. 141) and Meindert Hobbema's iconic *Avenue at Middleharnis* (fig. 49), to be discussed in the following essay.

Fra Angelico's calmly measured fresco is transfomed by Hockney into a bold rhythmic experience. It is the central 'panel' in a triptych of hexagonal canvases, entitled *Brass Tacks*, flanked on the left by a calm *Interior and Exterior with Flowers* and a life-cycle of *Birth, Copulation and Death* on the right (figs. 41–43).[20] The architecture of the courtyard of the Virgin's house is orchestrated into a vivacious optical dance in which our focus of attention on Mary reshapes the space in which she sits. The stretched and leaping arch seems to extend the instant of annunciation into another temporal dimension. It is as if Matisse's radiant colourism has been transported into a transformed Byzantium.

In *Something New in Painting*, the shaped canvases were joined by massive "photographic drawings" in which scanned objects were manoeuvred in computer-generated spaces with multiple vanishing points, in a manner akin to the chairs in the Dubreuil demonstration (see fig. 30). *Inside It Opens Up As Well* – how clever are his titles! – exemplifies the technique, as well as displaying an array of shaped canvases (fig. 44).

The procedure is nicely described by Weschler in *Something New* .... Working with Jonathan Wilkinson, his adept technological assistant,

> ... *Hockney turned towards the studio's back with all the paintings ranged along the walls ... and started taking photographs from hundreds of vantages .... Shifting to* 3D *software, they began making 360-degree tours of various individual objects – a stool, an easel, a chair ...(the tour of the stool, for example, comprising 196 separate shots) – and then waited as their laptop churned and churned, eventually generating notional digital objects that could be moved about the notional space .... Hockney himself stood still as his assistant loped all around him, snapping away. And then, like a child with a dollhouse, Hockney moved the objects about in the notional surround, pushing some of them forward, others back, centering himself in their midst. Once he'd gotten everything just so, he went in smooshing in the shadows, sliding in highlights.*[21]

The results were printed on large sheets of paper such that the compilation occupied the whole of the end wall.

An even more sophisticated space was constructed in *Viewers Looking at a Ready-made with Skull and Mirrors*, in which a tiny but sinister skull (a 'still-death'?) is mounted on a tower

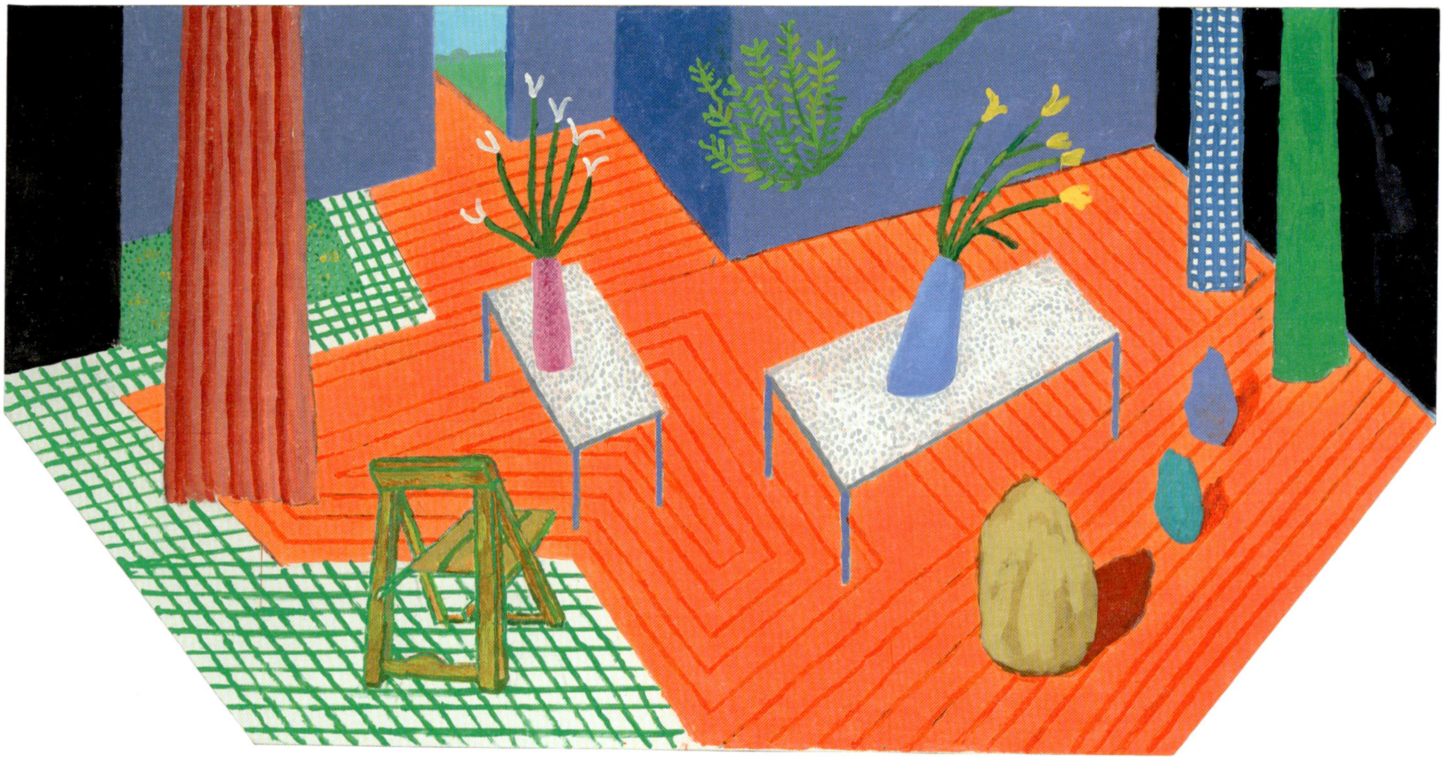

41 David Hockney, *Annunciation I, Interior and Exterior with Flowers*, from *The Brass Tacks Triptych*, 2017, acrylic on canvas 121.9 x 243.8 cm (hexagonal). Collection of the artist

42 David Hockney, *Birth and Copulation and Death. That's all the facts when you come to brass tacks.*, from *The Brass Tacks Triptych*, 2017, acrylic on canvas, 121.9 x 243.8 cm (hexagonal). Collection of the artist

43 | F David Hockney, *Annunciation II, after Fra Angelico*, from *The Brass Tacks Triptych*, 2017, acrylic on canvas, 121.9 x 243.8 cm (hexagonal). Collection of the artist

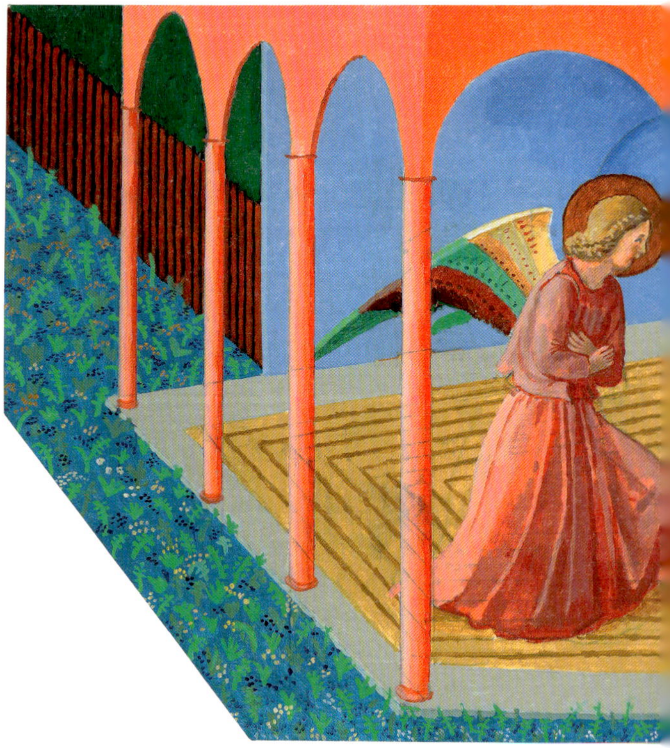

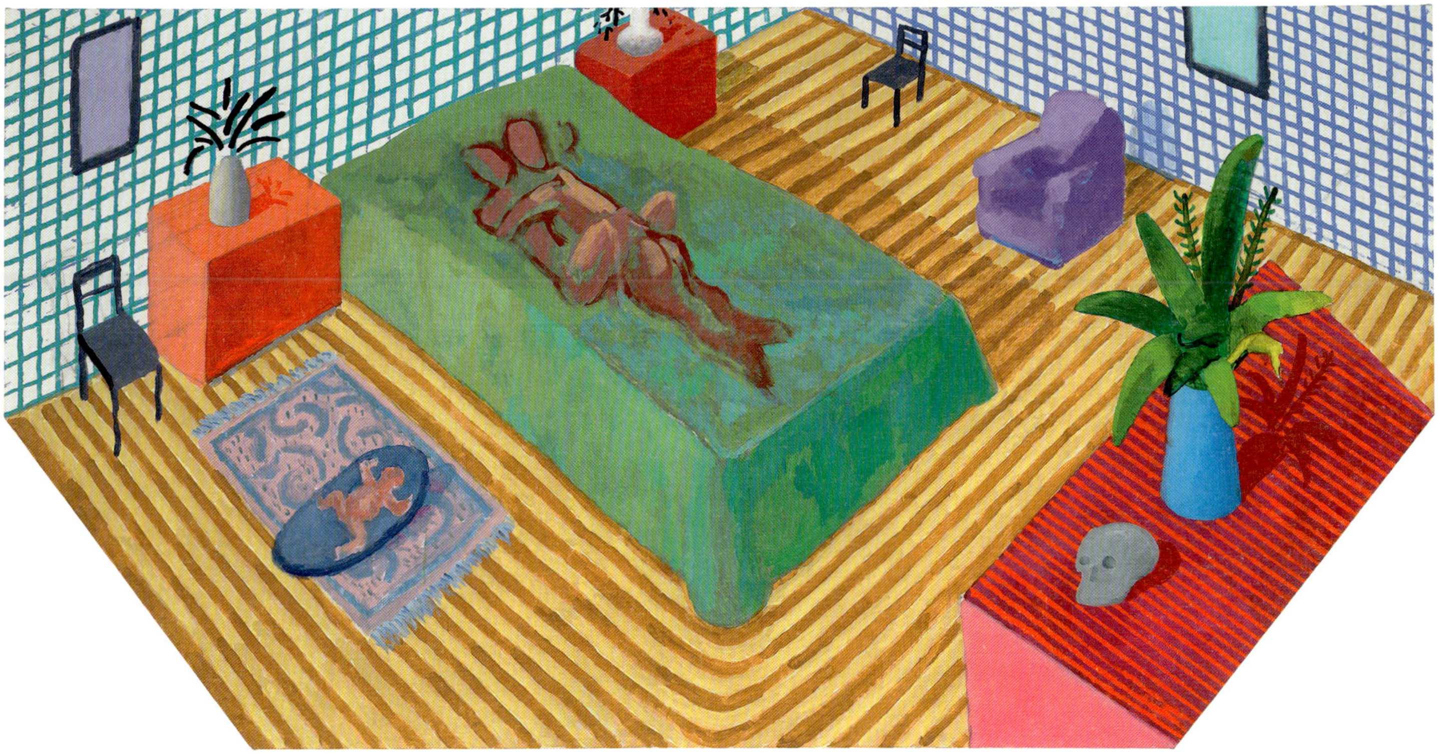

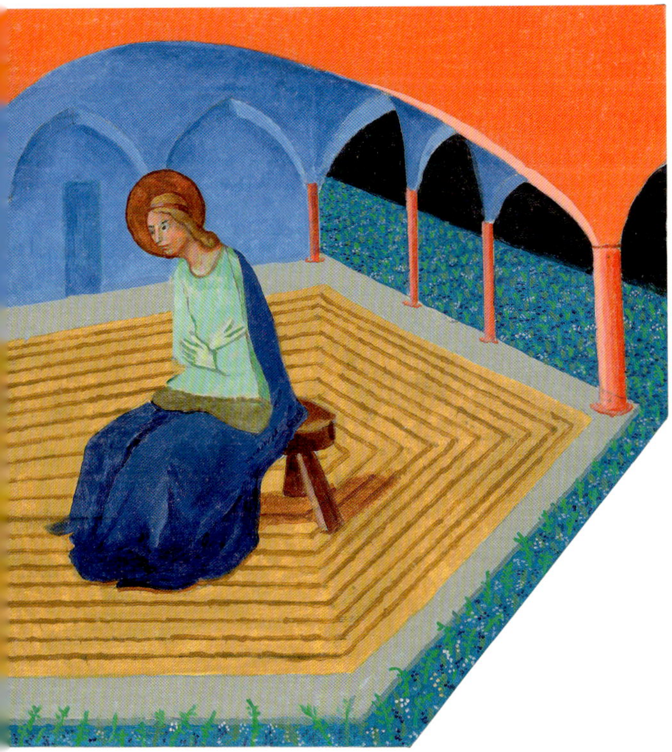

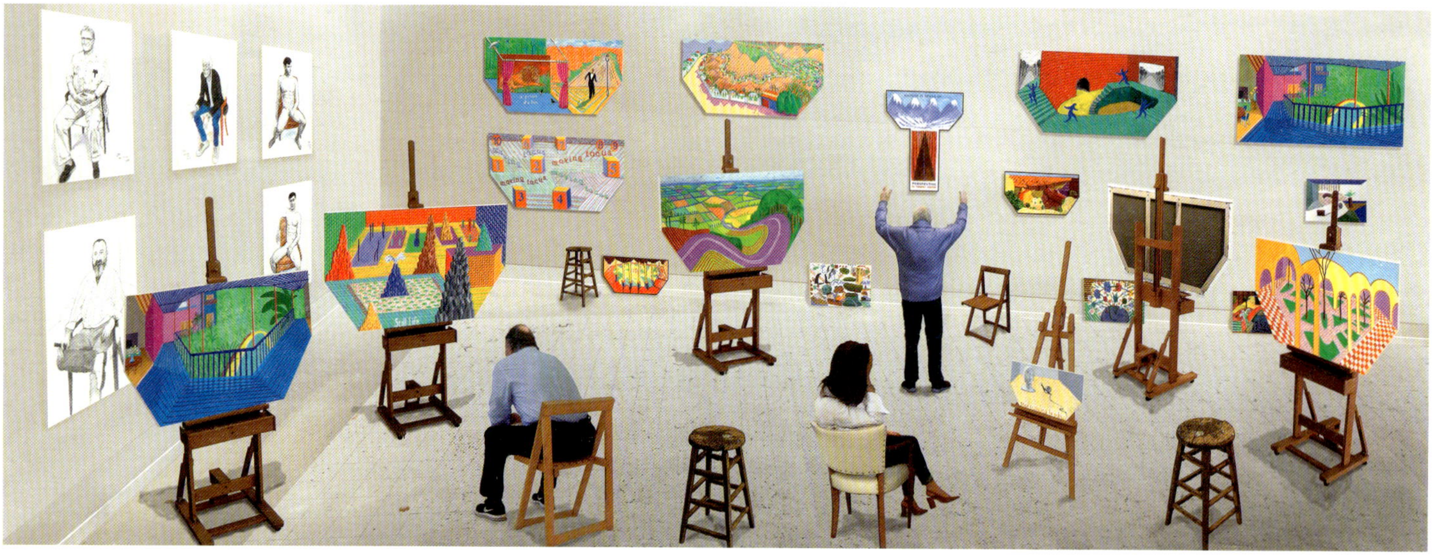

44 David Hockney,
Inside It Opens Up As Well,
2018, photographic drawing printed on 7 sheets of paper mounted on 7 sheets of Dibond, edition of 12 paper sheets 2.78 x 1.09 m, 2.78 x 7.6 m overall, assisted by Jonathan Wilkinson

built from a serially repeated trolley (fig. 46). The walls in this instance are largely covered by huge, inclined mirrors that reflect the reflecting spectators in surreal contemplation.

The computer-generated, optical ensemble actually corresponds in effect (if not in means or theory) to what painters have done since the Renaissance, studying each individual item freely from a chosen viewpoint before dropping it into the overall space within the picture. Wilkinson would have enjoyed comparing notes with Dubreuil, just as Hockney would have enthusiastically brought his bluff vigour into seventeenth-century debates about artificial and natural perspective.

There is an unexpected affinity between this high-tech chess game and the hand-made spaces that Nicolas Poussin was described as making in the seventeenth century. The great French master of classical composition placed small wax figures in a box that served as a kind of stage, with apertures that admitted light. He could then manoeuvre his waxen figures to achieve the most eloquent tableaux (fig. 45).[22]

Hockney's intense dialogue with the art of the past sets a challenge for a historian. At various points I feel like saying, 'yes, but ...'. This is particularly the case with 'reverse perspective'. However, I need to remind myself that Renaissance artists created brilliant optical effects that still beguile us, when the optical science they used was far from what we now know. I can accordingly say that I do not agree with Florensky's theory while delighting in Hockney's visual experiments. In fact, I can say that Hockney is using 'reverse perspective', even if, historically speaking, I do not think that was what Andrei Rublev was doing.

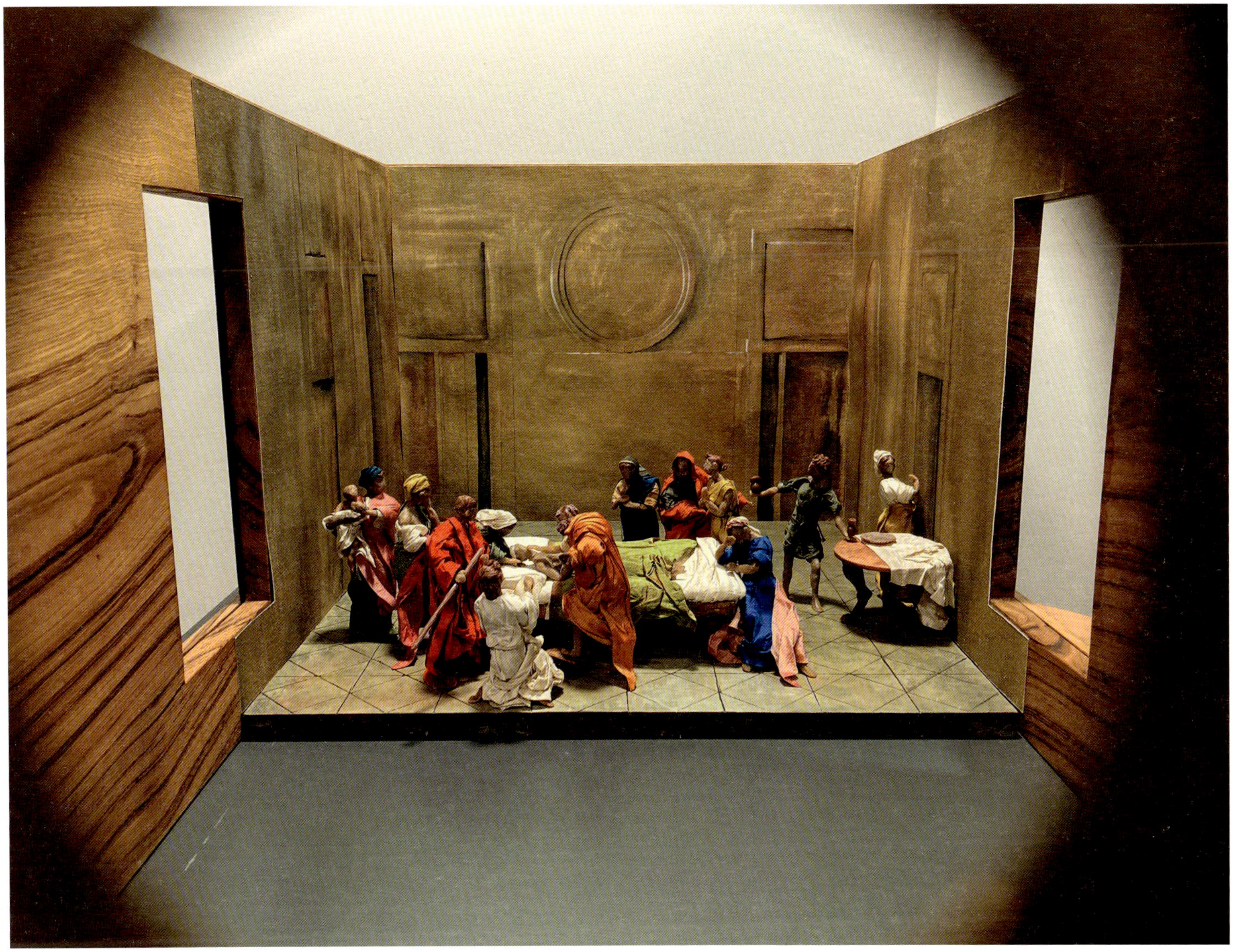

45 Andrew Lacey, Sian Lewis and Robin Williams, Reconstruction of Nicolas Poussin's 'grande machine', 2014 (detail), box: wood (sweet chestnut), metal (brass); interior: canvas, paint, board; figures: beeswax, metal wire, silk. Fitzwilliam Museum, purchased, 2014

Notes

1 For overviews of perspective in theory and practice, see Kemp 1992 and Anderson 2007. **2** Dubreuil 1691. **3** Dubreuil 1665, preface. **4** For strong advocacy about Vermeer using the camera obscura, see Steadman 2002 and Jelley 2017.
5 The category 'no perspective' largely consists of portraits and close-up still life/flower paintings. The category 'implicit perspective' includes scenes in which scaling, foreshortening and other spatial clues are present without obvious geometrical constructions, most notably in landscapes. The category 'perspectival motifs' involves paintings in which significant features are clearly perspectival but do not govern the whole composition. The category 'dominant perspective' denotes a composition in which the main impact is perspectival, as with townscapes and church interiors. This final category includes Domenico Veneziano's *predella* panels (figs. 143 and 144). The large number of flower paintings in the Fitzwilliam inflates the first category. **6** Piero della Francesca, *De prospectiva pingendi.* **7** Kemp 1992, 38–39. **8** Leonardo da Vinci, Codex Arundel, fol. 62r. . **9** Leonardo da Vinci, Windsor, Royal Library, RCIN 19102; Keele and Pedretti 1997–80, no. 198r. **10** Hockney and Gayford 2011, 50. **11** Hockney and Gayford 2011, 280. **12** Kemp 2004, 109–21; Kemp 2005, 84–89; and Kemp 2007, 31–46. **13** Press release by Viking Studio, October 2001. **14** Tinterow and Conisbee 1999–2000. **15** Hockney 2001, 185. **16** Kemp 2007. **17** Florensky 1919. **18** Antonova 2016. **19** Hockney 2018. **20** Hockney 2018, 28–33. **21** Hockney 2018, 18–19. **22** https://beyondthelabel.fitzmuseum.cam.ac.uk/labels/poussin.

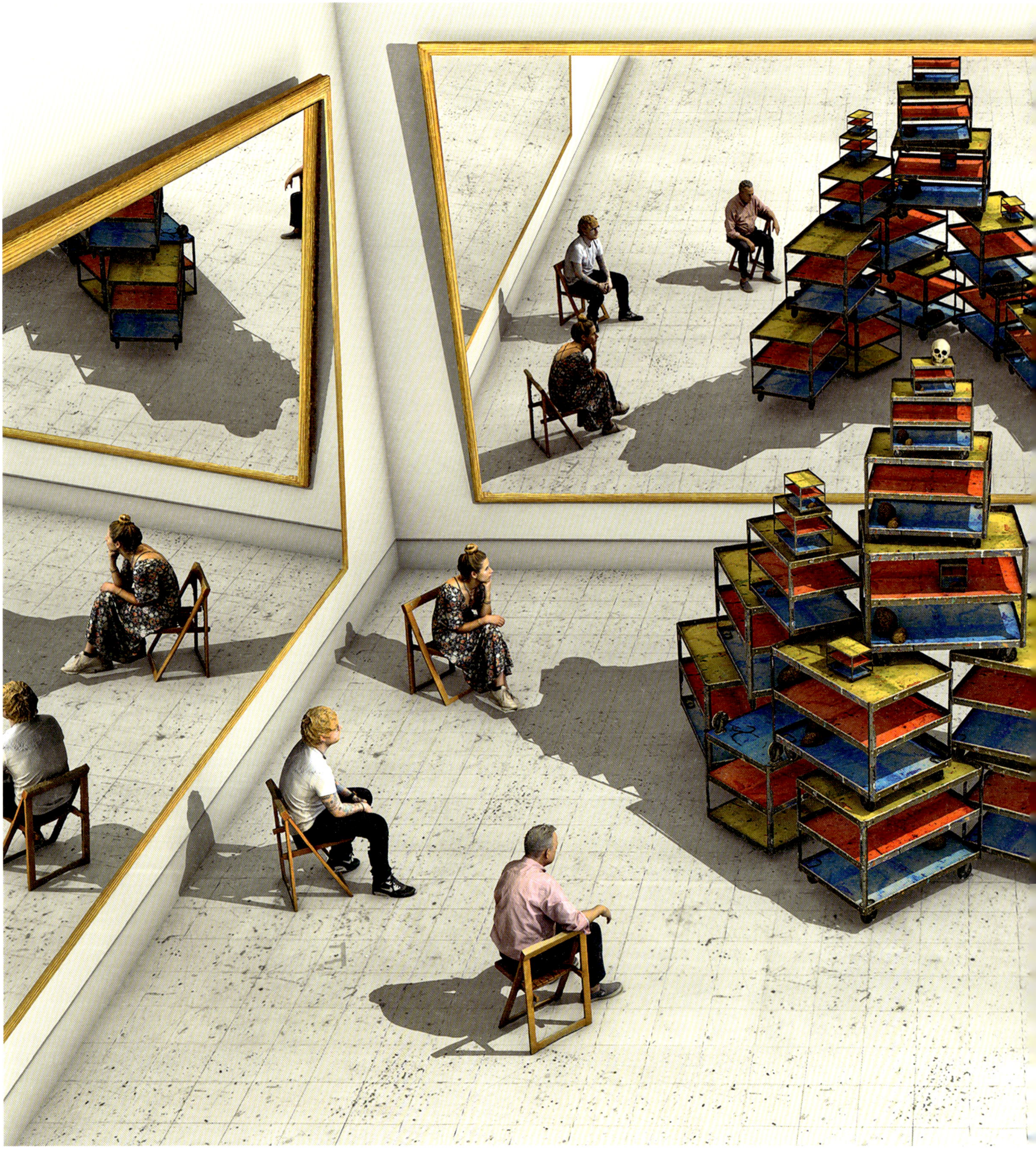

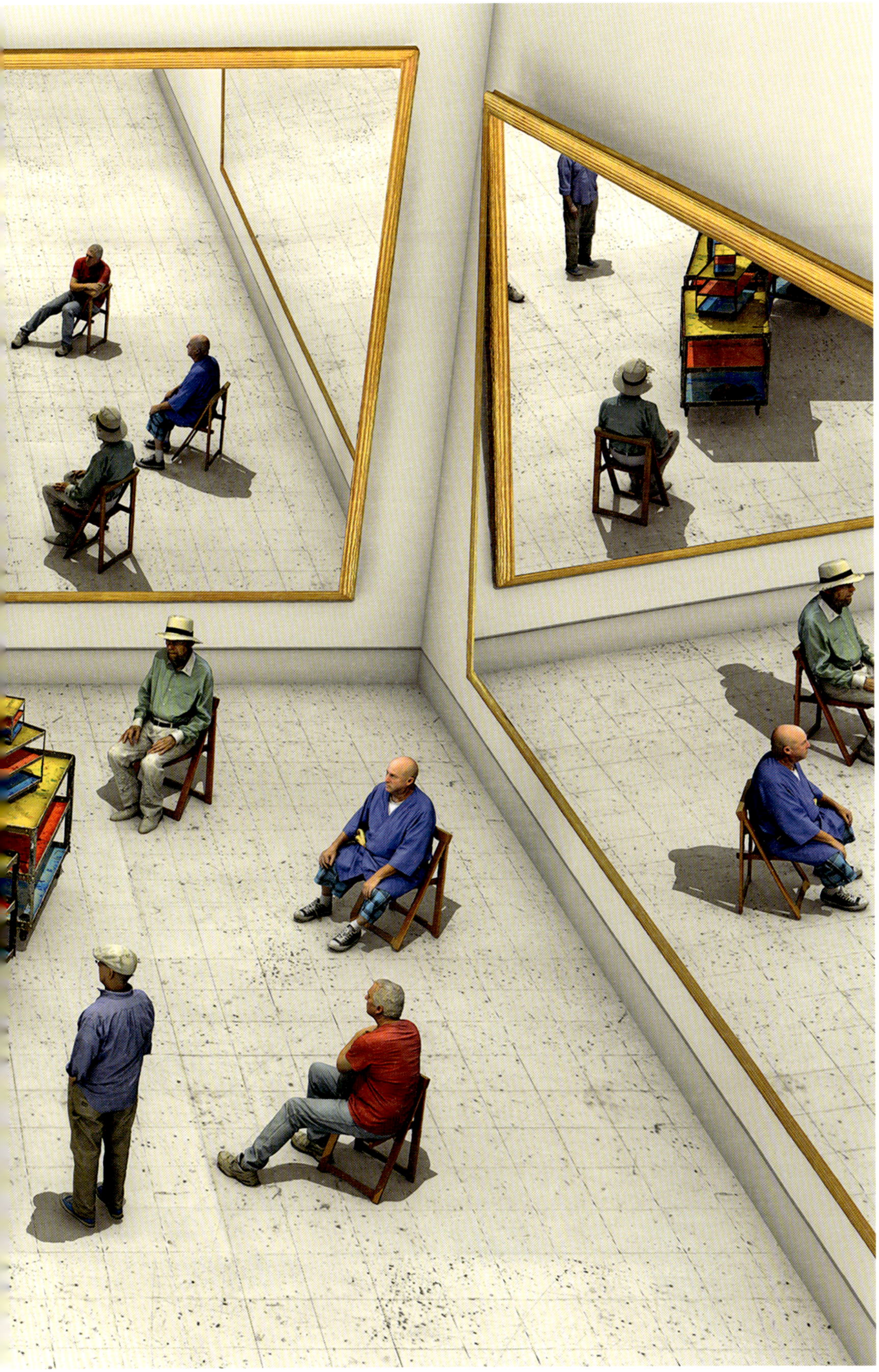

46 | H David Hockney, *Viewers Looking at a Ready-made with Skull and Mirrors*, 2018, photographic drawing printed on four sheets of paper, mounted on four sheets of Dibond, paper sheets 222.3 x 92.7 cm, 222.3 x 370.8 cm overall, assisted by Jonathan Wilkinson. Collection of the artist

Martin Kemp

Appendix: Where is the evidence?

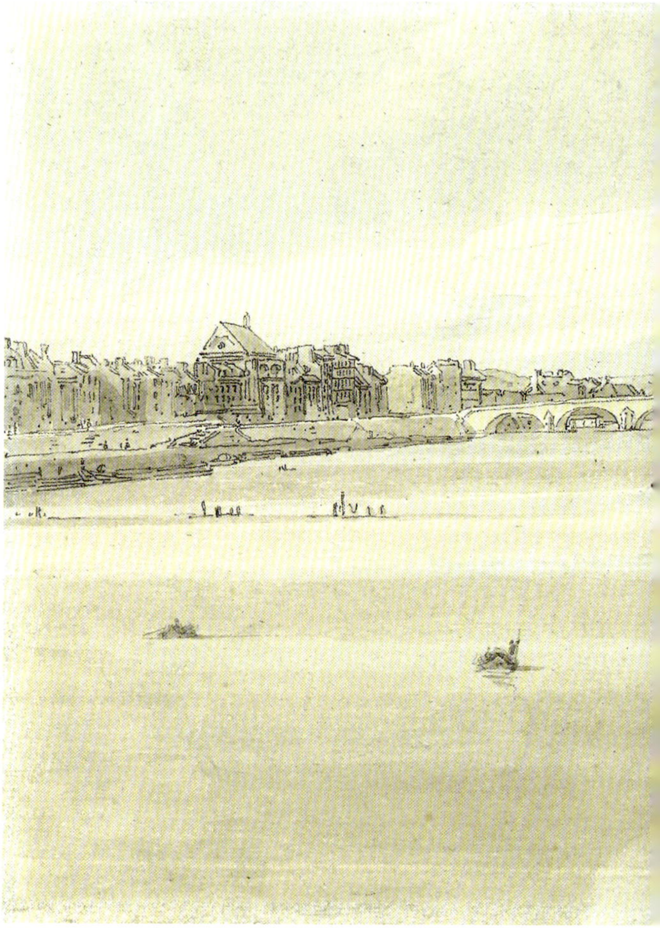

47 | F Thomas Girtin, *View of the Louvre and the Pont des Tuileries from the Pont Neuf, from A Selection of Twenty of the Most Picturesque Views in Paris and its Environs*, 1801, soft-ground etching, pencil and watercolour on paper, 17.5 x 44.9 cm. Fitzwilliam Museum, Purchased from the Biffen Fund, with contribution from the Victoria and Albert Museum Grant-in-Aid, PD.5-1983

An insistent question runs though the hypothesis that painters availed themselves of optical aids. Where is the evidence? From the seventeenth century onwards, we find illustrations of cameras in printed treatises (fig. 89), but there are only scarce records of cameras actually being deployed. That evidence becomes somewhat more plentiful in the eighteenth and early nineteenth centuries, particularly with regard to topographical studies and portraits. We must take into account that there are very few first-hand accounts of the actual process of portraying a landscape or producing a likeness of a sitter. The old saw that absence of evidence is not evidence of absence is highly relevant here.

Hockney's answer is two-fold. Professional artists deliberately kept their methods secret; and the pictures themselves are the evidence, if we know how to look. The historian necessarily has to work largely with the second answer. The problem is that the visual evidence is quite slippery, and often resides in the eye of the beholder.

Images made in early cameras do have a characteristic 'look'. The most strident tones in a lit subject are typically modulated in a soft manner. The camera image tends to translate areas of tone and colour into flat planes on the surface of the projection. Not least characteristic are powerful contrasts in scale between very close objects and those in the middle ground – contrasts that artists had generally sought to avoid. These visual characteristics correspond closely to paintings by certain Dutch artists in the seventeenth century (figs. 32–33), and are recognizable above all in Vermeer's domestic interiors. They also correspond to the *vedute* (view paintings) by Canaletto, as discussed by Philip Steadman. For Canaletto there is rich evidence of his exploiting a camera.

We gain a sense of how tricky matters are if we look at the area where supporting evidence is least thin, namely British topographical drawings in the late eighteenth and early nineteenth centuries. One immediate problem is that the various modes of making drawings with devices range from relatively sketchy to carefully traced.

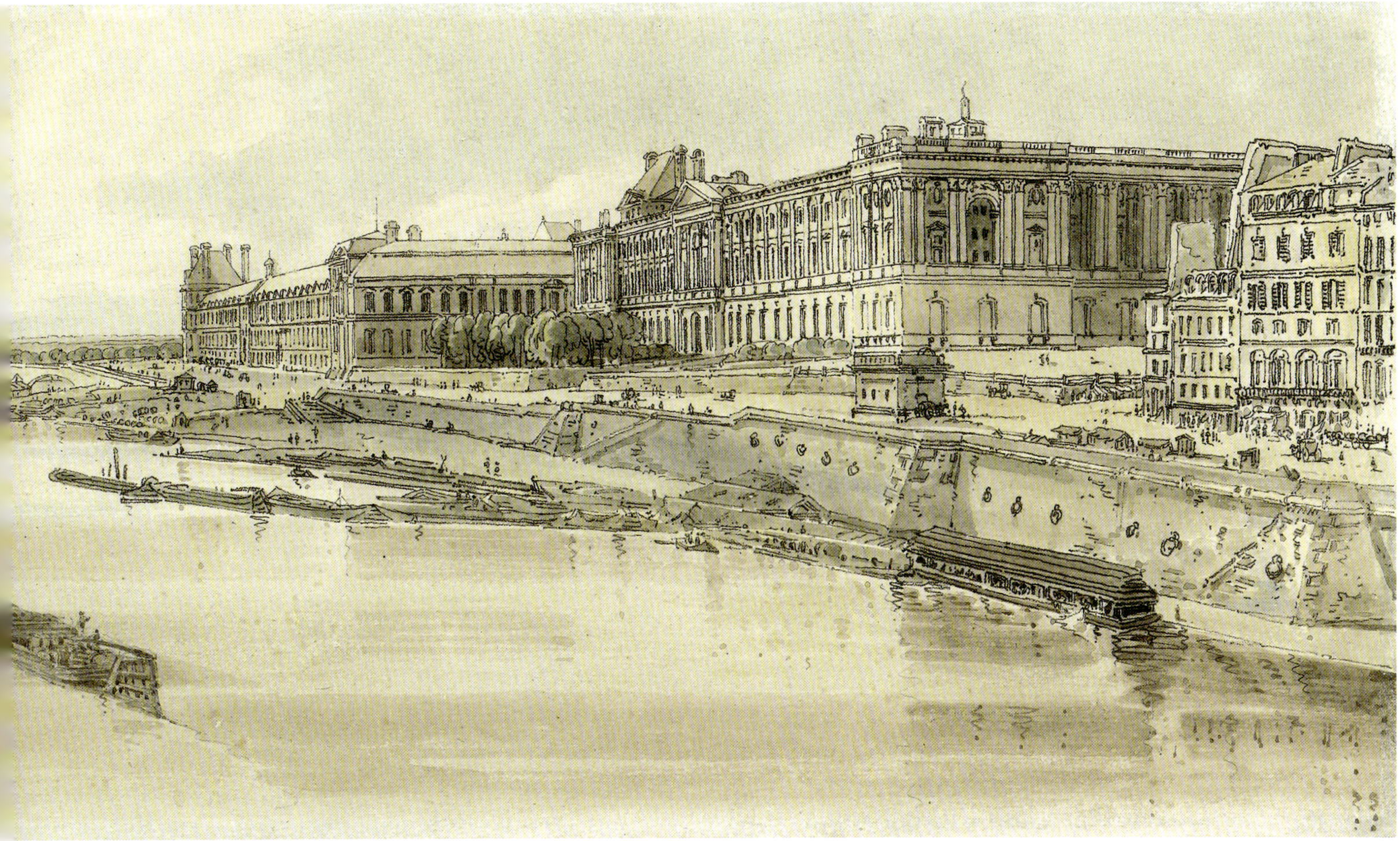

It is difficult (in the absence of an inscription or other evidence) to judge if particular drawings depended on such aids as cameras or the Graphic Telescope (see pp. 75ff.). There are good number of drawings, including several by Turner and Girtin (figs. 64 and 65), that share something of the 'traced look' of known camera drawings, a trait that becomes more readily recognizable with the greater number of drawings that are inspected. Without further direct evidence, we have to fall back on subjective judgement by eye. Anne Lyles thinks it unlikely Turner ever used a camera, and believes Girtin probably only used one in Paris. Martin Gayford and I say that some sketches 'look like camera drawings'. The sketches illustrated here are presented as hypothetical examples of camera drawings that still require firm proof one way or the other.

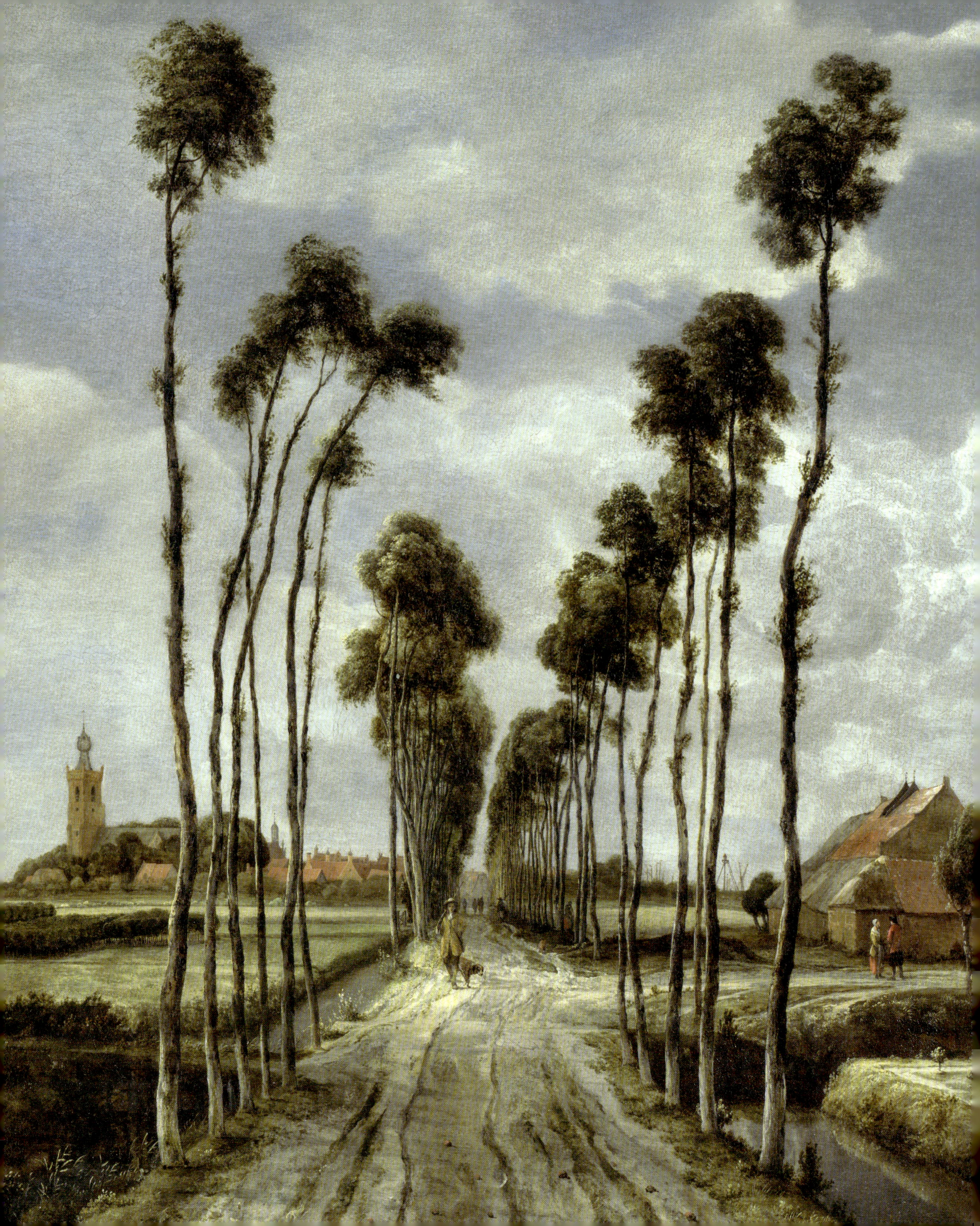

Martin Kemp and Gabriel Hemery

Hobbema's *Avenue* and the ordering of nature: arboreal and optical

Hobbema's masterpiece, *Avenue at Middelharnis* (1689, fig. 49), was much admired by Hockney as a young artist. More recently, he has undertaken two vivacious and iconoclastic riffs on the Dutch master's iconic scene, the first of which is entitled *After Hobbema (Useful Knowledge)* (2017, fig. 48).[1] The 'knowledge' involves the seeing and representation of space according to mechanisms of perception. Hockney challenges Hobbema's pictorial and optical order in a radical way, not least by totally omitting the rutted surface of the road leading to the port town. As we will see, Hockney has reconstituted his own kind of order, which speaks remarkably to Hobbema's Dutch orderliness.

The obvious way to enter the comparison is via the representation of space. Here we will enter down a different road, first exploring the zonal culture of trees in a characteristically flat Dutch polder. We will begin by concentrating on how nature is treated in a highly controlled manner, not just through the pictorial order of perspective but through the highly cultivated organization of the land itself.

Silviculture

In the seventeenth century, while tree-lined vistas became ever more popular in Europe as a measure of status for grand properties of wealthy individuals, their benefits to the prosperity and health of the wider countryside were also being realised. It has been suggested that France was among the first of many countries to embrace the benefits of lining its roads with trees, under King Henri II in 1522.[2] Although the landscape benefits are obvious, the main driver for lining roads with trees arose from a chronic shortage of wood. One or more of a wide range of factors led to this shortage, among them the fact that wood still heated the ovens and homes of most people, their needs competing with the ravages and demands of war, forest clearances for industry and agriculture, outbreaks of disease, harsh winters and summer droughts. All these factors combined to diminish tree resources across Europe. Other benefits of lining roads with trees were recognized, including their ability to stabilize road edges, delineate routes especially during inclement weather (e.g. fog and snow), and sometimes to provide shade and shelter to travellers, including a marching army.

The trees in Hobbema's painting of the avenue at Middelharnis, planted in 1664, are interesting to the student of the history of the management of trees in a number of respects.[3] Leaving aside for a moment the avenue that dominates the scene, to the right of the farmhouse in the middle distance is what appears to be an orchard, as might be expected near a rural dwelling. The right-hand foreground is dominated by a tree nursery, in which a worker is conducting 'formative pruning' on head-high young trees, removing forks and lower branches which would otherwise reduce future timber quality (fig. 50). A few paces in front of him is younger stock, perhaps one or two years old. The mature woodland on the left-hand side appears to be well managed, yet depicts a cropped browse-line typically arising from the heavy presence of deer. The area between the woodland and the church supports highly ordered coppices, most likely cut on a 12–16-year cycle, depicting coupes (parcels of woodland) in two stages of growth (i.e. 8 years and 16 years) (fig. 51).

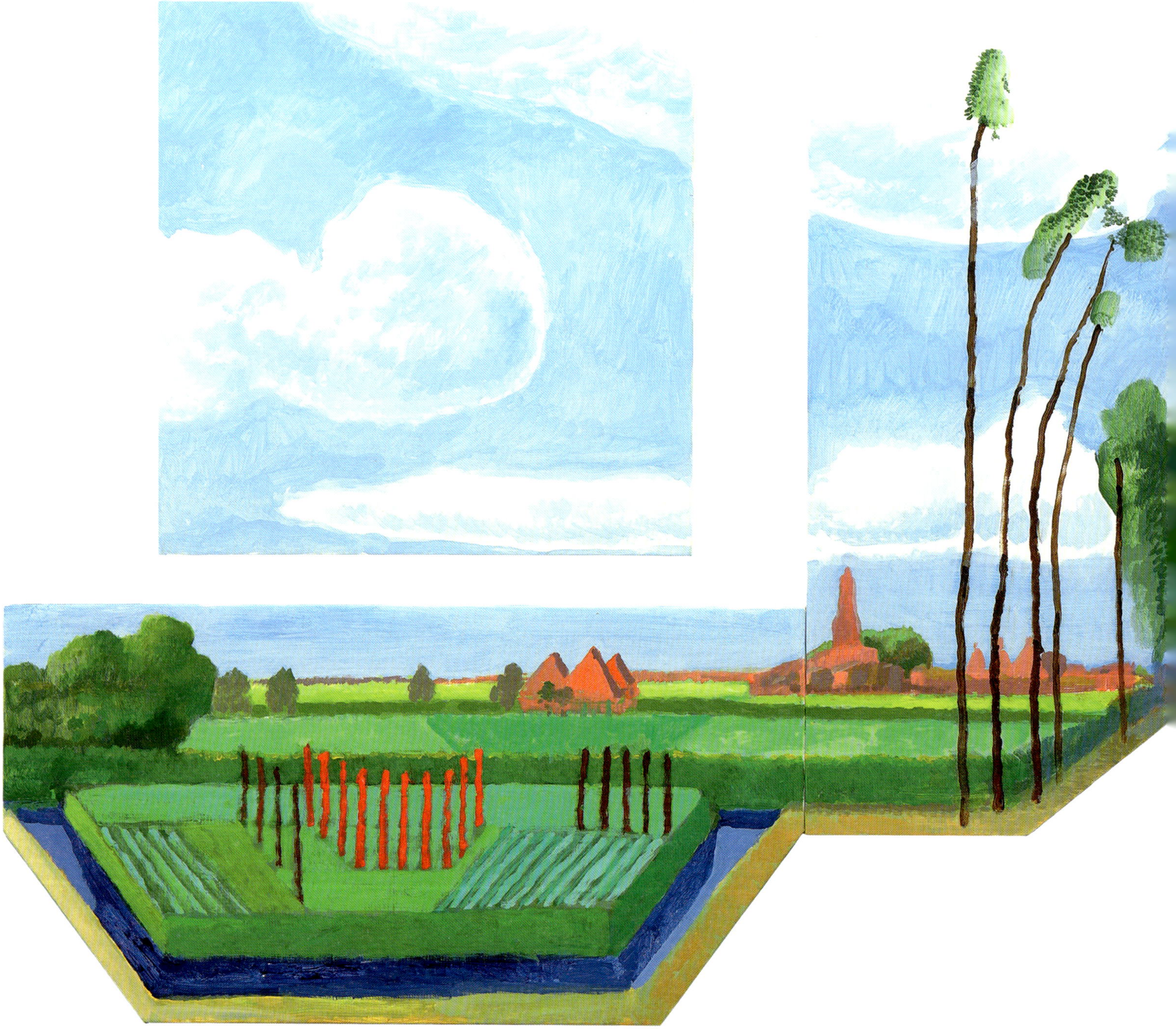

48 | F David Hockney, *After Hobbema (Useful Knowledge)*, 2017, acrylic on 6 canvases, 2 canvases: 61 x 61 cm; 4 joined hexagonal canvases: 113 x 277.5 cm. Collection of the artist

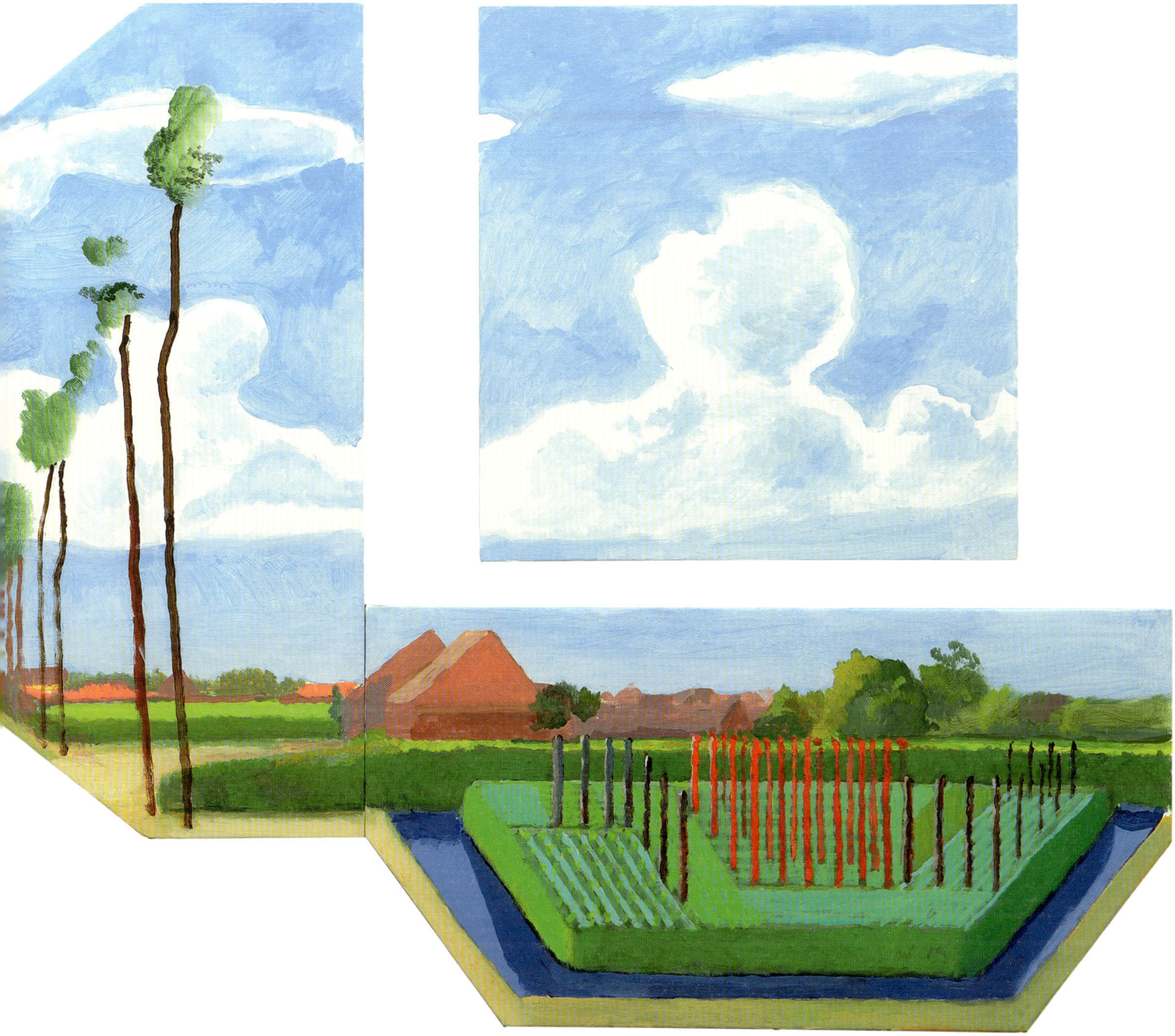

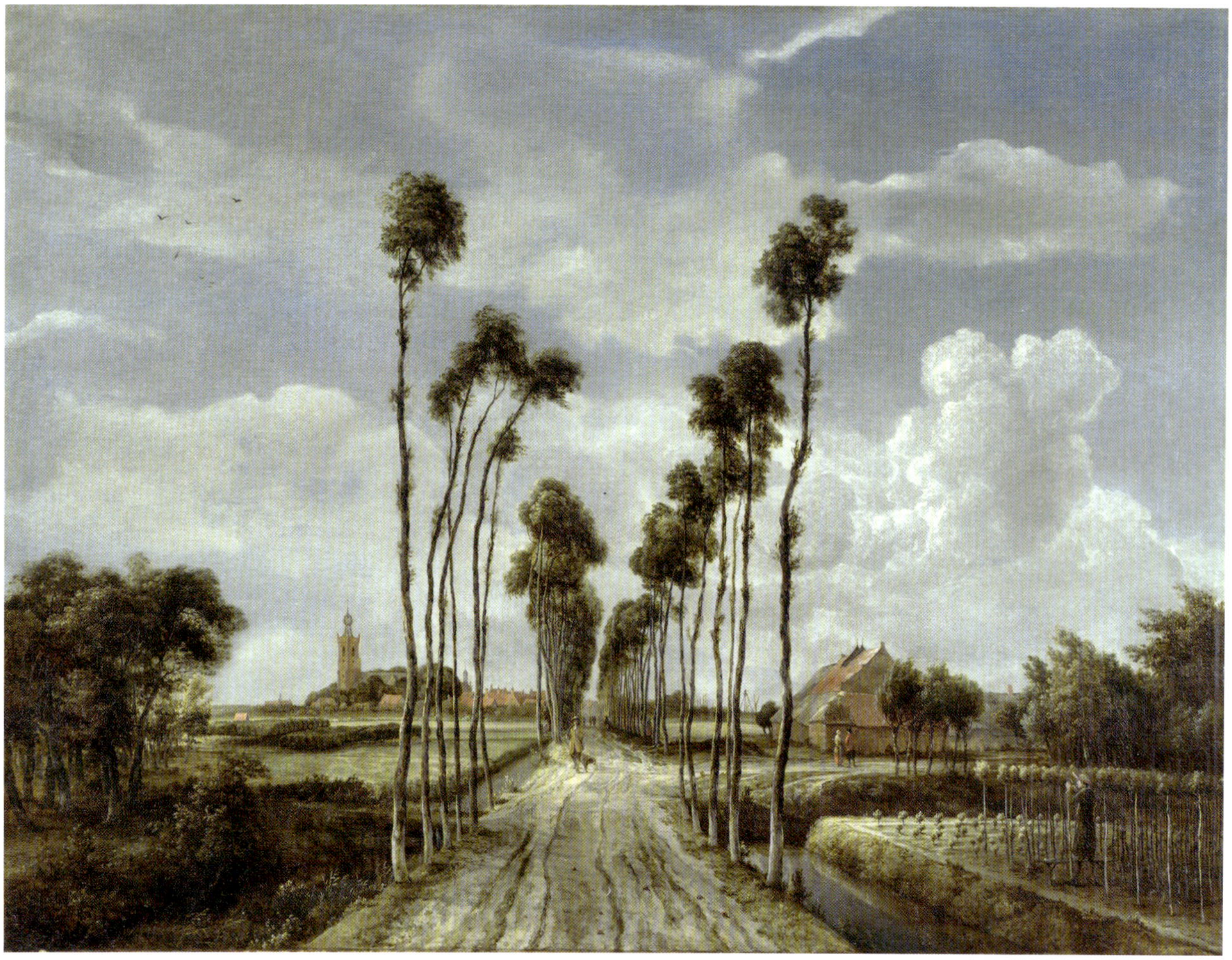

49 | F Meindert Hobbema, *The Avenue at Middelharnis*, 1689, oil on canvas, 103.5 x 141 cm. The National Gallery, London, Bough, 1871, NG830

50 Detail of *The Avenue at Middelharnis* (fig. 49) showing man pruning saplings

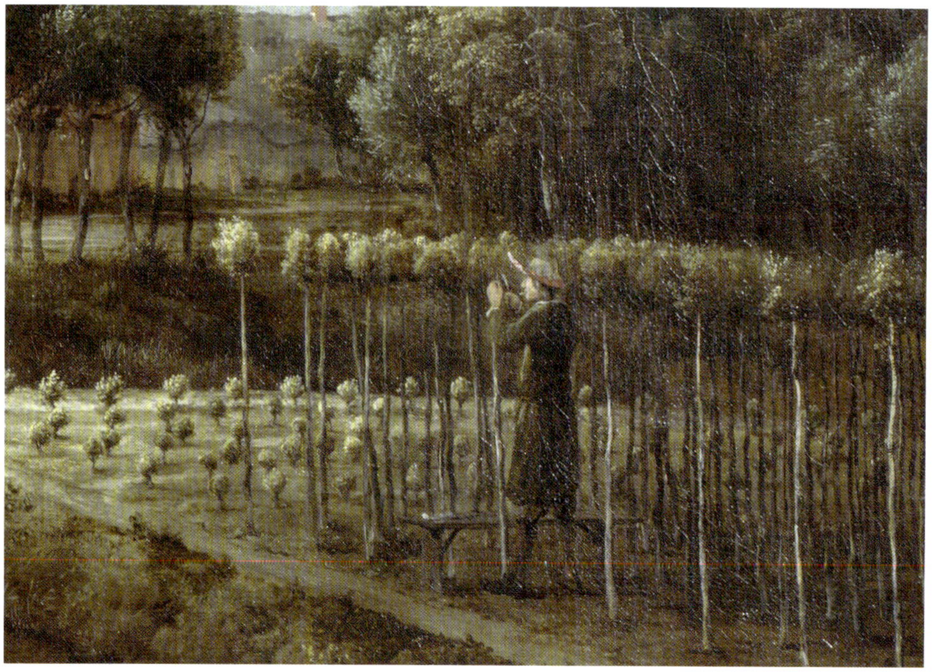

The lanky trees that line the avenue are very different from those in the coppices. They have been high-pruned to a greater height than used in modern practice, in which it is known such extreme pruning reduces tree health and growth. The removed lateral branches would have provided convenient material for the fagotters (e.g. for bread ovens), while high clearance would have kept branches from tangling with tall road traffic (e.g. hay wagons). In this case, the heavy pruning may have been a deliberate attempt to prevent over-shading of the highway, helping to create drier conditions and so less rutting. The clear stems would also provide fewer places for bandits or undesirables to loiter. The avenue trees were probably pruned the year before, as they are displaying a lot of healthy regrowth. This suggests again that this technique would have suited some sort of purpose, such as deliberate harvesting, and not been conducted merely as a cosmetic exercise for little utility (especially as this would have been hard work given the tools of the era).

The tree species of the avenue are the subject of debate. Some observers think the trees are alder or poplar trees, but this seems unlikely. Black alder (*Alnus cordata)* is water-tolerant, but a relatively short-lived tree of medium stature; it was also commonly coppiced to support the gunpowder industry and not pollarded. The foliage of the trees has the wrong appearance for poplar (*Populus* spp.), which would also have more vigorous and 'leggy' growth following pruning and very straight trunks or boles. The foliage looks light and feathery like ash (*Fraxinus excelsior)*, which would be a strong candidate, although the stems of this species typically grow straighter than depicted and its branches characteristically bifurcate (branch in pairs) which is not the case in the painting. Overall, it is most likely that the trees are pedunculate oak (*Quercus robur*) because this species has the greatest utility (both strength and calorific value) and could be high-pruned in the fashion depicted. Other clues are the regrowth on the high-pruned stems which is characteristic of the epicormic growth of oak when over-pruned, and the slightly wavering growth of the boles.

In short, every zone of the land speaks of the systematic and sustained management of trees, which redounds to the husbandry of the inhabitants and speaks of the moral framework

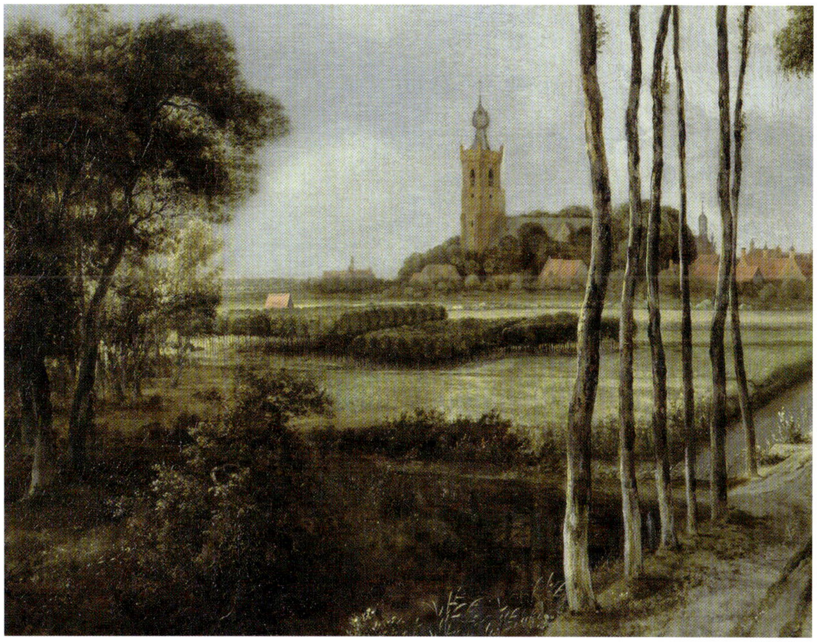

51 Detail of *The Avenue at Middelharnis* (fig. 49) showing the coupes

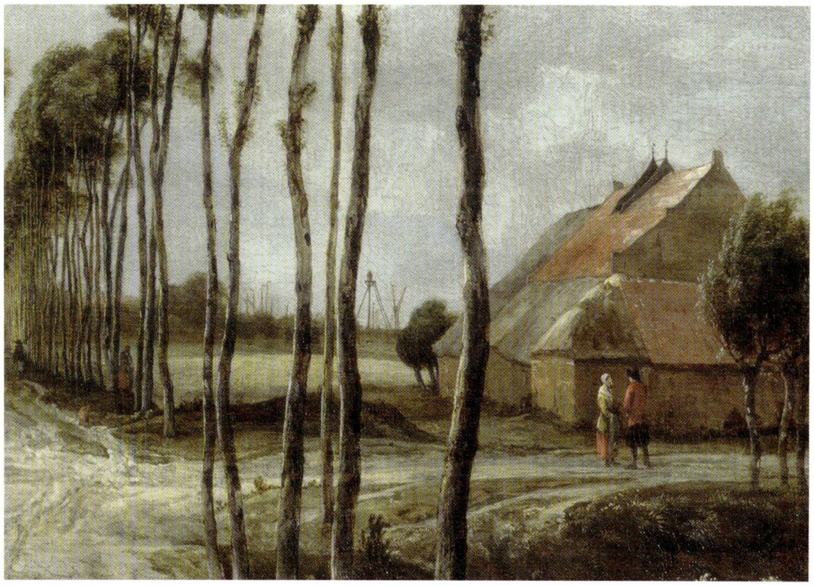

52 Detail of *The Avenue at Middelharnis* (fig. 49) showing the light and masts of boats in the harbour

of human order. The same religious and social values are declared by the tower of the church, the neat array of rooftops, and the welcoming harbour light on its lofty tripod (fig. 52). The dramatic avenue of trees that lines the straight road announces Middelharnis as an estimable destination that is firmly in charge of its land.

'Like tiled floors': Hobbema's perspective

There is a tendency to regard the use of strict perspective as essentially Italian, while Dutch art adopts more descriptively empirical ideals.[4] However, there were at least as many treatises on perspective published in seventeenth-century Holland as in Italy and France. Samuel Marolois's sophisticated treatise on perspective, first published in his *Opera mathematica* in 1614, which is replete with mathematical demonstrations and pictorial examples, went into ten editions.[5] Optics as a science played a conspicuous role in the Dutch scientific revolution, in which mathematics was brought into fruitful alliance with systematic observation. The great scientist Simon Stevin, writing in the Dutch vernacular, published a detailed analysis of geometrical perspective in 1605. If we look for related signs in Dutch art, we can obviously cite the perspectival delights of ecclesiastical and domestic interiors, and the geometrical spaces of townscapes with their tidy ensembles of religious, civic and domestic buildings. But rural landscapes seem to be something else, with their untidy relish of fecund nature and humble buildings, and most of Hobbema's paintings conform to this rustic mode.

However, Karel von Mander in the pioneering chapter on landscape in the introductory section of his influential 1604 collection of artists' lives, *Het Schilder-Boeck* (*The Book on Painters*), instructs the aspirational student to follow the rule that

the ditches and furrows we see in the field also taper and narrow as they recede from both sides towards the vanishing point, like tiled floors. Try to observe this without letting boredom get the better of you: it will give your backgrounds a lot of depth. I would like you to pay heed to foreshortening and reduction as it appears in nature. Even if [your subject] is not architecture, which demands strict rules, you must know how to place your viewing or vanishing point accurately on the horizon – that is, on the surface of the water. Everything that is below it is seen from above, and the rest from below.[6]

Indeed, if we look more carefully at the apparent disorder of rural landscapes, such as those by Hobbema, they keenly obey contrasts in scale and distance to create deep stage-sets for trees, human figures, roads, meandering rivers, watermills, wind-blown meadows and scattered buildings. This informal approach has served Hockney well in his more standard landscapes, such as *Huggate, St Mary's Church Spire* (fig. 56).

We are fortunate to have a compound drawing of suitable perspectival devices for landscapes and seascapes made in 1644 by Simon de Vlieger, who is mainly known for his marine subjects.[7] On a single sheet of paper he outlined ten demonstrations of how to observe rules of scale (fig. 53). The first demonstration provides the key technique. A geometrical 'height wall' proceeds from the bottom left to the vanishing point or 'eye point' on the horizon. The verticals of the wall are equivalent to the height of a person at each successive horizontal division. Everything in the picture can be scaled accordingly. The ten demonstrations show:

- *the principle of the height wall, using the height of a person for scaling;*
- *a height wall for sterns;*
- *height walls for the hulls of boats and the tops of two masts;*
- *vanishing points for towers orientated with their nearest plane parallel to the picture plane (right) and tilted to the picture plane (left);*
- *the lateral vanishing (or distance) points for towers orientated at 45% to the picture plan;*
- *a height wall that intersects with the hull or mooring platform of a boat;*
- *a height wall for trees in relation to the chimney of a house;*
- *a height wall used schematically for persons on a flat ground plane;*
- *a height wall for persons and a vanishing point for a house and the brickwork of a bridge;*
- *the relative scaling of boats of three different sizes without construction lines.*

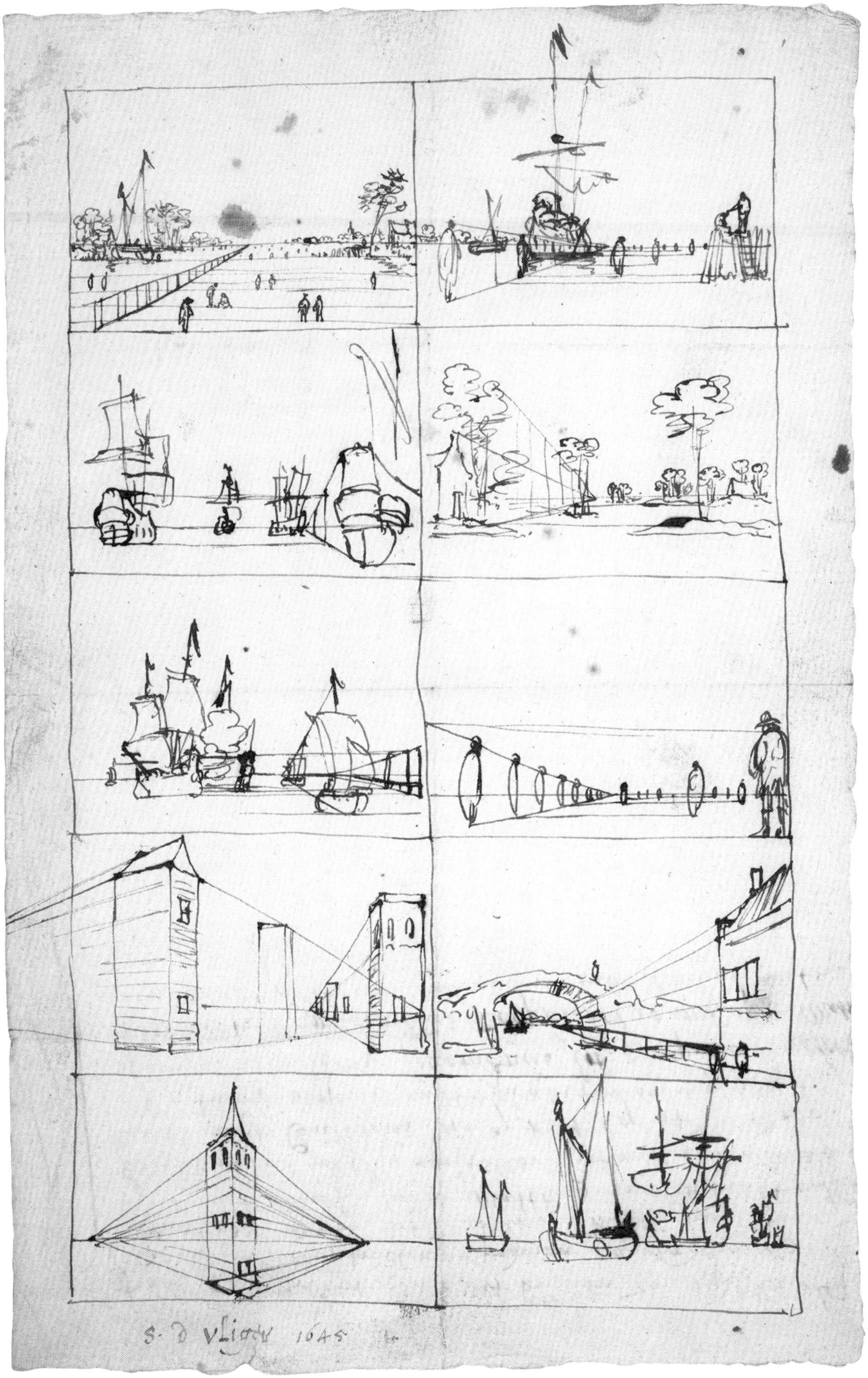

53 Simon Jacobsz. de Vlieger, *A sheet of ten studies in perspective*, 1645 pen and brown ink on paper, 32.1 x 21 cm. British Museum, London, 1874,0808.99

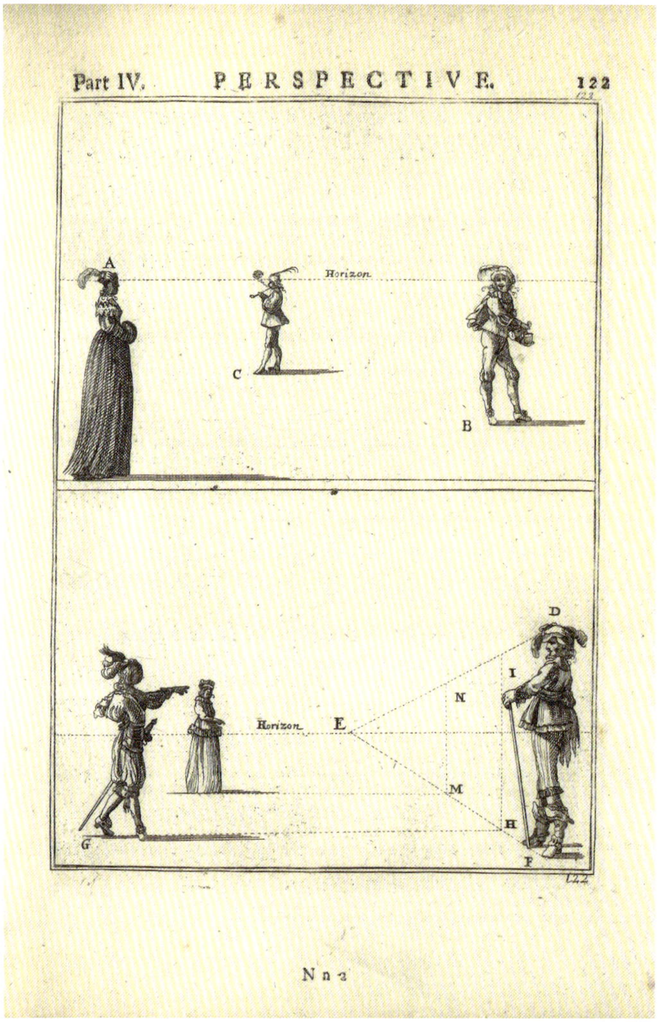

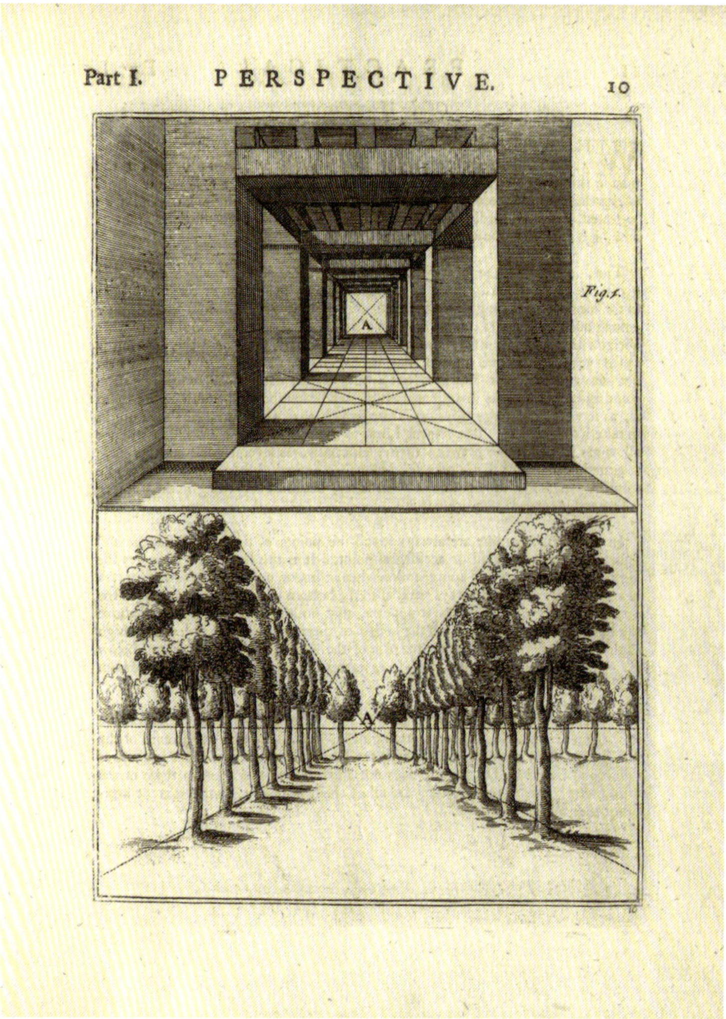

54 Jean Dubreuil, The scaling of figures with their eye level at and below the horizon, from Jean Dubreuil, *The Practice of Perspective: Or, An Easy Method of Representing Natural Objects According to the Rules of Art*, London, 4th edition, 1765, Part IV, p. 122

55 Jean Dubreuil, Perspective of a building and an avenue of trees, from Jean Dubreuil, *The Practice of Perspective: Or, An Easy Method of Representing Natural Objects According to the Rules of Art*, London, 4th edition, 1765, Part I, p. 10

De Vlieger's sketches are pedagogically effective. But were the techniques actually used? Marine sketches by Willem van de Velde the Younger at the National Maritime Museum in London show related constructions, but the overall evidence of their use is slight.[8] The demonstrations might have been used primarily to train the eye and hand. If they were actually used in making a picture, no developed underdrawings would be needed. A ruler and a stick of charcoal would do the job.

The scaling system of the height wall was a simple extrapolation from standard perspectival techniques. Something similar is shown in Jean Dubreuil's popular and well-illustrated *Perspective pratique* in 1642, where the height of a foreground figure is used to scale any other figure at a greater depth (fig. 54). He also shows early in his treatise that a regular avenue of trees behaves in a way comparable to a building (fig. 55).

If we take the method outlined by de Vlieger and Dubreuil's avenue, we have everything needed to construct the space in Hobbema's picture. The avenue itself looks as if could be an illustration of Van Mander's text. The figures of the man pruning the trees, the hunter with a hound and gun, the conversing couple in the side road, and the shadowy figures in the distance are inserted to look right in scale. However the scales do not appear to have been calculated precisely. If we take the hunter as the module, the pruner and talking couple are too small. Or we could better say that the hunter has been enlarged for the sake of emphasis. Like so many artists who plan their pictures with an armature

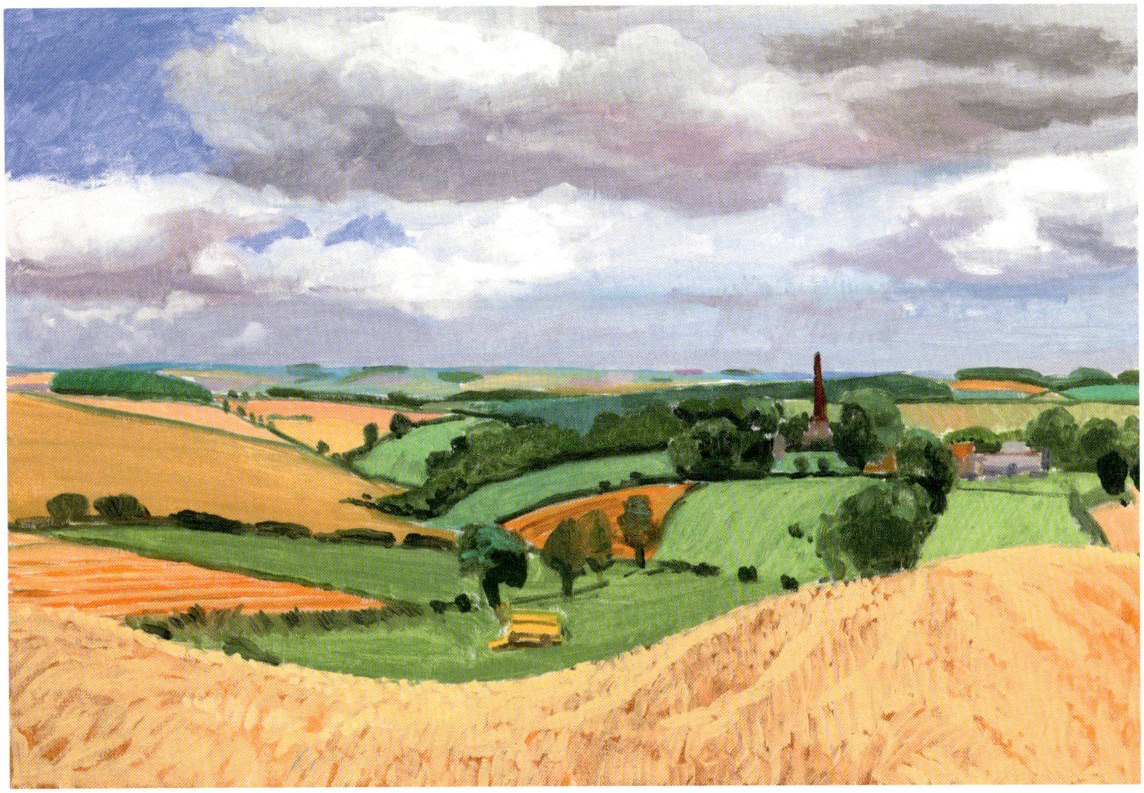

56 | F David Hockney, *Huggate, St Mary's Church Spire*, August 2005, oil on canvas, 60.9 x 91.4 cm. Fitzwilliam Museum, on loan from the Estate of the late Mrs Elizabeth Corob

of perspective, Hobbema ultimately turns to instinct rather than mathematics to make the image work to best effect.

'Useful knowledge'

We have already seen how Hockney has exploited 'reverse perspective' as championed by the Russian theorist, Florensky, to characterize a rectangular space as a trapezium, wider at the back than the front, in contradiction to standard perspective. Here Hockney eliminates the rutted road that compels us to read Hobbema's space in the prescribed way – *à la manière de Dubreuil*. Hockney's assertively shaped canvas even allows us (with a certain amount of effort) to invert the space of the avenue. When we look at the neat zones of inverted space in *Tall Dutch Trees* we are presented with neat orders of pictorial palisades with parallel furrows, which stand in front of pyramidal roofs painted brightly in red and compact trees in complementary green. The two lateral cloudscapes evoke what we see when we lift our eyes from the delineated land and to the free-wheeling fields of the sky.

Hockney's optical order is not the same as Hobbema's. But it has its own underlying organization that speaks eloquently of the underlying principles of visual and social cultivation that Hobbema so wonderfully exemplifies. Hockney says that we can look at this order in a different way.

Notes

1 The second version, also of 2017, is entitled *Tall Dutch Trees After Hobbema (Useful Knowledge)* (private collection). **2** Reverdy 1997. **3** Levey 1989a. **4** Alpers 1984. **5** For an overview of Dutch treatises and pictorial practice, see Kemp 1992, 109–19. **6** Karel van Mander, *Het Schilder-Boeck*, Haarlem 1604, as quoted by Ruurs 1983, 189. **7** Ruurs 1983, 189–200, provides a good account of the drawing by de Vlieger and related ones by Willem van der Velde the Younger **8** Ruurs 1983.

Fig. 2.

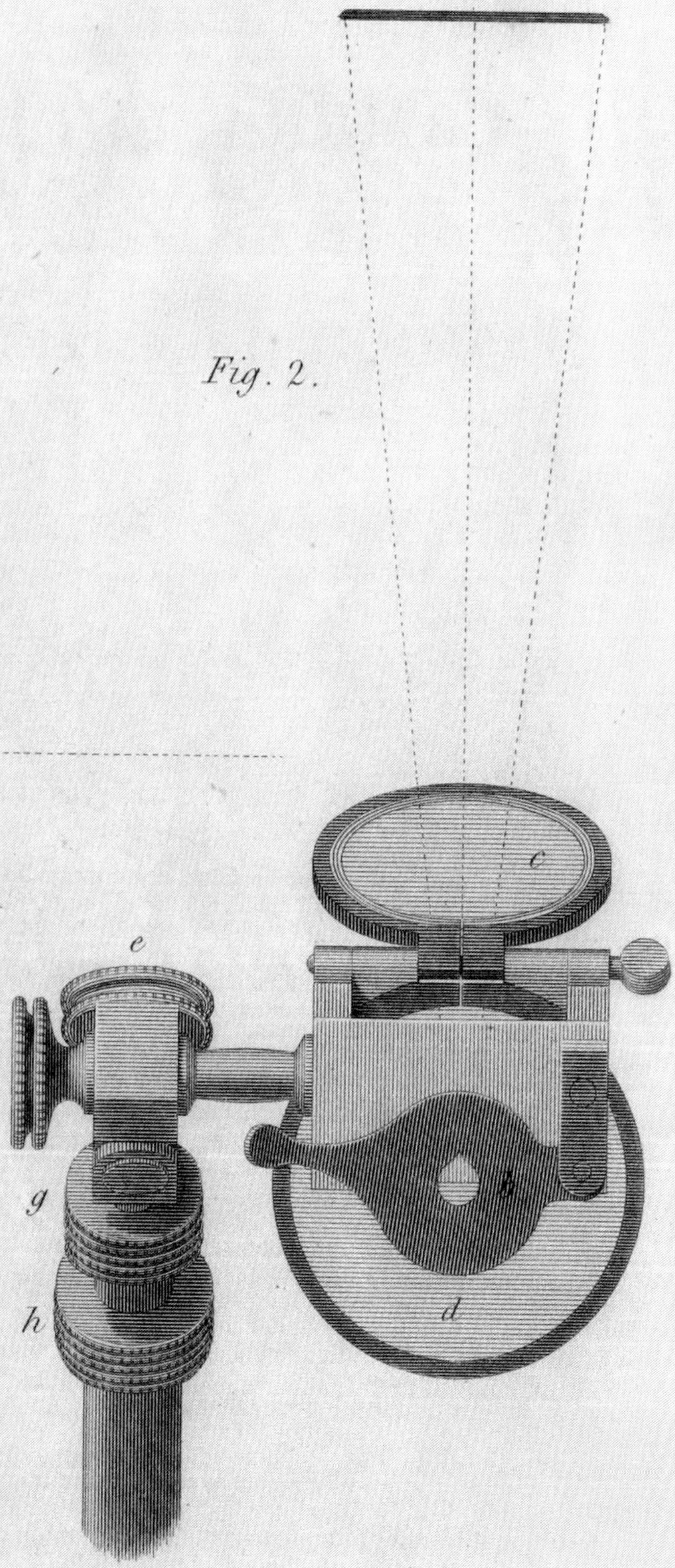

Fig. 1.

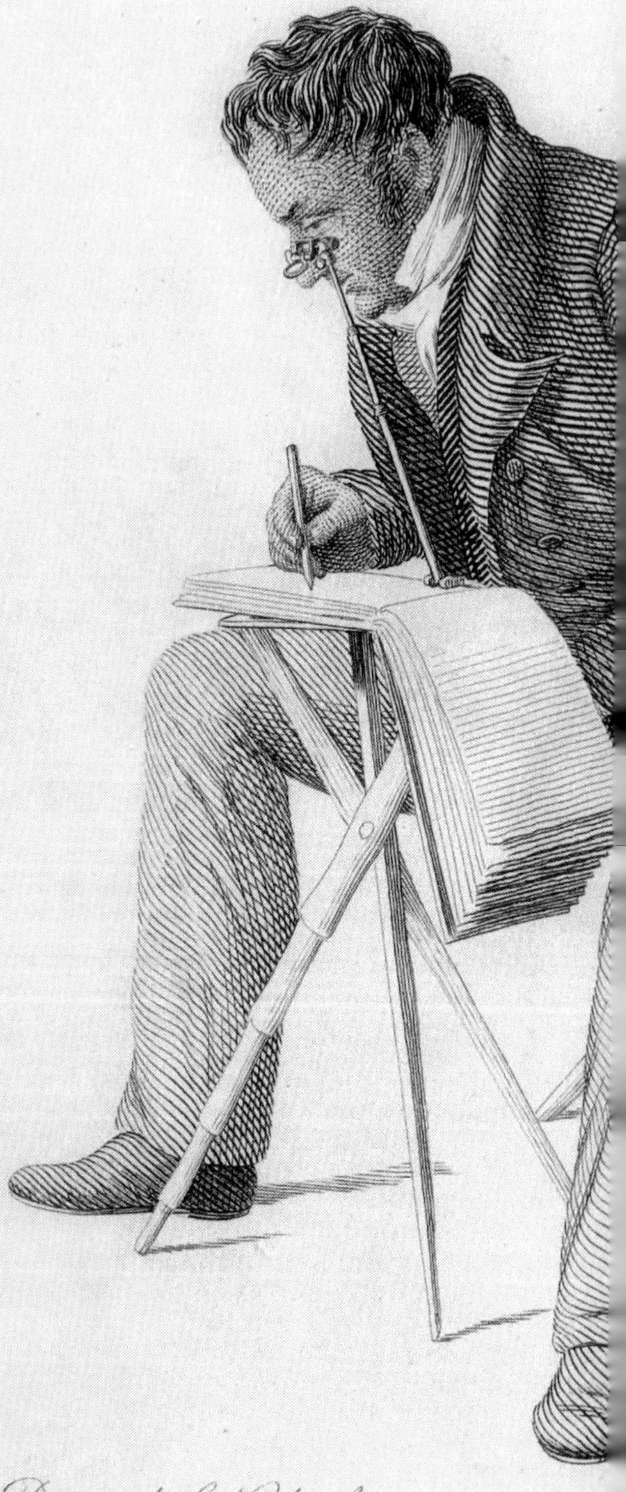

Drawn by C. Varley for G. Dollond, *with*

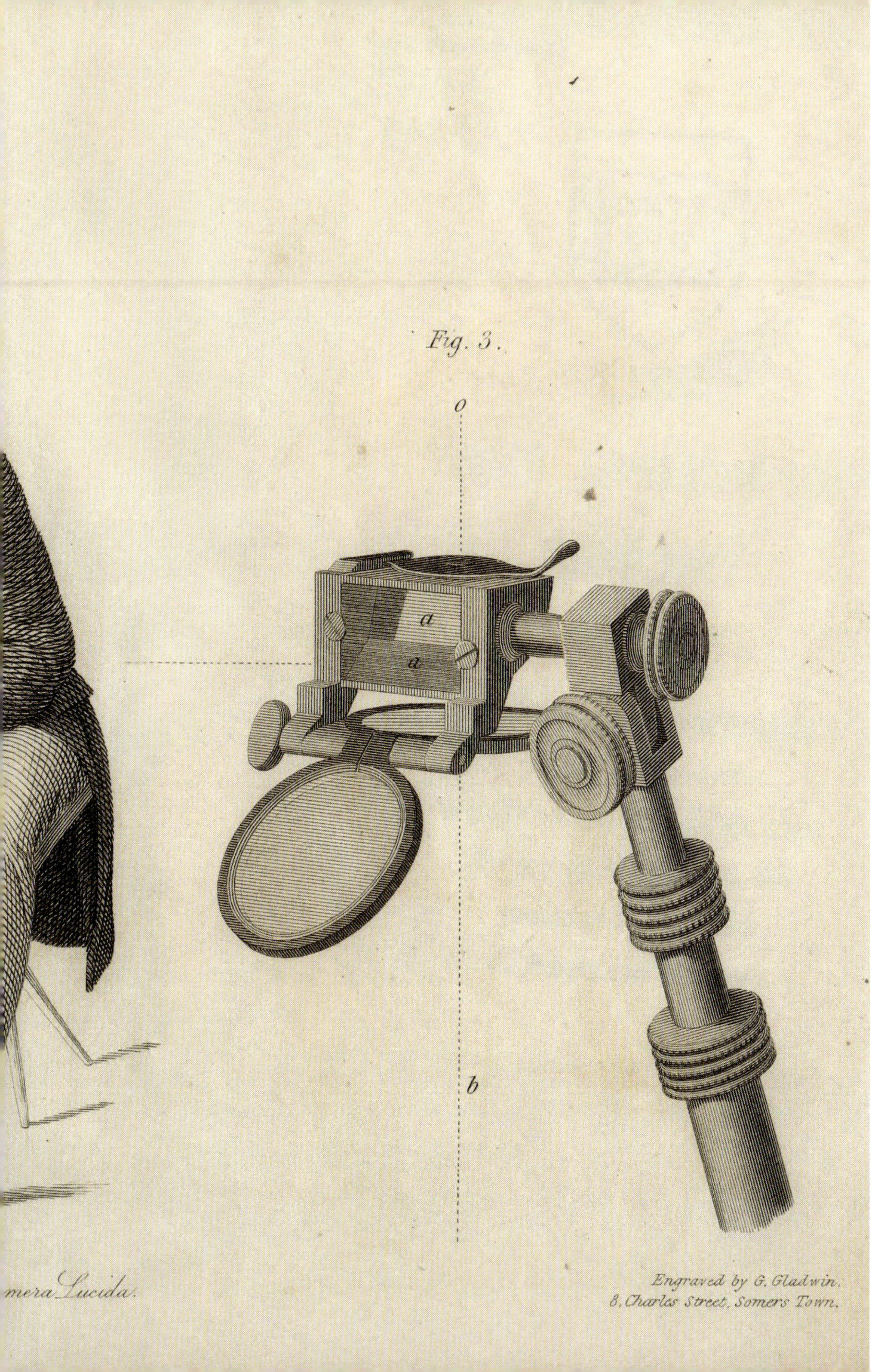

DEVICES FOR THE IMITATION OF NATURE

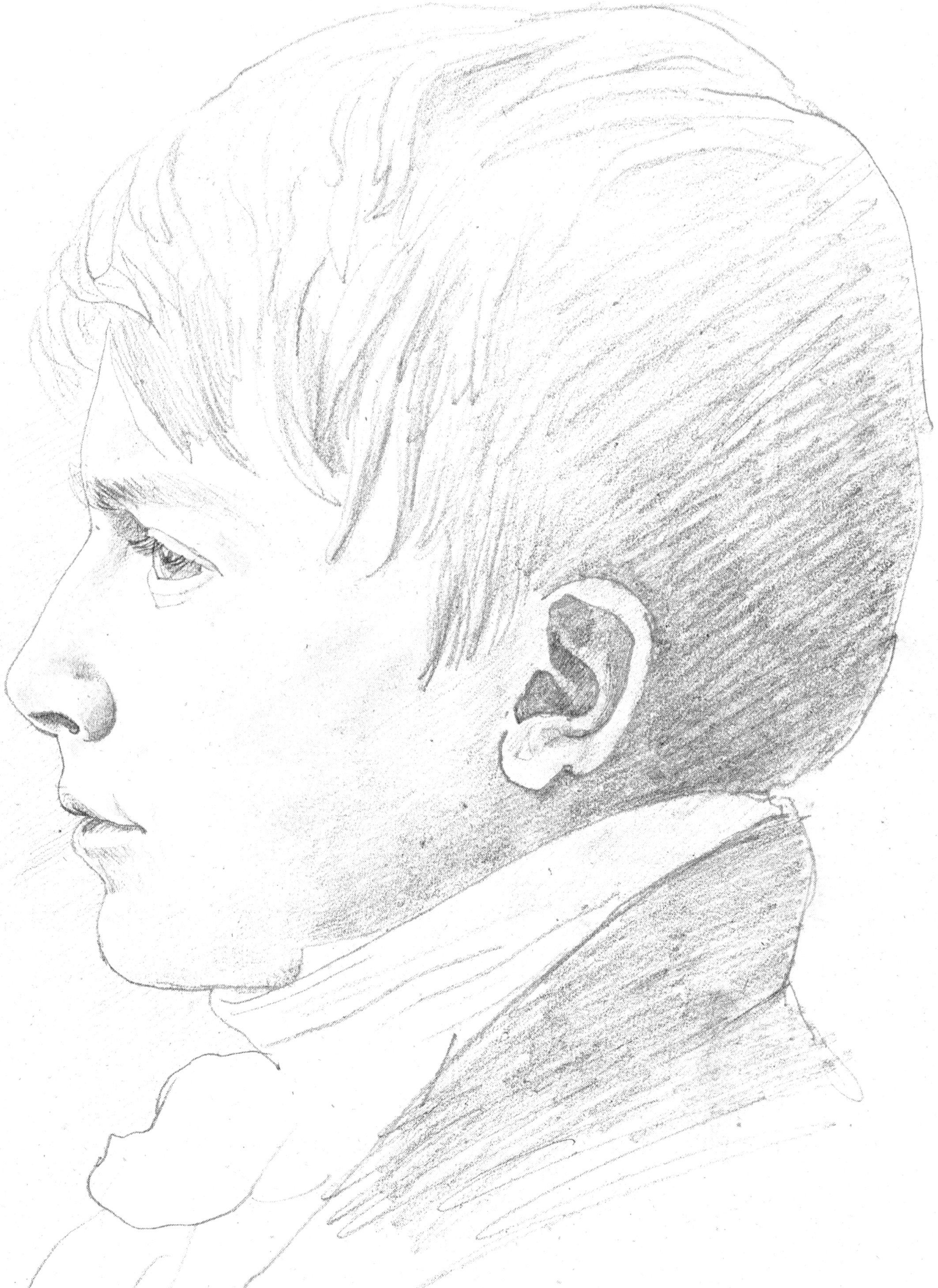

Anne Lyles

'All kinds of objects'

Cornelius Varley, the Patent Graphic Telescope and the use of optical instruments by nineteenth-century British artists

In 1818 the young painter John Linnell introduced his former tutor, the landscape watercolourist John Varley, to William Blake. Ebullient and somewhat credulous, Varley was fascinated by astrology, so was no doubt eager to meet Blake given the older man's legendary visionary powers. A drawing by Linnell made in 1821 shows Varley in animated conversation with a more quizzical Blake (fig. 57). Two years before, at Varley's house in Great Titchfield Street, Blake had started to draw for Varley – no doubt to satisfy the latter's curiosity – the famous sequence of 'Visionary Heads', comprising a group of biblical, historical and imaginary characters.

One of these 'Visionary Heads' is the celebrated image of the *Man Who Taught Blake Painting in his Dreams* (fig. 58). The correct identification of this character as a portrait of Blake's inspiration – thus, as Martin Butlin pointed out, a self-portrait as it were of his own imaginative, visionary self – was only eventually arrived at thanks to inscriptions on two other versions in the collection of Tate Britain. One of these is a counterproof. The other – in the same direction as the counterproof but with the head more prominently filling the page – is thought to have been made with the Graphic Telescope invented by John's younger brother Cornelius in 1809, and patented by him in 1811.[1]

Cornelius Varley, like John, was to become a talented artist in his own right. Indeed the two brothers were amongst the founding members of the Old Watercolour Society in 1804. Cornelius, however, was brought up from the age of twelve by his uncle Samuel Varley, a watchmaker based in Clerkenwell noted for his fine lenses and philosophical instruments. By the age of fourteen, the precocious Cornelius had already perfected his own pocket microscope, complete with accompanying lenses. When the budding young scientist's interests shifted to art around the turn of the century, he began to apply his experimental skills to the development of an instrument that would help facilitate one of his own favourite artistic activities, sketching from nature.

The Graphic Telescope is a type of camera lucida designed like its immediate predecessor, the instrument of that name patented by William Hyde Wollaston in 1806, to be used in full daylight and enabling an object or scene to be projected on to a flat surface to be traced. It combined the

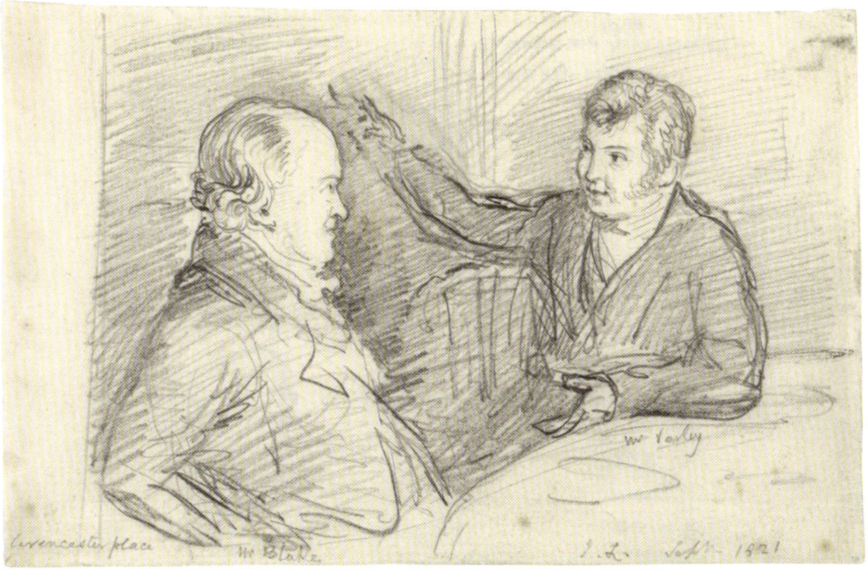

57 John Linnell, *William Blake in conversation with John Varley*, 1821, pencil on paper, 11.3 x 17.6 cm, Fitzwilliam Museum. PD.59-1950

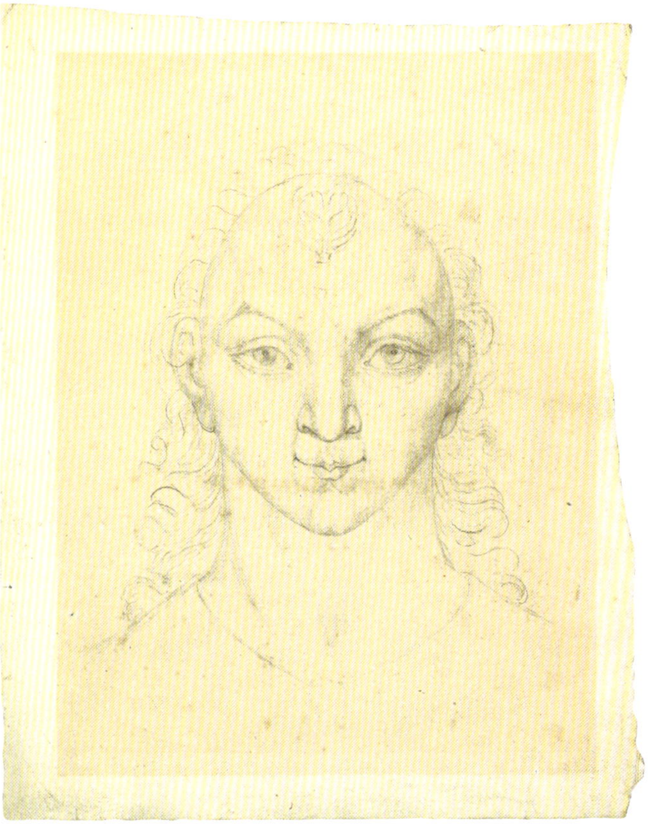

58 William Blake, *The Man Who Taught Blake Painting in his Dreams*, c. 1819, pencil on paper, 30.0 x 24.5 cm. Fitzwilliam Museum, PD.166-1985

optics of a telescope with an eyepiece similar to that used in the camera lucida (see below, p. 97). By Varley's own account he invented his Telescope in 1809, though it was not until 1811 that he sought to patent it. He claimed to have been initially reluctant to seek a patent owing to the likely expense, but his friends apparently urged him to do so given the instrument's novelty and potential usefulness.[2] Varley was awarded a patent on 4 June 1811, only then to find himself saddled with the extra costs of having to manufacture the Telescope as well, unable to find any other maker capable of the task.[3]

There may have been another reason why Cornelius Varley was initially reluctant to seek a patent. The Telescope was similar in function, even in its mode of operation, to the camera lucida itself, both instruments dependent on a two-way mirror arrangement. In both cases the user would look at the object or scene with one eye (through a prism and aperture in the case of the camera lucida, or downwards through an aperture in the case of the Telescope), whilst at the same time looking with the other eye at the pencil and paper, a procedure which often proved difficult for the user to master. There were of course various differences. Varley's telescope

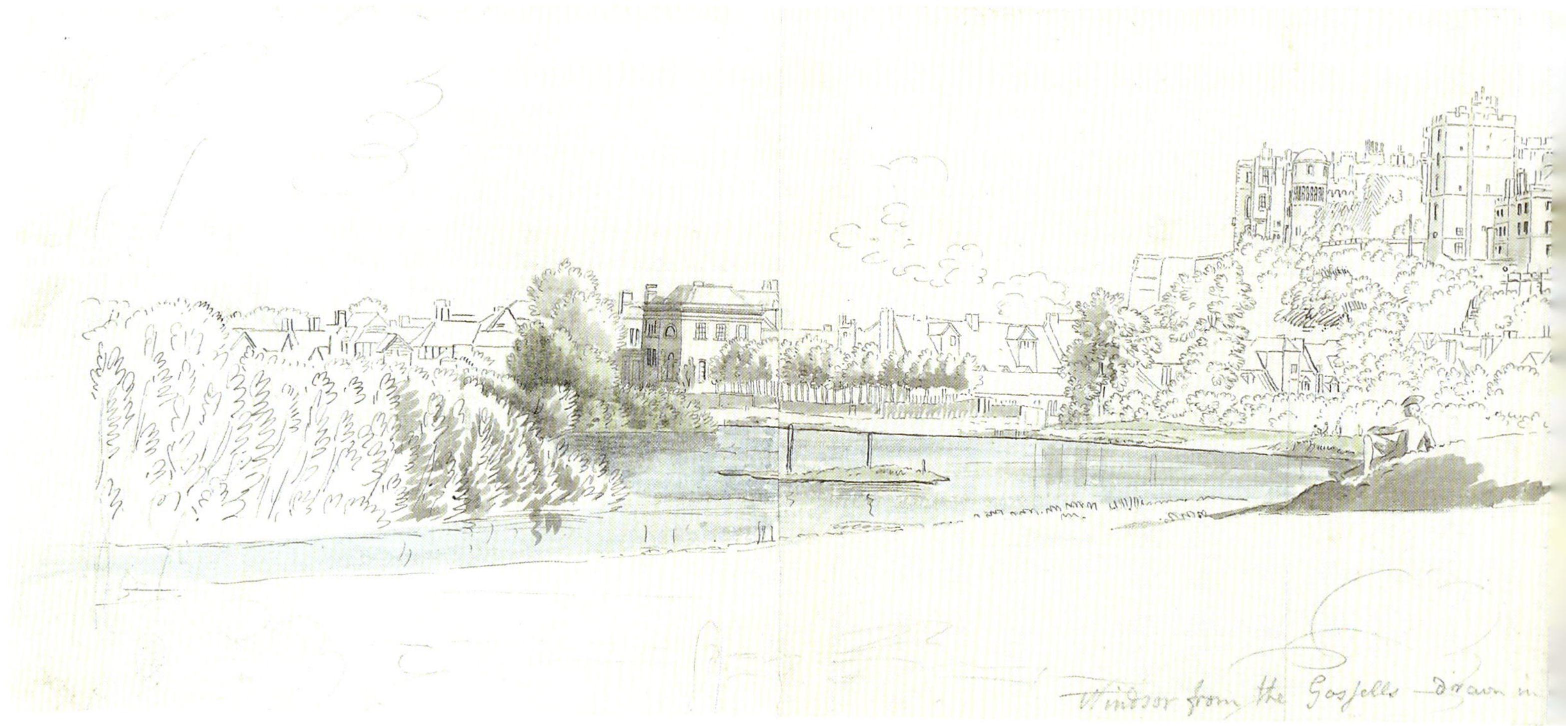

offered much greater powers of magnification (ranging from five to 60 times). Moreover, whilst Wollaston's device incorporated its small viewing prism on a narrow arm that could be clamped to a flat stand or table, Varley's telescope came with its own portable table to allow for maximum stability and thus minimize the problem of vibration in the field. Nevertheless, Samuel Varley was sufficiently worried that Wollaston might sue for infringement of copyright that he wrote to his nephew in 1810, when the application was still under consideration, to encourage him to meet Wollaston to ensure he could make no objection.[4]

Wollaston would no doubt have been reassured to discover that Varley's Telescope was more expensive than his own camera lucida, though the price of his rival's device depended on the model. Indeed, according to Varley's own list of published prices, the Telescope was available in seven models, ranging from £5 to £15, depending on its powers of magnification. Varley wrote that it could capture "all kinds of objects", from "the most distant" (towns, perhaps, or "positions and fortifications of the enemy beyond gunshot") to those at closer range such as carts, wagons, boats and shipping – or even smaller foreground details such as "flowers, plants and weeds" (and we know Varley himself used the device when making a detailed drawing of the flowerhead of a rhododendron in Chelsea Physic Gardens in 1828). Some of these objects, he noted, could even be drawn through a window for added convenience. Finally, he added, it could be used for drawing portraits "from much larger than life down to miniature". Moreover, as well as being able to reduce or enlarge an image in the same direction (in common, as it happens, with the camera lucida), Varley emphasized that the Telescope was capable of reducing or enlarging an image "the reverse way for drawing on stone and for engravers, whereby they may copy a picture or print, line for line, to print the right way". [5]

Following the award of a patent for the Telescope, Varley often inscribed the drawings he himself made with the device with the abbreviation PGT (for Patent Graphic Telescope). Sometimes he appears to have added these initials retrospectively to drawings, even to drawings made a year or two before the device was actually patented. For example, a landscape drawing he apparently made through a window, judging by its high horizon line, carries two annotations, one an inscription describing the view, *Hyde Park from Paddington P.G.T.,* and

59 | F Thomas Sandby, *Windsor Castle from the Goswells drawn in a camera*, c. 1760–70, pencil, pen and ink and watercolour on paper, 12.4 x 57.8 cm. Royal Collection Trust, RCIN914602

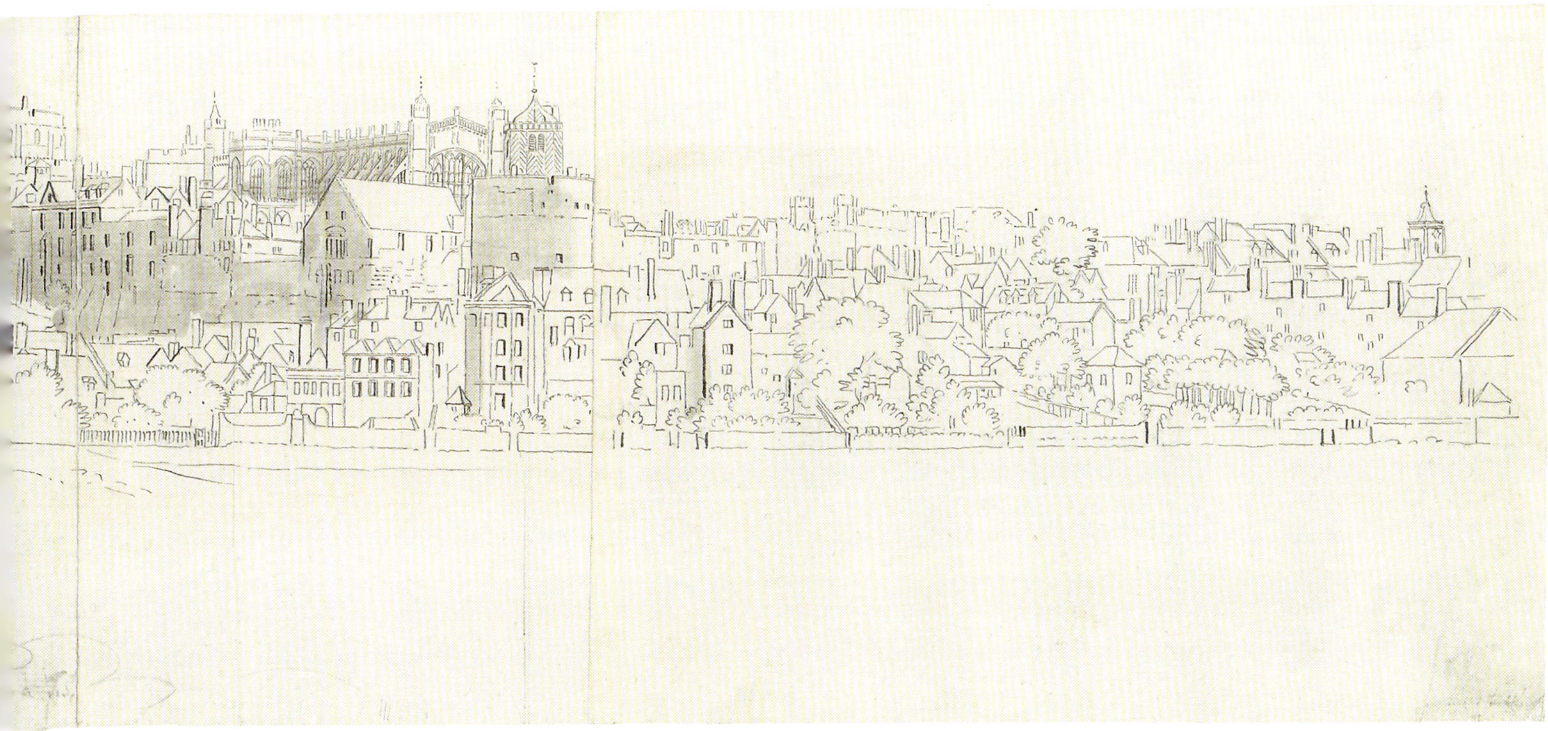

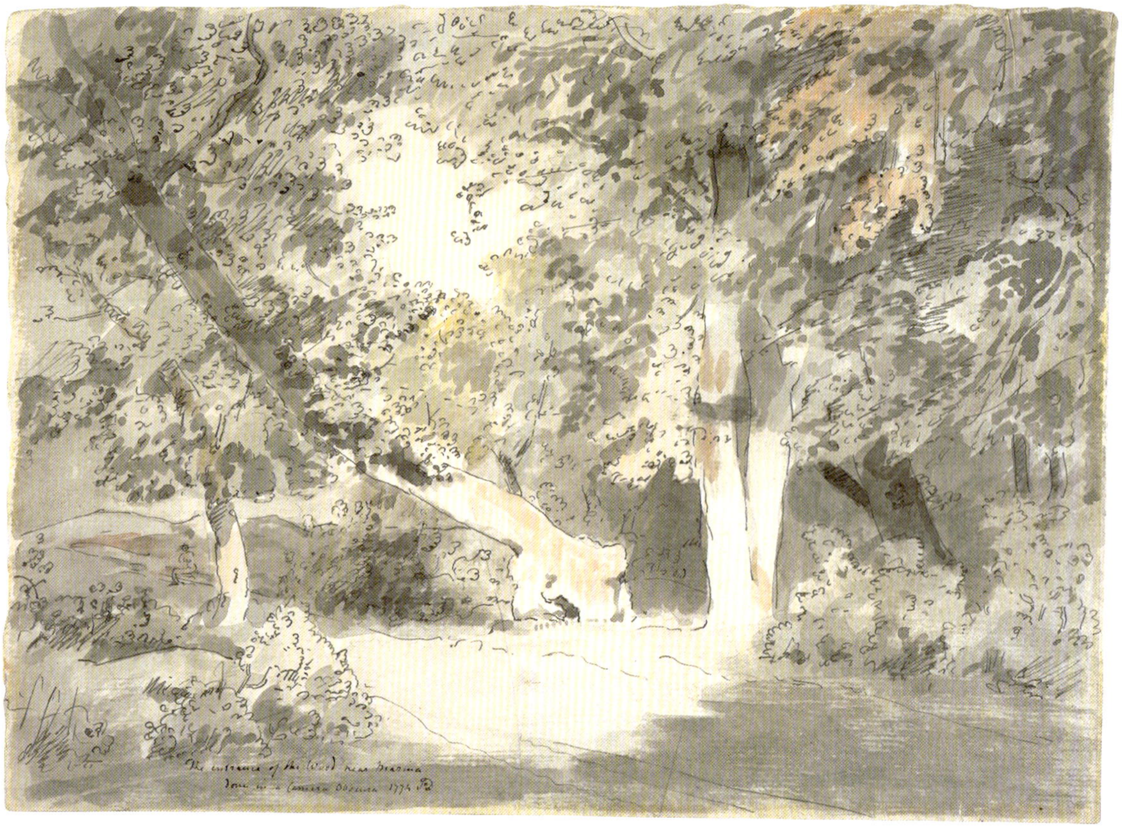

60 John Downman, *The Entrance to a Wood near Marino*, 1774, pen and brown ink and watercolour on paper, 26.2 x 36.0 cm. Whitworth Art Gallery, Manchester, D 1999.18

another, a signature in small neat letters, *C.Varley 1810*. Sometimes Varley noted on a drawing the power of magnification he had used, or even the time of day (one drawing he made with the Graphic Telescope in 1820 is annotated *12'oclock shaddows* (sic), which tends to confirm that, as for the camera obscura, midday was probably the best time of day to use the device).[6] The fact that Varley often inscribed these drawings as having been made with the Graphic Telescope means that – together with similar drawings produced by other artists in his immediate circle – they prove particularly suitable for closer examination as a group. For previous artists did not generally specify on their drawings if, or when, they had even used an optical aid when making them.

There are, however, a few earlier documented camera drawings which can usefully be examined to help provide important context and comparison for these Graphic Telescope images. Indeed these earlier drawings provide key visual clues as to what one might expect a drawing made with a mechanical aid to look like, even if they also serve to caution as to the extent that such drawings can vary in appearance. For example, Thomas Sandby's drawing of *Windsor Castle from the Goswells*, c. 1760–70 (fig. 59) – which he inscribed as having 'made in a camera' – shows the use of rather careful, mechanical looking outlines to trace the contours of the buildings on the castle mound. The drawing extends over four overlapping sheets, which indicates where Sandby had to turn his camera through four different positions to embrace the wide sweep of the view.[7] By contrast, John Downman's drawing of a more enclosed view at the entrance to the woods near Marino outside Rome in 1774 – which he similarly inscribed as having 'done in a camera obscura' – shows the use of much freer lines in pen and wash (probably reinforcing lighter pencil lines below) so as to capture the general contours of trees, path and distant hills (fig. 60). This prompts the question as to whether stylistic differences such as these can be explained as being the result of the two artists' differing drawing styles or else be attributable to the likely function of the drawings in question – or perhaps a combination of both these factors.

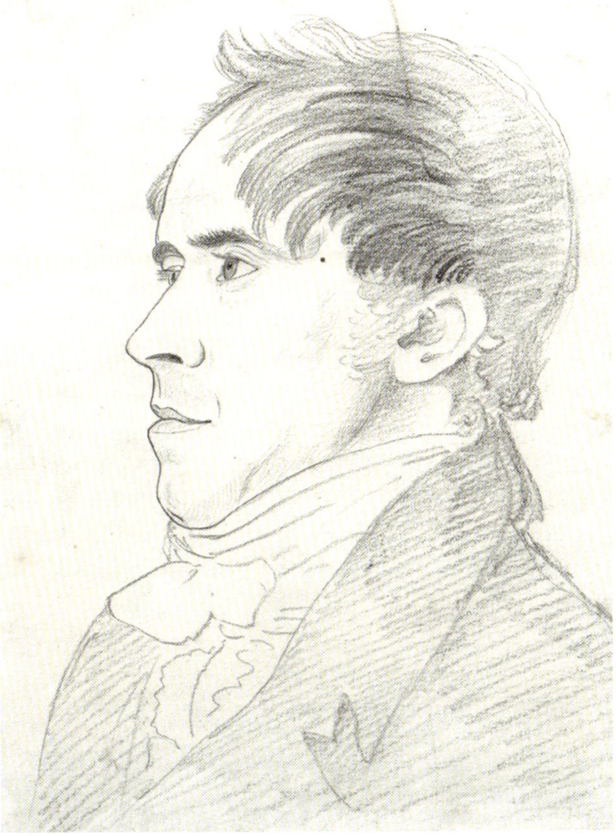

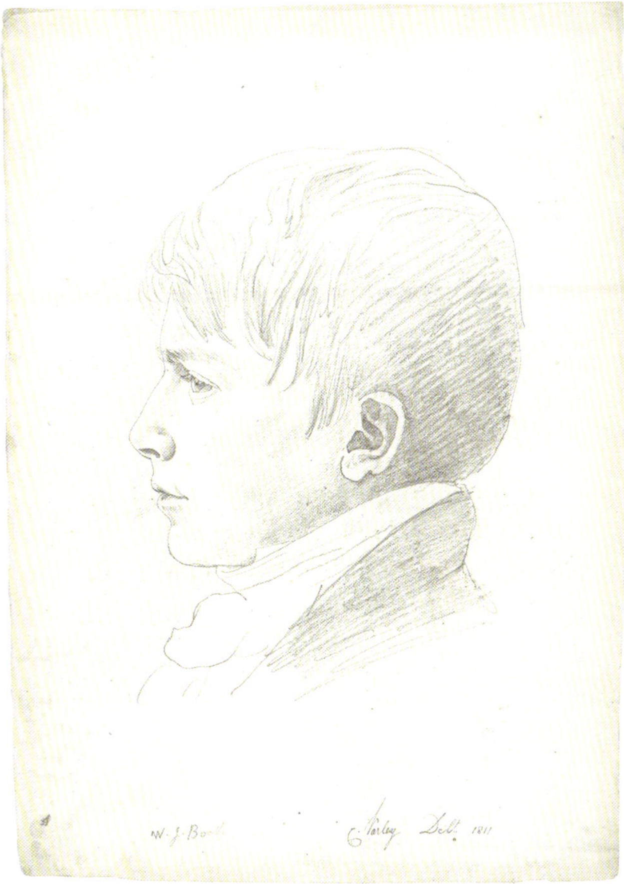

Thomas Sandby was trained as an architectural draughtsman, and was skilled in mapping and surveying. The careful drawing style seen in *Windsor Castle,* though partly explicable by his use of a camera obscura, must also owe much to the fact that his work falls within a distinct late eighteenth-century topographical tradition which prized accuracy. Moreover, Sandby may even have made this drawing in preparation for a more detailed design he intended to work up later. Downman, by contrast, was primarily a portrait draughtsman (see below, pp. 125, 127), and *The Entrance to a Wood near Marino* – together with other landscape drawings he made on his travels abroad at this date – show him off duty, working apparently for his own pleasure. HIs fluid pen-and-wash lines defining the features of *Entrance to a Wood* are in any case partly a response to the more organic nature of his subject, lacking in any buildings (and thus any straight lines). Not only, then, can camera drawings vary according to subject (and also perhaps according to whether an artist later overworked them), they can also vary according to the extent to which artists, especially professional artists, felt free to improvise stylistically even when working from a virtual image designed to be 'traced'.

Some of the earliest drawings made with the Graphic Telescope are of portrait heads, and these were made by both Cornelius and John Varley. John apparently drew the first portrait head after the Telescope had been patented in 1811.[8] However, as there are other portrait drawings by him made with the Telescope dated to 1810, clearly the instrument was used for this purpose – as we have seen it was by Cornelius for landscapes – before it was patented.[9] As Timothy Wilcox has pointed out, the portrait heads made by John Varley are usually of artists (or of figures associated with the art world) such as that of his fellow watercolourist William Havell (fig. 61). Those by Cornelius meanwhile tend to represent figures from a wider circle of scholars or scientists such as, for example, his uncle Samuel

61 | F John Varley, *Portrait of William Havell*, c. 1810–11, pencil on paper, 21.3 x 15.4 cm. The Wordsworth Trust, Dove Cottage, Grasmere, 1997.2.2

62 | F Cornelius Varley, *Portrait of William J. Booth, head in profile*, 1811, pencil on paper, 37.8 x 27.7 cm. Fitzwilliam Museum, Sir Ivor and Lady Batchelor Bequest, 2015, PD.178-2015

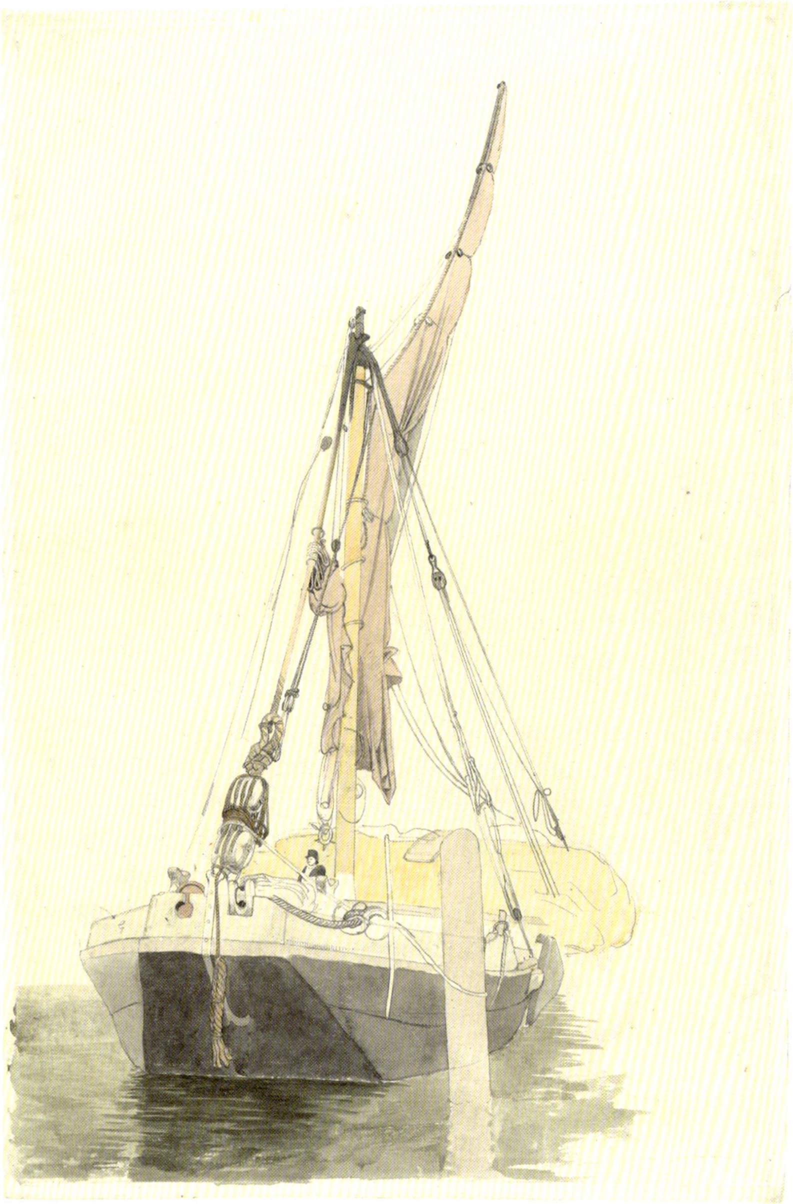

63 | F Cornelius Varley, *Study of a Masted Boat*, c. 1823, pencil and watercolour on paper, 47.8 x 32.5 cm. Fitzwilliam Museum, Purchased from the Biffen Fund, 1993, PD.42-1993

Varley or the architect William J. Booth (fig. 62), surveyor to the Draper's Company estates in County Derry from 1827 to 1855.[10] Not surprisingly the portrait drawings made by both brothers with the Telescope share an emphasis on silhouette, and on firm lines for the contours of the heads modified by looser shading probably added later by hand. However, the portrait heads by Cornelius tend to have crisper outlines and a greater clarity of finish whilst those by John generally have a more hesitant, softer touch. Cornelius Varley's portrait of Samuel Varley is known in two nearly identical versions, as are examples of other portraits drawn both by him and by John using the Telescope. This suggests that – as with some of Blake's 'Visionary Heads' – the brothers made replicas of some of the portrait heads, usually on a similar size as the originals, again with the aid of the Graphic Telescope.[11]

At this early stage of his career, Cornelius Varley was spending a fair amount of time teaching watercolour and drawing, and indeed many of his travels at this date – including a trip to Ireland in 1808 – seem to have been undertaken in connection with teaching commitments. It was no doubt for the benefit of pupils that in 1809, together with his brother John (a life-long and more prolific teacher of watercolour), Cornelius published the first (and, as it was to transpire, only) part of his *Etchings of Shipping*. This contained eight prints of boats, five etchings and three early pen lithographs, based on sketches he had made on the banks of the River Thames. In 1847 he embarked on a follow-up publication, Varley's *Drawing Book of Boats,* and for this he clarified that many of the vessels had been "drawn by his Graphic Telescope ... so as to secure both truth of form and perspective".

There is no reason to doubt Cornelius Varley's assertion, especially as we know that, again thanks to their inscriptions, in 1823 he was certainly using the Telescope for drawing boats "with all [their] minutiae of rigging". [12] The example in the Fitzwilliam Museum (fig. 63) was probably made by Varley in 1823 as well, especially as – like others dating from that year – it has additional watercolour washes. Meanwhile, one wonders whether the images of boats Varley had included in the earlier treatise, *Etchings of Shipping*, 1809, might also have been made – like some of his landscapes and John's portrait heads – with the

Telescope before it was patented. Alternatively, it has even been suggested that Cornelius Varley might have been using Wollaston's Camera Lucida to make the boat drawings for his 1809 publication.[13] Certainly at some stage Varley would have wanted to experiment with Wollaston's device before working out what improvements he might make to any appliance of his own invention; that he knew it well is evident from the print after his drawing showing an artist sketching with the device that was used to illustrate the frontispiece of George Dollond's *Description of the Camera Lucida* (1830) (see fig 72).

It is hard to know for sure what drove Cornelius Varley to invent his Graphic Telescope in the first instance. It may have been his frustration in attempting to draw distant details in panoramic vistas he saw on trips to Wales in the early years of the century that motivated him to develop a device which would enable him to sketch such scenes with greater accuracy and in true perspective.[14] Certainly in the specification he wrote for the patent for the Telescope in 1811 Varley described it as "an instrument for Viewing distant objects"; and, as Charlotte Klonk has pointed out, he was later to write that it was the application of superior lenses to drawing instruments such as the Telescope that allowed for greater lateral definition as well.[15] From the earliest years of his training as an artist Varley had been attracted to landscape and to sketching in the open air, in pencil and watercolour, inspired – he later wrote – by the powerful example of Thomas Girtin. On those same trips to Wales, and elsewhere in his early career, he made highly expressive watercolour sketches of clouds, trees and mountains which follow in the same naturalistic vein injected into British landscape depiction by Girtin at the turn of the century. Perhaps Varley believed he was taking Girtin's example one step further by inventing an instrument that would enable artists to capture natural details with even greater precision.

Of course Varley was not the only artist at this time to be influenced by Girtin's powerfully naturalistic watercolours. Cornelius's own brother John had been strongly affected by Girtin's example at the turn of the century, adopting for a few years a style of naturalistic painting far removed from the rather formulaic classical landscapes he was later to produce for annual exhibitions at the Old Watercolour Society. J.M.W. Turner spent time in the 1790s making drawings alongside Girtin at Dr Thomas Monro's 'academy' in the Strand in London. Indeed the style of the pencil or pen-and-ink drawings made by both artists in the 1790s – using short, cursive strokes, and lines which are alternately thick and thin – ultimately derives from their experience of copying drawings by Canaletto in Monro's collection. It was a style they continued to use for making topographical drawings throughout the decade, whether on individual sheets (fig. 64) or even in sketchbooks when on tour (fig. 65). However, unlike Canaletto himself (see below, pp. 103–11), Turner seems unlikely ever to have used a camera obscura, whilst Girtin appears to have employed it only late in his life, in 1802, when making panoramic drawings along the banks of the Seine in Paris from a hackney carriage.[16] John Constable, whose work was to become a keystone of natural painting over the next two decades, was also significantly influenced by Girtin in his early career. In his personal pursuit of a more naturalistic art, however, rather than using optical instruments like Cornelius Varley, Constable experimented with tracing landscapes on glass in the open air.[17] For example, he made such a tracing of the mill at Flatford in Suffolk, which he later used in the preparation of his famous painting of *Flatford Mill* in the collection at Tate Britain. Not surprisingly, these ink tracings have a highly utilitarian character, and are a far cry from the remarkably fine drawings Constable made freehand in sketchbooks throughout his lifetime.

By contrast to Constable's tracings on glass, Cornelius Varley's landscape drawings made with the Graphic Telescope, though technically also 'tracings', reveal much more of the artist's personal drawing style and vocabulary. They also vary one from another, or at least more than one might expect for drawings made with a mechanical aid. The majority of them (and they mainly date from between 1810 and 1825) feature open, panoramic landscapes seen from ground level and at some distance. Some of their more obvious differences can probably be explained by the varying distances or viewpoints Varley adopted when making them, and thus the power of magnification he used. *Vale of the Exe from Tiverton*, made on 7 June 1824 (fig. 66), for example, is a classic Graphic Telescope landscape

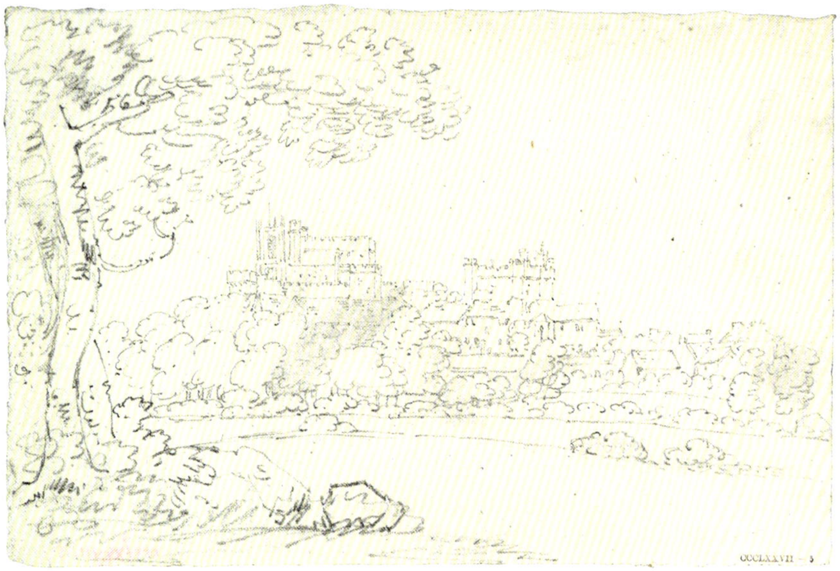

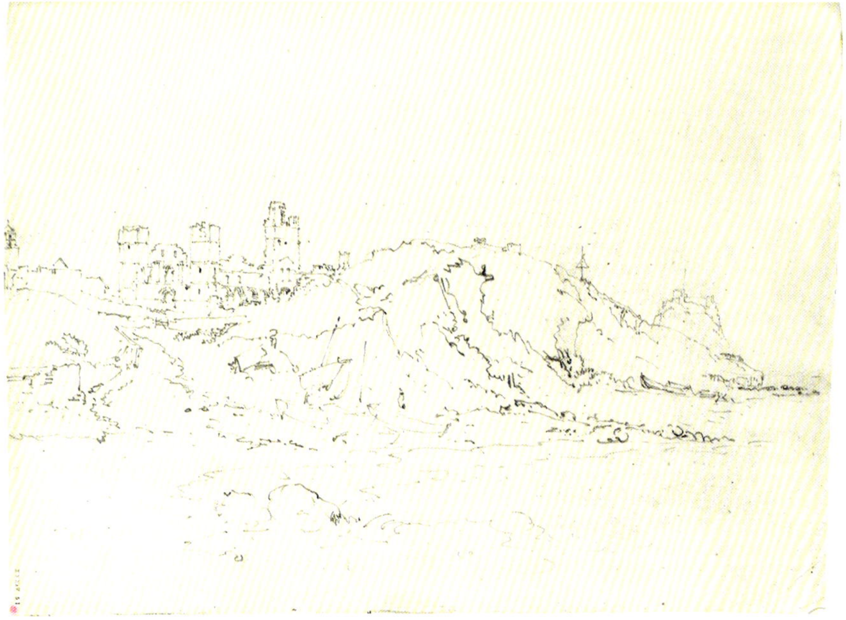

64 | F Thomas Girtin, *View of Lancaster*, c. 1797, pencil on paper, 14.3 x 21.8 cm. Tate, Accepted by the nation as part of the Turner Bequest, 1856, D36575

65 | F J.M.W. Turner, *Holy Island, Northumberland – a page from the 'North of England' sketchbook*, 1797, pencil on paper, 21.0 x 27.0 cm. Tate, Accepted by the nation as part of the Turner Bequest, 1856, D 00959 / TB XXXIV 51

drawing in which Varley has rendered the middle to far distance in remarkably fine detail but left the rest of the foreground almost entirely empty, with the exception of a few grazing cows (a tendency to omit details in the foreground is a distinct characteristic of drawings made with the Graphic Telescope). Moreover, given that *Vale of the Exe* has no obvious 'compositional' features framing the view, it is strikingly unmannered and indeed highly naturalistic. However, not all of Varley's Telescope drawings have this sense of refreshing naturalism. Some can verge on the hyperreal, even surreal. An example in the British Museum depicting *Patshull House, Staffordshire*, 1820, includes rather strange but solid looking low-level clouds which appear to hover just above the tops of similarly rounded trees, creating a distinctly unreal effect.[18]

Cornelius Varley appears to be the only artist to have used the Graphic Telescope for making pure landscape drawings. However, he might have influenced his brother's former pupil, John Linnell, to take up some sort of mechanical device for drawing landscapes around this date, albeit apparently not the Telescope itself. In 1811 Cornelius took Linnell to the Baptist Chapel in Keppel Street, Bloomsbury, where, not long afterwards, Linnell committed himself to the Baptist faith. From about this time Linnell started making landscapes in watercolour – of simple, unassuming 'slices' of nature – in the vicinity of Kensington Gravel Pits in Bayswater, whether of brick kilns, perhaps, or the corner of a house, *Alpha Cottages* (designed by the architect Charles Heathcote Tatham, also a Baptist), seen in open fields (fig. 67). These watercolours were, it seems, inspired by Linnell's spiritual awakening and new-found belief in painting the simplest of subjects, which he saw as a reflection of God's handiwork.[19]

Given, however, the way in which details in some of these Bayswater watercolours appear somewhat flattened, and details arbitrarily cropped, it has often been suggested that Linnell might have made them with the aid of a camera obscura, an example of which he is known to have acquired in 1811.[20] This is entirely possible. However, it is also possible that these watercolours – like the small landscapes made by Welsh artist Thomas Jones in oil in Rome and Naples in the 1780s or else in pencil in

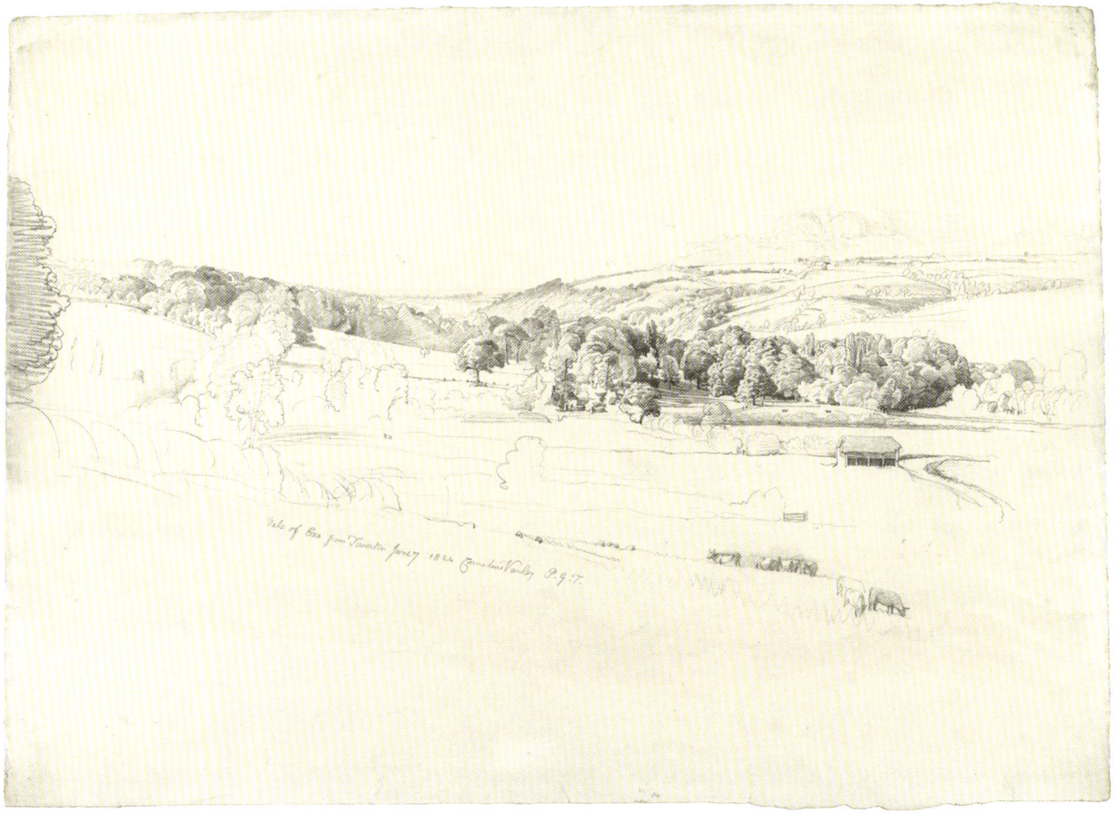

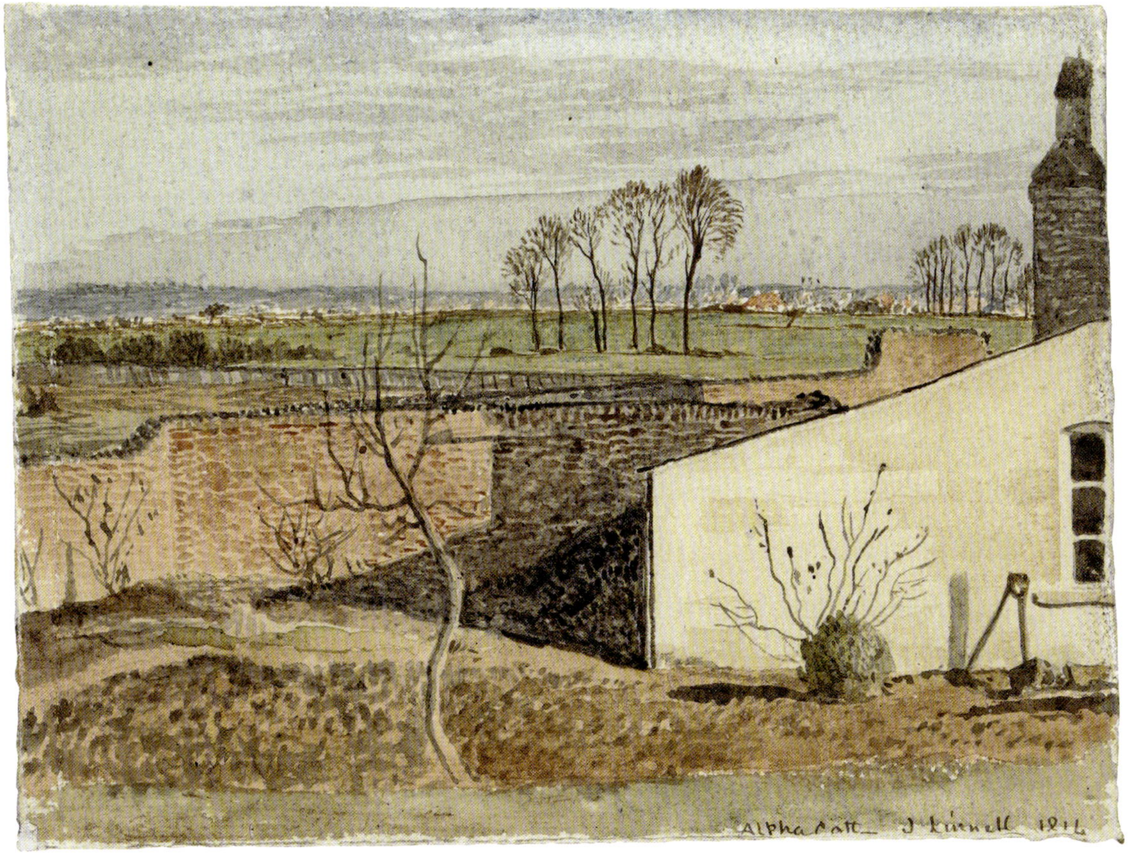

66 | F Cornelius Varley, *Vale of the Exe from Tiverton*, 1824, pencil on paper, 38.5 x 54.8 cm. Fitzwilliam Museum, Sir Ivor and Lady Batchelor Bequest, 2015, PD.179-2015

67 John Linnell, *Alpha Cottages*, 1814, watercolour on paper, 10.6 x 14.4 cm. Fitzwilliam Museum, PD.13-1995

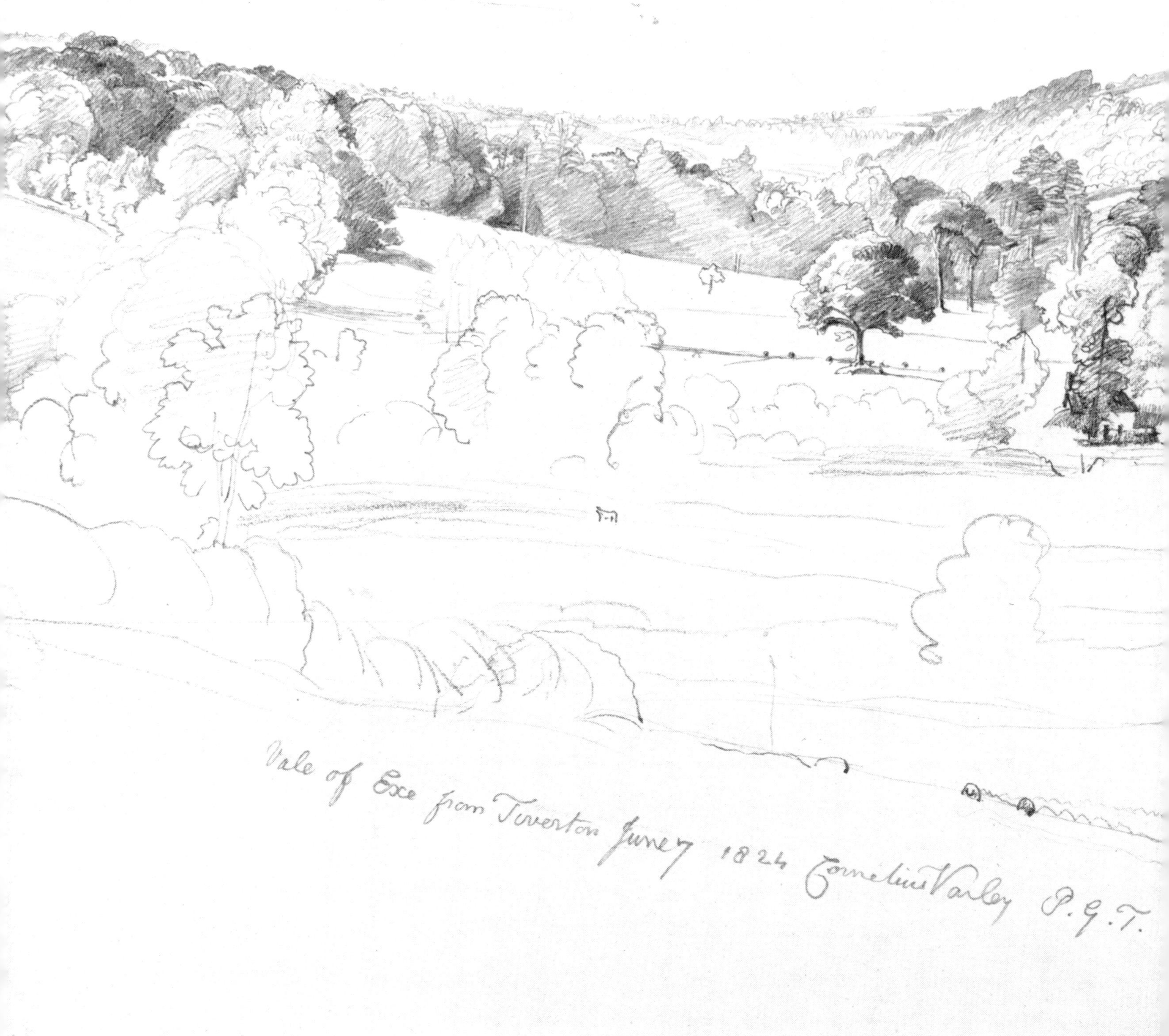
Vale of Exe from Tiverton June 7 1824 Cornelius Varley P.G.T.

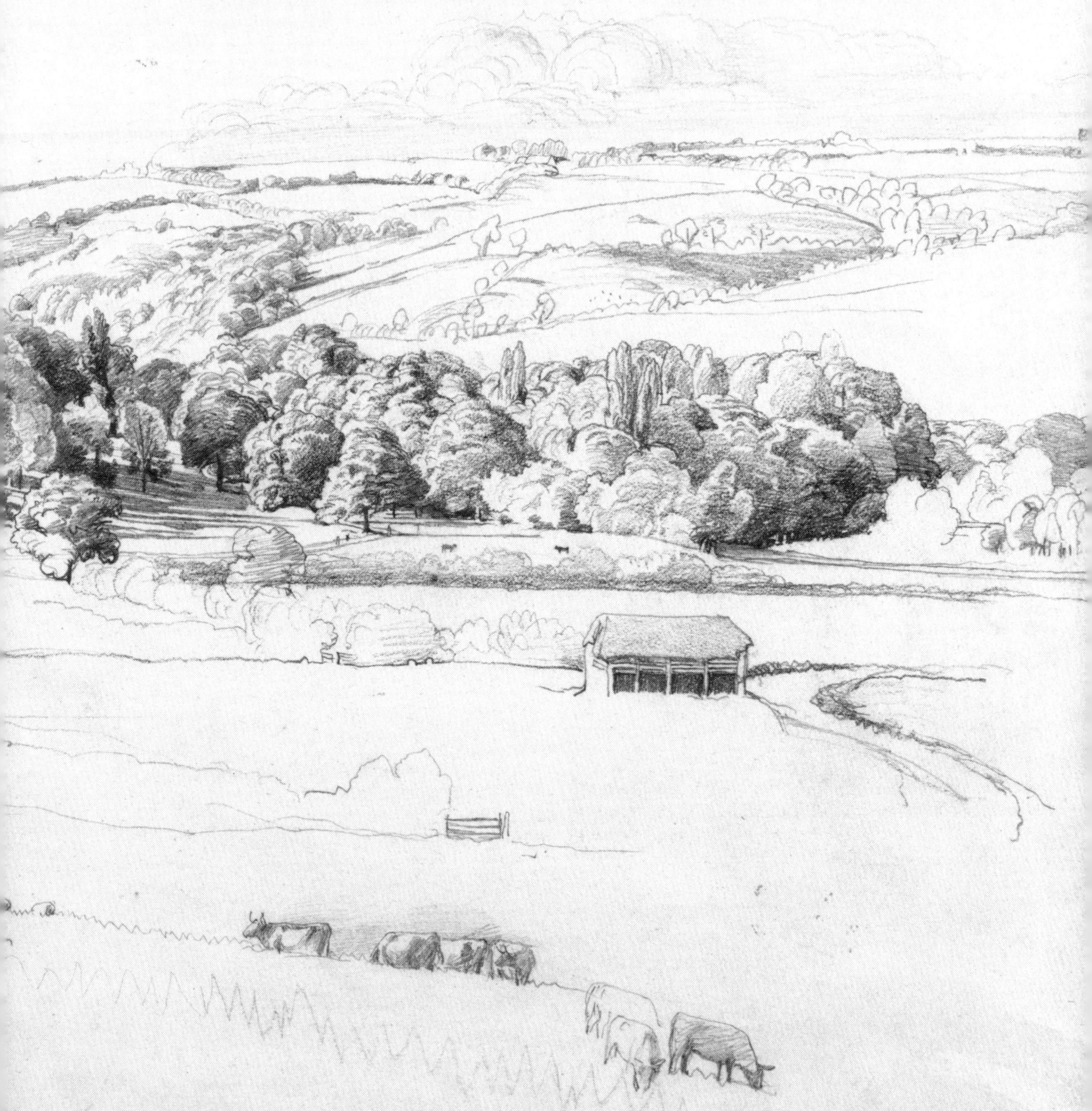

68 Thomas Jones, *View from Behind a Low Wall with Villa Mondragone in the distance*, 1777, pencil on paper, 21.5 x 27.7 cm, page from Large Italian sketchbook. British Museum, 1981.01516.18.33

69 Thomas Jones, *Scene near Naples*, 1783, oil on paper, 24.1 x 34.6 cm. Fitzwilliam Museum, PD.21–1954

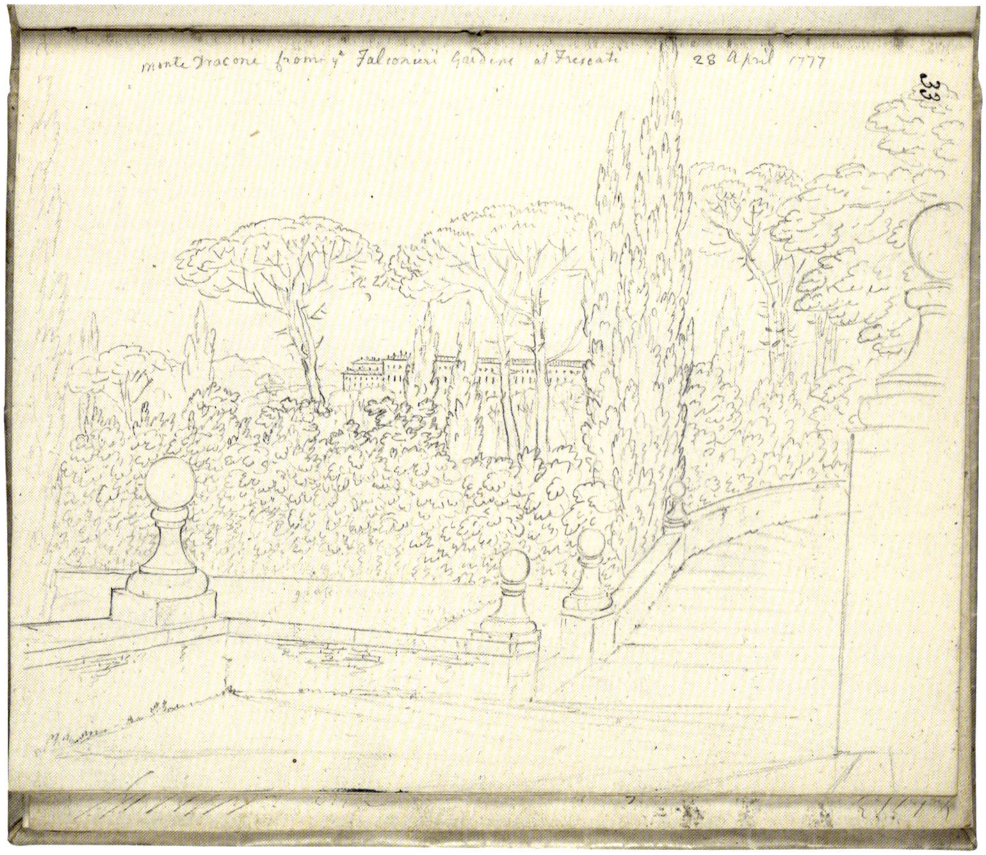

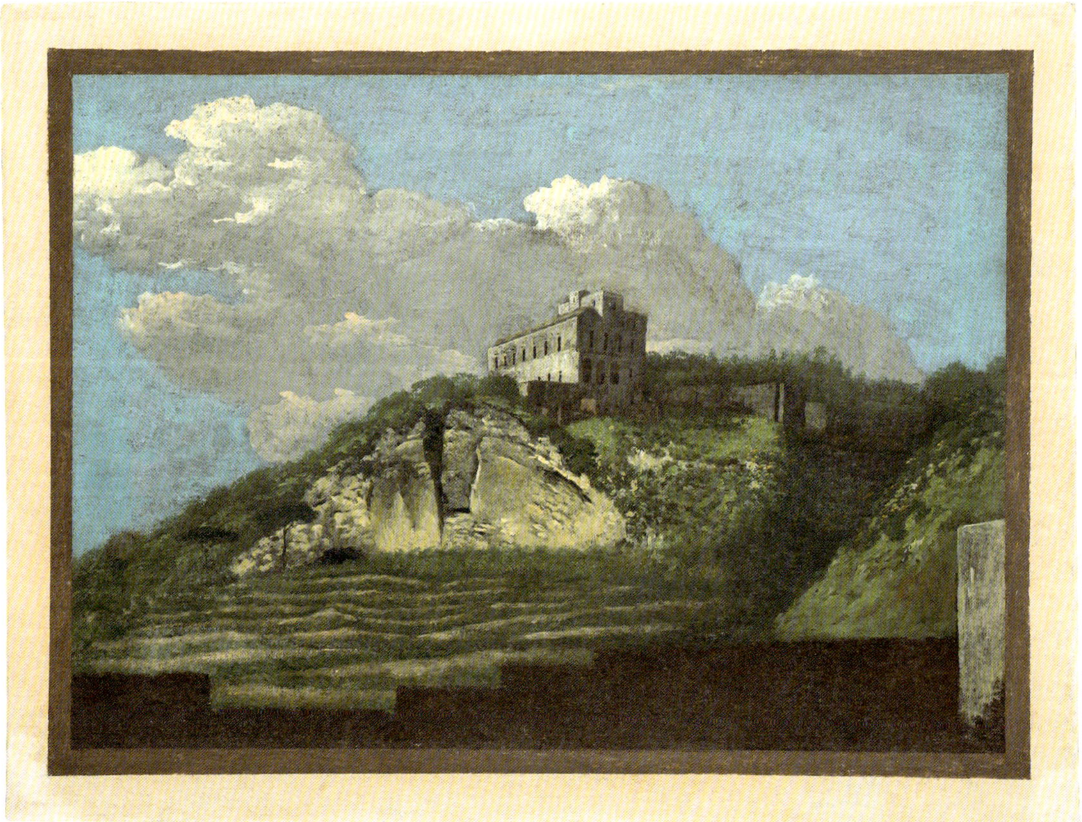

sketchbooks (figs. 68 and 69), similarly depicting views with unusual croppings of buildings or balustrades – can be explained by both artists having learnt to see the world through a camera – and thus with what has sometimes been called the 'proto-photographic gaze'.[21]

In 1826 Linnell went on to acquire an example of the Graphic Telescope itself but apparently used it for a very different sort of purpose than drawing landscapes.[22] For around this time he began to collaborate with his former tutor John Varley in engraving some of his drawings of heads of zodiacal signs and also some of Blake's 'Visionary Heads' for John Varley's *Treatise on Zodiacal Physiognomy*.[23] It seems that Linnell used the Telescope to reduce and reverse Varley's drawings directly on to the copper plate, so that they would subsequently be printed in the right direction.[24] Only the first part of John's *Treatise*, with six engraved plates, was ever published, in 1828. However, a unique impression of an engraving attributable to Linnell shows the front of the *Coin of Nebuchadnezzar* after Blake alongside a profile head of *Cancer* after John Varley (fig. 70). This plate was presumably intended for the *Treatise*, but never published.

Given that Cornelius Varley had originally been encouraged to patent his Graphic Telescope by friends, including no doubt some fellow artists, it is interesting to note which professionals are also recorded as having used the instrument – apart, that is, from those in his own immediate circle. One of these was John Sell Cotman, a landscape watercolourist with whom Varley had been well acquainted in London in the early years of the century but who subsequently moved back to his native Norwich. Cotman is known to have been given a Graphic Telescope by their mutual patron Sir Henry Englefield around 1817, and used it that year when making drawings of medieval cathedrals in France for Dawson Turner's *Architectural Antiquities of Normandy*. The as yet little known architect Charles Barry recorded in his diary that year that Cotman was using the Telescope to draw Rouen Cathedral, albeit Barry himself referred to it as "a very large and new-invented Camera Lucida by Varley", apparently using this term in its more general, generic sense. In fact Cotman found the Telescope rather difficult to use that summer. When he returned to Rouen the following year he fared much better, Dawson Turner's wife recording that he managed to secure "an upper apartment opposite the South transept of the Cathedral" from which to operate the device (to which, like Barry, she also referred as a 'Camera Lucida').[25]

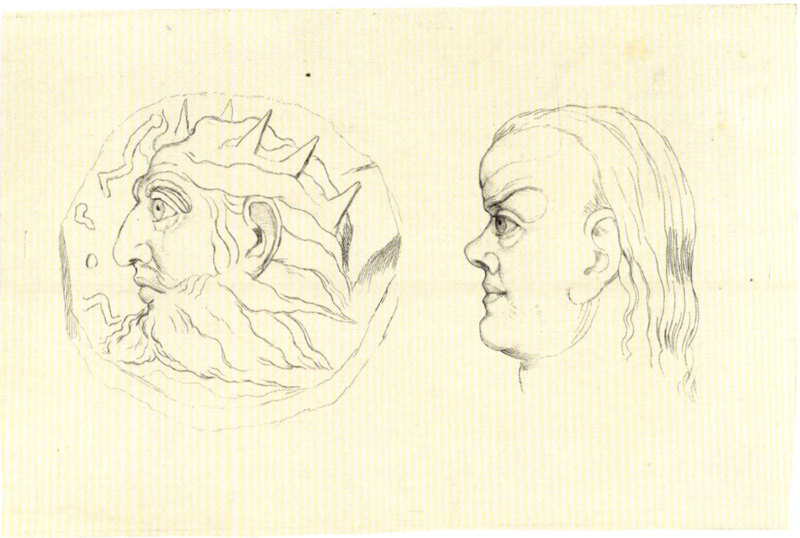

70 John Linnell after William Blake and John Varley, *Obverse of the Coin of Nebuchadnezzar and a Head of 'Cancer'*, c. 1828, etching, 16.2 x 25.3 cm, unpublished plate for John Varley's *Treatise on Zodiacal Physiognomy*. Fitzwilliam Museum, P.535–1985

There are a few references to other artists using the Telescope around this time, especially for recording architectural subjects or panoramas in correct perspective, in the same way that Thomas Sandby had availed himself of the camera obscura over fifty years before when drawing the buildings on the mound of Windsor Castle. In the 1820s, for example, Thomas Horner employed the Telescope when working on a panorama of London from the dome of St Paul's Cathedral, Joseph Cartwright used it for making a panorama of Corfu, and Edward William Cooke utilized it when recording the construction of the New London Bridge.[26] Amateurs may even have used the Telescope too, for we know that Dawson Turner's daughter Elizabeth learnt to operate it after minimal instruction from Cotman,[27] albeit she may have been untypical in mastering it with such rapidity and indeed – as a non-professional – in using it at all.

In the latter half of his life, Cornelius Varley became increasingly absorbed in scientific matters. However, the Telescope continued to serve him as a useful tool. In 1814, he had been elected to the Society of Arts and, over a period of forty years, in addition to writing many papers for the Society's *Transactions*, produced mechanical drawings for engravings in the same publication.

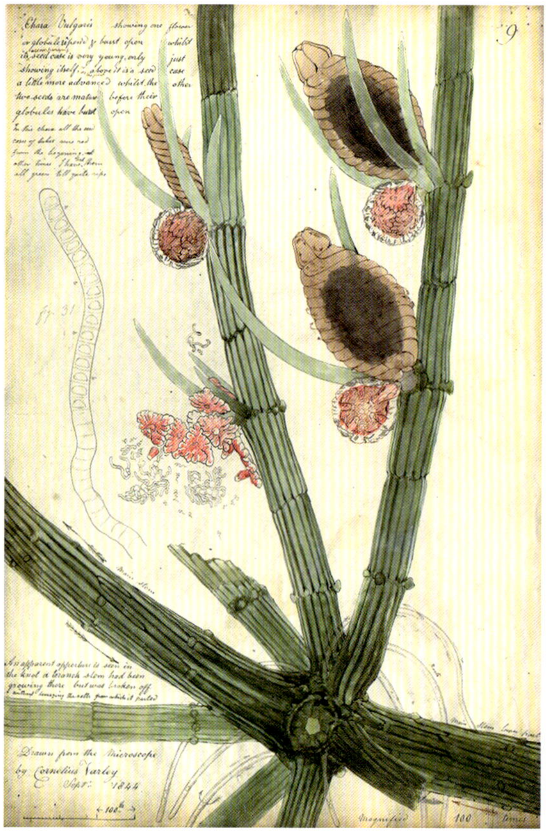

71 Cornelius Varley, *Chara Vulgaris: one flower or globule open (male reproductive part)*, 1842, watercolour with pen and ink on paper. American Philosophical Society

Many of these illustrations, he later wrote, were "drawn to the exact scale without measurements being traced from the instruments or models with my Graphic Telescope".[28] Then in 1839 he was a founder member of the Microscopical Society, and again contributed papers with diagrams of botanical and plant specimens which he also drew with the aid of the Graphic Telescope albeit a Telescope now adapted to the microscope (this instrument is generally referred to as the Graphic Microscope and Telescope or – for short – the Graphic Microscope).[29] Many of Varley's watercolours made in connection with these illustrations – such as of the *Chara Vulgaris* or common stonewort (fig. 71), *Nitella Translucens* and *Nitella Flexilis* – are remarkably fine drawings in their own right. [30] Nevertheless, his priorities by now had clearly changed. If, in Varley's early career, science had been at the service of art, in his later life art was now serving science.

Notes

1 See Butlin 1978, 135–36; and Butlin 1990, 162–64. **2** Libson 2005; see cat. no. 1, p. 60, *An Autograph portion*. **3** Ibid. **4** Letter from Samuel Varley to Cornelius Varley, 27 September 1810, National Art Library, Victoria & Albert Museum, MS L 74/11–1984; discussed by Huon Mallalieu, 'Varley the Optician', in Libson 2005, 27. **5** Varley's list of published prices (Science Museum Library, London; 1934–0121) is illustrated by Huon Mallalieu in Libson 2005, 29. This (undated) list also gives locations in London where the Telescope could be purchased, including directly from the 'Inventor and Patentee, C Varley' at no. 228, Tottenham Court Road. The rhododendron head is illustrated in Pidgely 1972, 784, fig. 63. **6** See Libson 2005, cat. no. 64, *Llangollen Bridge, Denbighshire, North Wales*, inscribed by Varley *12 oclock shaddows* just above his ink inscription giving the drawing's location. **7** Kemp 1990, 198.
8 John Varley made a drawing of a 'Miss Hayes' which he inscribed *Nov 25 1811 the first Portrait Drawn in the Patent Graphic Telescope*. **9** Portrait heads made by John Varley with the Graphic Telescope and signed by him as made in 1810 are of Anthony Vandyke Copley Fielding and John Sell Cotman (see Libson 2005, cat. nos. 94 and 95); and of *Mr Lorrain* in the Huntington Museum and Art Gallery, San Marino, Ca.
10 Timothy Wilcox, 'The Art of Cornelius Varley' in Libson 2005, 15. **11** Cornelius Varley's Graphic Telescope portraits of Samuel Varley are in the collections of the Science Museum and British Museum. Near identical replica versions also exist of his two famous portrait heads in the Graves Art Gallery, Sheffield, of John Sell Cotman and of J.M.W. Turner (for the latter two, see Seddon 1945, albeit the identification of the sitter as Turner is now disputed). In addition, two near identical versions are known of John Varley's Graphic Telescope portrait head of the watercolour collector John Wheeler.
12 For examples of his boat studies made in 1823, see Libson 2005, cat. no. 77, *A Thames Sailing barge being loaded*, pp. 142–43 (where there is a reference to another example in Birmingham Museums and Art Gallery, 154.23). **13** Libson 2005, 14–15. **14** For a particularly interesting sketchbook used in Wales in 1803 containing some fine panoramic landscapes, see Ryskamp 1990. Another sketchbook by Varley used in Wales the previous year is in the Fitzwilliam Museum (PD.78–1972). **15** His exact description reads: "A New Construction of a Telescope or Optical Instrument for viewing distant objects, & for other useful purposes, with a suitable table or stand for the same". A full transcription of Varley's patent specification, complete with his illustrations, is given in Libson 2005, Appendix III, 186–91. See also Klonk 1996, 134, citing Cornelius Varley's *A Treatise on Optical Drawing Instruments,* London 1845. **16** When Turner was plotting perspective for his elaborate drawings of English cathedral interiors in the 1790s, Maurice Davies argues (Davies 1992, 58–62 passim) that the artist often used ruled "frameworks"; but that even when Turner did not adopt this system, the use of a camera obscura – Davies believes – can be ruled out where a given cathedral drawing could not have been made from a single viewpoint. Smith 2002, 122, argues that, when sketching in Paris from a carriage, Girtin sometimes (and uncharacteristically) used two or three pieces of paper joined together to form a panoramic format, suggesting the use of a portable camera obscura which only took small pieces of paper. By contrast, Smith argues that Girtin is unlikely to have used a camera obscura or any other optical device when making detailed line drawings for his slightly earlier *Eidometropolis*, or Panorama of London, but rather that in this case the artist would have trusted to his eye (p. 191). **17** See Fleming-Williams 1990, 118–23, for a fuller description of these tracings.
18 The drawing is inscribed by Varley *Patshul Staff – Seat of Sir George Pigot. Bart. Augt 16.1820* (1978.0722.2). Klonk (1996, 133) refers to an anonymous pamphlet published in 1874 which records the names of the places Cornelius Varley drew with the Telescope from 1809, speculating that many of the drawings of country houses or estates would surely have been done on commission from the owners of the properties in question.
19 See, especially, Payne 1982, 131. **20** Crouan 1982, 11. Linnell acquired a camera obscura in August 1811 for 1½ guineas (Diary, 5 August 1811, MS 5–2000, Fitzwilliam Museum, Cambridge; see Libson 2005, 16). **21** Camera obscuras were recommended in treatises not only as aids for drawing but also as a way of studying atmospheric perspective and colour, given that colours looked more vibrant inside a camera. Cameras also served to provide the viewer with an automatic 'picture', a slice of the world outside, reduced in scale and in two dimensions. Thus the very process of using a camera obscura as a visual aid may have influenced some artists to see the world differently than with the naked eye. **22** Wilcox (in Libson 2015, 16) notes that in 1826 Linnell acquired a Graphic Telescope for 5 guineas. This, the most basic version, was advertised in Varley's list of published prices as capable of magnifying five times, and as being ideal for "drawing portraits" albeit only "shewing the reverse way" (unlike the slightly more expensive version of the Telescope, at 6 guineas, with the same magnification but "shewing the right way or reverse"). Given that the model Linnell acquired was only capable of reversing the image, it would have been ideal for use in connection with making engravings, so that they ultimately printed in the correct direction. **23** Butlin 1969, 9–12; Kauffmann 1984, 39–45. **24** Martin Butlin, 'Blake, the Varleys and the Patent Graphic Telescope', in Paley and Phillips 1973, 294–304; Martin Butlin, 'Blake, Linnell and Varley and *A Treatise of Zodiacal Physiognomy*', in Dethloff, Murdoch, Sloan and Elam 2015, 126–35. **25** For a full discussion of Cotman's use of the Telescope in Normandy, see Pidgley 1972, 785–86.
26 Varley Jeffery 1997–98, not paginated; and Pidgley 1972, 785.
27 Pidgley 1972, p. 786. **28** Libson 2005, Autograph portion, p. 62. **29** Libson 2005, Autograph portion, p. 62. **30** There is a group of these in the Library of The American Philosophical Society, Philadelphia, some of which were included in their exhibition, *Through the Looking Lens: Cornelius Varley's Wondrous Images of Art and Science, 1800–1860*, 17 May–19 December 2013. This exhibition was organized by Sue Ann Prince with K.M. Frederick-Frost, but there was no related publication.

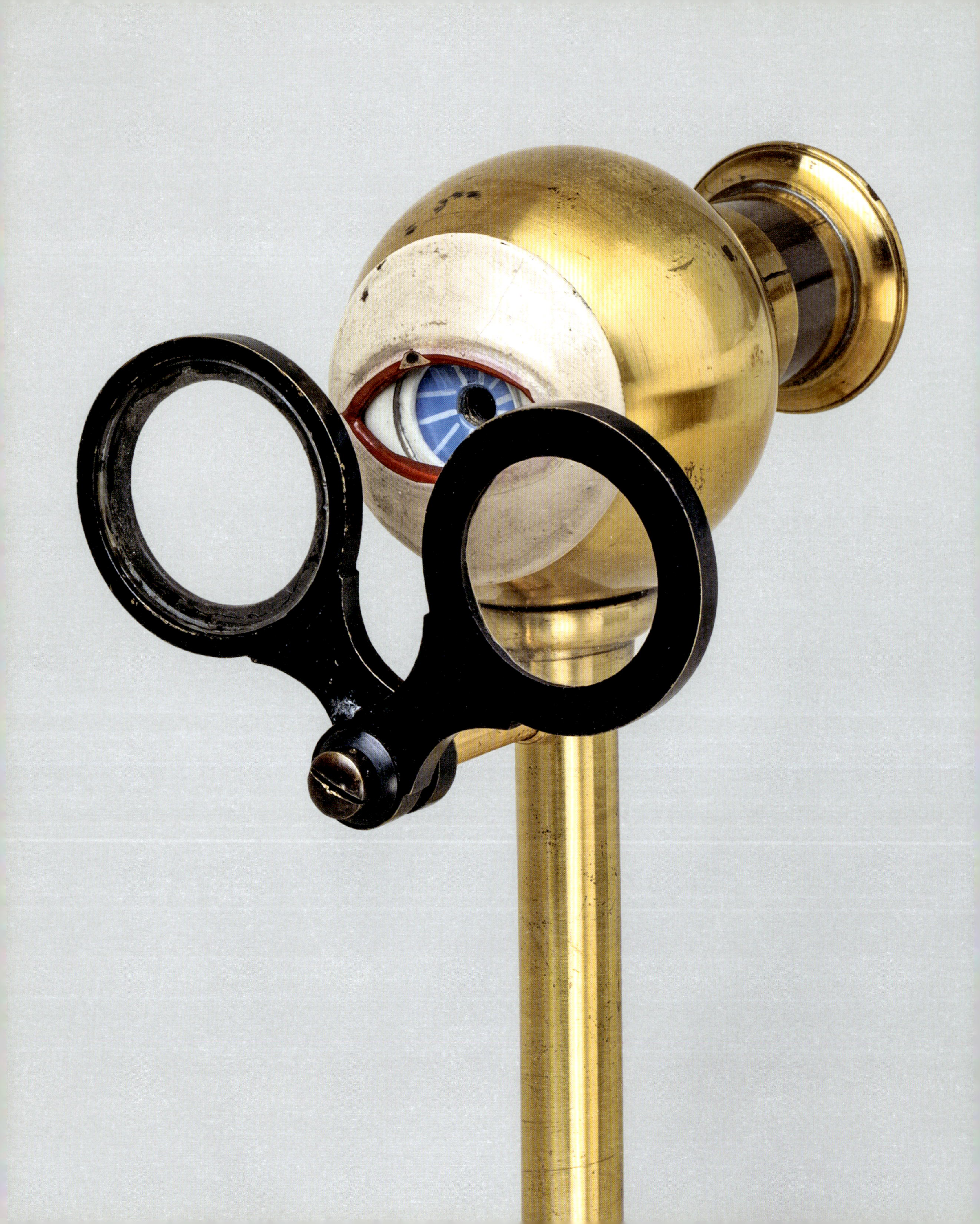

Boris Jardine

The camera lucida and the technologies of imitation

In short, if Dr. Wollaston, by his invention has not actually discovered a Royal road to drawing, he has at least succeeded in Macadamising the way already known—Francis West, *Description of the Camera-Lucida*, 1831[1]

The period 1800–1840 witnessed an extraordinary flourishing of theoretical innovation, practical invention and popular interest in optics – a discipline encompassing optical theory and the development and use of optical instruments. The revival and ultimate triumph of the wave theory of light; investigations into the refractive powers of every material under the sun; the discovery of polarization; the invention of the kaleidoscope, stereoscope, spectroscope and others; improvements in the production of optical glass and the correction of aberration in microscope lenses – these are just some of the events that propelled optics into the public consciousness and placed it at the pinnacle of the physical sciences. In the arts, one invention of the period stands out for its mass appeal and close relation to physical optics: the 'camera lucida', invented by William Hyde Wollaston at the beginning of the century, and immediately popular as a tool enabling its user to sketch a scene while simultaneously observing it though a prism (fig. 72).

Tempting as it has been to connect the arts and sciences in this period through high theory, the philosophy of classification or the nature of the perceiving individual, there is another route – a royal road paved with macadam, perhaps – in which transformations in both domains are understood in terms of the technologies and practices of image-making.[2] In this view, an explanation that works for the so-called 'optical revolution' in physics will also apply to the changed disposition of hand, eye and subject-matter that is in evidence in the arts, both fine and applied. In addition to the flux of innovative theory and practice in the early nineteenth century, there is one striking continuity with the eighteenth: optics was 'public property' – a fashionable subject of study, an integral part of technical training, and a lucrative area of commerce.[3] It is the last of these – the world of the optician, instrument maker, industrial designer, engraver and artists' supplier – that provides the clearest view of the complete interrelation of science and art in this crucial period. Broadly speaking, optical instrumentation was transformed from apparatus of demonstration to apparatus of investigation, with the surprising consequence that image-making itself became an area of intense invention and experimentation.

Even if we begin with high theory – for instance the revival of the wave theory of light at the beginning of the nineteenth century – we are still immediately thrown back into the mangle of practice.[4] In 1800 the polymath Thomas Young proposed an entire experimental programme exploring the relationship between sound and light, and in 1802 he introduced his famous theory of interference, providing a range of experimental demonstrations to show the doubling and negating interactions of two 'undulations' propagating through the 'luminiferous ether'.

72 The principles, design and use of the camera lucida, from George Dollond, *Description of the Camera Lucida, and Instruments for Drawing in True Perspective* (London: George Dollond, n.d. [c. 1830]). The text under the central illustration reads 'Drawn by C. Varley for G. Dollond, with the camera lucida'

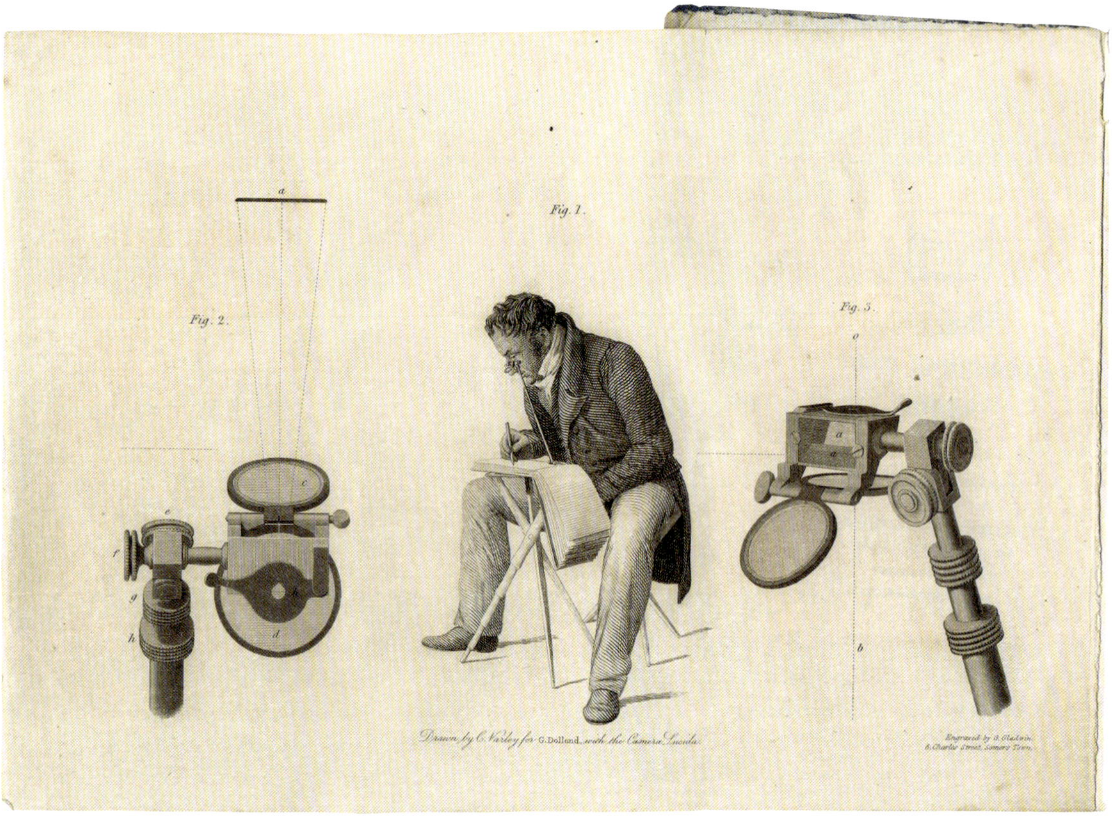

A year later Young concluded his series of papers on a confident note, announcing a stunning proof of interference:

I think it will not be denied by the most prejudiced, that the assertion is proved by the experiments I am about to relate, which may be repeated with great ease, whenever the sun shines, and without any other apparatus than is at hand to every one.[5]

Young's demonstration (fig. 73) was indeed simple: sunlight is admitted to a darkened room through small hole (ideally directed first to the hole by a mirror). A thin card (a) is held perpendicular to the window, splitting the beam of light. This split beam is observed on another piece of card (b) held square to the window, which can be brought towards and away from the card that splits the beam. Within the shadow of first card (a) Young observed coloured parallel 'fringes'. These fringes, crucially, could be made to disappear or reappear by moving the second card (b). The fringes, argued Young, are produced by the interference of undulations from either side of the split beam; the movement of the card (b) can obliterate or create them as it meets their points of divergence or convergence. This cannot be explained by the movement of particles of light, on the older Newtonian account, but it *is* consistent with the wave phenomenon of interference, in which meeting waves either amplify or cancel each other out. A new science of optics, then, for a new century.

In fact the ultimate success of the wave theory of light did not take place until the 1830s and relied – more than it did on Young's work – on the influence of the mathematics and experiments of the French investigator Augustin-Jean Fresnel.[6] Instead Young's homely experiments are typical of the extraordinary range and vitality of optical experimentation around 1800. It is in the triumphant tone of demonstration in Young's slit experiment that this can be seen most clearly. Young and his contemporaries – especially William Hyde Wollaston in London and David Brewster in Edinburgh – were almost pathologically concerned with the empirical foundation of their challenges to the established Newtonian paradigm. But at the same time there is a breathlessness to the experiments they conducted that threatens to take them – by the force of sheer invention – into the realm of speculation. The range of subjects investigated is truly impressive. Young himself had begun his research into optics with a study of 'accommodation' – the ability of the eye to maintain focus at a range of distances. Wollaston, meanwhile, introduced an ingenious new device to measure the refractive indices of materials, bringing such everyday substances as amber, sugar and alcohol into the purview of the exact sciences.[7] Brewster, like Young, spent time examining the diffraction of light, but by the 1810s his research had proliferated into almost every conceivable aspect of optics, with a striking combination of mechanical invention and law-like reasoning.[8]

More even than Young, Brewster and Wollaston came to embody the spirit of invention and mechanical ingenuity that characterizes physical optics at this time, and it was Wollaston, in 1806–07, who produced the decisive image-making tool of the nineteenth century – the 'camera lucida' (figs. 74 and 75). Wollaston was a slightly older friend of Young: both began in medicine, ranged widely in their studies, and benefited from independent wealth. Also like Young, Wollaston turned to optics in the 1790s and found himself at the forefront of this revolutionary science. The exact date at which he invented the camera lucida is hard to discern, and this difficulty is itself instructive. In 1806 Wollaston received a patent "for an Instrument whereby any person may draw in Perspective, or may copy or reduce any Print or Drawing".[9] But this was not quite the camera lucida as we know it, which uses a prism to allow its user to look down at their drawing in progress and simultaneously see the scene ahead. Instead the patented instrument was to use reflective surfaces to create the desired effect.[10] The distinction is small but important: Wollaston was clearly still at work on his invention between 1806 and 1807, when he published a description of the prismatic device that is still in use to this day. Yet there exist two anecdotal invention narratives that put the moment of inspiration somewhat earlier. One has Wollaston on a sketching tour with his friend Henry Hasted, failing to depict geological features accurately, and busying himself when back at his home laboratory to devise a system of lenses and/or prisms to allow the hand and eye to co-ordinate without too much or little talent getting in the way. In the other version Wollaston simply took inspiration from a cracked mirror: could the reflected scene not be drawn behind the mirror, through the crack, if one came in close and moved one's eye while drawing? These two stories are the Janus face of invention: in one story necessity plays the maternal role; in the other we have sheer happenstance and brilliance. Given the wide range of options for the design of the instrument suggested in the patent and the ongoing process of tinkering we can, frankly, dismiss both. The camera lucida was hard won – a combination of an inventive mind, skilful manipulation, a desire to create a marketable tool for image-making and the presence of highly skilled craftsmen. It is in this context that we can make sense of the strange 'prototype' camera

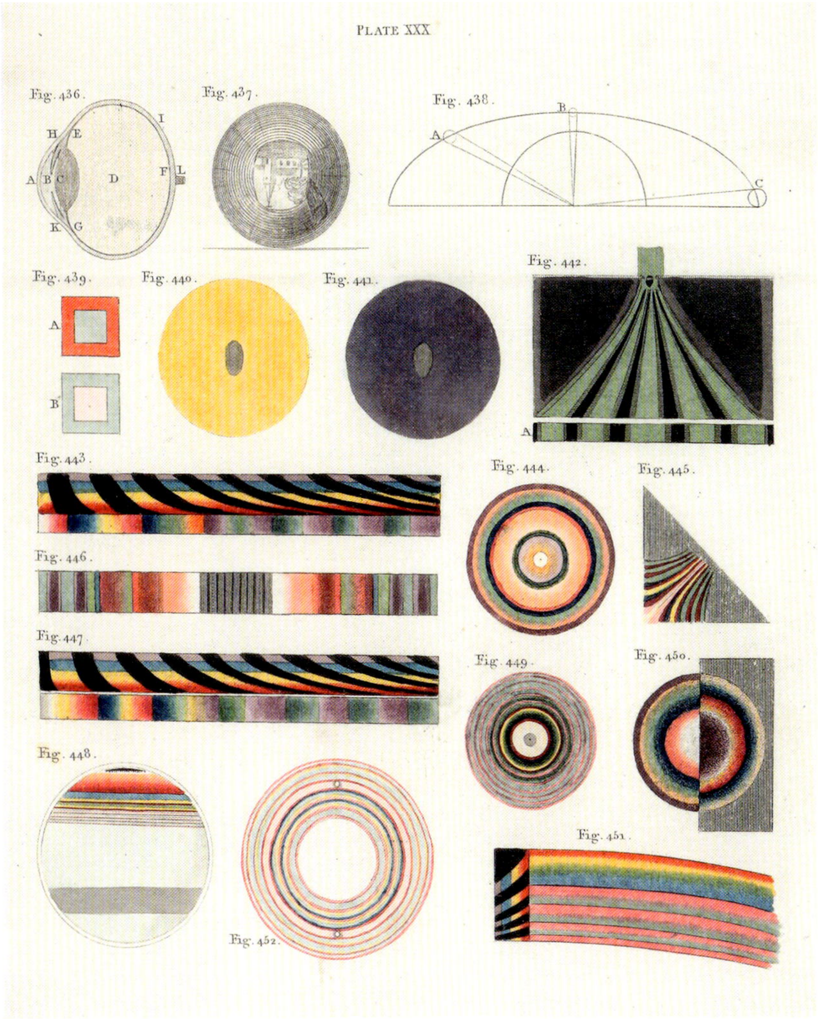

73 Plate XXX from Thomas Young's *A Course of Lectures on Natural Philosophy and the Mechanical Arts* (London, 1807). Fig. 442 in the plate shows a version of the slit experiment, with 'A' showing a schematic of the interference pattern. Other observations include the effects of colours on one another (figs. 439–41), coronae around the sun and moon (fig. 444), and "the coloured stripes of a film of soapy water, covering a wine glass" (fig. 448)

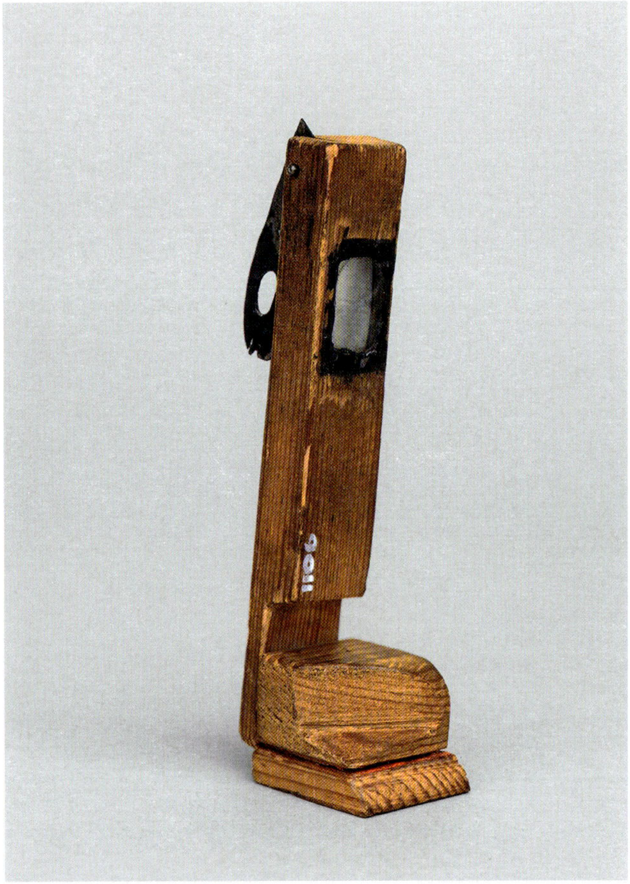

74 William Hyde Wollaston, Camera lucida, experimental prototype, c. 1802, wood, glass, wax, metal, 10 x 2.3 x 4 cm. Whipple Museum of the History of Science, University of Cambridge, on loan from the Cavendish Laboratory, 1106

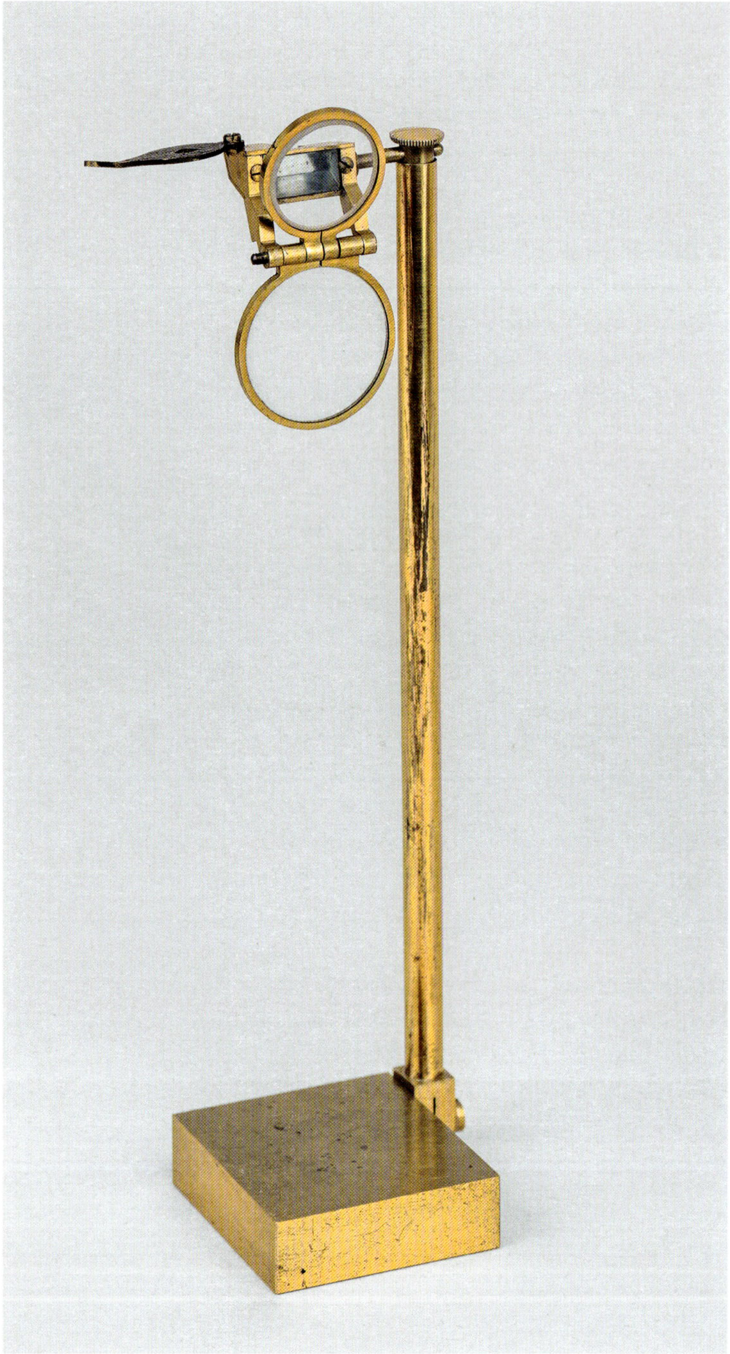

75 | F Camera lucida, 1850, metal (brass), glass, 19.1 x 5.5. x 4.9 cm. 19.1 x 5.5. x 4.9 cm. Whipple Museum of the History of Science, University of Cambridge, 0093

lucida preserved at the Whipple Museum (fig. 74). This instrument uses a lens to enable the accurate sketching of fine detail, at a distance of only a few centimetres – suggesting that around the time of its invention Wollaston was experimenting with even more forms of the device than eventually appeared in his patent or for retail.[11]

Before it could be marketed several problems with the design of the camera lucida had to be solved: first, which of the various forms of the instrument's basic optical apparatus should be used? And how could the *principle* of the device be translated into a design, with stand, clamp, screws and mount, to be used conveniently by an unsuspecting sketching public? As the instrument was designed to facilitate *plein air* drawing (see fig. 111), we can imagine that in the months following his patent Wollaston was eager to resolve these matters in time for the 1807 summer season. Sure enough the June issues of *Philosophical Magazine* and *Journal of Natural Philosophy, Chemistry and the Arts* carried articles by Wollaston with the title 'Description of the Camera Lucida'. Not only had the instrument acquired a catchy (and, as we will see, significant) brand name, but it had also been fixed into a neat brass and glass design, with the prismatic version now the sole design on sale. We might guess that Wollaston had collaborated with an instrument maker to solve the design problems – but the initial description of the instrument throws even this innocent speculation into doubt.

In the two magazine articles the camera lucida was offered for sale solely by James Newman – not an optician but a highly successful artists' colourman, then trading from Soho Square in London. Although Newman is listed as the sole retailer in the earliest descriptions of the camera lucida, he clearly was not the only commercial party involved in its development, and Wollaston issued a quick correction stating that the instrument makers P. & G. Dollond also sold the instrument. Later instruction sheets also include the optician William Cary, and some even leave a blank space for the retailer to fill in. The simplest explanation would be that the Dollonds – who already had an agreement with Wollaston for the manufacture of another of his instruments – were the designers and then makers, and the others were simply retailers. But even that is not the whole story, because a little later an enthusiast for the instrument confided, in the pages of the *Mechanics' Magazine*, that "from good authority, I learn that they are all chiefly *made* by an obscure journeyman in the neighbourhood of Whitechapel".[12]

The instrument must have been hot property, at least if the serial numbers that appear to be etched on to the lenses of early instruments are simply sequential. By around 1830 the numbers are above 3,000.[13] Certainly this is possible: the Newman/Dollond situation speaks to some competitiveness over Wollaston's license; the cost of production was apparently low but the retail cost was definitely high; and there is extensive evidence of its early use, critique, celebration and application. Some of the success of the instrument can be put down precisely to the context of its invention – the turn, around 1800, to the faithful record of natural and man-made features of the landscape, sketched *in situ* on tours at home and abroad. The camera lucida must be both product and then contributor to this phenomenon. We have already seen that Wollaston was attempting accurate delineation of geological features when the idea came to him – even if this is apocryphal it speaks of a situation all too easy to imagine, and much in evidence in contemporary fine art, amateur sketching, book illustration and of course scientific imagery. Subsequent events show that the camera lucida was not a flash in the pan. The instrument was taken up quickly by a wide range of practitioners. Not only did it allow the quick and accurate portrayal of a landscape, but it could also be used at closer proximity, especially

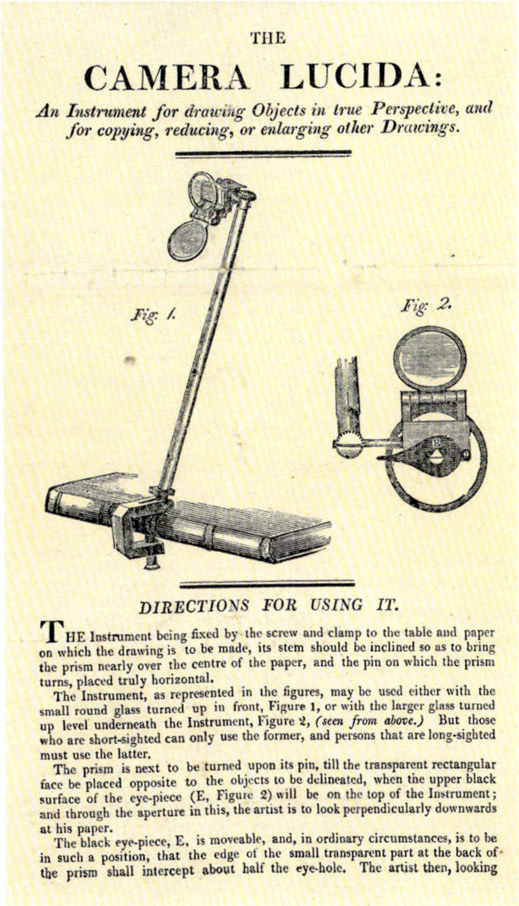
THE

CAMERA LUCIDA:

An Instrument for drawing Objects in true Perspective, and for copying, reducing, or enlarging other Drawings.

DIRECTIONS FOR USING IT.

THE Instrument being fixed by the screw and clamp to the table and paper on which the drawing is to be made, its stem should be inclined so as to bring the prism nearly over the centre of the paper, and the pin on which the prism turns, placed truly horizontal.

The Instrument, as represented in the figures, may be used either with the small round glass turned up in front, Figure 1, or with the larger glass turned up level underneath the Instrument, Figure 2, *(seen from above.)* But those who are short-sighted can only use the former, and persons that are long-sighted must use the latter.

The prism is next to be turned upon its pin, till the transparent rectangular face be placed opposite to the objects to be delineated, when the upper black surface of the eye-piece (E, Figure 2) will be on the top of the Instrument; and through the aperture in this, the artist is to look perpendicularly downwards at his paper.

The black eye-piece, E, is moveable, and, in ordinary circumstances, is to be in such a position, that the edge of the small transparent part at the back of the prism shall intercept about half the eye-hole. The artist then, looking

76 J. Barfield, London (printer), *The Camera Lucida: An Instrument for drawing Objects in true Perspective, and for copying, reducing, or enlarging other Drawings*, c. 1800–50, engraving and letterpress on paper, laid down on card, 32.2 cm x 35.6 cm. Whipple Museum of the History of Science, University of Cambridge, 3498

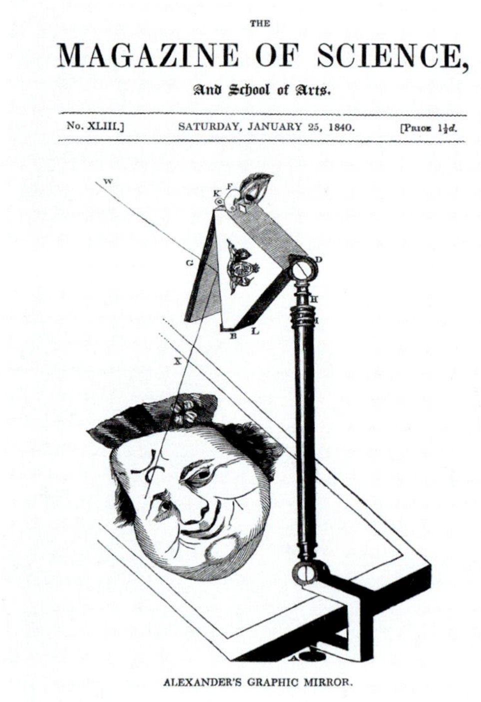
THE

MAGAZINE OF SCIENCE,

And School of Arts.

No. XLIII.] SATURDAY, JANUARY 25, 1840. [Price 1½*d*.

ALEXANDER'S GRAPHIC MIRROR.

77 'Alexander's Graphic Mirror', wood engraving and letterpress, front cover illustration for *The Magazine of Science, and School of Arts*, Saturday, 23 January 1840. Cambridge University Library, CUL00514075

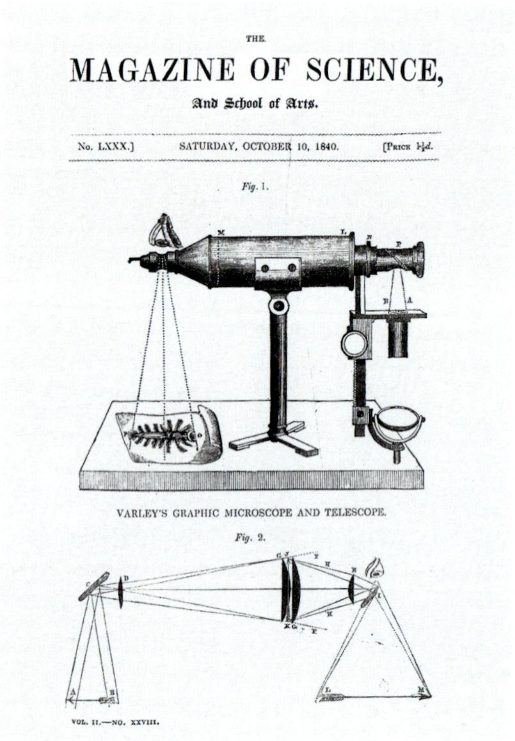
THE

MAGAZINE OF SCIENCE,

And School of Arts.

No. LXXX.] SATURDAY, OCTOBER 10, 1840. [Price 1½*d*.

Fig. 1.

VARLEY'S GRAPHIC MICROSCOPE AND TELESCOPE.

Fig. 2.

VOL. II.—NO. XXVIII.

79 'Varley's Graphic Microscope and Telescope', wood engraving and letterpress, front cover illustration for *The Magazine of Science, and School of Arts*, Saturday, 10 October 1840. The Whipple Museum of the History of Science, University of Cambridge, Robert Whipple Collection, 0069

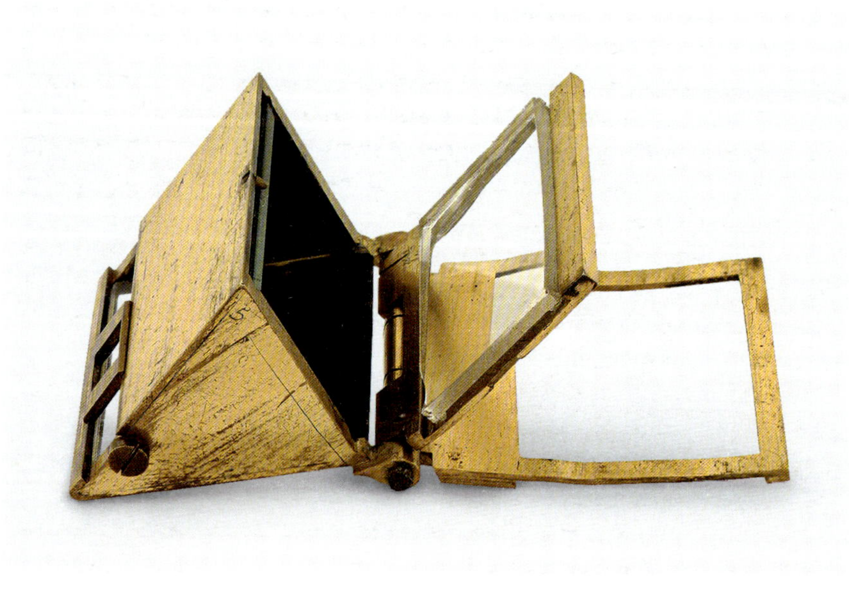

78 | F Camera lucida, owned by the Herschel family, 19th century, glass; brass, 3.7 x 6.0 x 5.2 cm. National Maritime Museum, Greenwich, London, Herschel Collection, AST0794

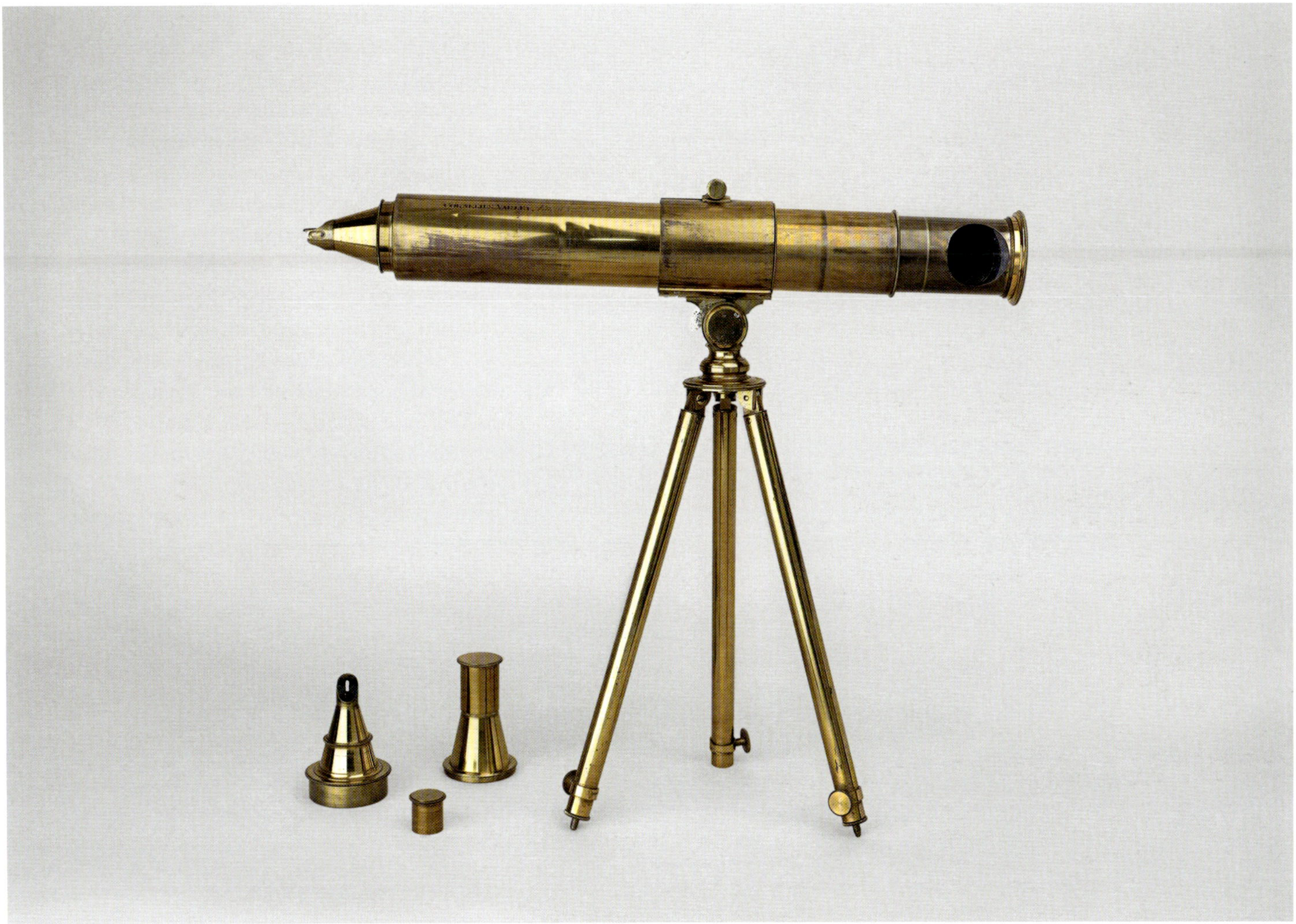

in portraiture. A repeated refrain in promotional material for the instrument is that it allowed the copying of other images – and not only images, but patterns, for use in the decorative arts. Although the technologies of imitation are as old as mimesis, again the camera lucida arrived at a pivotal moment, responding to a demand for accuracy and in turn contributing to a fervent period of invention. Wollaston had attempted to cover his bases in the patent, which described a range of optical arrangements. But this did not deter competitors. On the Continent a number of improvements and modifications were quickly suggested, the most significant being Giovanni Battista Amici's investigation, in the late 1810s, of a wide range of optical design (see below, p. 123). A far simpler device was invented in the 1830s by Alexander Alexander, an optician working in Exeter: this uses two mirrors – or three if the intention is to create a reversed image (for example for drawing directly on to lithographic stone for printing) (fig. 77). A variant on Alexander's Graphic Mirror was owned by the great scientist Sir John Herschel, who is known to have used a camera lucida to record topography and scientific specimens (fig. 78). He was closely involved in Talbot's invention of photography.[14]

In general the trend in these adaptations was towards affordability, simplicity of manufacture and also of use. But there is one striking counter-example: Cornelius Varley's Patent Graphic Telescope (figs. 79 and 80), which was intended as a direct challenge to the camera lucida – replacing the prism with mirrors and the optical range of unaided vision for that of a low-power

80 | F Cornelius Varley, *Patent Graphic Telescope*, c. 1840, metal (brass), bronze, copper, glass, telescope 31.0 cm, max. diameter 6.3 cm; tripod 43.5 x 13.0 x 6.0 cm; eyepiece 1: 8.6 cm, max. diameter 5.7 cm; eyepiece 2: 8.2 cm, max. diameter 5.7 cm; eyepiece 3: 8.4 cm, max. diameter 5.7 cm. Whipple Museum of the History of Science, University of Cambridge, 0069

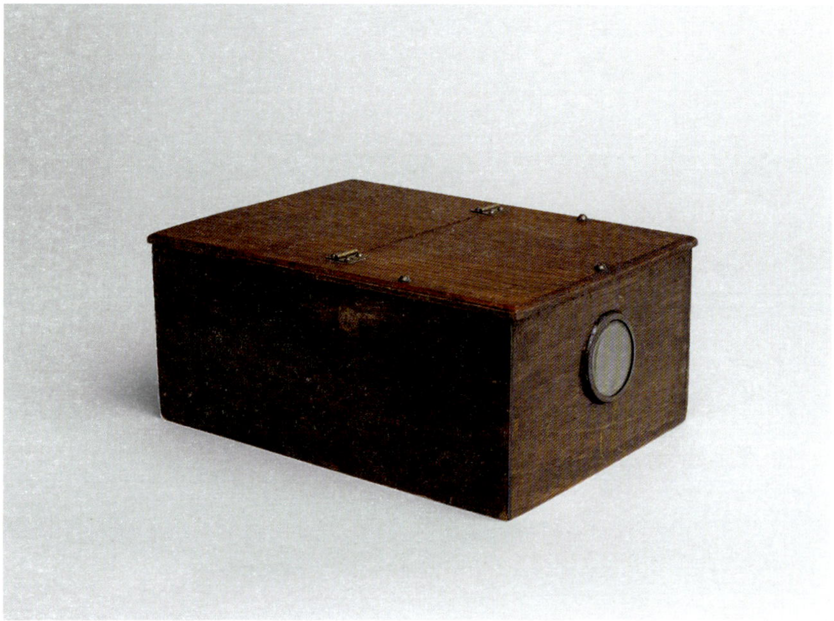

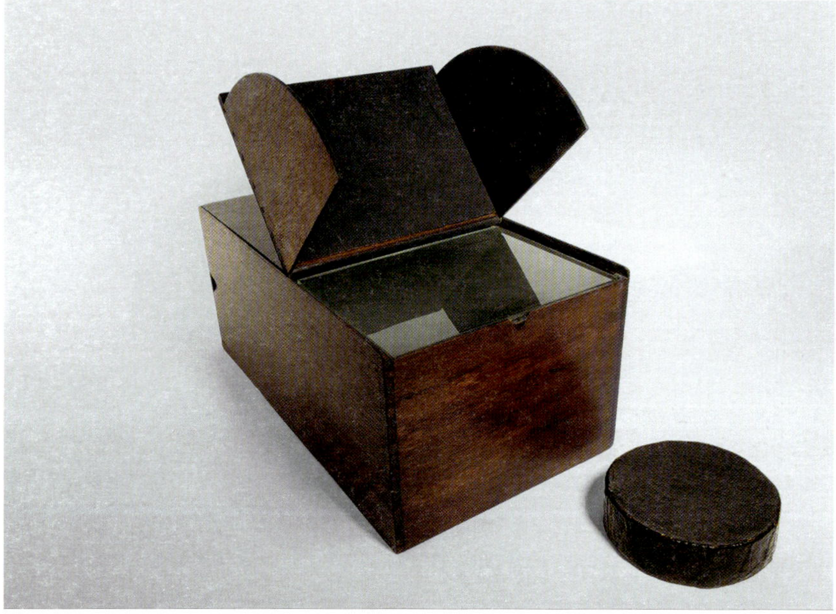

81 | F Box camera obscura, 19th century, wood, metal, glass, 8.7 x 26.8–19.0 x 14.4 cm. Whipple Museum of the History of Science, University of Cambridge, 6492

82 | F Reflex camera obscura, c. 1820, wood, glass, paper, 37.5 x 19.8 x 21.5 cm. History of Science Museum, University of Oxford, 78618

telescope. Varley's invention could be used for an unusual range of purposes – portraiture, image reproduction, microscopic drawing, sketching animals at a distance, and so on. But it seems to have found its most consistent application – not least in the watercolours of Varley himself – in the inclusion of fine, distant detail in landscape sketching (see above, pp. 81–82, fig. 66).

All of these instruments share one important feature: they bring the artist/observer into close contact with the instrument itself (see fig. 72). This simple fact of comportment brings us to a deeper understanding of optical instrumentation in this period. Here we have to pause and consider the general applicability of the camera lucida. The name offers a clue to its versatility. Wollaston offered no explanation for calling it a 'camera lucida', but the contrast must be with the much older camera obscura (figs. 81 and 82). The latter operates by projecting an image on to a screen; it therefore needs some darkness in order to be used. But the camera lucida, typical of the instrumental tradition that Wollaston, Young and others pioneered, brought the eye directly into the instrumental set-up itself: the camera obscura produces an image that can be copied; the camera lucida allows its user to enter into a visual-manual situation in which the scene is produced only for the user, for as long as the act of reproduction takes place.

This is a profound difference. 'Lucida', in this sense, does not simply refer to the fact that the instrument can be taken out into the light: it refers to the whole instrument-user set-up, in which light beams, prismatic reflections, experiences and depictions become a single phenomenon.[15] This places the camera lucida squarely in the tradition of optical invention in which the human eye is seen as the paradigm or perfect optical instrument (fig. 83), and man-made optical instruments are therefore to operate within the system of human vision itself, rather than creating or manipulating phenomena beyond or different to human sight. The mechanical metaphor is therefore two-way: we can easily grasp that scientists understood the operation of human physiology by analogy with the products of the workshop, but the camera lucida shows that instrumental set-ups were also brought into the physiological realm through their design and optical construction.[16]

This might seem to imply that the camera lucida's user becomes a kind of cyborg, but it is much more accurate to say that they become an automaton, or a piece of machinery, and we should see the use of the instrument not from the point of view of the mechanics of physiology but of the physiology of mechanics: the camera lucida was just one part of a system of image-making and reproduction in which parts of the production process communicate with each other more fully and directly than they do with nature or the perceiving mind. It has been tempting to ponder the automatism of artistic creation when devices like the camera lucida are in use – and certainly, in an age preoccupied with individual genius this detained contemporary observers – but in fact the question of agency is far more extensive than that. The camera lucida, after all (and much like the photographic camera later), was to be used in the service of whole systems of reproduction that do not necessarily refer to the world outside their own conventions at all. An illustration of this is given in the *Encyclopaedia Londinensis* article on 'optics', which subordinates the camera lucida to other optical instruments, like Brewster's sensational new 'kaleidoscope', whose phenomena it can help depict:

As the kaleidoscope is of great use in the ornamental arts, particularly to carpet and lace manufacturers, calico printing, paper-staining, jewellery, &c. &c. its adaptation to their purpose is effected by occasionally furnishing the instrument with a stand, in order that the pattern may be fixed whilst the artist is engaged in copying it. It is also capable of being used with Dr. Wollaston's camera lucida, by which means those who would otherwise be unable to copy the patterns may do it with perfect facility and accuracy.[17]

This commercial imperative was combined, especially in the work of Brewster, with an intense desire to popularize optical inventions, and to proselytize on the refinement and extension of human vision. This culminated in Brewster's modified stereoscope, which drew on Charles Wheatstone's earlier invention but was specifically intended as a means of seeing the sensational new invention of photography in 3D.[18]

Earlier I called the camera lucida the "decisive" invention of nineteenth-century image-making

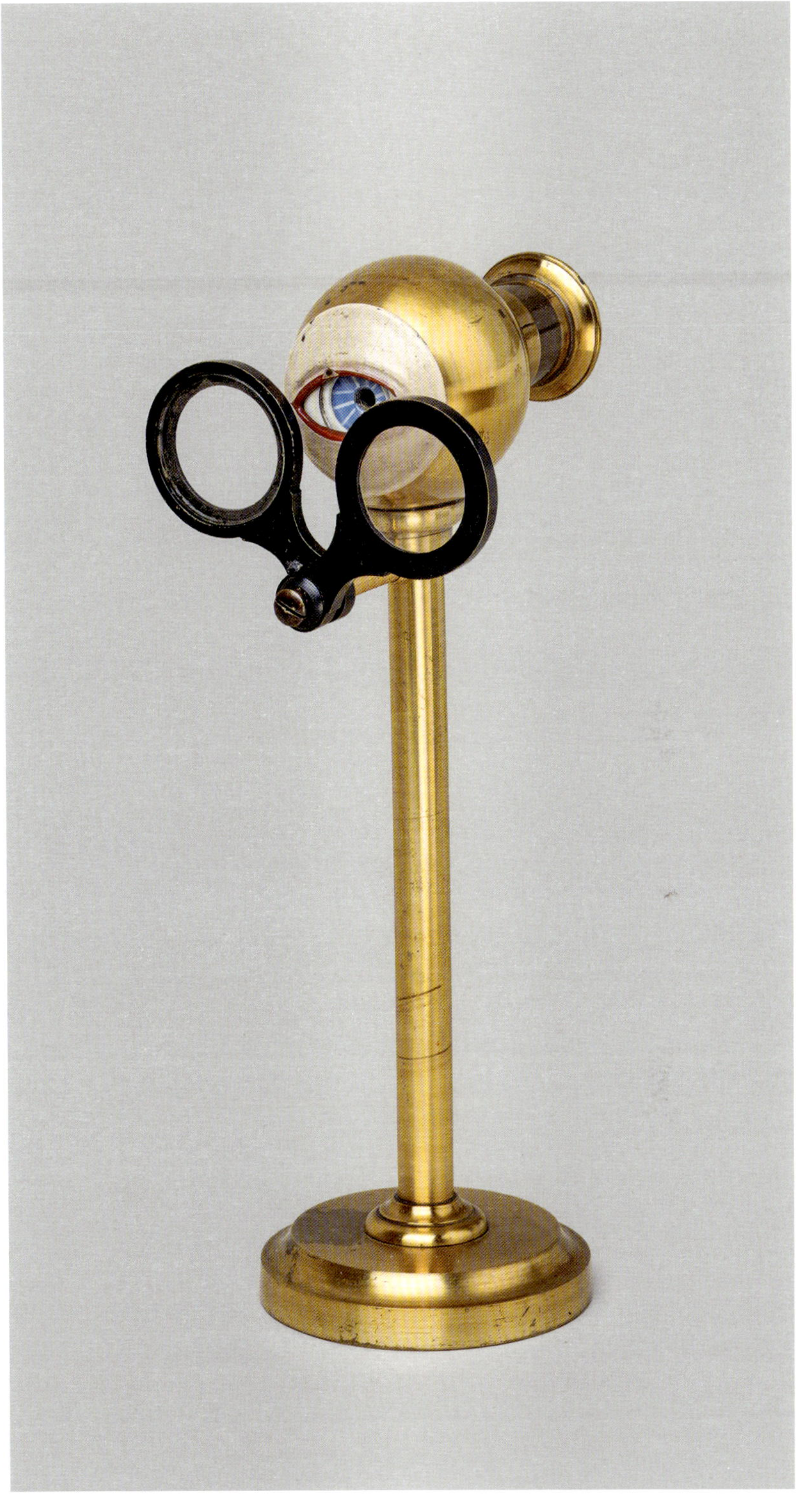

83 | F Model of the human eye in the form of a camera obscura, c. 1850–1900, metal (brass and lead alloy), glass, enamel, 23 x 7.7 x 11.4–12 cm. Whipple Museum of the History of Science, University of Cambridge, 5984

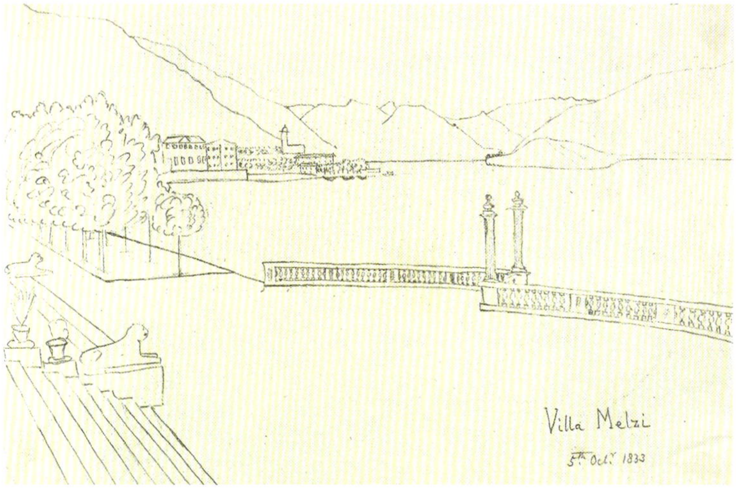

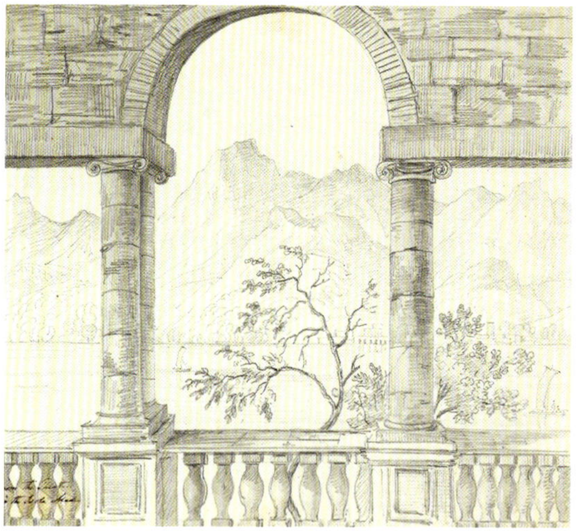

84 | F William Henry Fox Talbot, *Villa Melzi*, 5 October 1833, pencil on paper, 14.2 x 21.8 cm. Science Museum Group, 1937-2537/06

85 | F Caroline Augusta Fielding, *Lago Maggiore from the Theatre in the Isola Madre*, n.d., pencil on paper, 27.5 x 38.5 cm. The Bodleian Libraries, University of Oxford, MS. WHF Talbot 74, fol. 25

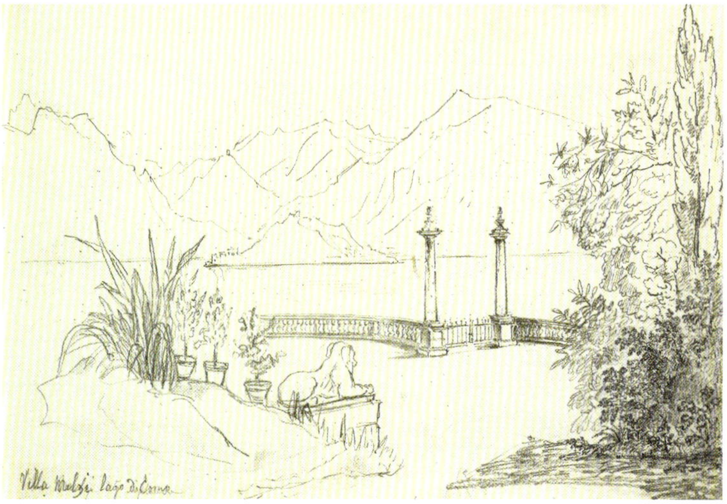

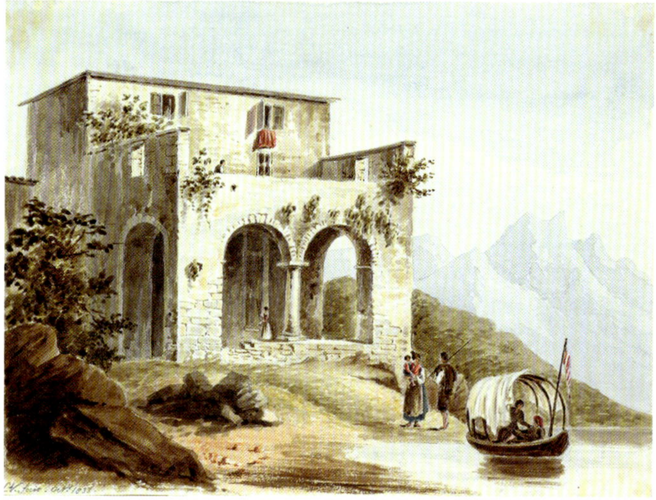

86 | F Caroline Augusta Fielding, *Casaccia a Bellagio, Lago di Como*, n.d., pencil on paper, 27.3 x 37.6 cm. The Bodleian Libraries, University of Oxford, MS. WHF Talbot 89, fol. 14

87 | F Constance Fox Talbot, *Villa Melzi lago di Como*, 1833, pencil and watercolour on paper, 19 x 27.6 cm. The Bodleian Libraries, University of Oxford, MS. WHF Talbot 98, fol. 9

– a statement that, in light of photography, may seem either provocative or simply absurd. In a number of respects, however, the camera lucida stands behind photography and gives meaning to the later invention. In a straightforward sense the camera lucida will always be tied to photography, because it was through failed attempts to use the former that William Henry Fox Talbot was inspired to experiment with the latter. Henry's laboured and gauche attempts to render the view from the Villa Melzi on the shores of Lake Como (fig. 84) compare badly with the more gracious efforts of his women companions, his sister Caroline and Constance, his wife (figs. 85–87). It was the gulf between what the view looked like through Henry's camera and what he was able to lay down on paper that induced him to consider how to fix the optically generated image – using what was to become known as photography.

The camera *lucida* represents a shift towards the 'mechanical objectivity' of photography.[19] We have seen that it embodies at least three key ideas: the need to make accurate records of antiquities, natural features of the landscape; the desire to reproduce other images, to record and transfer patterns; the bringing together of hand, eye and instrument into a single system. The first and second of these show that the camera lucida was part of the same general movement as photography, but the last point reveals that it was not simply a precursor, and had a logic and form of practice that is distinctive and typical of the early nineteenth-century optical arts.

Notes

1 'Macadam' was a road surface consisting of compacted small stones, developed around 1820 and named after John Loudon McAdam; the addition of tar as a binding agent after the advent of motor vehicles gave us 'tarmac'. **2** See Jones and Galison (1998) 2013, especially the introduction. **3** Geoffrey Cantor, 'Physical Optics', in Olby, Cantor, Christie and Hodge 1990, 627–38, esp. 632. **4** The phrase is Andrew Pickering's: see Pickering 1995. **5** Young 1804, quotation 1–2. **6** Cantor 1975. **7** See Usselman 2015. **8** See Geoffrey Cantor, 'Brewster on the Nature of Light', in Morrison-Low and Christie 1984, 67–76. **9** *The Repertory of Arts, Manufactures, and Agriculture, second series*, LVII (February 1807), pp. [161]–164 and Pl. VII. **10** Wollaston did include the prismatic version in the patent as another possibility. **11** For a full account of this instrument see Jardine 2020. **12** Quoted in Hammond and Austin 1987, 25. **13** Hammond and Austin 1987, 21. Caution must be taken with numbers like these, as serial numbers can begin in the thousands, or use the first number to indicate some difference in design or manufacture (hence 1000+ would be one type, 2000+ another). However for the camera lucida the numbers do seem to be sequential: they are found in the hundreds and thousands, and the sequence of numbers is at least plausibly correlated with dates of manufacture. **14** For a comparison of the various modifications see [Anonymous], 'Wollaston's Camera Lucida ...', 1840, 338–39. **15** For 'instrumental traditions' in optical research – a fruitful notion for considering the use of instruments in the arts as well – see Chen 2000, 212ff. **16** Chen 2000, 121ff. **17** 'Optics' in *Encyclopaedia Londinensis; Or, Universal Dictionary of Arts, Sciences, and Literature* ..., vol. 17, London 1820, 541–673, quotation at 651. **18** See Martin Kemp, '"Philosophy in Sport" and the "Sacred Precincts": Sir David Brewster on the Kaleidoscope and Stereoscope', in Castel, Leith and Riley 1994, 203–32 (with Appendix by B. Pert). **19** Daston and Galison 2010, ch. 3.

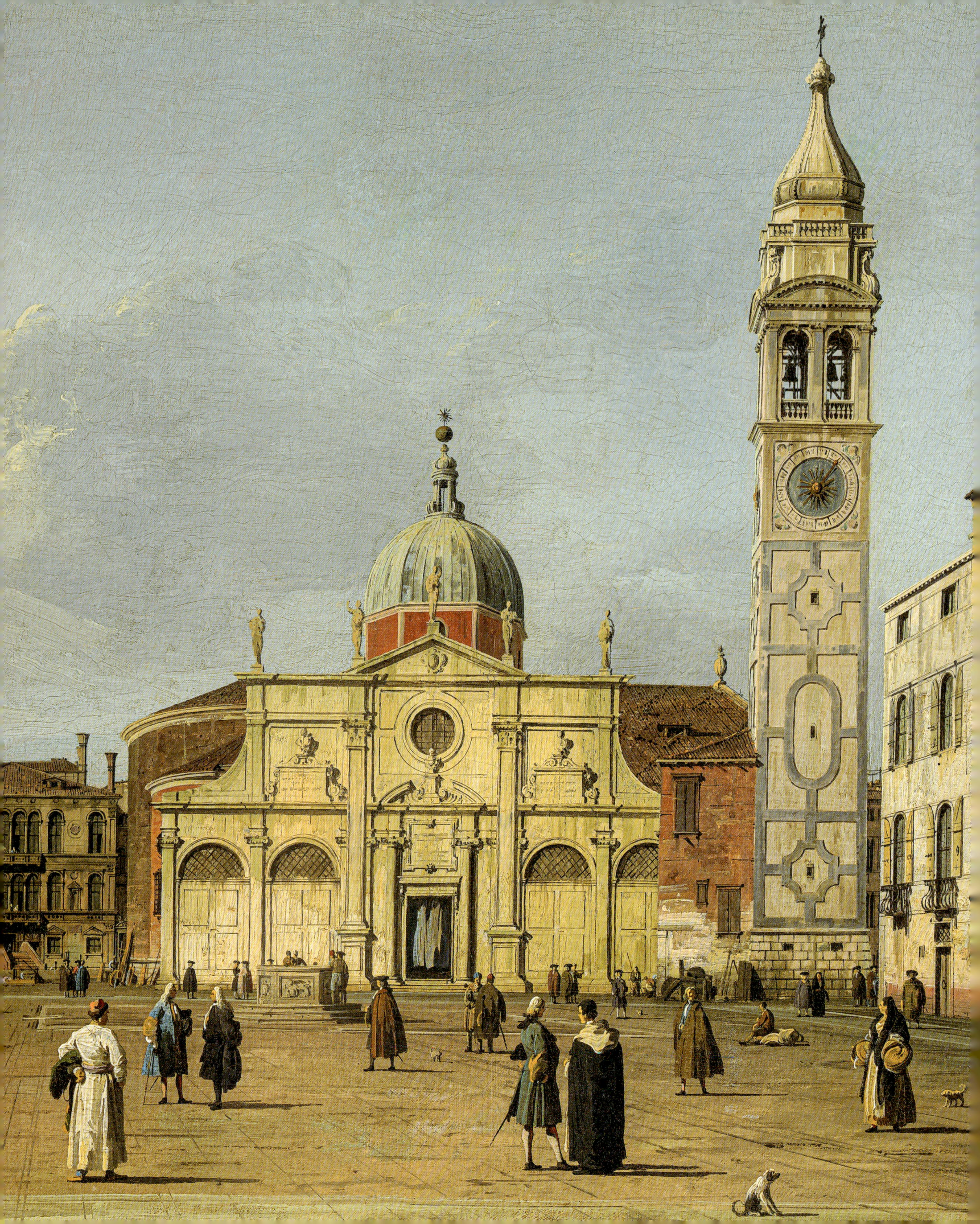

Philip Steadman

Canaletto's camera

The popular idea, in caricature, is that Canaletto was a supplier of superior postcards of Venice to English aristocrats on the Grand Tour. There is some truth in this, especially for those paintings produced in quantity in Canaletto's studio in the 1730s and early 1740s. The apparently 'proto-photographic' character of the works can, it is tacitly assumed in this idea, be attributed to the use of an optical method. The reality is more complicated, and more interesting. Canaletto certainly made many view paintings or *vedute*; but he also produced large numbers of finished drawings for sale, as well as pictures of apparently fantastic buildings in imaginary settings, the *capricci*.

We know that Canaletto was a camera user. His contemporaries said so.[1] There is a small box camera in the collection of the Correr Museum in Venice labelled 'A. Canal', meaning of course that its owner was Antonio Canaletto.[2] Most important, there survive more than a hundred pencil sketches made with a camera by Canaletto and perhaps also by his nephew and assistant Bernardo Bellotto. The majority of these are in a single notebook or *quaderno* now in the collection of the Gallerie dell'Accademia.[3]

Typically, Canaletto divides a panoramic view into a series of sections, traced on successive pages of the book. There can be between four and ten sketches for a single picture. Figure 88 reproduces four pages of drawings from the *quaderno,* of San Simeone Piccolo and buildings either side of the church, along the Grand Canal. This is the view that still confronts visitors to Venice today who arrive by train and step out of the station, straight into the eighteenth century. Because Venice is in many parts so little changed, it is often possible, as here, to compare the works directly with the scenes they depict. Canaletto and Bellotto both made finished drawings of this subject. There is no known painting.

The four sketches are made on the fronts and backs of two pages. The paper is thick and opaque. This means that they could *not* have been made with a box camera of the type in the Correr, which demands transparent paper. The pages of the *quaderno* must have been placed *under* the projected image of a larger camera, taking the form of a tent or booth. Such cameras were illustrated in contemporary books with which Canaletto could have been familiar, as for example W.J. 's Gravesande's *Essai de Perspective* of 1711 (fig. 89).[4] Decio Gioseffi built a tent camera of this type in the 1950s and demonstrated something of the way Canaletto might have worked.[5]

Several qualities of the graphic character and layout of the sketches in the Accademia *quaderno* are strongly suggestive of a camera method. It is clear that the drawings were executed quickly, only rarely with any shading. The images are flattened and lack depth. Lines can run continuously around many overlapping buildings and roofs, even though these are at very different distances. There are few corrections or second thoughts. The majority of the sketches have no guidelines, ticks or dots to set out the regular spacing of openings – although there are places where Canaletto uses construction lines to straighten up columns or position rows of windows, some of which are ruled. The elliptical curves of domes are drawn smoothly without kinks or wavering.

All this is suggestive, but not definitive proof of a camera being used. Such characteristics could be the product of extreme skill in making freehand

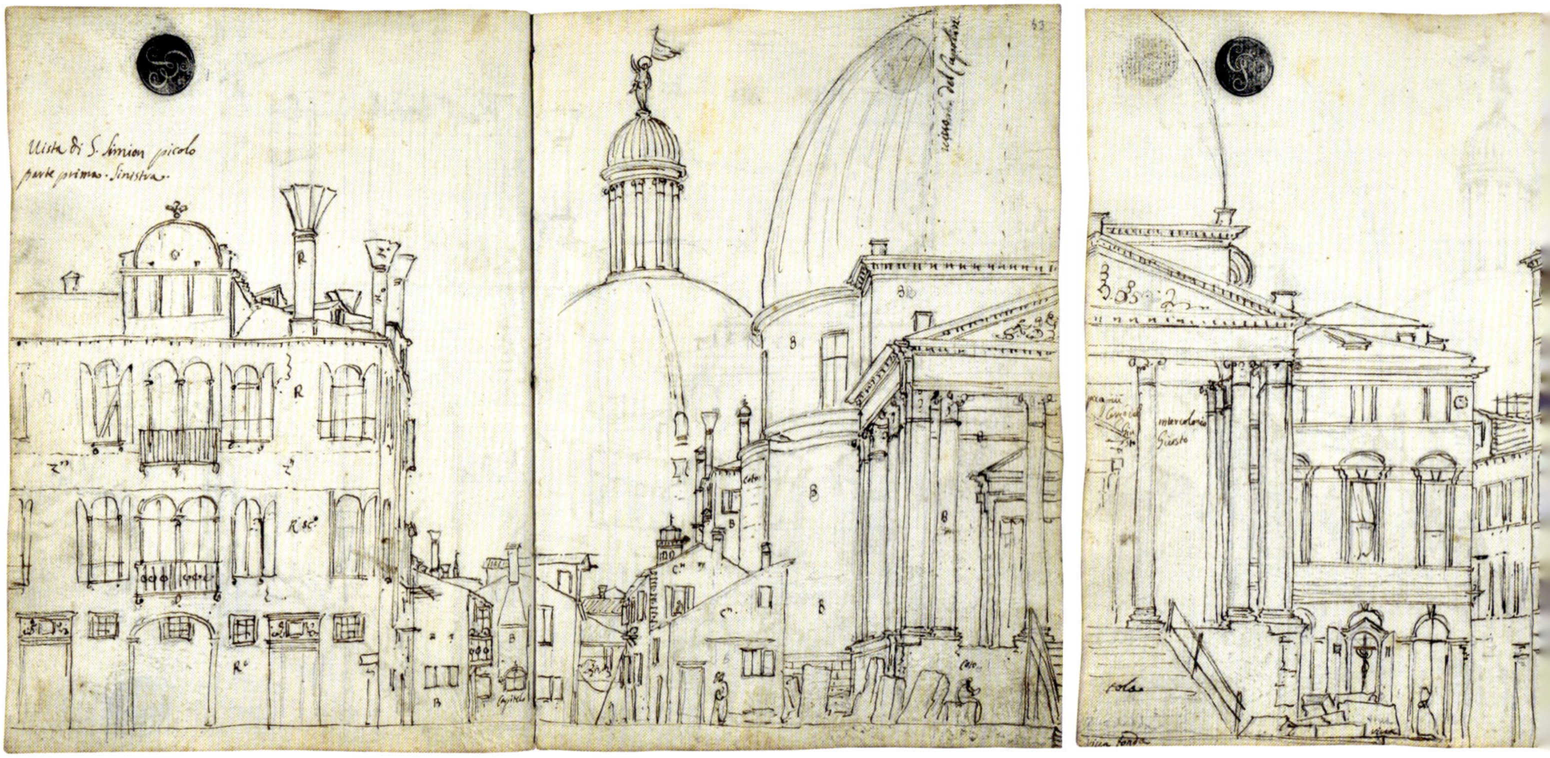

88 Four pages from Canaletto's *quaderno* (52V to 54R) in the Gallerie dell' Accademia (see note 4), showing the church of San Simeone Piccolo in Venice, and adjoining buildings

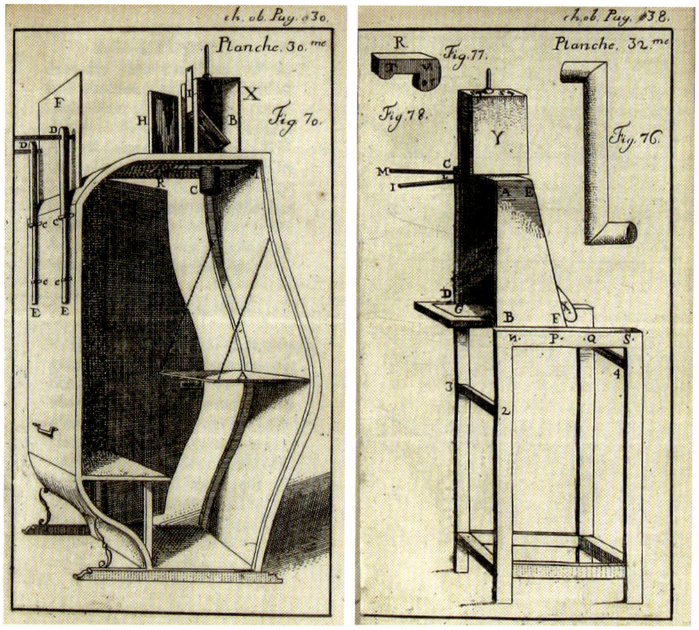

89 An enclosed booth type of camera obscura (left) and a tent type (right): from W.J. 's Gravesande, *Essai de Perspective*, 1711

sketches by eye; there is no doubt that Canaletto was a highly accomplished draughtsman. There are further features, however, that are much more difficult to explain other than by reference to the camera. They have to do with the placing of images on the page, and the sizes of these images.

Look at the four sketches of figure 88. In every case the page is completely filled to the bottom and sides. Buildings are cut off arbitrarily at the extreme left and right, where the optical image reaches the edges of the sheets in question. The church of San Simeone Piccolo itself is split between two sheets. The cupola on top of the dome is too high up to fit on its sheet, so is drawn separately in the sky – presumably by shifting the sketchbook under the optical image. The same happens with other domes and campaniles elsewhere in the *quaderno*.

A draftsman working by eye would surely judge the overall size of a subject first, and would want to make sure that all of it fitted on his page. Here by contrast the standard size page is placed under

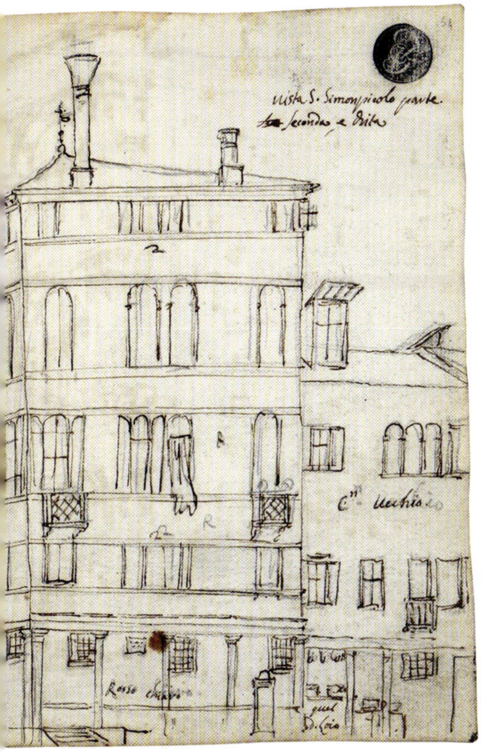

the lens, and Canaletto draws just what the lens catches. Despite the overall view being broken up in this way, the drawings on the different pages all match up precisely at the joins, not just across double spreads, but even where they are on front and back of the same sheet.

One final test: do the sketches match the actual scene? Figure 90 shows them superimposed digitally over a photograph taken from Canaletto's viewpoint. The correspondence is close throughout. Many experienced draughtsmen could reproduce local detail by eye with high accuracy. I do not believe that they would be capable of preserving relative sizes, proportions and alignments across the whole of an extended view in this way, especially if it was drawn on four separate sheets.

Both Canaletto and Bellotto made paintings of another scene, the Campo Santa Maria Formosa, for which there are again sketches in the *quaderno*. Figure 91 reproduces one of Canaletto's versions. Figure 92 shows the relevant sketches superimposed over a photograph of the Campo. Here there are several contrasts with San Simeone Piccolo. The camera drawings are made at different scales, depending on the depths of the various parts of the scene, perhaps using different lenses. They have to be altered in scale to fit

90 The camera sketches of figure 88 superimposed over a photograph of San Simeone Piccolo and adjoining buildings, taken by Philip Tabor from Canaletto's viewpoint

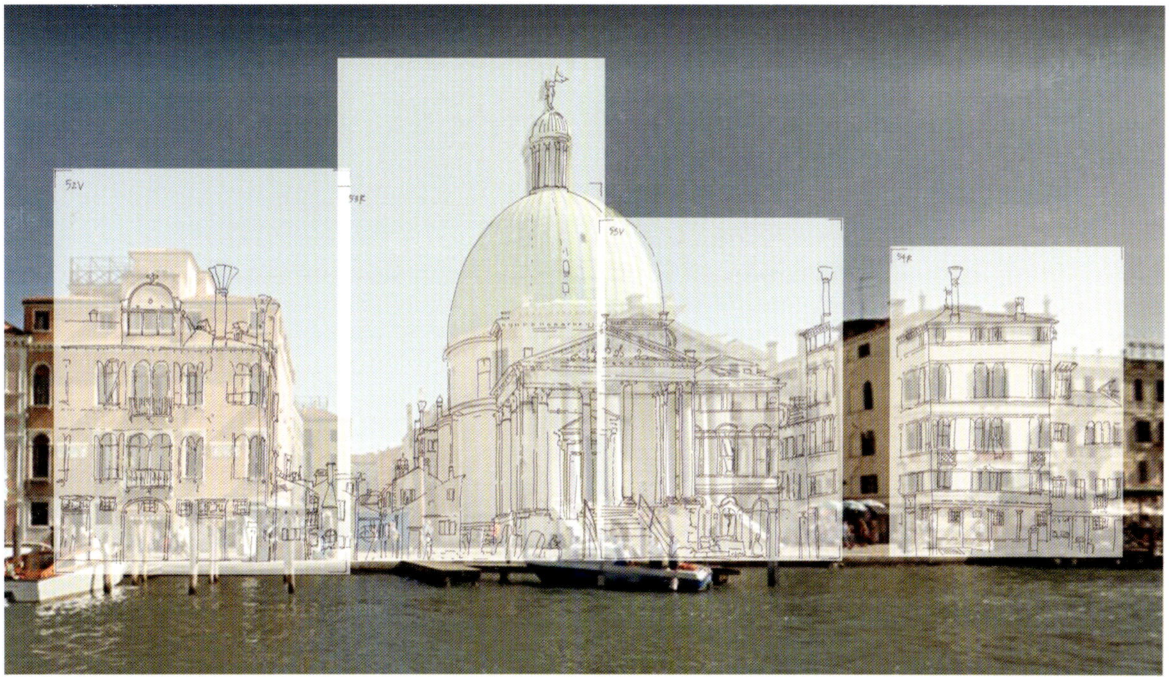

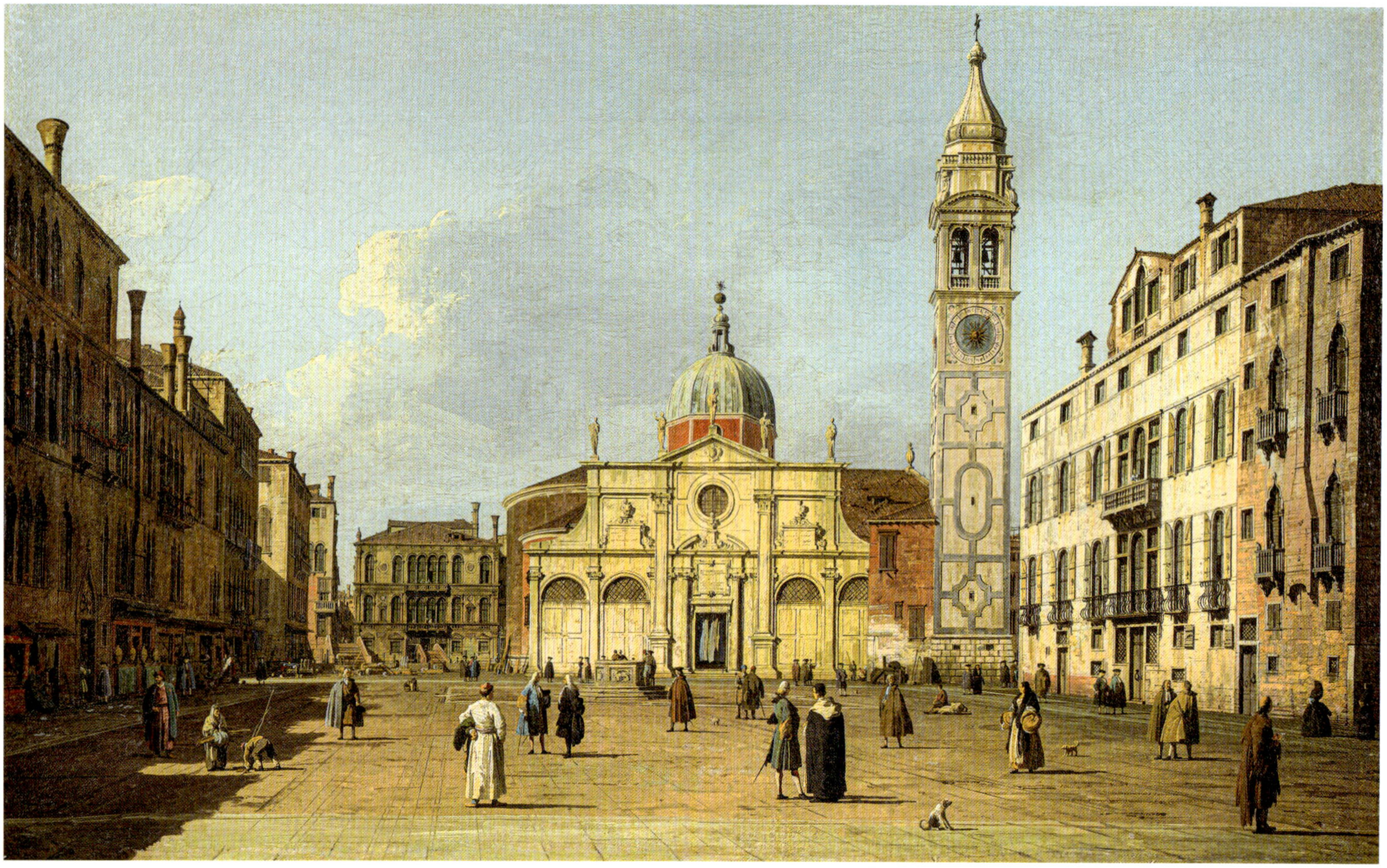

91 Canaletto, *Campo Santa Maria Formosa*, 1730s, oil on canvas, 47 x 80 cm. Woburn Abbey

92 Camera sketches on six pages of the *quaderno* (36V to 39R), superimposed over a photograph of the Campo Santa Maria Formosa, taken by Philip Tabor from Canaletto's viewpoint

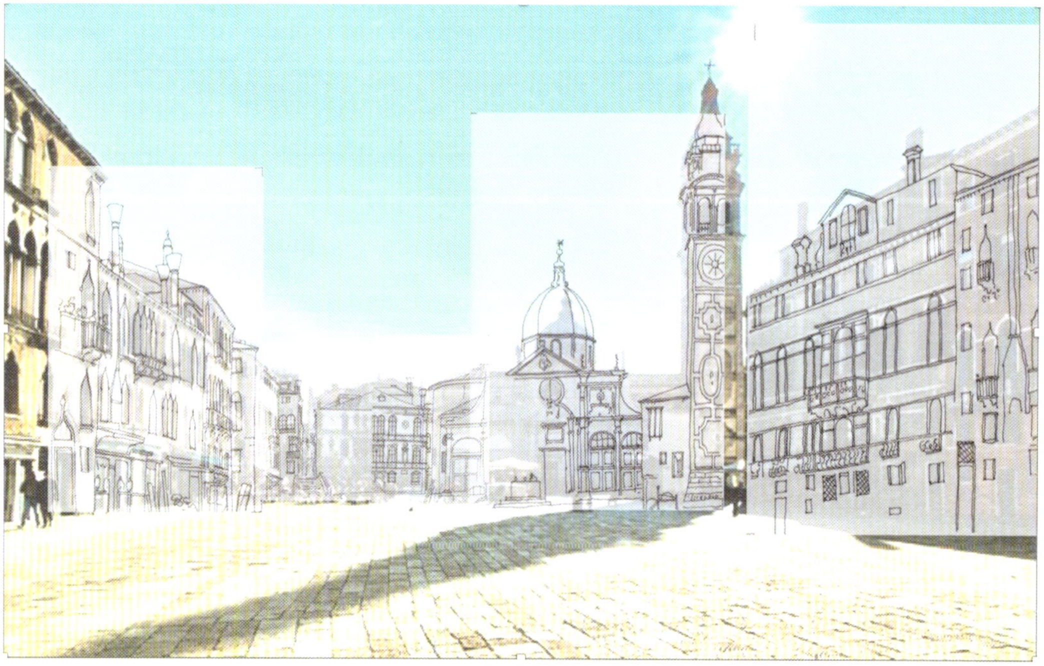

over the photo. With the church itself, and the building to its left, both of which are seen frontally, Canaletto draws just one half of the façade, and presumably is planning to mirror the sketch to provide the missing half, back in the studio.

The perspective of the sketch at extreme right does not exactly match the buildings, suggesting perhaps that the camera has been turned slightly. Similar discrepancies are found at the edges of other scenes. The outstanding way in which both sketches and painting differ from the photograph, in this case, is that Canaletto has greatly enlarged and raised the dome of Santa Maria, to give it the visual prominence it deserves. He does this with churches and campaniles in many pictures.

Canaletto's painting of the church of Santi Giovanni e Paolo illustrates similar graphical habits (fig. 93). There is again a slight divergence in the buildings at the extreme right – seen in very steep perspective – between sketches and painting. The west front of the church is captured in three sections, with some overlap, and the pinnacles on the roof are drawn separately in the sky. Canaletto has greatly enlarged the dome. The building at the left, the Scuola di San Marco, is not traced at all in the camera – although the silhouette of its far corner is outlined at the left of the church. The same happens with many *palazzi* and architectural monuments in other groups of sketches. Is it possible that Canaletto had access to architectural drawings or engravings of such buildings, from which he worked? There were architectural folios in the library of his patron and agent Joseph Smith. If so, Canaletto would have needed some method of turning elevation drawings into oblique views.

Gregorio Astengo and I have made superimpositions of all the camera sketches in the *quaderno* over the corresponding paintings, finished drawings and engravings. Our conclusions so far are that Canaletto is in general extremely faithful to the everyday fabric of Venice, especially in the less well known and less frequented parts of the city. Departures from reality – enlargements of important buildings, shifting of campaniles from their true positions – tend to increase in

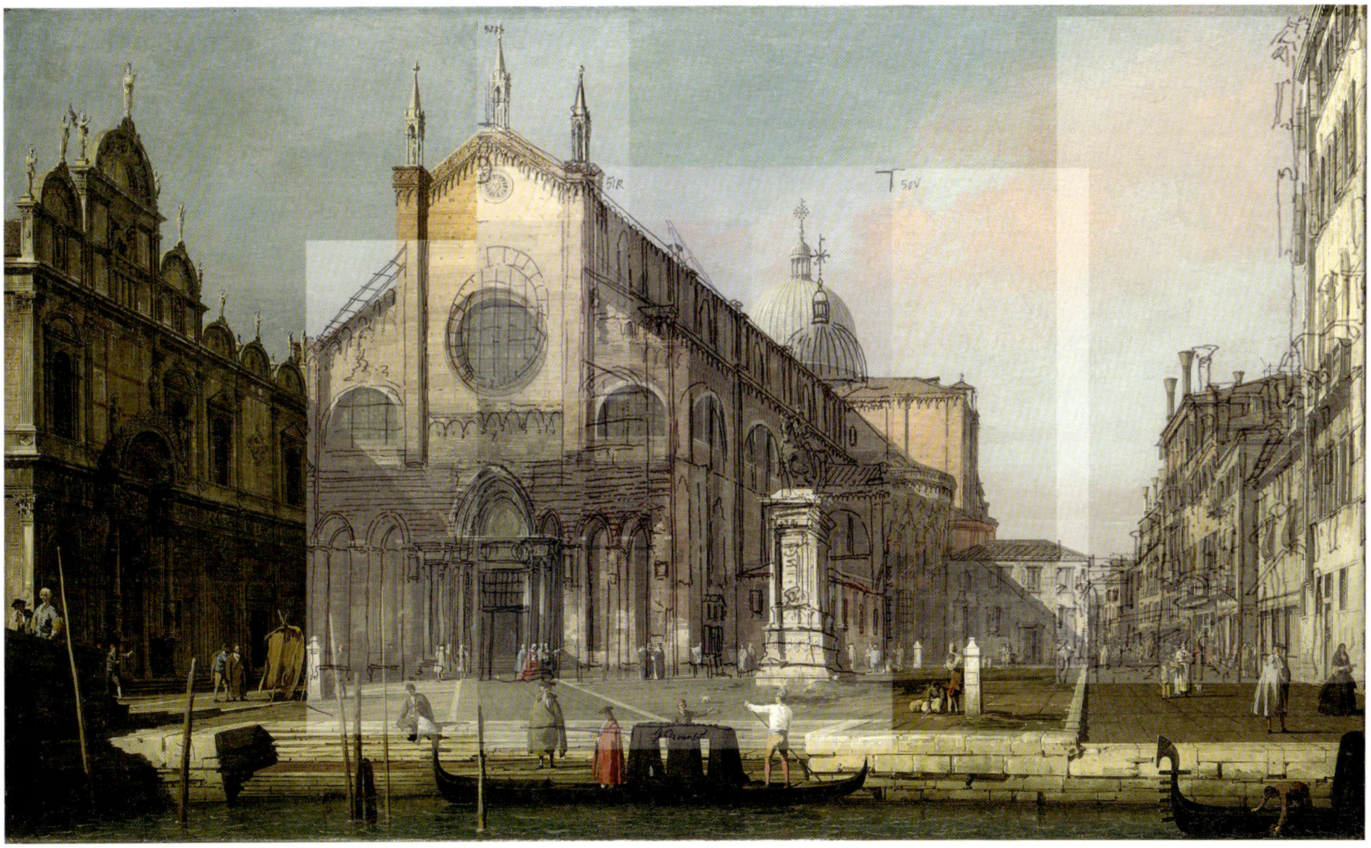

93 Camera sketches on four pages of the *quaderno* (50V to 52R) superimposed over Canaletto's *Church of SS. Giovanni e Paolo*, late 1730s, oil on canvas, 46 x 78 cm. Royal Collection, Windsor

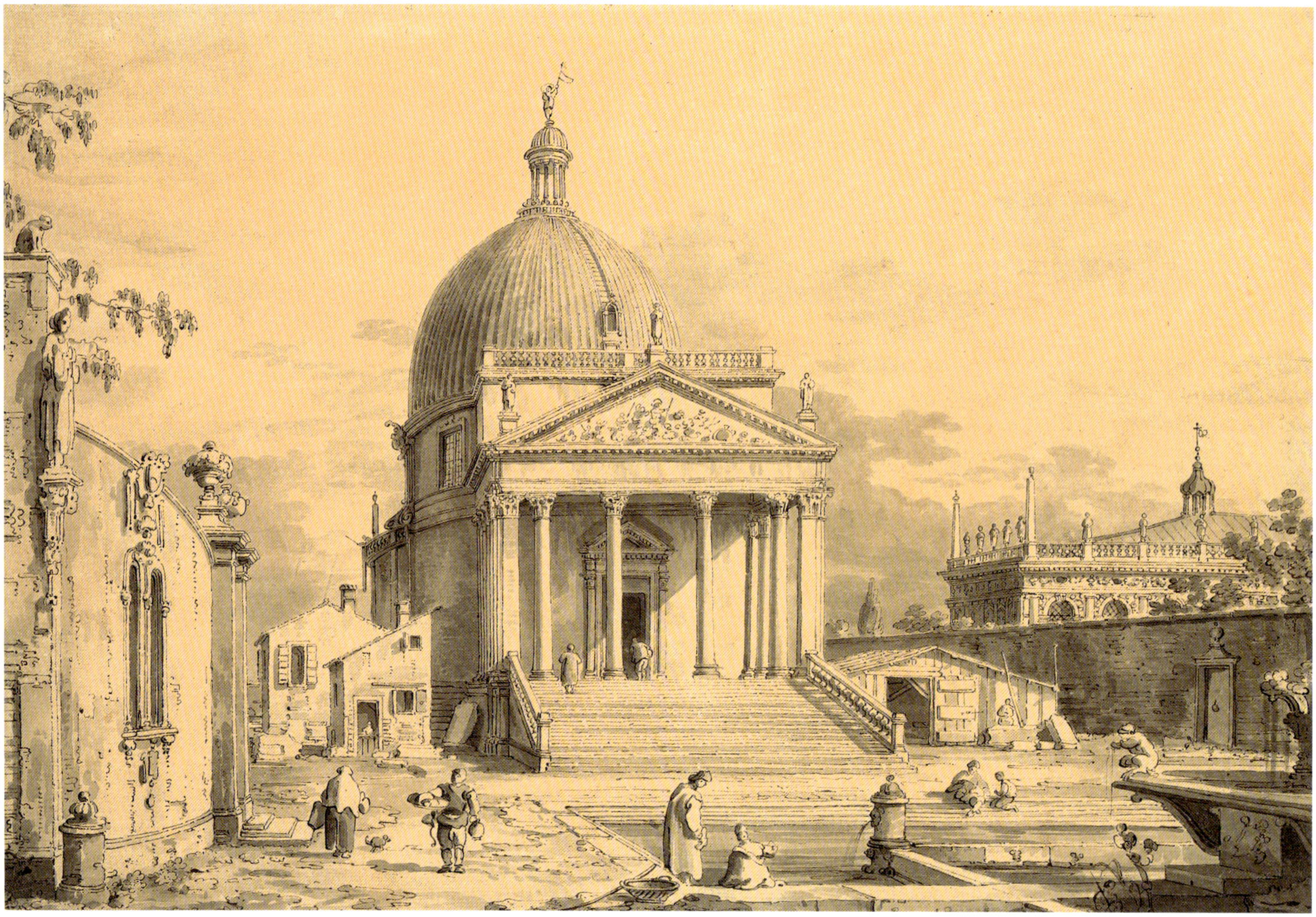

94 Canaletto, *Capriccio with San Simeone Piccolo*, c. 1735, pen and brown ink with grey wash over traces of black chalk on yellow antique laid paper, 31.1 x 46.7 cm. Detroit Institute of Arts, 29.171

frequency towards the Grand Canal and the Piazza San Marco. The Piazza in particular is a difficult space in which to obtain satisfactory views – as photographers find today – and Canaletto is quite happy to alter the angles between the corners of the square, distort its shape, move or remove buildings altogether, and even take viewpoints from positions that are in reality inaccessible.

I plan to build a camera or cameras, working from 's Gravesande's designs and other types described in the eighteenth century, to test whether it is possible to recreate these procedures of Canaletto's, and to understand what problems he faced.

Going back to San Simeone Piccolo: figure 94 shows a finished drawing, a *capriccio*, in which Canaletto has picked up the church and dropped it on to some unknown garden site. The building is exactly as it appears in the *quaderno* sketches, and has even carried along with it two small houses at the left. The building over the garden wall to the right is Jacopo Sansovino's Libreria Marciana, which in reality is opposite the Doge's Palace, and for which Canaletto perhaps had the architect's drawings.

Matters become yet more curious in a second picture, *Capriccio with an oval church* (fig. 95), set in the Venetian lagoon. Here the houses on either side of San Simeone are inherited wholesale from the original *quaderno* sketches (compare fig. 88). The ghost of the façade of the church itself is still vaguely recognizable, and its hemispherical dome has been squashed into the shallow saucer of the oval church's roof. The Gothic tower might come from another source. André Corboz has studied Canaletto's *capricci* intensively: he calls this kind of series a "linear chain" of progressive transformations.[6] It becomes clear from this

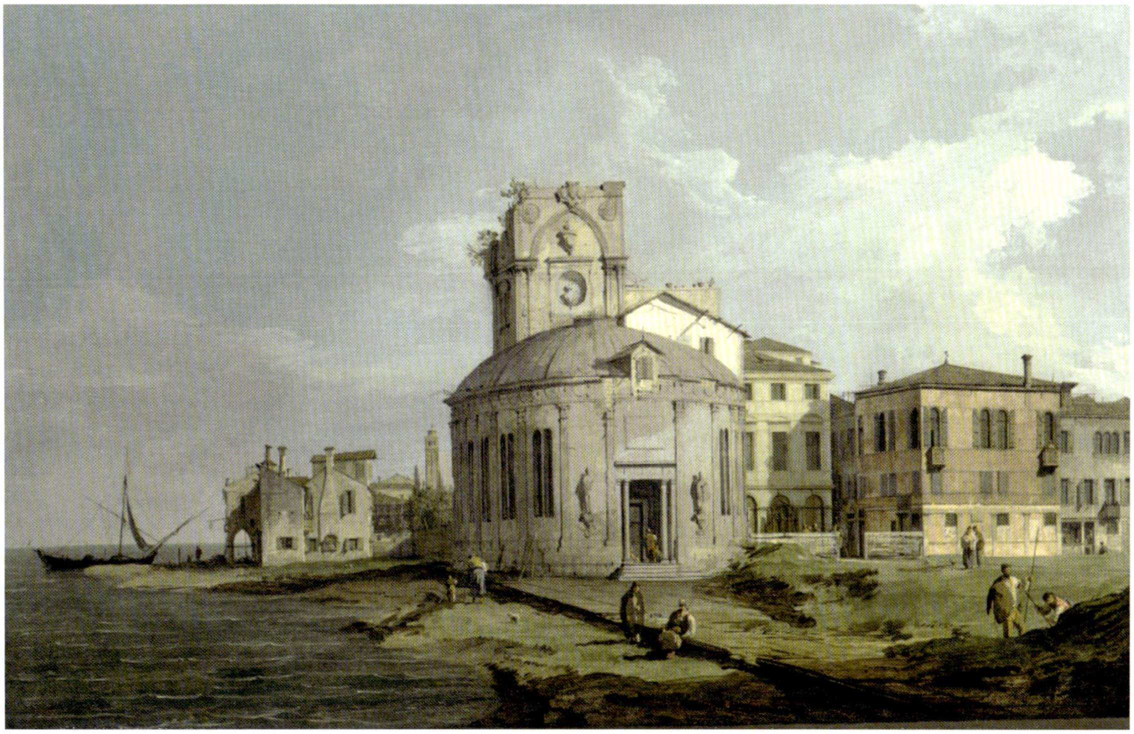

95 Canaletto, *Capriccio: An Oval Church by the Lagoon*, early 1740s, oil on canvas, 61 x 95 cm. Private collection, New York

and many other *capricci* that Canaletto has a characteristic method in which he starts from camera sketches, cuts them up, permutes them and reassembles them, like some kind of eighteenth-century Photoshop. After studying the oeuvre for a time, one begins to look for departures from reality in the *vedute*, and vestiges of reality in the *capricci*.

Mysteries remain, in particular the issue of how Canaletto might have transferred the camera tracings to paper for the finished drawings, and to canvas for the paintings. No underdrawing has been found beneath the paint layers. One standard method of transferring drawings was to square them up and transfer them using grids: but there are no grids on the *quaderno* tracings. Another method was to prick small holes along the outlines, and sift powdered charcoal through ('pouncing'); but there are no pinholes in the *quaderno* sheets. There *are* pinpricks in the finished drawings, but their function has not been explained.[7]

Examination of these drawings under infrared reflectography has also revealed receding orthogonals and horizon lines in pencil, made with a ruler. Rosie Razzall has claimed this as evidence of geometrical perspective construction, and that Canaletto was therefore *not* a camera user.[8] This is a misunderstanding. It is the sketches in the *quaderno* that are made with the camera, of course. What is happening in the underdrawing for the presentation drawings is that Canaletto is tidying up and straightening the images transferred from the *quaderno*, so that the perspective of the view as a whole is coherent and consistent.

Lawrence Gowing wrote that Vermeer is alone among users of the camera in "putting it to the service of style rather than the accumulation of facts".[9] Did Canaletto use the instrument just to accumulate facts? Were there no effects on his style of painting, his use of colour, or his treatment of tone? These questions have not been much studied. Leading twentieth-century Canaletto scholars such as J.G. Links and Michael Levey, who were sceptical about or hostile to the camera thesis, declared that the instrument, if used, served only to account for a mechanical quality in some of the paintings.[10] At the most basic level, one needs strong light to work with a camera: Canaletto's are paintings of a sunlit Venice. Both Canaletto and his nephew paint distant human figures as little twists and blobs of bright colour, resembling nothing so much as

96a,b Bernardo Bellotto, *Castello Sforzesco, Milan*, c. 1744, oil on canvas, 61 x 98 cm. National Heritage Institute, Brno, Czech Republic (and black and white reproduction)

the luminous images of clothes and faces on the camera screen. In Bellotto's later paintings of northern Europe he shows a sensitivity to tonal values that make his paintings look, precisely, like photographs, especially in black and white reproduction (figs. 96a,b).

Canaletto is barely mentioned in the main text of David Hockney's *Secret Knowledge*, and none of his paintings features in Hockney's 'Great Wall' of pictures, designed to illustrate an increasing naturalism in Western painting from 1300 to 1900; indeed, the density of images along the 'Wall' thins out very noticeably in the eighteenth century, at the zenith of European view-painting.[11] Half a dozen pages are devoted to Canaletto in Hockney's book with Martin Gayford, *A History of Pictures*.[12] However, the informative text here is largely by Gayford, and Hockney's few remarks are mildly negative. He talks about the fact that both the camera obscura and the photographic camera serve to distance an artist from the scene. Taking the example of one of Canaletto's many paintings of the Piazza San Marco, he says "we are fixed in position ... in a sense we are outside this space, not in it".

Gayford mentions the 'collage' technique adopted by Gaspare Vanvitelli, the Dutch/Italian view-painter and precursor of Canaletto, through which both artists combined the use of the camera with drawing by eye. Gayford also makes the comparison with Photoshop. It would be interesting to have Hockney's comments on the *capricci* and their relationship to his own 'joiner' photographs and paintings. Vanvitelli and Canaletto aimed to create 'collaged' pictures that still had overall perspective coherence, while Hockney's purpose has precisely been to pull the viewer closer into each separate part of the picture.

Notes

1 For example Zanetti 1771, 463. **2** https://correr.visitmuve.it/en/home/. **3** The sketchbook was donated to the Gallerie in 1949. Facsimiles have been edited by Terisio Pignatti (Pignatti 1958) and Annalisa Perissa Torrini (Torrini 2012). **4** 's Gravesande 1711, 'Usage de la chambre obscure pour le dessein'. A copy of the first edition is in the library of the Correr Museum in Venice. **5** Gioseffi 1959. **6** Corboz 1985, 350. **7** Parker 1948, 22, 24. **8** In publicity associated with an exhibition in London in 2017, *Canaletto and the Art of Venice, 18th century art in the Royal Collection* (Razzall and Whitaker 2017). **9** Gowing 1952, 23. **10** See, for example, Links 1977, 61; Michael Levey, 'Canaletto as Artist of the Urban Scene', in Baetjer and Links 1989, 17–29, at 24. **11** Hockney 2006. There are some mentions of Canaletto in the collected texts at the back of the book. **12** Hockney and Gayford 2016, 219–21.

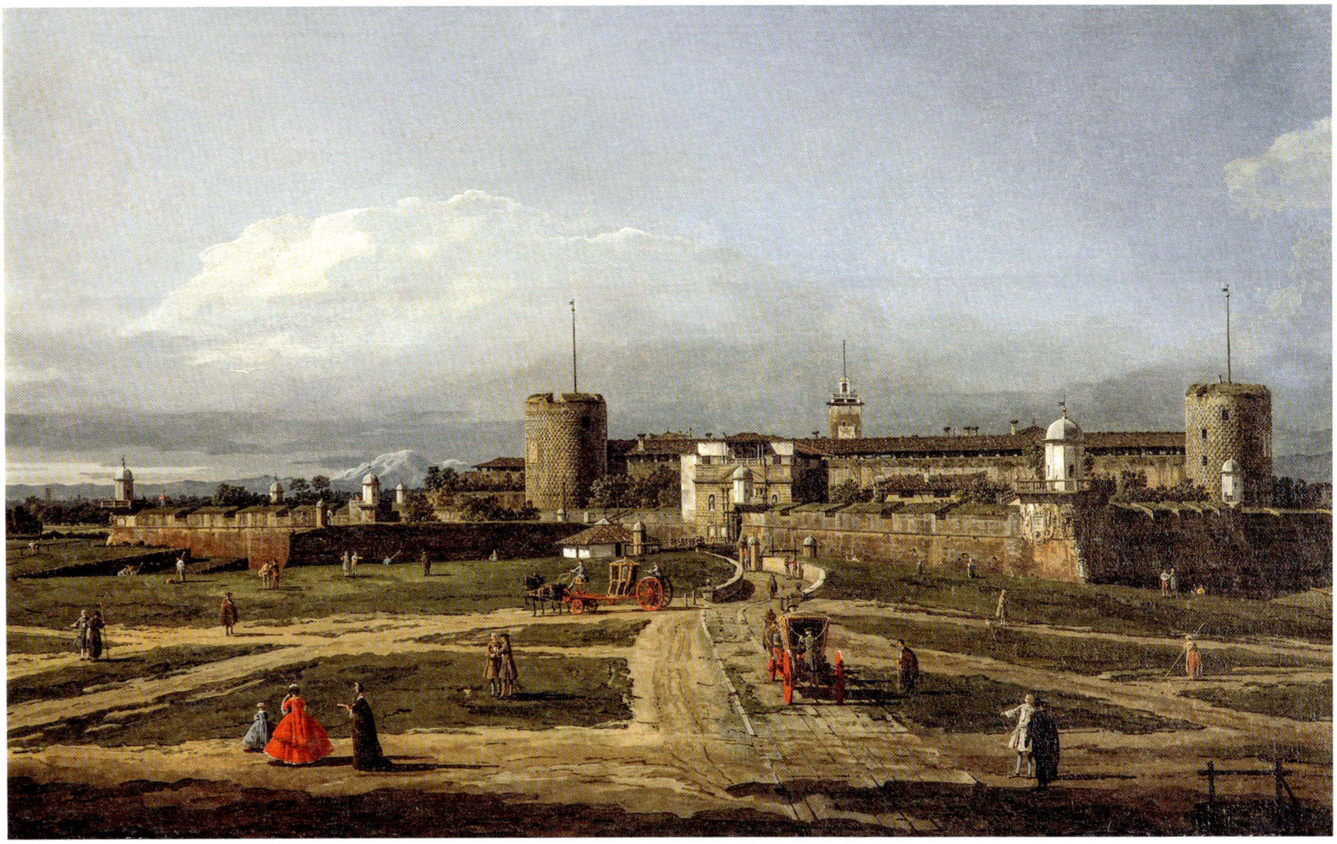
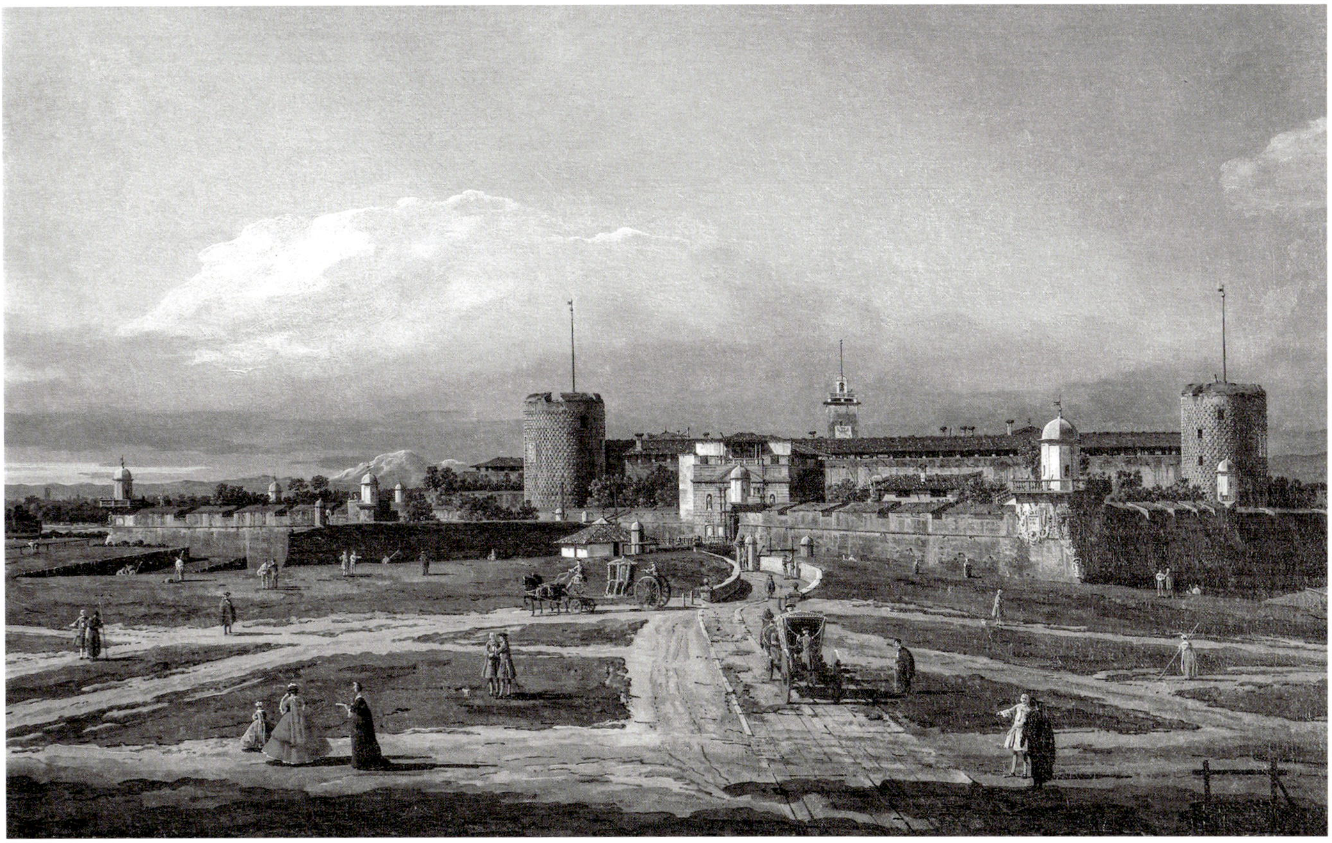

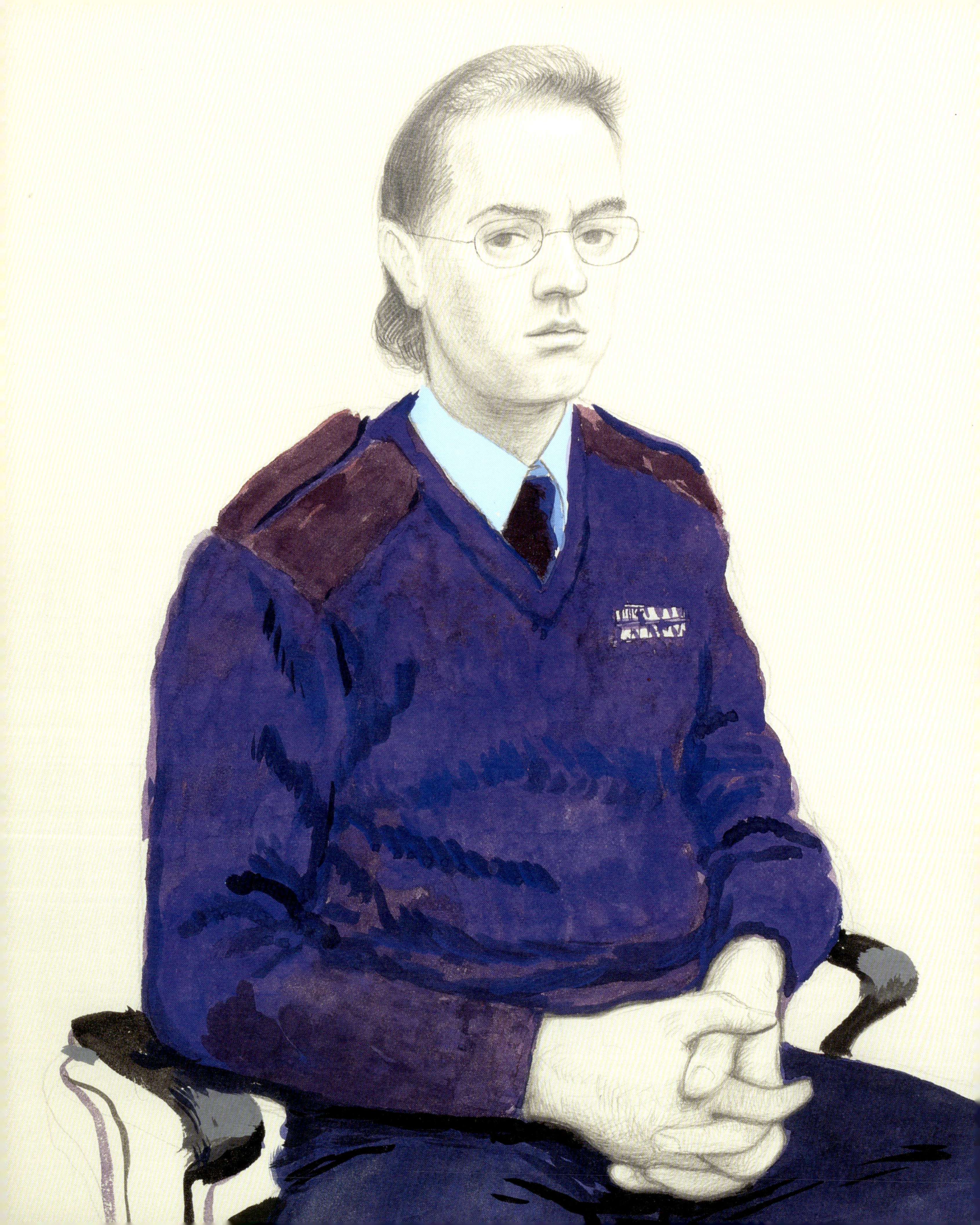

Jane Munro

Ingres and Hockney: Art, science and uniformity

In 1861, six years before Ingres's death, a group of the octogenarian artist's friends and admirers staged an exhibition of his work that would prove revelatory. Organized at speed and acknowledged as consequently "*provisoire*",[1] the exhibition in the sumptuous rooms of the Salon des Arts-Unis in rue de Provence, Paris, featured nearly one hundred of Ingres's drawings, divided into three categories: preliminary studies for commissioned paintings, independent portraits and a small group of assorted sketches. Almost all were in private hands and were seen by the public for the very first time. Reviews, mainly by Ingres's greatest champions, were predictably enthusiastic, their authors at pains to stress the once-in-a-lifetime opportunity to see a group of "priceless drawings" that would re-enter private collections after the exhibition, and so become once again inaccessible to artists and public alike.[2] As it transpired, the claim proved exaggerated, since not long after many of the same collectors were persuaded to lend their drawings again to the posthumous exhibition of Ingres's work held at the École des Beaux-Arts in 1867.

By the 1860s critical responses to the excellence, but also the eccentricity ("*bizarrerie*"), of Ingres's drawing style had become a commonplace.[3] A pillar of the academic establishment, Ingres upheld its key classicizing tenets and in his own teaching insisted on the fundamental importance of mastering drawing skills, but at the same time routinely deviated from idealizing norms. In his portrait drawings, a similar tension was perceived to exist between the precision with which Ingres was able to capture a likeness and his bravura handling of the pencil, at once assured and as "light as air".[4] As much as they were praised for their artistry and "calculated lack of finish",[5] so Ingres's drawings also seemed to reflect something of the scientific, conveying the minute particulars of a sitter's appearance with breath-taking, if at times unforgiving, verisimilitude.

Ingres's future biographer, the painter and art critic Henri Delaborde – also principal organizer of the 1861 exhibition – detected in the artist's approach to portraiture a "scientific disinterest" which he compared to portraits by Hans Holbein, an artist whom Ingres greatly admired.[6] For Charles Blanc, first professor of aesthetics and art history at the Collège de France and founder of the *Gazette des Beaux-Arts*, the extraordinarily lifelike quality of Ingres's portrait drawings ultimately demonstrated the power of art over science, and in particular the superiority of drawing over photography. His portrait drawings offered the definitive proof that "art is, when it wants to be, more exact than science, more precise than mathematics ... more sensitive than collodion, more subtle than chloride, more clear-sighted than light", Blanc wrote, "truer, at last, than truth itself".[7] When it came to penetrating observation and a realistic rendering of the thing seen, science could not teach art new tricks, he believed.

Many of the drawings exhibited in 1861 are now dispersed in museums throughout the world, so in the public domain, but this does not make

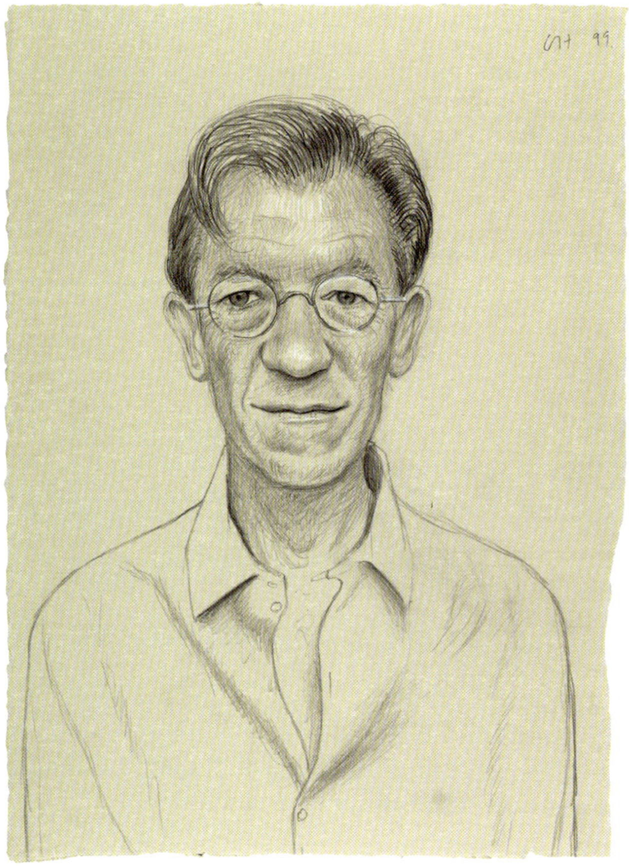

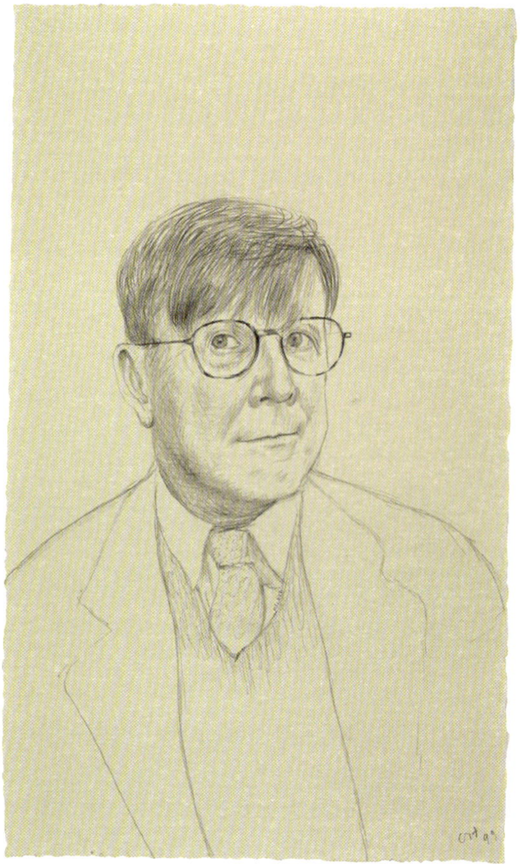

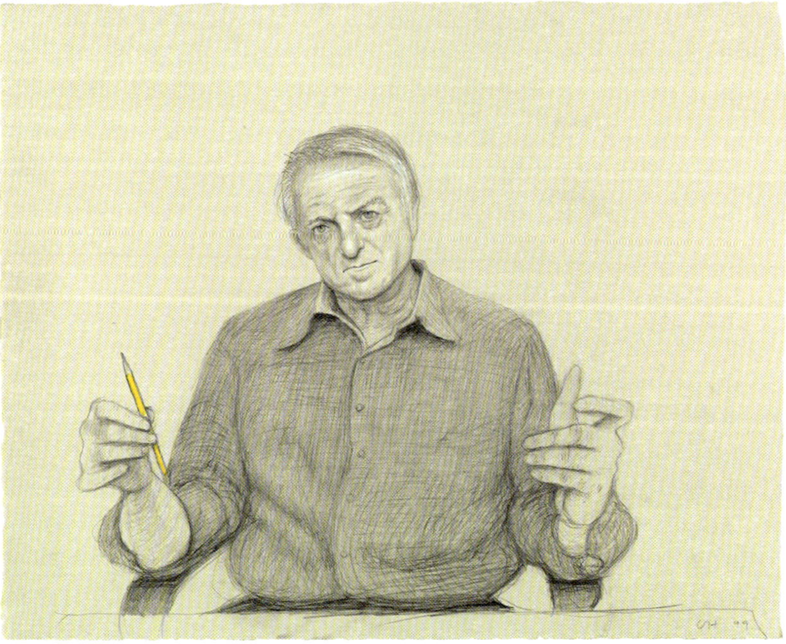

97 | F David Hockney, *Ian McKellen. London, 27th May 1999,* pencil and coloured pencil on paper using a camera lucida, 38.1 x 28.6 cm. Collection of the David Hockney Foundation

98 | F David Hockney, *Alan Bennett. London, 25th May 1999,* pencil on paper using a camera lucida, 38.1 x 23.5 cm. Collection of the David Hockney Foundation

99 | F David Hockney, *Colin St John Wilson, London. 3rd June 1999,* pencil and coloured pencil on paper using a camera lucida, 38.1 x 48.6 cm. Collection of the David Hockney Foundation

100 | F David Hockney, *Martin Kemp. London. 22nd June 1999,* pencil and coloured pencil on paper using a camera lucida, 38.1 x 36.8 cm. Collection of the David Hockney Foundation

The subject is one of the curators of the exhibition Hockney's Eye.

101 | F David Hockney, *Damien Hirst. London, 18th June 1999,* pencil on paper using a camera lucida, 38.1 x 43.5 cm. Collection of the David Hockney Foundation

102 | F David Hockney, *Margaret Hockney. Bridlington, 16th May 1999,* pencil on paper using a camera lucida, 29.8 x 20 cm. Collection of the David Hockney Foundation

a curated assembly of several of Ingres's finest drawings any less of a rarity. David Hockney is one of a long line of artists from Degas and Cézanne to Picasso and Lucian Freud to have been dazzled by Ingres's astonishing pencil portraits – "these marvels of the human spirit"[8] – in his case as a result of repeated visits to the exhibition *Portraits by Ingres. Images of an Epoch*, held at the National Gallery, London, in 1999. Fascinated by their "uncanny accuracy" and intrigued by the technical means by which Ingres had accomplished it, Hockney's most immediate response was to experiment with a camera lucida, having concluded that Ingres himself had used this or a similar optical device to achieve his ends (figs. 97–102). Ultimately, as we have seen, his scrutiny of Ingres's drawings led to nothing less than an entire and highly personal theory of optics and perspective, published in his book *Secret Knowledge* (2001). Fittingly, Hockney's most thoroughgoing engagement with the camera lucida in his work, the magnificent series of portraits of National Gallery warders

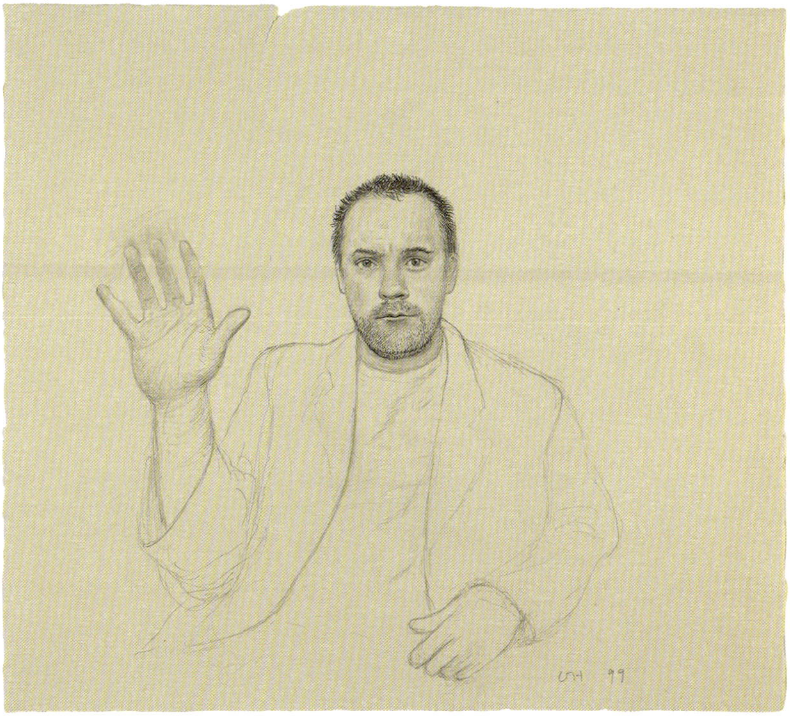

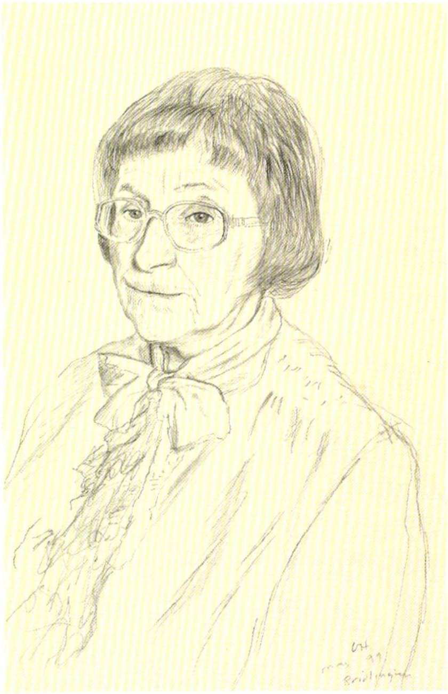

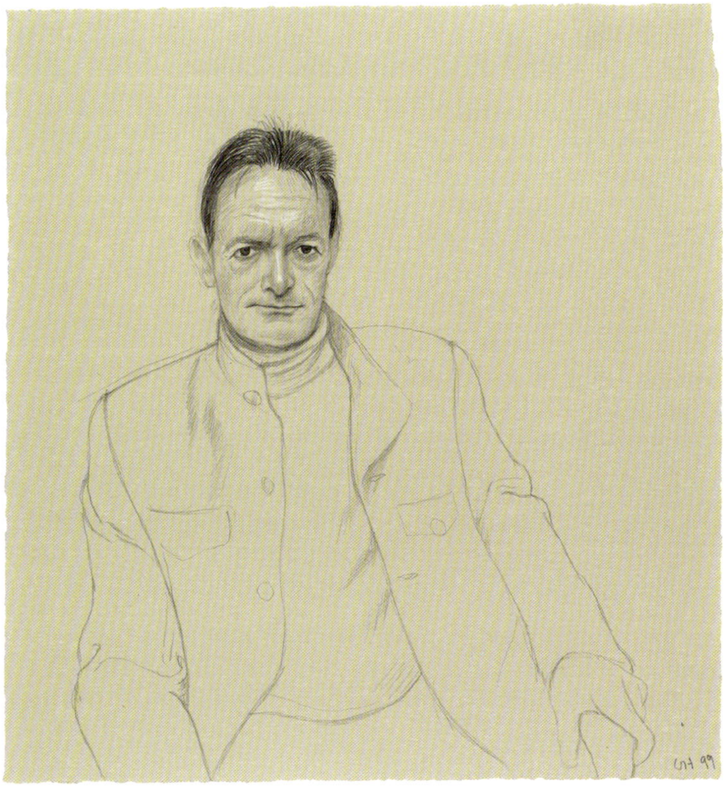

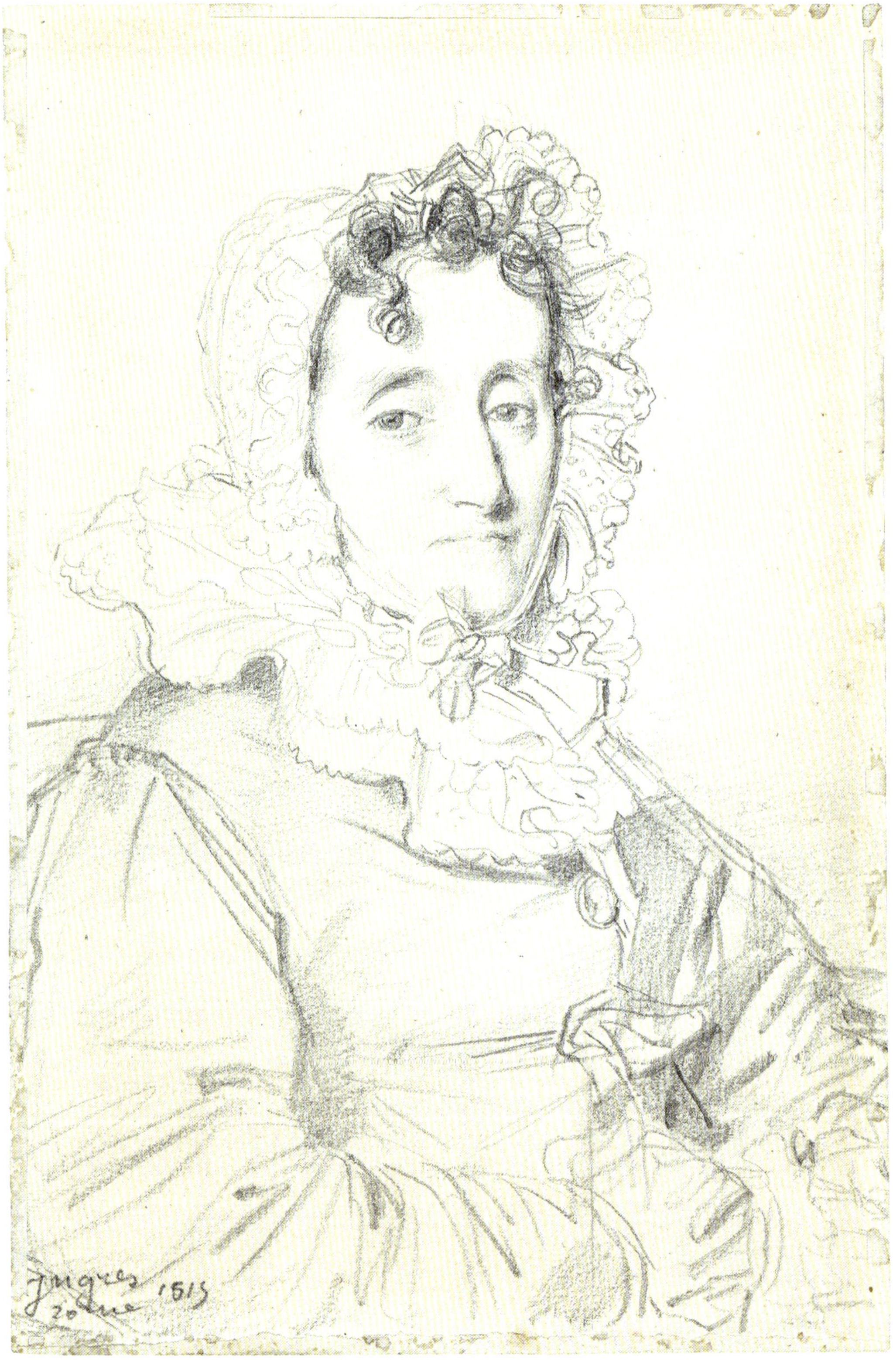

103 | F Jean-Auguste-Dominique Ingres, *Portrait of Maréchale Kutusov*, 1815, pencil on paper, 13.2 x 8.7 cm. Fitzwilliam Museum, Accepted by H.M. Government in lieu of Inheritance Tax and allocated to the Fitzwilliam Museum, 2010, PD.40-2010

(figs. 115a–l), expressly acknowledges Ingres as his source of inspiration, while punning on and interrogating the notion of uniformity.

Ingres: portraits of 'the lean years', 1815–17[9]

Ingres made independent portrait drawings from an early age, while still a pupil at the Académie Royale in Toulouse and from 1797 when studying with Jacques-Louis David in Paris, but it was only after moving to Rome in 1806 at an otherwise fallow period in his budding career that he began to produce them in significant numbers. During the fourteen years he spent in Italy, Ingres estimated that he had made around three hundred portrait drawings, for which he had earned around 8,000 francs, an amount he implicitly considered poor reward for his efforts.[10] While he disliked his growing reputation as "the man who draws little portraits",[11] believing that it deflected from his more elevated ambition to become a history painter, he recognized that his options had become limited after the defeat of Napoleon in 1815, putting paid to potentially lucrative painting commissions from the French community. Newly married and in debt due to paintings left unsold or unpaid for, he turned to producing "innumerable quantities" of small portraits, executed almost entirely in graphite pencil, which guaranteed him a steady source of income.[12] Some of those he portrayed were friends of fellow artists, but many others were no more than fleeting encounters with a transient international clientele – *"un belge, un suisse"*[13] – eager to have a souvenir of their Italian trip, whose names Ingres quickly forgot.[14]

French and British citizens were prominent among the international tourists who beat a path to the door of the "famous artist" M. Ingres,[15] but there was also a substantial Russian community, many of whom sought out the company of artists, writers and musicians then resident in the city. Among the most distinguished of these, Catherine Kutusov, née Bibikov (fig. 103), was the widow of one of Russia's most distinguished military commanders, who had become a national hero after repelling the invasion of the Napoleonic armies in 1812.

Highly cultured, Princess Kutusov was a renowned society hostess and passionate theatre-goer, who had been a precocious actress in her youth. Ingres appears to have drawn her portrait soon after she arrived in the city in the latter half of 1815, accompanied by her eight-year-old grandson.[16] It may be a sign of her approval or disapproval of this portrait (unusually small by comparison with others of the period) – or perhaps of Ingres's dissatisfaction with his first attempt – that she sat to Ingres again the following year for a second portrait in which her face, if not her body, is turned more directly towards the artist.[17]

Probably around the same time, in November 1815, Ingres drew the first of his portraits of the many British visitors who came to Rome, some returning to the city after an absence of ten years due to the war with France. Between then and 1817, he made around thirty drawings of these Grand Tourists, among the earliest of which were those of the Hon. Frederick North, later Earl of Guildford (1815; Gallery of New South Wales, Sydney) and his nephew the Hon. Sylvester North Douglas (1815; Portland Art Museum), who would die four years after his portrait was drawn, aged only 27. North has been credited with actively promoting Ingres's skills among his contemporaries, a role otherwise said to have been filled, initially at least, by a member of the artist's household, paid a percentage of the cost of each drawing to drum up custom.[18] The following year Ingres also drew North's sister, Lady Glenbervie, and her husband Sylvester Douglas, Lord Glenbervie, either before or after the couple travelled to Naples (March to May 1816); both drawings are now in the Pierpont Morgan Library, New York.[19] At some point after 1820 – the date of the watermark on paper – and before Lord Glenbervie's death in 1823, all four portraits were grouped on one lithographic stone that was printed and published in London by Charles Hullmandel, a partly posthumous memento of the extended family's time together in Italy (figs. 104–07).

Documentary evidence related to another portrait of 1816, that of Mrs John Mackie (fig. 108), provides us with the clearest idea of the time Ingres took to make these drawings. In her published journals, Mrs Mackie's daughter Sophia, who seems to have commissioned the

104 | F Charles Joseph Hullmandel, after Jean-Auguste-Dominique Ingres, *Katherine Anne (North) Lady Glenbervie*, c. 1815–23, lithograph on paper, 31.3 x 22.4 cm. Fitzwilliam Museum, Given by John Charrington, 1933, P.14248-R

105 | F Charles Joseph Hullmandel, after Jean-Auguste-Dominique Ingres, *Sylvester (Douglas) Baron Glenbervie*, c. 1815–23, lithograph on paper, 31.3 x 21.5 cm. Fitzwilliam Museum, Given by John Charrington, 1933, P.14249-R

106 | F Charles Joseph Hullmandel, after Jean-Auguste-Dominique Ingres, *The Hon Frederic Sylvester Douglas*, c. 1815–23, lithograph on paper, 30.1 x 22.1 cm. Fitzwilliam Museum, Given by John Charrington, 1933, P.14250-R

107 | F Charles Joseph Hullmandel, after Jean-Auguste-Dominique Ingres, *Frederick (North) Earl of Guilford*, c. 1815–23, lithograph on paper, 30.5 x 22.1 cm. Fitzwilliam Museum, Given by John Charrington, 1933, P.14251-R

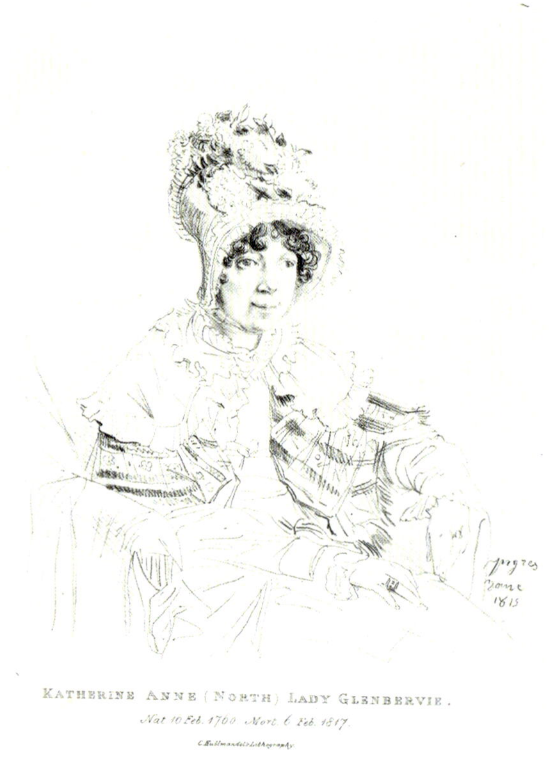

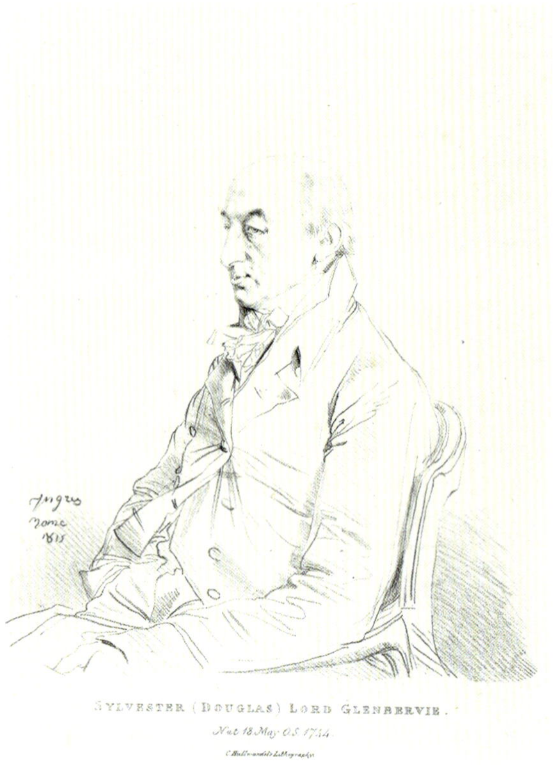

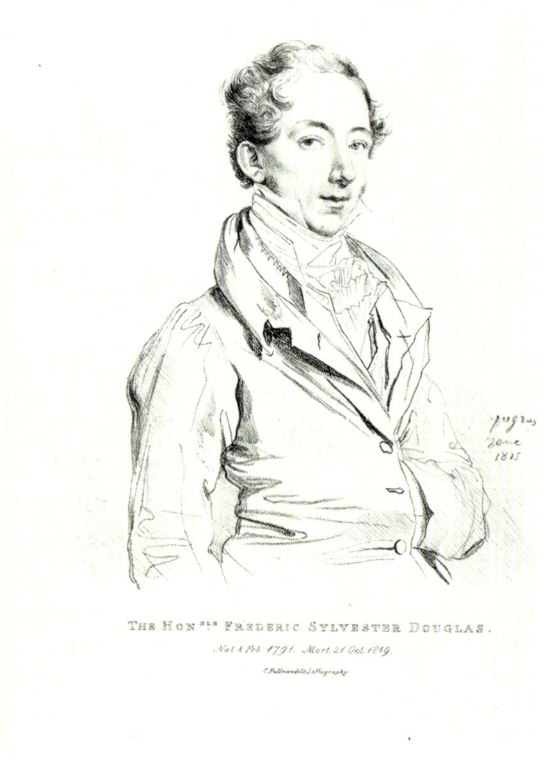

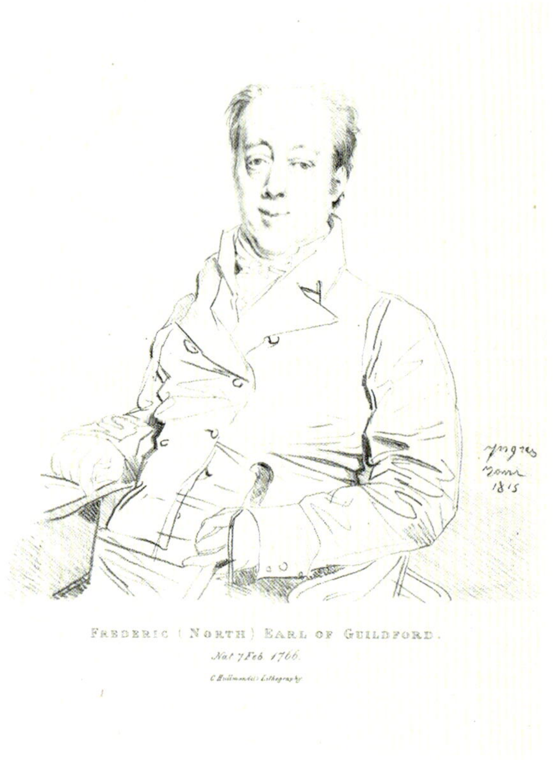

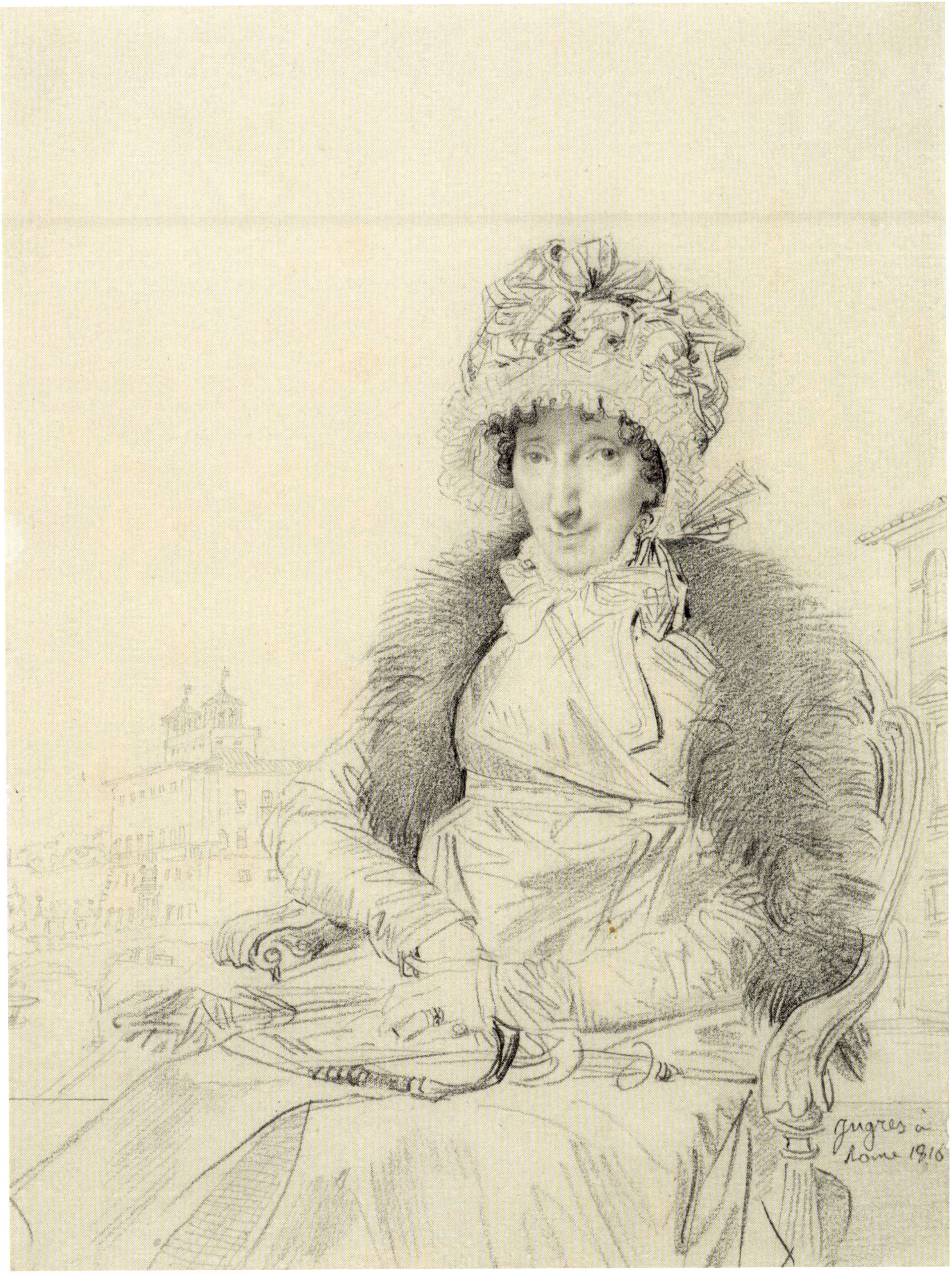

108 | F Jean-Auguste-Dominique Ingres, *Portrait of Mrs John Mackie*, 1816, pencil on paper, 27.7 x 22.7 cm. Victoria and Albert Museum, Gift of Miss Winifred M. Giles through the Art Fund, E.230–1946

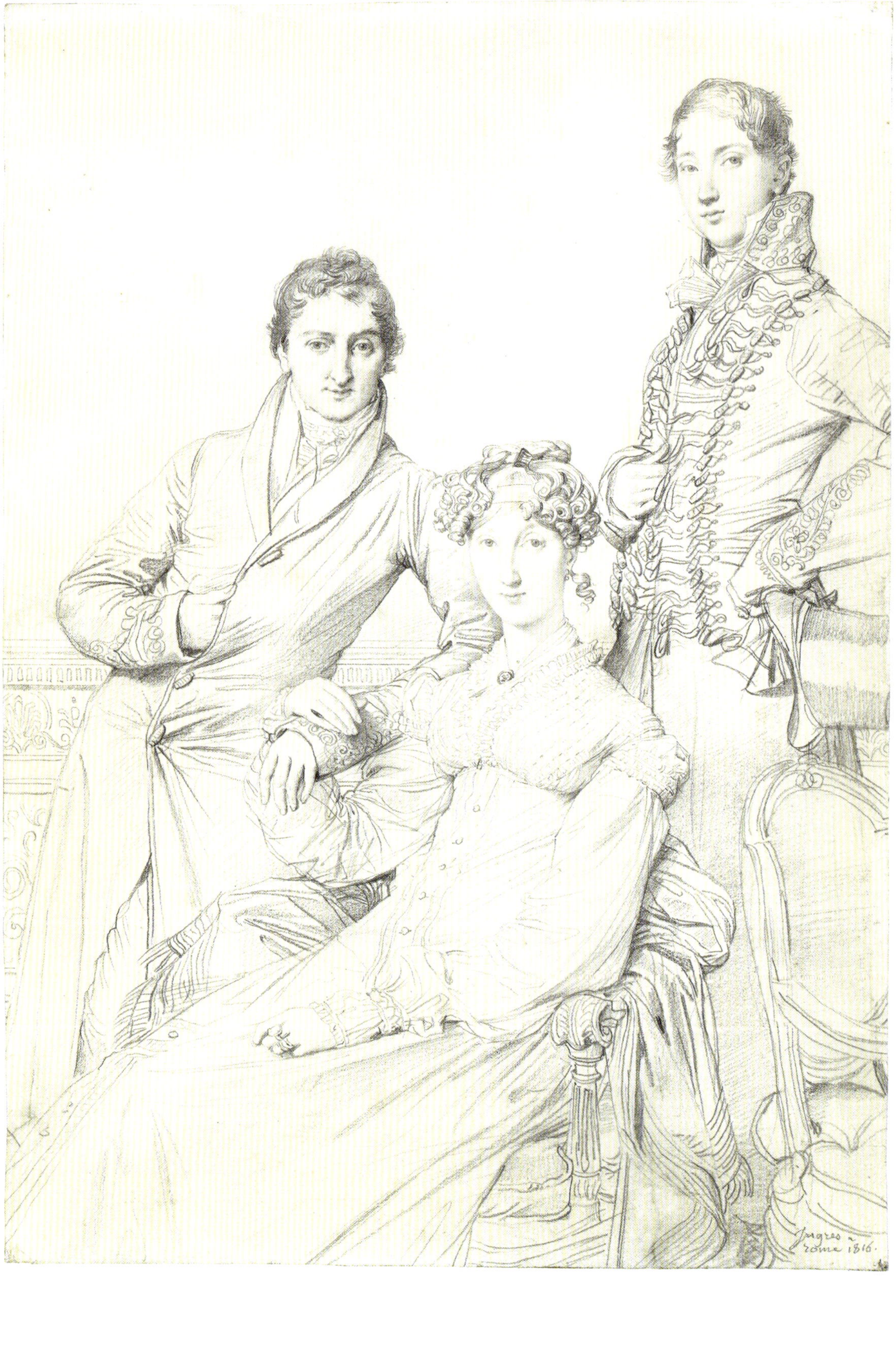

109 | F Jean Auguste Dominique Ingres, *Mr and Mrs Joseph Woodhead and Mr Henry Comber in Rome*, 1816, pencil on paper, 30.4 x 22.4 cm. Fitzwilliam Museum, Given by the National Art-Collections Fund, 1947, PD.52-1947

portrait, recorded that her "dear Mama" sat to Ingres on 9 April and that she took possession of the drawing on 18 April – nine days from sitting to delivery.[20] After Ingres's death, his pupil Raymond Balze recorded that Ingres was able to draw his friends even more speedily, in less than a day, taking care to record details of his sitters' expressions over lunch when they were more relaxed, although it may be that this applied only to portrait drawings made later in his career and that lengthier sittings were needed for commissioned portraits which required a higher degree of finish.[21] While some parts of Mrs Mackie's portrait are sketchily drawn, in particular her hands, arms, and the lower part of her dress, Ingres lavishes attention on her soft facial features, fur stole and elaborate English bonnet, complete with ribbons and trim. Like Lady Glenbervie, Mrs Mackie was a woman of a certain age – just over sixty at the time she sat for this portrait. Ingres makes no attempt to regulate the physical imperfections of these mature women, but instead sympathetically evokes their astuteness, gentle charm, and the spirited self-deprecation that allowed one, Lady Glenbervie, wittily to quote a *bon mot* of the philosopher La Bruyère in relation to her own appearance: "One falls hopelessly in love only with ugly women".[22]

The majority of Ingres's Roman portraits depict a single sitter, but he occasionally made drawings of family groups, some close acquaintances, others patrons, such as Lucien Bonaparte and his wife, whom he was keen to impress.[23] A rare example of a threesome of British visitors depicts the recently wed Joseph and Harriet Woodhead, on honeymoon in Italy, with Harriet's brother, Henry Comber (fig. 109); as such, it doubles as a souvenir of the couple's new-found marital status and of their travels to Rome. An agent in the Royal Navy, Woodhead would have been almost double the age of his 23-year-old wife, Harriet, daughter of the rector of the Yorkshire parish of Oswaldkirk, at the time they married; her younger brother Henry went on to study in Cambridge and eventually took over his father's parish. All three fix their gaze on the artist/viewer, the apparently legless Comber towering above his brother-in-law and sister, whose improbably supple right arm is fondly interlaced with her husband's. Oddly proportioned though the sitters are, these anatomical and perspectival infelicities do not disturb. Instead the eye is drawn to their engaging and characterful features, to Ingres's detailed rendition of their dress and the rhythmic graphite flurries with which he delineates the buttoning on Comber's coat and the poised wayward curls of Harriet's hair. For some of Ingres's contemporaries, the taut balance he preserved between painstaking exactitude and astonishing freedom of execution had its most

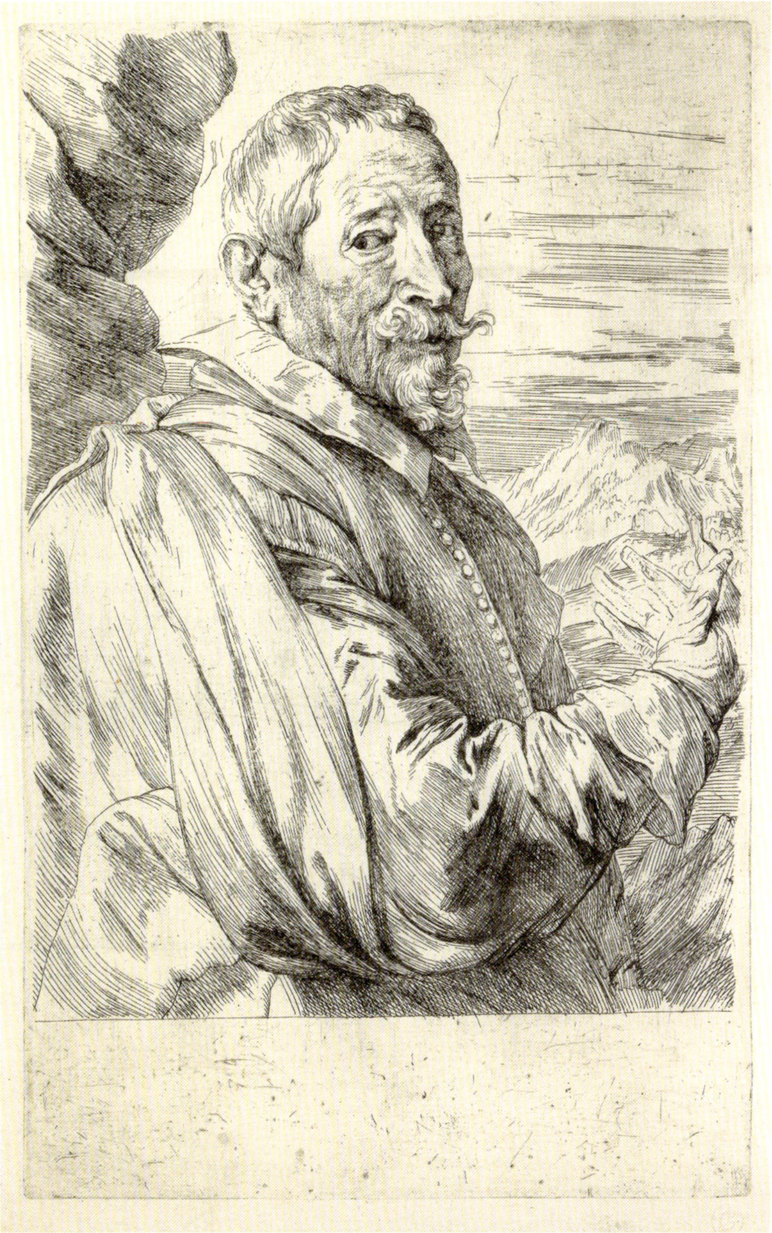

110 Anthony van Dyck, *Joos Momper*, 1641, etching on paper, 28.7 x 22.0 cm. Fitzwilliam Museum, Given by John Charrington, 1933, P.2759-R

direct parallel in the portrait etchings by Van Dyck (fig. 110), each artist achieving a "perfect harmony between the approximate and absolute definition".[24]

What of the camera?

There is no documentary evidence that Ingres used a camera lucida. No mention of it is made in accounts of his life and work, in his correspondence, in the memoirs of his students or in the reminiscences of any of his sitters. Ingres's acknowledged brilliance as a draughtsman and his highly individualized portraiture have made it difficult for many to accept, or even envisage, that he would have resorted to the support of an instrument designed as much for the amateur artist as for the professional. As one rhapsodic admirer wrote, Ingres created likenesses that were so penetrating and authentic that the paper or canvas seemed to disappear before our very eyes, allowing us to see an individual who "fixes you with their gaze, whose mouth is about to open, [and] whose thoughts speak to your own". Ingres's portraits went beyond being two-dimensional representations, in other words, to become a vivid reflection, a projection, an immaterial evocation of a living being: life was "born under his fingers".[25]

Hockney's conclusion that Ingres had used an optical aid to help him fix the main features of his sitters was based on a "hunch", albeit that of a seasoned practitioner and unaltered after his own experimentation with the instrument.[26] However, long before him it appears that others sensed its presence in Ingres's portraits. Writing in fulsome praise of the draughtsmanship of the eroto-decadent artist Louis Legrand, Gustave Kahn contrasted his drawings with the precise but emotionally desiccated work of artists who relied on optical instruments of various kinds to achieve their hyper-realistic ends, be it photography, microscopes (Ernst Meissonier) or "Monsieur Ingres and his camera lucida [*chambre claire*]".[27] A leading Symbolist poet and art critic, Kahn would no doubt have been taking a swipe at what he considered to be the stultifying tenets of naturalism as well as the "falsely beautiful" drawing style promoted by the academic art establishment in order to reinforce his somewhat inflated estimation of Legrand's abilities.[28] But the suspicion that Ingres had made use of the device seems to have arisen much sooner, perhaps during the artist's lifetime. Barely a decade after he had written in glowing terms of the Ingres exhibition at the Salon des Arts-Unis, Charles Blanc addressed head-on the suggestion that his hero's drawing was underpinned by an optical aid. If Ingres's "graphic truth [*verité graphique*]" seemed disturbing or strange, he argued, it was not the result of using any such device, but rather because it had passed through the prism – the camera lucida – of his own perspicuous and sensitive soul.[29]

As was the case with other common pieces of studio equipment, use of, or over-reliance on, an optical device could be wielded as a slur on an artist's competence and creative skills.[30] Indeed the camera lucida was dogged from the outset by the perception that it was a lowly crutch to support those of lesser or no ability, and its practitioners were "apt to feel a sort of humiliation" when relying on "instrumental assistance".[31] Whether or not Ingres harboured such inhibitions is unknown. In general, though, he expressed disdain for the "era of mechanism" in which he had come to live, and in particular the obsession of contemporary artists with new-fangled methods and techniques, be it in painting, sculpture or, especially, drawing and printmaking. [32] That said, Ingres was not averse to calling on the help of friends, pupils or the support of studio equipment to complete his paintings, notably in the case of types of work for which he felt ill-equipped or in which he simply had no interest.[33] His friend François-Marius Granet, for example, painted the landscape background in several of Ingres's portraits executed during his early years in Rome; and, where backdrops of the Eternal City were required for his drawn portraits (see fig. 108), Ingres has been shown to have copied the drawings of a yet-to-be-identified landscape draughtsman, some evidently made using a camera obscura.[34] There is evidence, too, that even in portraiture, a genre of painting in which he was an acknowledged master, Ingres was prepared *in extremis* to resort to studio tools.

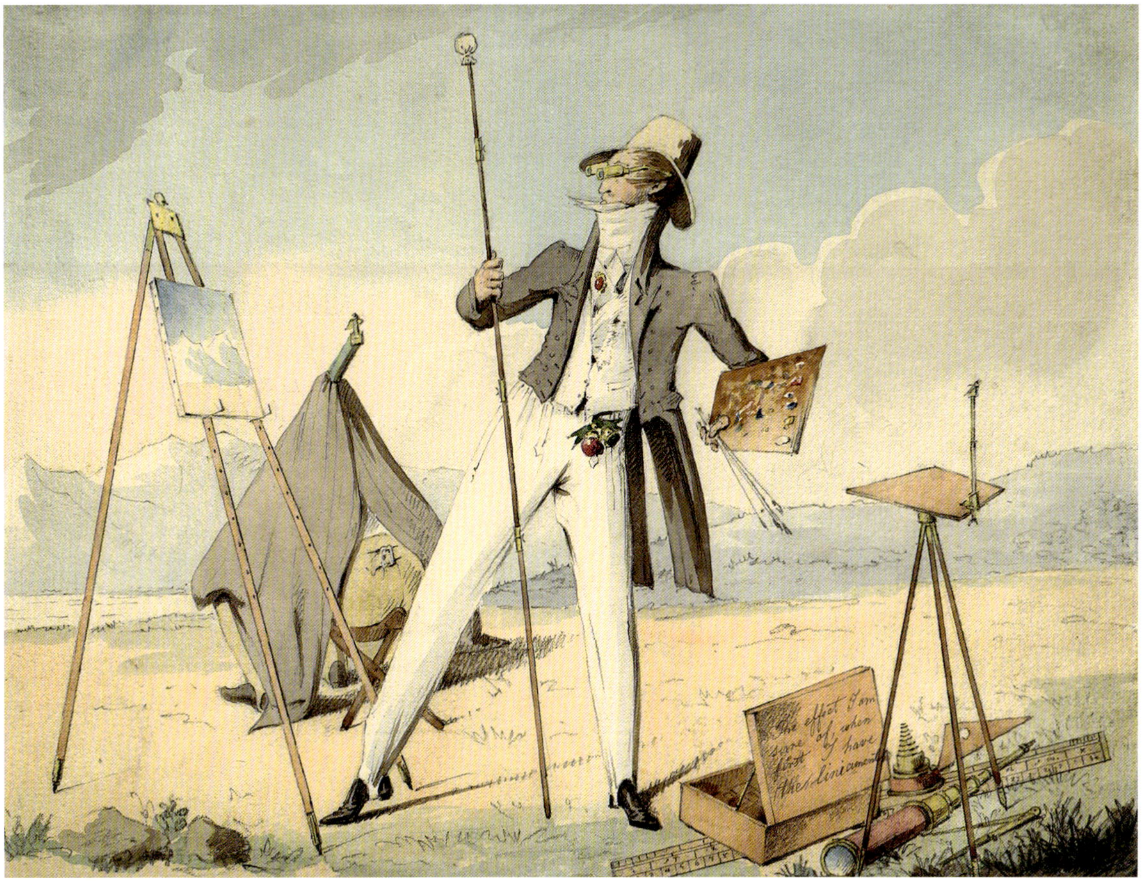

111 Carl Jacob Lindström, *Den engelske konstnären* (The English artist), c. 1810, watercolour on paper, 19.3 x 25.8 cm. Nationalmuseum, Stockholm, NMH 73/1876

A case in point was the lifeless lay-figure, which Ingres advocated be "banned", except in the case of portraits, and then only in order to draw or paint women's decorative jewellery which required a higher degree of finish (see figs. 104–07 and 108).[35] Expediency was at times a necessary compromise.

By the time Ingres came to be in demand as a portrait draughtsman in Italy, Wollaston's camera lucida had been in production for around ten years, rapidly replacing the more cumbersome camera obscura as the artist's optical instrument of choice (see above, pp. 75–101). In the interim, as Erna Fiorentini has shown, a number of variants were produced across Europe, by far the most successful of which was the camera lucida developed in Modena by the physicist, astronomer and optician Giovanni Battista Amici, based on a model imported from Paris in 1815.[36] Unlike his predecessors and competitors, Amici adopted a high-profile marketing campaign which involved making presentations in cities throughout Italy that attracted widespread interest from scholarly communities and the public alike. So successful was his tour of Florence, Rome and Naples in the early part of 1817 that Amici struggled to keep pace with the orders he received from those who had come to test the instrument, or others to whom they had vaunted its merits. We cannot know whether Ingres was among the enthusiastic throng of artists to attend these demonstrations, but by this date the use of the camera lucida (not necessarily Amici's) was widespread among by contemporary German and Italian landscape painters and, if Carl Lindstrom's witty caricature is to be believed (fig. 111), was especially keenly taken up by dandified, paraphernalia-loving English *plein air* painters.

Amici's model quickly gained favour in Paris, where it was further refined and "perfected" by Vincent Chevalier, a member of a leading French family of opticians and microscope makers. As the fabrication of the camera became

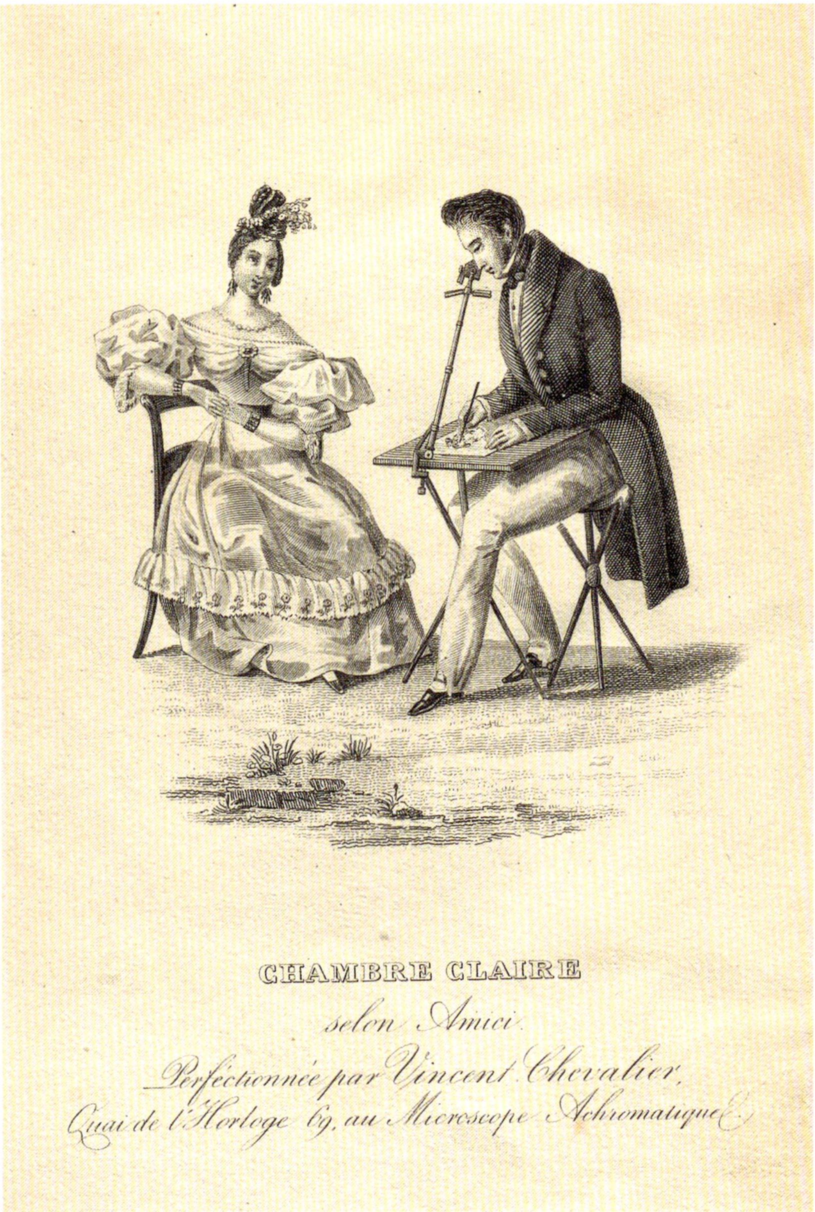

112 Unknown printmaker, *Chambre Claire / Salon Amici / Perfectionné par Vincent Chevalier / Quai d'Horloge / 69, au Microscope Achromatique*, from Jacques- Louis-Vincent (Vincent) Chevalier, Notice sur l'usage de la chambre Claire ... perfectionné par Vincent Chevalier, printed de Petit, Paris, 1834. Bibliothèque nationale de France, bpt6k325135p.f11

increasingly sophisticated, so the range of optional equipment enlarged, and accompanying printed instructions gave more detailed guidance as to how to adjust lenses, eye-pieces, stands, lighting, the distance between instrument and object etc. to achieve best results.

Portraits presented a particular set of challenges when using the camera. Good lighting evenly distributed between the sheet of paper and the sitter was essential to avoid glare, and the contours of the figure could be more sharply distinguished by using a white fabric as a backdrop behind their clothing and hair.[37] When drawing a person's features, the artist's eye, and so the lens of the camera, needed to be placed at the same level as the model being 'traced'; it was recommended that the latter also have a support or prop to maintain the position of the head "because a small movement would take away any resemblance".[38] One of the principal advantages of using the camera lucida was the ability to maintain a degree of uniformity, and to conquer one of "the most tormenting difficulties in drawing", proportion.[39] Inverting the lenses or adjusting the distance between the device and sheet of paper and the sitter allowed the artist to achieve a pleasingly "uniform scale". So, for example, if the device was twice as far from the subject as it was from the paper, the end result would be half life-size, if three times, a third, and so on proportionally. To represent the entire figure, some recommended a distance of "around ten feet",[40] which presumably also ensured an appropriate degree of decorum, although the user also had the flexibility to enlarge the scale of the image by adjusting concave and convex lenses, or by using a grid.[41] If the person was to be represented seated, positioning the body side-on to the artist was also critical, since, if the sitter faced the artist directly, the respective distances from their feet and head would "produce distortion in the drawing" (fig. 112).[42]

With commissioned portraits, uniformity of scale often reflected an artist's pricing structure. Ingres is recorded as having two fixed charges for his portrait drawings, eight *écus* for a half-length and twelve for a full-length figure,[43] although it is reasonable to imagine that the price would have varied for larger or more complex groups

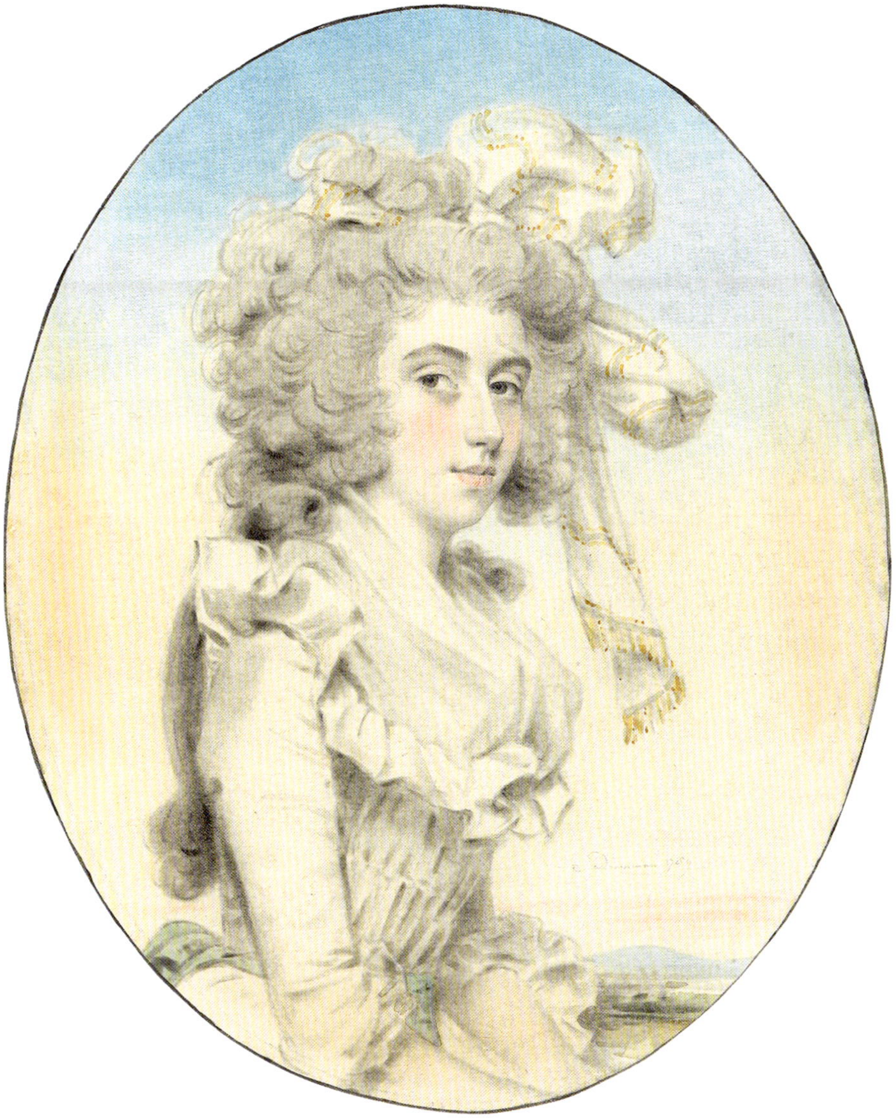

(see fig. 109). Uniformity could also be a response to consumer demand. In the series of portraits Ingres made of the North-Glenbervie family, for example, consistency of scale and proportion would have been especially important in ensuring a compact compositional arrangement on the lithographic stone.[44] Drawn over a period of some months, all four portraits are almost identical in size and in perspective, the sitters occupying proportionally the same space on the sheet. The end result is a truly family affair, the touchingly devoted Lord and Lady Glenbervie turning inwards, mirroring each other's seated pose; nephew and uncle positioned to face one another as their gaze meets our eye (figs. 104–07).[45]

Although reproduction through print media was a long-established mode of replicating an artist's work, other portraitists of the period resorted to different forms of technological innovation to standardize their production. A particularly fascinating case is the British artist John Downman, who enjoyed enormous popularity for his watercolour portraits of 'Distinguished persons' in the first years of the nineteenth century (fig. 113).

At the beginning of the 1780s, Downman began to use a lightweight paper supplied by mills in Kent and Gloucestershire that was also used from

113 John Downman, *Miss Elizabeth Monro*, c. 1789, black and red chalk, with stump, watercolour and white highlights on paper, laid down on recto of album sheet, 21.3 x 17.6 cm. Fitzwilliam Museum, no. 2314.14

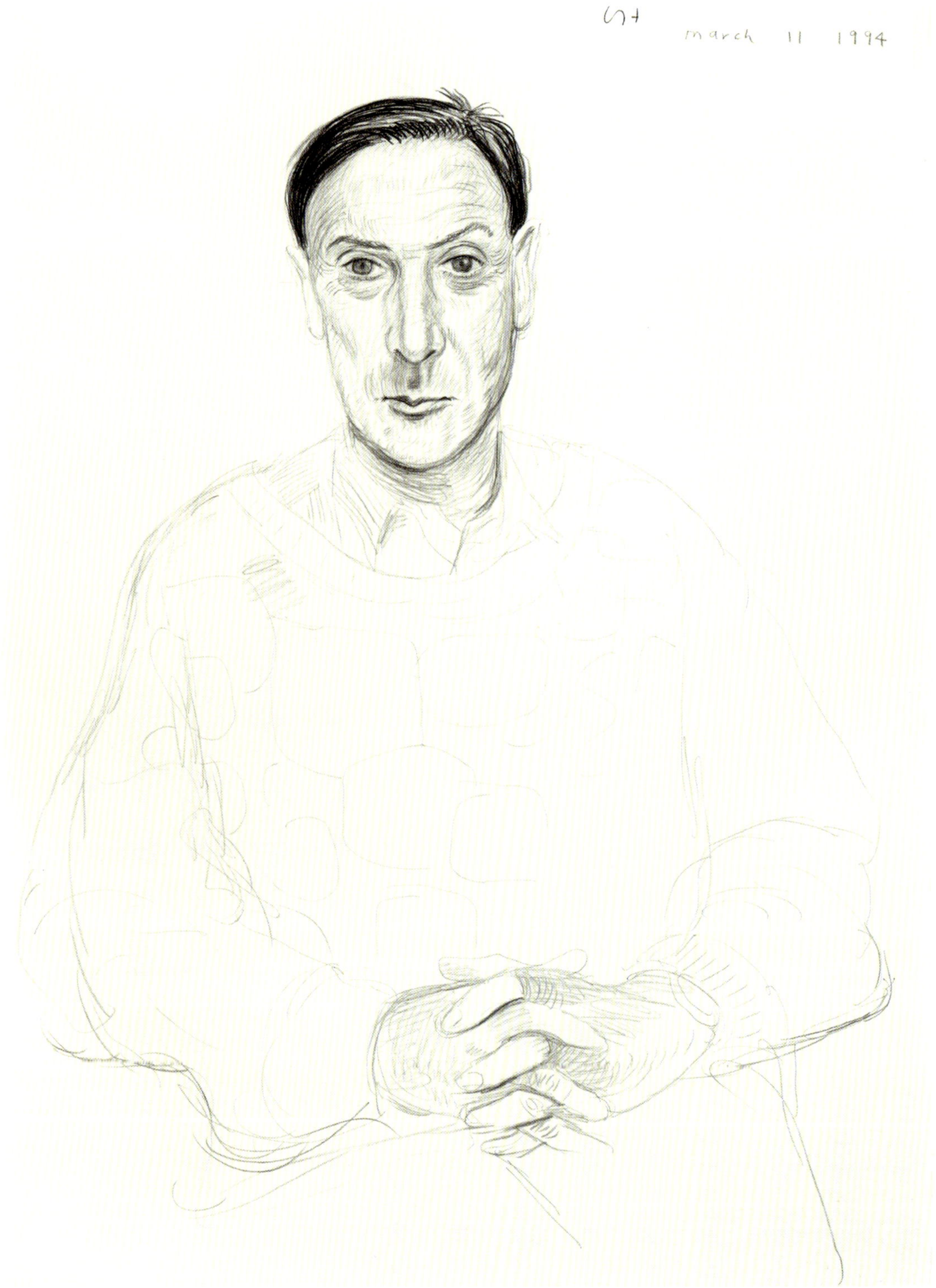

114 | F David Hockney, *William Hardie, March 11, 1994*, pencil and crayon on paper, 76.8 x 57.2 cm. Private collection

c. 1779 by the engineer James Watt for a machine that reproduced copies of his correspondence and other documents. Downman exploited the thinness of the paper to allow him to produce multiple versions of a single portrait – sometimes as many as twelve – by tracing the original and adding coloured chalk or watercolour to the back of the paper to give the face a distinctive healthy glow. In this way, he was able to satisfy the huge demand for his portraits without the expensive intervention of a printmaker.[46] For all their contemporary appeal, Downman's production-line portraits today seem blandly formulaic, not least by comparison with Ingres's extraordinarily expressive and characterful drawings. However, they serve as a useful example of the willingness of portraitists to engage with new media and technological advances to maintain a reputation and satisfy market demand.

"There is no art without science," Ingres once proclaimed.[47] By this he meant not to glorify the contribution of the sciences to the visual arts, but rather used the French term *science* in the wider sense of 'knowledge', as a way of dispelling the Romantic notion of unfettered artistic genius and upholding the academic tradition in which he had trained; creative endeavour should be founded on assiduous study, both practical and intellectual, he insisted. All the same, it would be surprising – not least given his evident interest in the reflected image in his portraits – if in the course of his long career Ingres did not come to know of, and perhaps even be curious about, the plethora of optical instruments and technological advances in seeing, representing and reproducing that became available in the first part of the nineteenth century, even if his brief engagement with photography and the daguerreotype was limited to the last decade or so of his career.[48] Opinion is likely to remain divided on the question of whether or not Ingres used a camera lucida to attain the marked "truth and ... feeling of accuracy" of his portrait drawings.[49] Would it have helped him? While with practice the device could prove time-saving, enabling a proficient draughtsman to reproduce perspectival lines "with a mathematical exactitude",[50] the instrument was not without its disadvantages. It was tricky to master, extended use proved extremely tiring on the eye and, whatever improvements were made to different models in the course of the nineteenth century, it was acknowledged that the lines it produced were inevitably hesitant and faltering ("*troublés*").[51] And as almost all publications on the use of the camera lucida reminded would-be users, the device was no substitute for sound artistic training, nor could it compensate for those who "by nature are destitute of these gifts".[52] But the degree of precision it facilitated did not preclude "the most perfect freedom of execution"[53] any more than the prism could replace the individual experience of looking.[54] A similar view has been repeatedly expressed by Hockney with respect to Ingres: a "master of the pencil", Ingres did not need the camera in order to draw, Hockney has written, but used it only to position key facial features before completing the portrait by direct observation:[55] optical instruments did not make the art – "they do not draw for you".[56]

Uniformity and diversity

When invited to contribute to the exhibition *Encounters: New Art from Old* at the National Gallery, London, in September 2000, Hockney chose not to reinterpret art from the gallery's permanent collection, but instead responded to portraits by Ingres that hung in the temporary exhibition then running concurrently. After long experience in making rapidly drawn portraits of friends and acquaintances (fig. 114, for example), he was well practiced in the format he adopted for camera lucida portraits. Using a camera lucida combined with an element of freehand 'eyeballing', he made twelve portrait drawings in pencil, crayon and gouache of the gallery staff whose job it was to watch members of the public as they looked at art (figs. 115a–l).

By creating this series of drawings in a "uniform style", Hockney paid a witty and insightful homage to Ingres, in the process exploring diversity through uniformity and the potential of multiple portraiture as a single art work. Consistency in size, poses and props anchors the ensemble, accentuating difference, highlighting individuality. Seated in the same green chair, the models' hands either folded

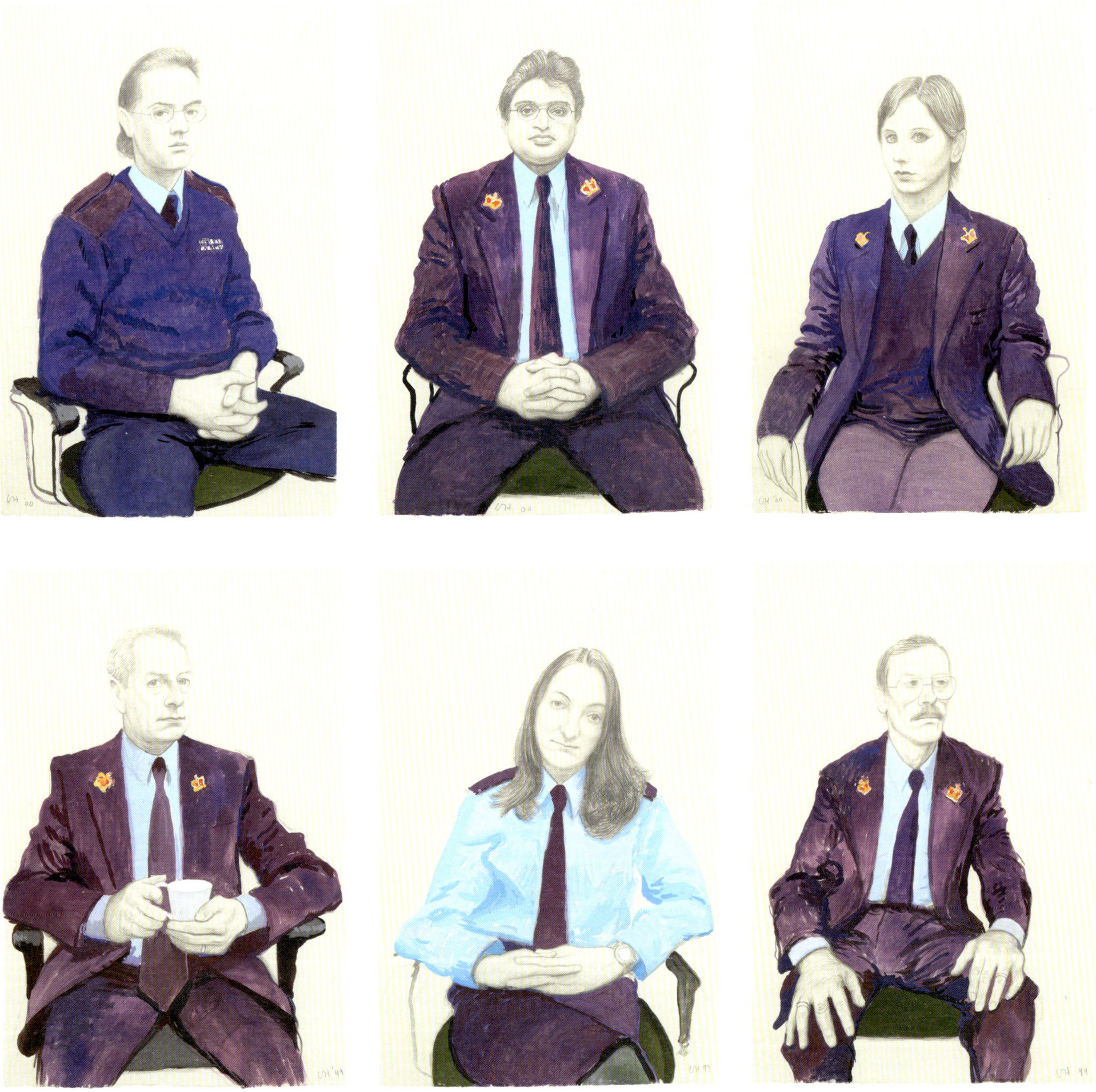

115a–l | F David Hockney, *12 Portraits After Ingres in a Uniform Style:* [top row from left] *Devlin Crow, London, 11th January 2000; Pravin Patel, London, 5th January 2000*; *Katherine Dooley, London, 6th January 2000*; *Graham Eve, London, 7th January 2000; Brian Wedlake, London, 10th January 2000; Lena James, London, 3rd January 2000;* [bottom row from left] *Ron Lillywhite, London, 17th December 1999; Maria Vasquez, London, 21st December 1999; Ken Bradford, London, 20th December 1999; Jack Kettlewell, London, 13th December 1999, Fazila Jhungoor, London, 18th December 1999; Vincent Simon, London, 16th December 1999,* all pencil and coloured pencil and gouache on paper, 56.2 x 38.1 cm each, 112.4 x 229 cm overall. Private collection

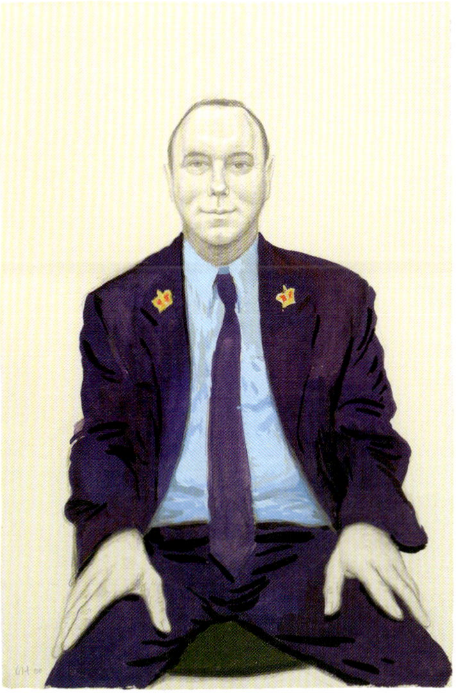
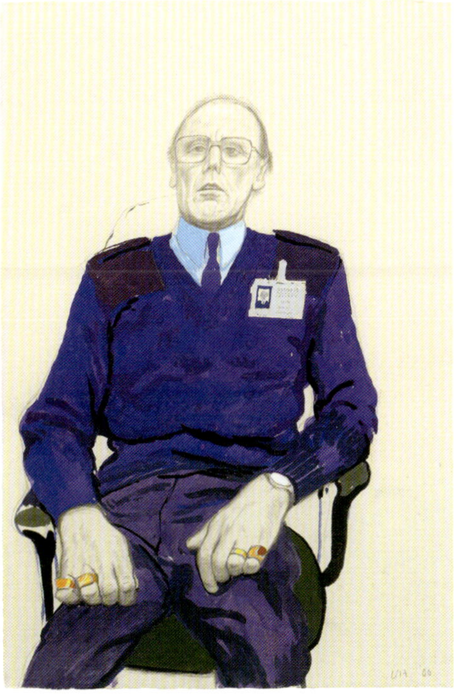
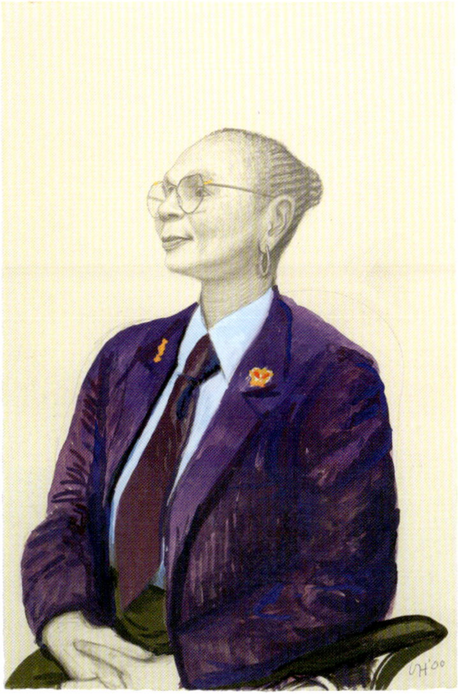
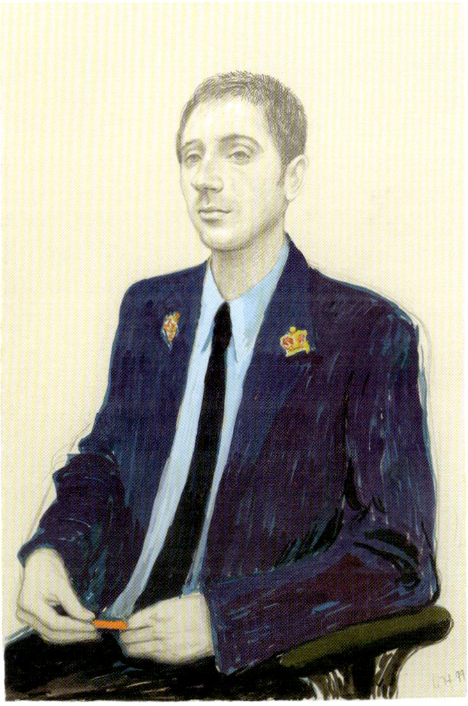
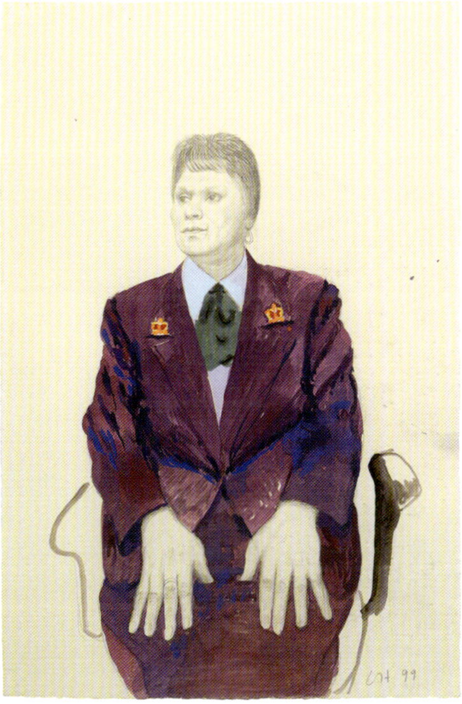
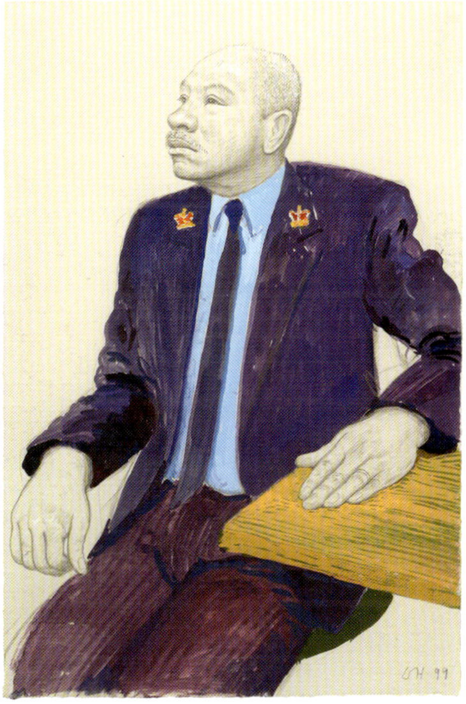

116 | F David Hockney, *Martin Gayford, 4th, 5th, 6th December 2013*, from *82 Portraits and 1 Still Life,* 2013, acrylic on canvas (one of an 82-part work), 121.9 x 91.4 cm. Collection of the artist

The subject is one of the curators of the exhibition Hockney's Eye.

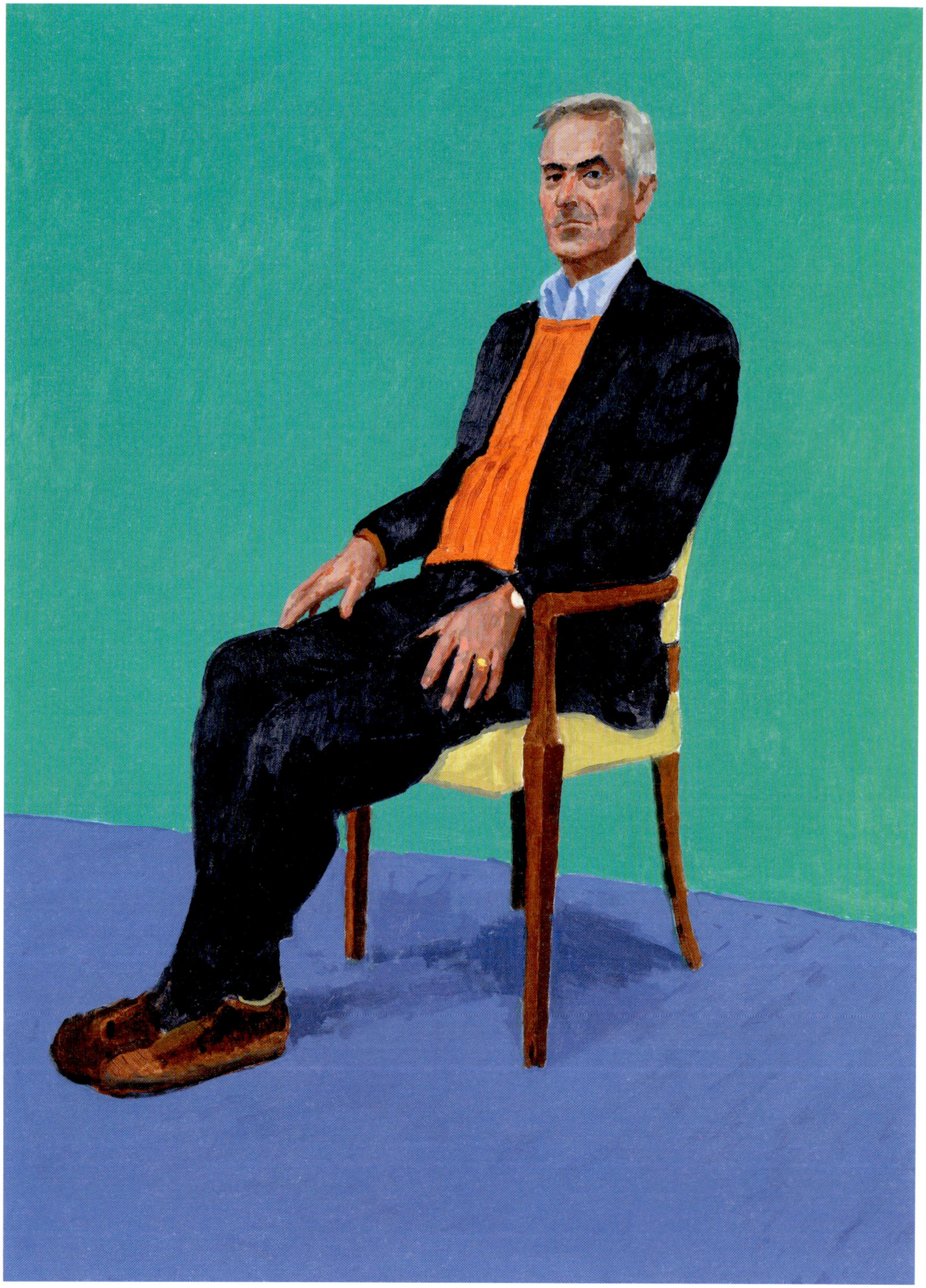

or resting on knees, chair arms or table-tops, this uniformed assembly of warders looks out more or less directly at the artist, and at us. The tilt of their heads and angle of their gaze – sometimes open, sometimes guarded – conveys a strong sense of the sitters' personalities; they have uniqueness in numbers. Instead of clutching a fashionable top hat, one holds a cup of tea, another twirls a pencil. Frock coats and voluminous bonnets are replaced by unisex regulation blazers and ties; the rosette of the Légion d'Honneur by security badges and institutional insignia. Brought together by the artist in fictive unity, each performs a distinctive role in a wordless pictorial drama. Some years later, in 2013, Hockney returned to the idea of creating variations on a theme, painting a number of otherwise unconnected friends and acquaintances in his studio in Los Angeles, in the series '82 Portraits and 1 Still Life' (fig. 116). One by one, sitters mounted a platform – literally took the stage – and, like the warders, posed in the same chair; keenly observed, their posture, body language and footwear speak as much of the Balzacian *Comédie Humaine*, the "infinite variety of human nature", as their facial features.[57]

Portraying the warders, Hockney employed resources prismatic and perceptual, psychological and artistic. "Life is born under his fingers", the paper fades away ....[58]

Notes

1 Galichon 1861a, n.p. **2** Blanc 1861, 190. **3** Shelton 2005, 233–34. **4** Blanc 1861, 190, 191. **5** Delaborde 1861, p. 265. **6** Delaborde 1870, 86. **7** Blanc 1861, 191 (my translation) "...[qui d'avance ont prouvé à la photographie que] l'art est, quant il veut, plus exacte que la science, plus précis que les mathématiques, plus pénétrant que la chimie, plus sensible que le collodion, plus subtil que la chlorure, plus clairvoyant que la lumière, plus vrai, enfin que la vérité même". **8** Degas to A. Bartolommé (no date), Guérin (1945) 1995, 133. **9** Conisbee 1999, 217. **10** Delaborde 1870, 36, n. 1. **11** Boyer d'Agen 1909, quoted in translation Conisbee 1999, 111, n. 40. **12** Lapauze 1901, quoted Ford 1939, 3. **13** Delaborde 1870, 287, 288. **14** "*entrevues tout accidentelles*": Delaborde 1870, 286. **15** Conisbee 1999, 212, under no. 72. **16** Naef 1978, 29–31. **17** Naef 1978, 26–27, fig. 1. **18** Delaborde 1970, 35–36. **19** Naef 1977, 551. **20** Naef 1978, 85–88; Hans Naef in Tinterow and Conisbee 1999–2000, 195–96. **21** See Ford 1939, 13. When making his camera lucida drawings, Hockney was aware of reports that Ingres limited the time he devoted to his portrait drawings to sittings before and after lunch: Hockney (2001) 2006, 23. **22** "On n'aime que les laides éperduement", quoted Naef 1977, 554–55. **23** Notable examples are the portraits of the family of Ingres's one-time fiancée, Julie Forestier (1806, Louvre) and the family of Lucien Bonaparte, commissioned by Mme Alexandrine Bonaparte in 1815 (Harvard Art Museums/ Fogg Art Museum). **24** Delaborde 1870, 87–88, 265. **25** De Montrond 1868, 34. **26** Hockney (2001) 2006, 12. **27** Kahn 1907, 3. **28** Kahn 1907, 1. **29** Blanc 1870, 43–44. **30** This applied notably to the use of lay figures: see Munro 2014, esp. 75–93. **31** Basil Hall in Dollond 1830, 11. **32** "époque de méchanisme", Balze 1880, 22. **33** Georges Vigne, 'Ingres and Co.: A Master and his Collaborators', in Tinterow and Conisbee 1999–2000, 523–42. Vigne referred to the anonymous artist as 'The Master of the Little Dots', 528–29. **34** Vigne in Tinterow and Conisbee 1999–2000, 526–27. **35** Quoted Cogniet 1947, 8. **36** Erna Fiorentini, 'Popularity Despite Anti-Popularization. Thinking of Optical Drawing Devices in the Early 19th Century', in Fiorentini 2021, 381–82. **37** Amici 1819, transl. *Annales* 1823, 141–42. **38** Amici, translated online at https://static1.squarespace.com/static/5a12448cd74cffd6f6b03d2f/t/5bb52c697817f707000365b8/1538600043428/GiovanniBattistaAmici_Some+advice+for+using+the+Camera+lucida+1819.pdf . Accessed 1 September 2021. **39** Dollond 1830, 7. **40** Dollond 1830, 9. **41** Amici (*Annales* 1823), 141. **42** Dollond 1830, 9–10. **43** Quoted Ford 1939, 13. **44** Impressions of the original lithograph showing the foursome are relatively rare, since the sheet was later cut to sell impressions of prints of individual sitters, as is the case with the four prints at the Fitzwilliam, all of which were acquired by John Charrington in February 1933 and given to the museum the same year. **45** Naef 1977, 554–55. **46** See Munro 1996, 13–14. **47** Quoted Gounod 1896, 301. **48** Most famously Mme Moitessier (1847, National Gallery, London); see also Prieur 2012, 41–50, 135–36. **49** The comment is made of the camera lucida in Dollond 1830, 11. **50** Lami 1882, 539. **51** Lami suggested this defect could be simply overcome by light rubbing out of the lines drawn with a camera lucida and reinforcing with a more assured and fluid pencil line (1882, 539). Hockney has suggested Ingres made a few notations on the paper to fix key aspects of the sitter's physiognomy – hair, eyes, nostrils and the edges of the mouth – then completed the face from direct observation – 'eyeballing': Hockney (2001) 2006, 29; see Martin Kemp, above, pp. 47–48. **52** Dollond 1830, 7. **53** Basil Hall and Augustin Creuze, 'Drawing and Description of the Capstan Lately Recovered from the Royal George', *The United Service Journal and Naval and Military Magazine*, Part III (1839), 376–80, quoted Fiorentini 2021, 377. **54** Fiorentini 2006, 39. **55** Hockney (2001) 2006, 133, 203. **56** Letter to the editor, *Daily Telegraph*, 28 December 2001. My thanks to Anne Lyles for drawing this letter to my attention. **57** For the 'Comédie Humaine' series see Gayford 2011, 254–69. **58** De Montrond 1868, 34.

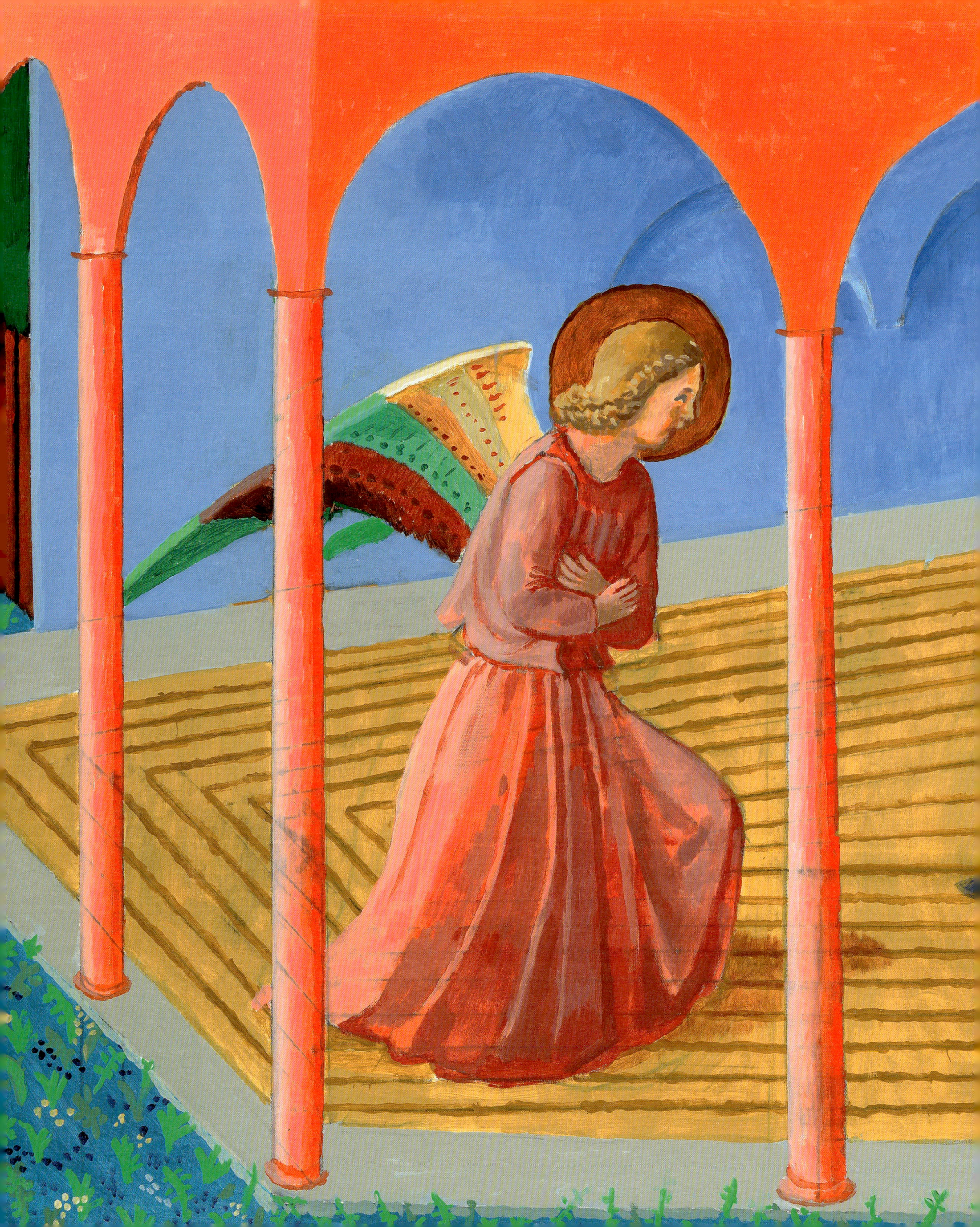

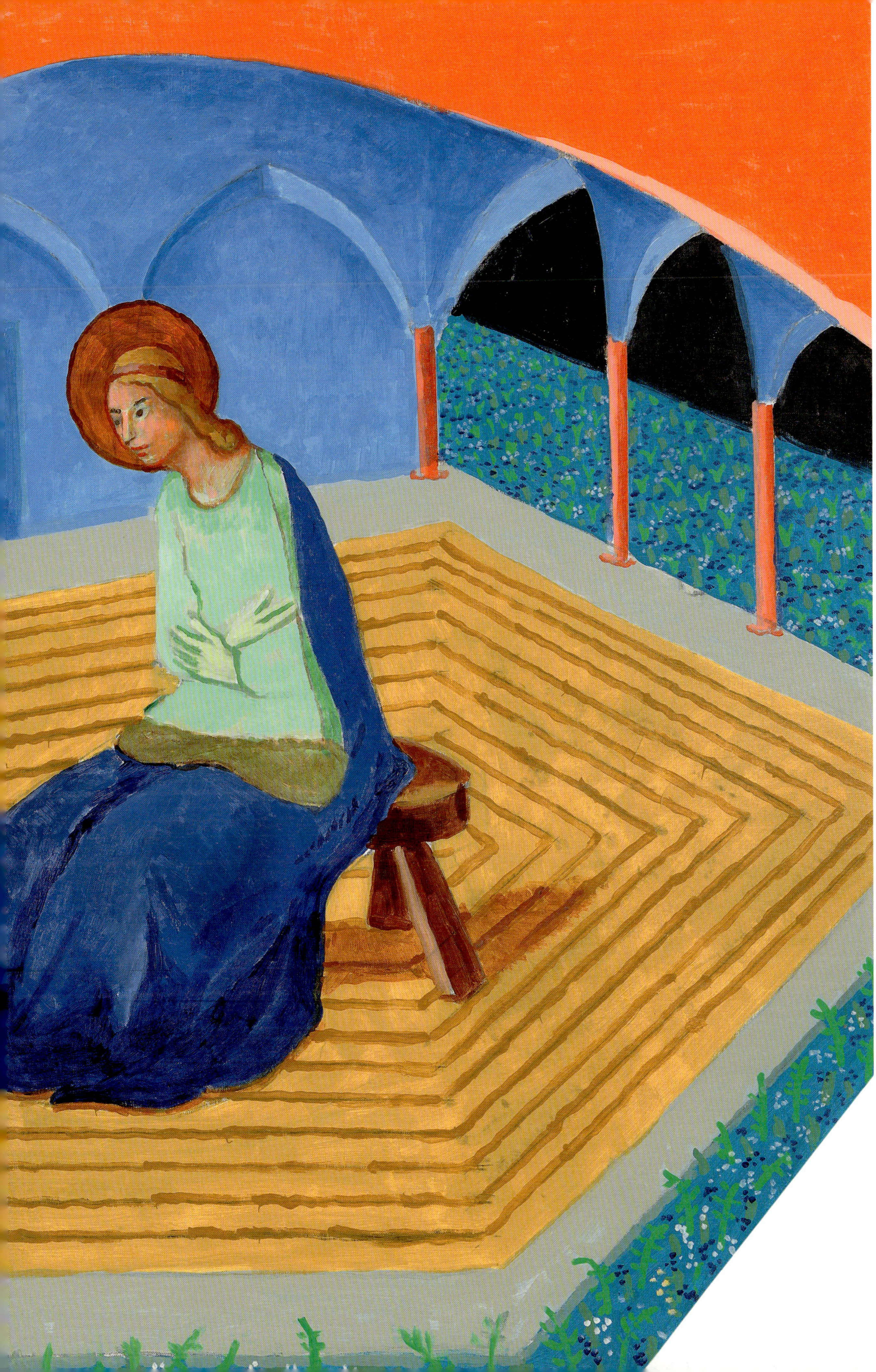

THE SCIENCE OF SEEING AND PICTURING

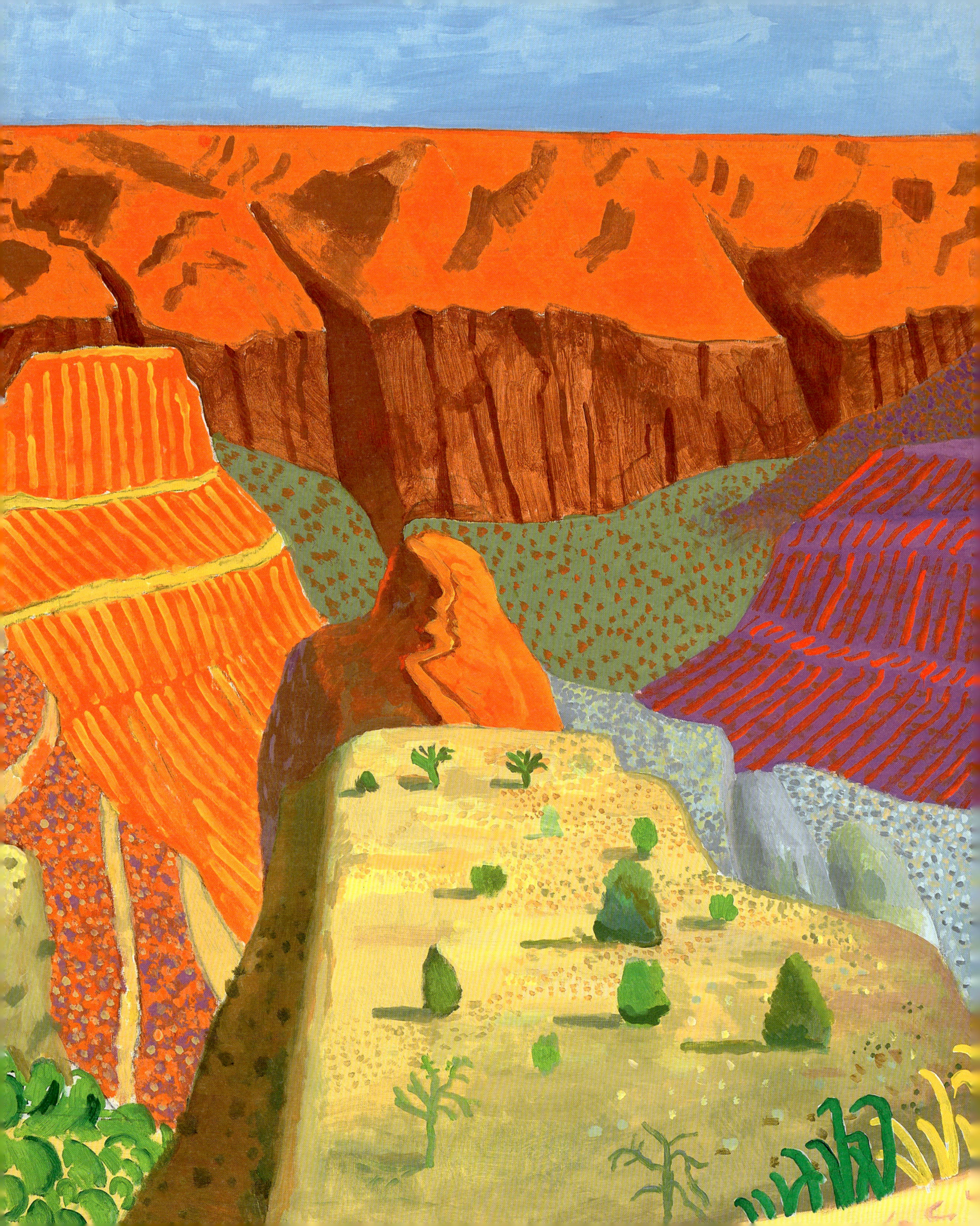

Zoe Kourtzi, Andrew Welchman and Martin Kemp

Hockney through the mind's eye

All vision is three-dimensional, that is, it depends on complex interactions between objects, illuminants and viewers that occupy different locations in space. In a remarkable way, we even vividly experience three-dimensional (3D) structures under diverse impoverished conditions, including those of the random magic-eye stereograms and the aesthetically beautiful, but objectively flat paintings viewed away from the artist's centre of perspective projection. In the stereograms, a pattern of random dots is shown to one eye, while a similar pattern with tiny variations, is shown to the other. Seen simultaneously, the variations in each eye are improbably merged into a single image in which 3D forms are apparently present. In all this, our sensory apparatus (the eye) samples the surrounding environment by projecting it into a lower dimensional measurement space, resulting in a puzzling question: how can we estimate the 3D world using a 2D projection on to the retina?

The answer to this question may appear straightforward: we have two eyes and we can triangulate the true depth of an object from the subtle differences in positions registered on the two retinae (binocular disparity). Disparity can be used to infer 3D structure, break camouflage,[1] estimate surface reflectance,[2] or control grasping.[3] In addition, we have access to a range of visual signals related to depth (e.g. perspective, shading) that in isolation or combination give rise to an impression of 3D structure. Thus, perhaps the answer to the challenge of perceiving three dimensions is trivial: a rich natural world gives us more than enough information to resolve ambiguity and explain our impression of depth.

Yet, this solution poses a challenge to the neurons of the brain, which will have to deal with two main sources of uncertainty when interpreting the 3D world: first, the mapping from the world to the senses is incomplete and ambiguous, so the same sensory events can be compatible with multiple physical events; and second, sensory events are subject to stochastic (random) noise: look at the same object twice and your brain will register slightly different information. So, how does the brain translate locally ambiguous signals to the perception of 3D surfaces and objects?

To understand how the brain performs this complex inverse inference (i.e. perceiving the most likely state of the world from incomplete and randomly varying signals) we need to think about a number of different pieces of information: what is the input to the system, how is it encoded and represented, what does our brain already know about the structure of the environment, and what are the costs/benefits of a particular interpretation or decision. Bayesian statistics provide a useful way of answering these questions by quantifying probabilities to estimate the (unknowable) state of the world. For instance, first, given the current image I am viewing, what is the most likely object to have produced it (known as 'the posterior')? To calculate this conditional probability, we can combine things that we could have established from past experience. Second, what is the probability of encountering the object in the first place (known as 'the prior') and third, given a particular object, what is the probability

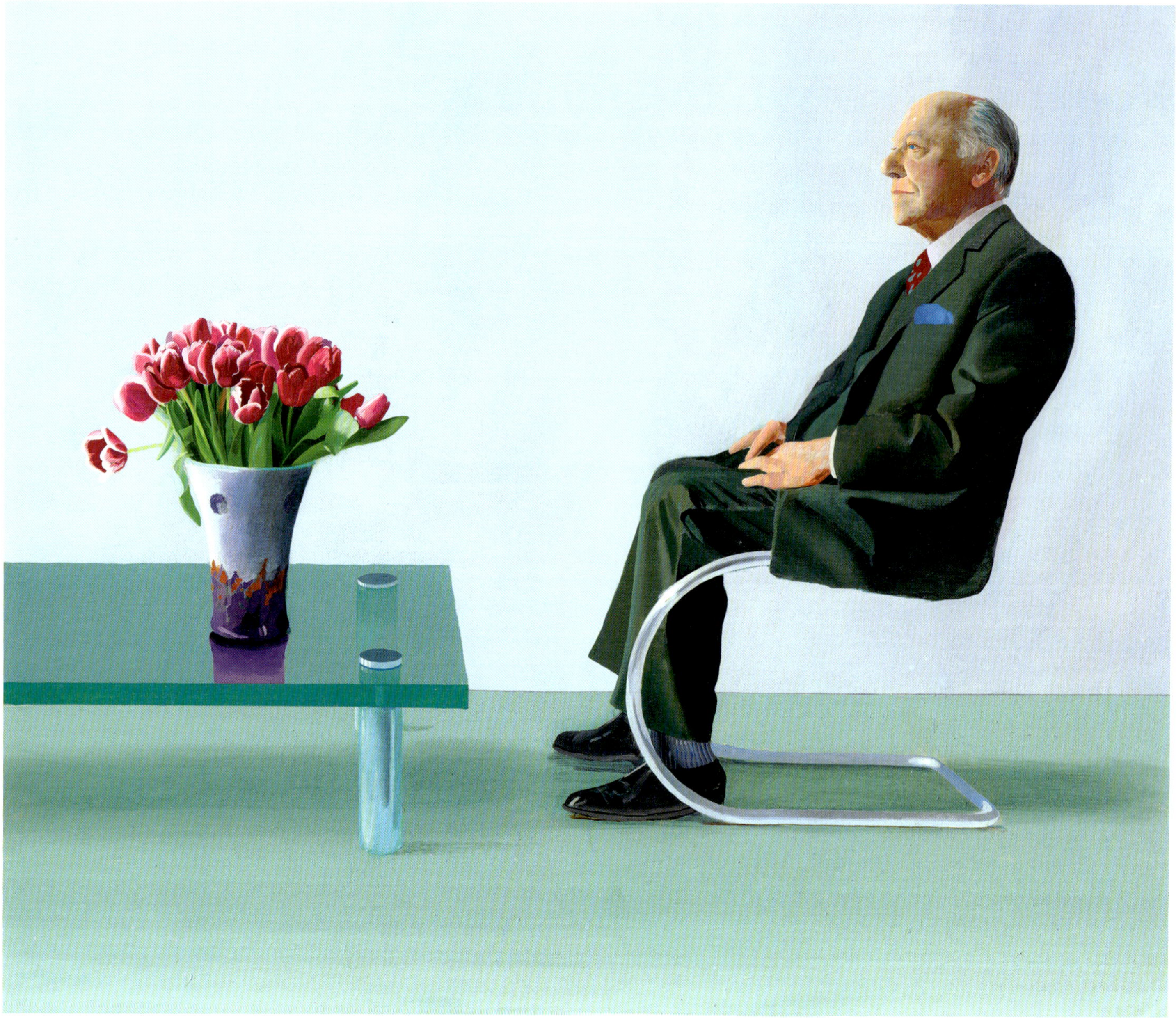

117 | F David Hockney, *Portrait of Sir David Webster*, 1971, acrylic on canvas, 144.8 x 182.9 cm. Ross Foundation

of producing the current image (known as 'the likelihood').

We consider how the brain interprets 3D environments from flat shaded images — as in Hockney's paintings — within this Bayesian framework. The images that are registered by our eyes depend on three principal elements: (i) the position of the viewer, (ii) the position and properties of the object, and (iii) the position and properties of the light source. When thinking about the properties of the object, we need to consider two main elements, (a) what is the 3D shape (or more technically, the orientation of the surface normals at each point on the surface of the object) and (b) how does light get reflected by the object (technically, the surface albedo): does it scatter in all directions as happens with a matte object (e.g. chalk) or does more light get reflected in particular direction, as happens with glossy objects (e.g. metal kettles and brass doorknobs). The image registered by the eye is the result of the combination of all of these factors – how could the brain have any chance of unpicking them? The single measurement confounds

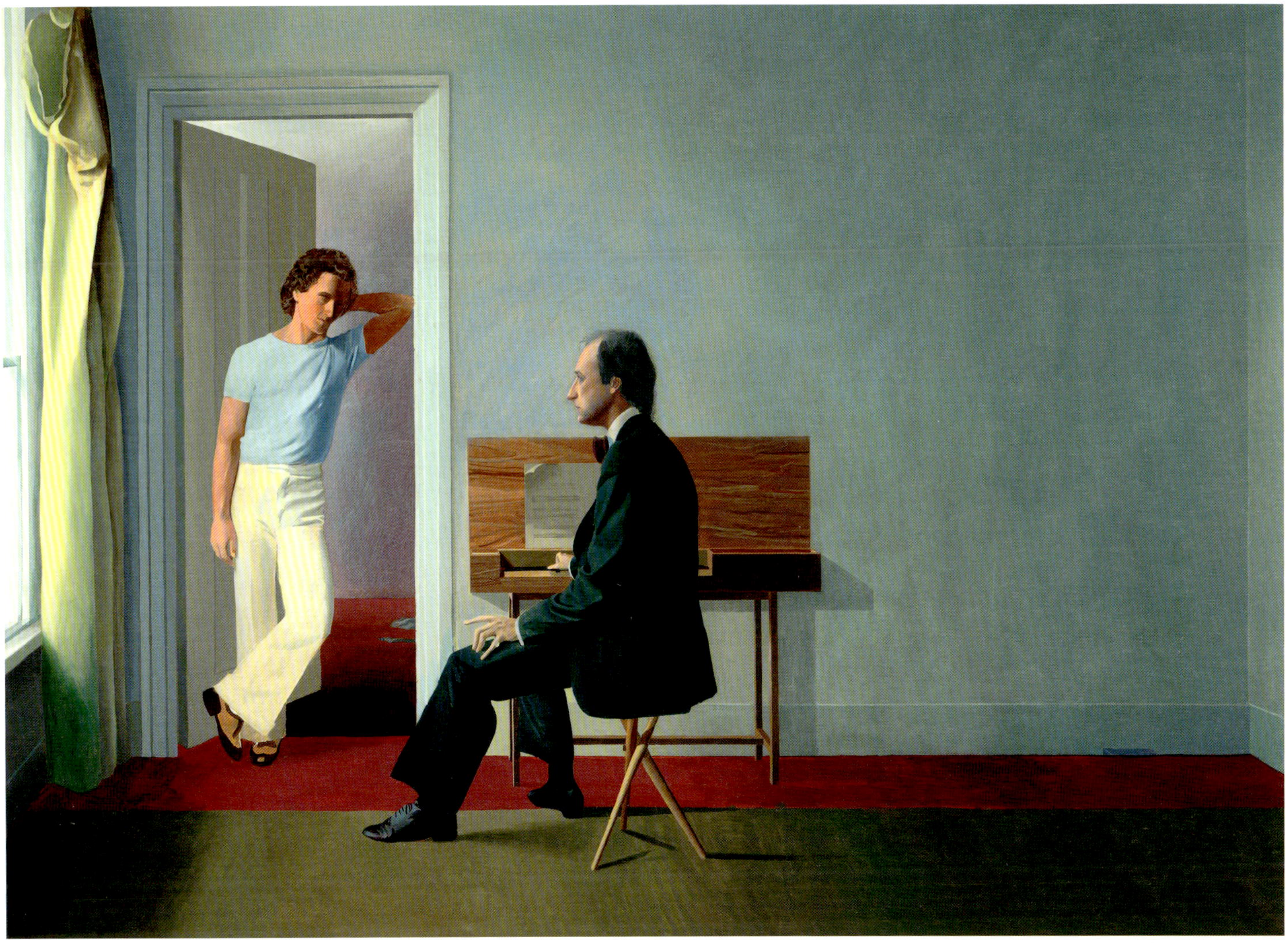

118 David Hockney, *George Lawson and Wayne Sleep*, 1972–75, acrylic on canvas, 203 x 304 cm. Tate, T14098

information about the illuminant, the surface material and the surface orientation. The task of recovering the shape of an object from variations of image intensity (i.e. shading) is strongly underconstrained.[4] Empirically, our interpretation of a shaded image can be ambiguous – for instance, inverting a shaded pattern often leads to a change in the interpretation of the 3D shape. For example, there are some apocryphal stories about NASA scientists finding mountains on the surface of the moon on which to site probes, only to find they were craters. There is evidence that some animals have countershading (i.e. lighter surfaces on their lower parts) to camouflage themselves.

We can think about shading patterns as providing ambiguous likelihood information, that is constrained with the help of prior knowledge. In this case, the brain appears to employ a prior assumption that scenes are lit from above. More particularly, the direction of assumed lighting appears to be slightly to the left,[5] which might relate to the way in which we routinely orient ourselves to light sources. This perceptual assumption appears to be something that painters have incorporated into their work since the fifteenth century.[6] Prior information about the light source direction seems to be something that is entrenched into visual systems. For instance, Wayne Hershberger conducted a classic study on chicks raised in a light-from-below environment.[7] He found they interpreted shading patterns as if lit from above, suggesting that light-source direction was hardwired and, perhaps, inflexible. Yet recent work has questioned the inflexibility of priors, showing that light-from-above assumptions

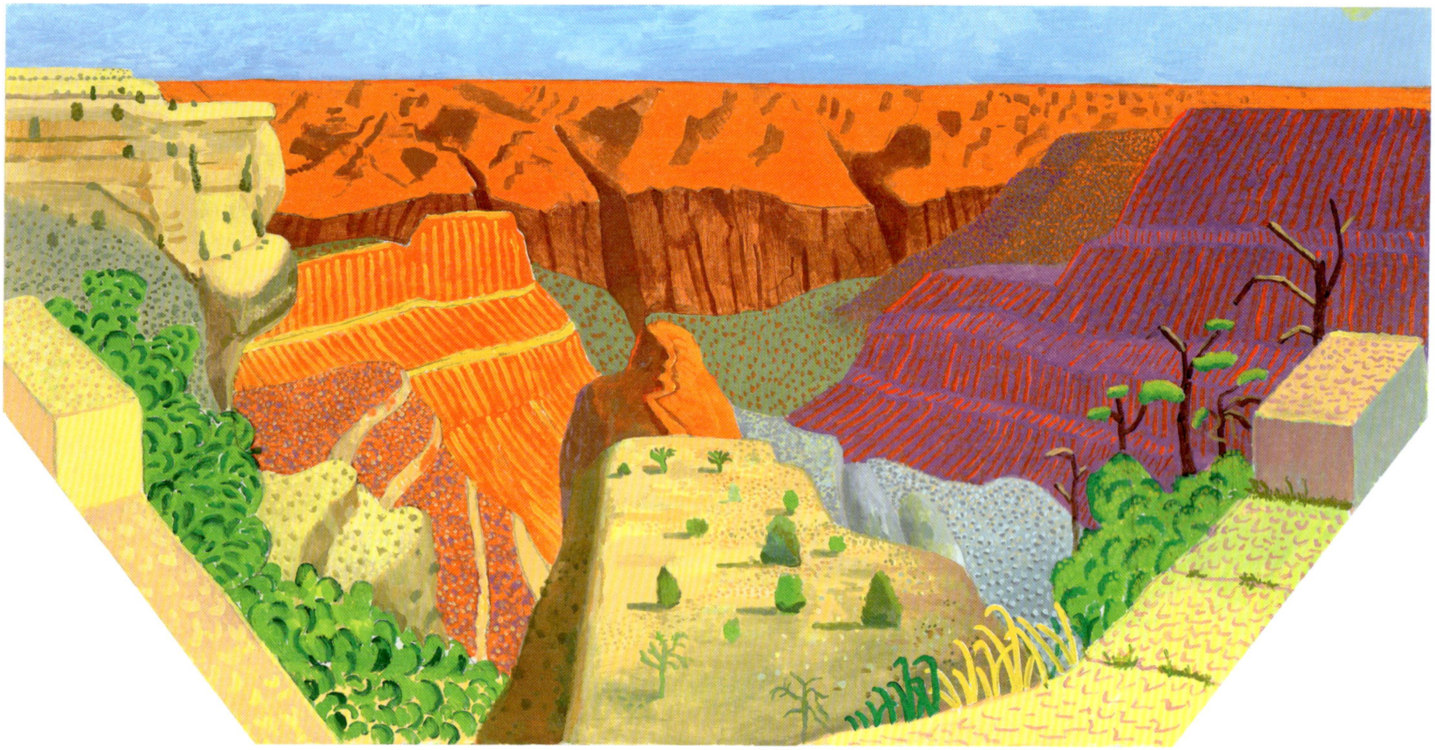

119 | H David Hockney, *Grand Canyon I*, 2017, acrylic on canvas, 121.9 x 243.8 cm (hexagonal). Collection of the artist

were modified by haptic feedback about the 3D shape of objects.[8]

To see Hockney's paintings through the lens of the brain rather than simply the eye – this requires our brains to transform incomplete and randomly varying signals to the most likely state of the 3D world. Perhaps even more impressive is that it does this in a way that can rapidly adapt to new knowledge and changes in the environment. This flexibility in solving the inverse inference problem is something that many computer systems struggle to achieve. Yet human perception *is* remarkably flexible. We inhabit a world of illuminated physical objects. The visual system is tasked with appreciating the properties of these objects from a distance so that we might move among them and engage with them. It tackles this challenge by capitalizing on knowledge that we have built up from previous experience that alters what we perceive. This adaptive process underlies not only our skills in navigating in new environments and interacting with objects but also our engagement with works of art.

Given the extraordinary complexity, flexibility, agility, adaptability and potential ambiguity of how we see and make visual sense of the myriad spatial clues that bombard our eye and mind, we may say that orthodox linear perspective as rejected by Hockney acts radically to stabilize our acts of seeing in a way that plays selectively towards certain key features in our perception of space (see figs. 22 and 49).

We have noted the most important of the parameters that govern our perception of objects in space: the position and orientation of the object; the position of the viewer in relation to the object, and the position and nature of the light source. In painting and photography, we have to add the relative position of the 'window' (or plane) through which we look at the object and on which we portray it. These parameters comprise the fundamentals for expositions of perspective in the many handbooks for artists.

As we have seen, light is generally characterized as coming from above the subject and to the left. Such acts of radical stabilization in perspective pictures were grist to mill of the classic and much-loved Hockneys of the 1960s and early 1970s. We see this in the *Portrait of Sir David Webster* (fig. 117), although in the famous painting of *Mr and Mrs Clark and Percy*, the two designers and their dignified cat are

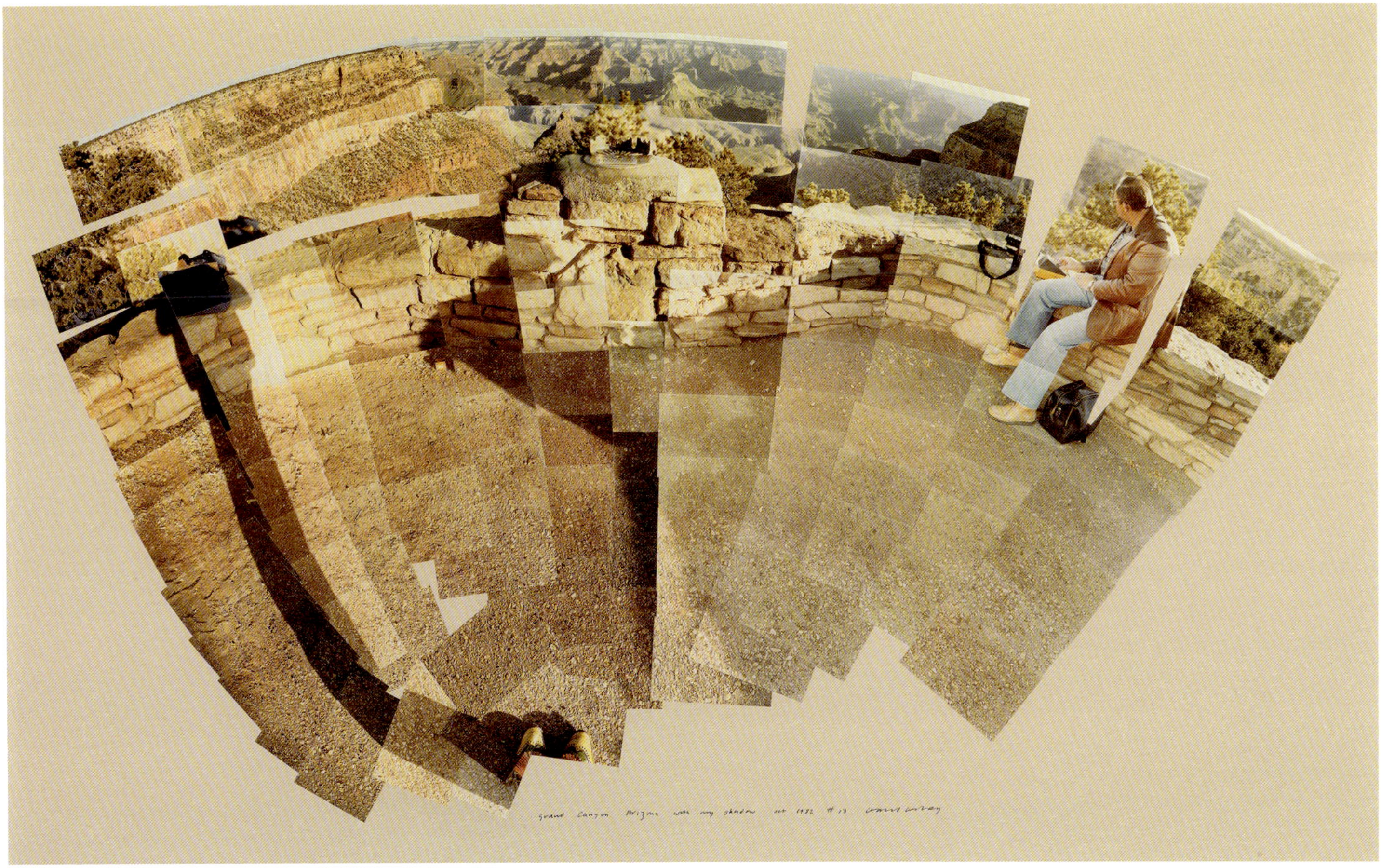

lit unusually from a centrally placed window. Hockney's growing disillusionment with standard perspective came with the double portrait *George Lawson and Wayne Sleep* (fig. 118), begun in 1972 but abandoned three years later as he became disillusioned with his mastery of naturalistic techniques.

If perspective is not the dominant optical rule to be followed, other graded signals of pictorial depth come into more prominent play. There are texture gradients, in which the texture of a surface gradually becomes less evident as it moves away from the viewer. There are related gradients of detail, in which (say) the individual leaves in a tree become less discernible at greater distances. There is also colour perspective, according to which separately coloured surfaces lose their distinctness. And there is aerial or atmospheric perspective in which moisture in the air progressively veils objects. These graded signals are notable features of Chinese scrolls, much admired by Hockney for their non-perspectival vision of foreground and distant spaces. His landscapes (figs. 56, 134–40) richly exploit a variety of non-linear ways of constructing depth.

Over the course of the visual journey taken by Hockney from the time he lost confidence in standard perspective, he has explored in an extraordinary way a variety of perceptual modes and instabilities – or perhaps it is better to call them dynamic physical and perceptual dimensions. The relationship between sensory events and physical events becomes a matter of 'feeling' the forms, spaces and colours under the scrutiny of our mobile eyes and subject to our mobility as a spectator. The 'joiners' (figs. 25–27) rely upon a series of perceptual 'shots' with cameras over intervals of time that we mentally assemble into a coherent image. He exploits vertiginous instabilities in his images of the Grand Canyon and Garrowby Hill (figs. 119, 120 and 121). The colonnade of the *Hotel Acatlan* (fig. 122) takes us on a merry perceptual dance in time and motion rather than static depiction.

120 | H David Hockney, *Grand Canyon Arizona with my Shadow, October 1982*, 1982, photographic collage, edition 13 of 15, 96.5 x 158.8 cm. Collection of the artist

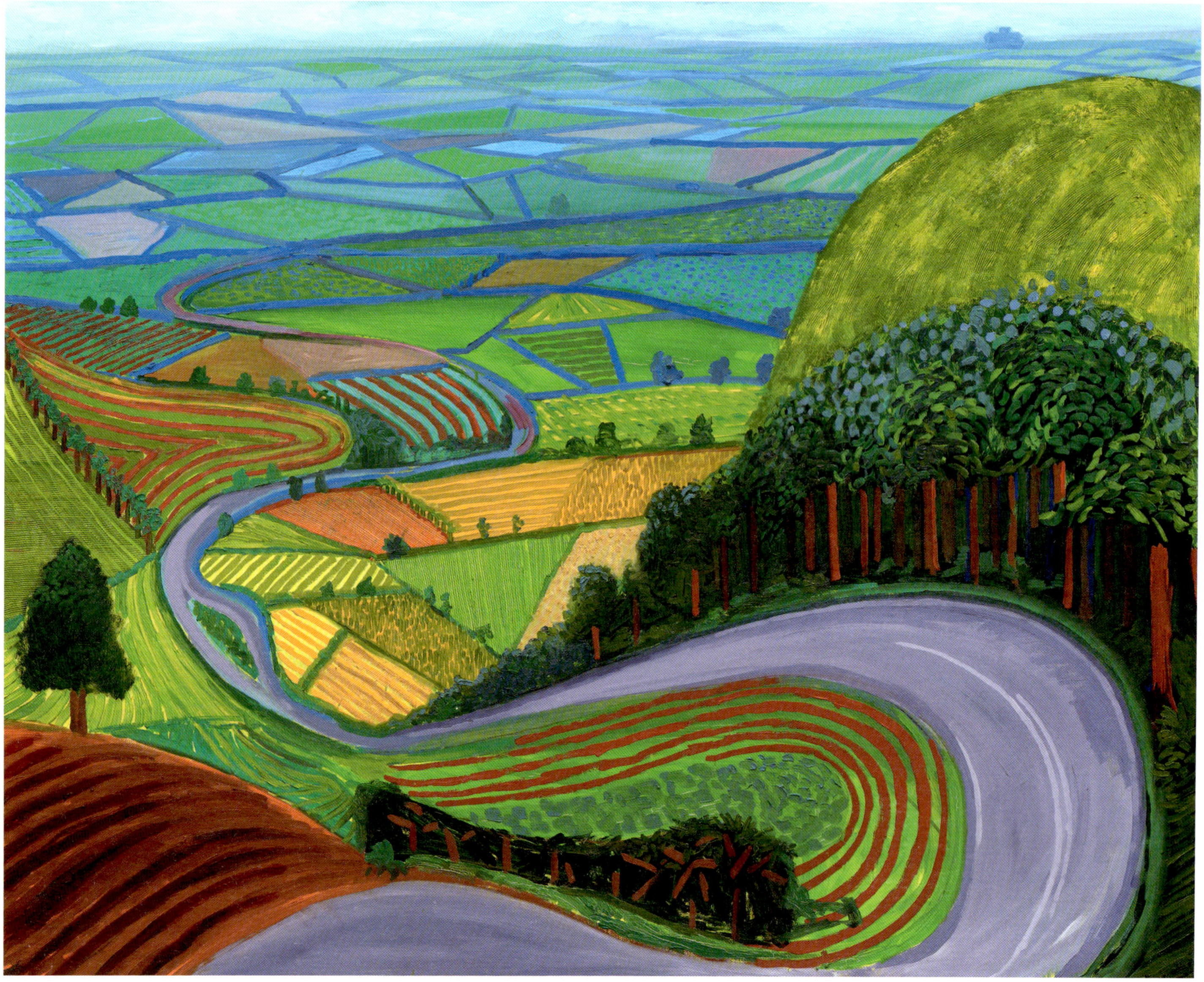

121 David Hockney, *Garrowby Hill*, 1998, oil on canvas, 152.4 x 193 cm. Museum of Fine Arts, Boston, 1998.56

The crucial factor of *knowing* (or thinking we are knowing) what we are looking at is exploited brilliantly by the economical painterly and graphic marks with which Hockney summons up the existence of (say) a shiny surface (figs. 20, 38, 124, 137). Like Chardin, whom he greatly admires, a judiciously placed comma of impasted white can transform a matt object into a glossy one – without *describing* the surface as more generally shiny. If we look at the details in Hockney's iPad images, we witness the extraordinary brevity and facility of the artist's mark-making in which details only become visually coherent in the context of our assumption about what the total image represents. If the stripes on his cap, resting on a wooden shelf (fig. 123) were to be viewed in detail and in isolation, they would not be coherent. The minimal description of veins on a leaf and the stamens of a lily work brilliantly in concert, but only because we operate with the context of our knowing overall what we are looking at (fig. 124). We perform the same visual operation of the 'beholder's share' on all the iPad images. They achieve the paradox of being both rich in painterly vigour and impoverished in their degree of actual description.

Any representation of the "visible world" (a favoured phrase of the artist) is on the face

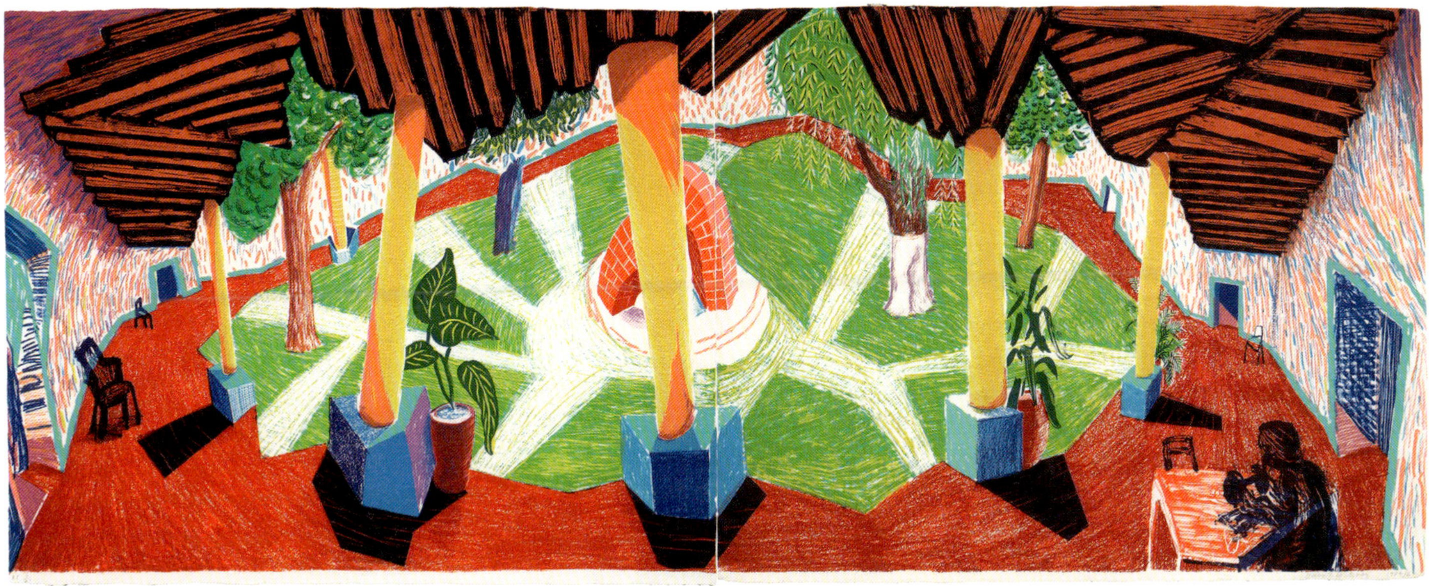

122 David Hockney, *Hotel Acatlan: Two Weeks Later*, 1985, lithograph on paper, edition of 98, 73 x 188 cm. (Pictured: A.P. I from the Collection of the David Hockney Foundation)

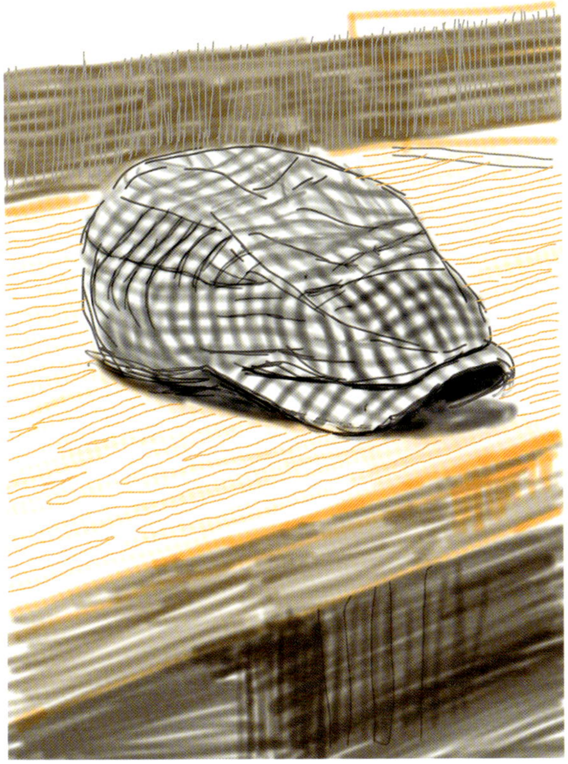

123 | H David Hockney, *12th November 2010,* iPad drawing. Collection of the artist

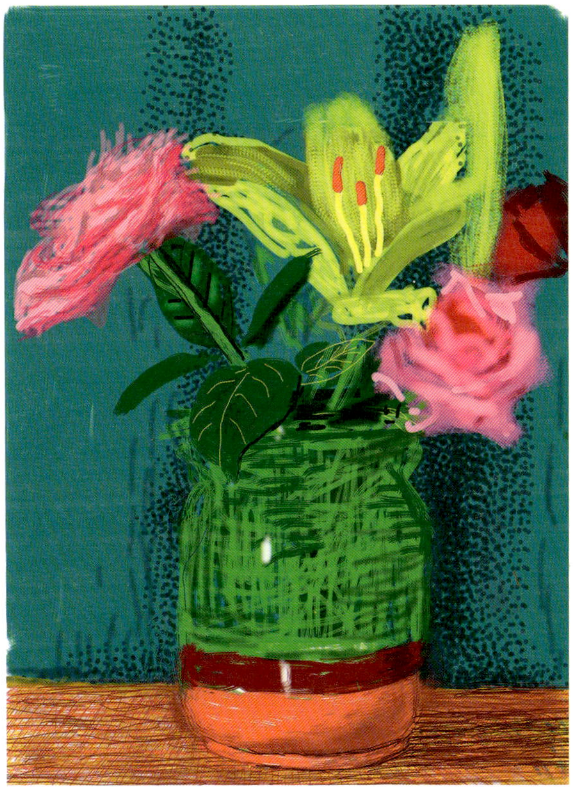

124 | F David Hockney, *14th July 2010,* iPad drawing. Collection of the artist

of it absurdly impoverished compared to the real space, real light and real colour of the real thing – not to mention binocular vision and the mobility of the spectator's eyes. Yet somehow, by dropping carefully calibrated visual clues, artists have learnt how to transcend their limitations. What Hockney has done is to eschew one or more of the standard and time-honoured clues that allow the stable management of space and light in pictures. He has replaced them with vibrantly colourful forms that surge in spatial and temporal dimensions, playing to various kinds of perception.

Testimony that Hockney has been exploring a visual territory simultaneously occupied by neuroscientists of vision is his relationship to Sir Colin Blakemore, whom the painter visited in Los Angeles in 2017. One of Blakemore's concerns has been how our perception of depth and size from perspective clues can be misleading. This misperception was music to Hockney's ears. The distinguished brain scientist has also been looking at how we assemble a coherent perception of space from a series of scattered visual 'shots' of a dynamic kind, a procedure that resonates with Hockney's desire to escape from the 'prison' of static, monocular perspective. Blakemore has been leading a wide-ranging project on 'Rethinking the Senses: Uniting the Philosophy and Neuroscience of Perception', which is studying sight in the context of the all the faculties of the brain, an agenda that is much in line with Hockney's insistence that our perception of space is not just a matter of the geometry of optics in isolation. Not the least result of the interchange was the striking portrait of Blakemore (fig. 125).

Our juxtaposition of Hockney's painted spaces with the sciences of seeing raises the fundamental question, do representations on flat surfaces correspond with how we see things in nature? Yes and no – an answer that signals that it is not the right question. What is happening is that a pictorial representation plays selectively towards one or more of a series of perceptual acts in such a way that the pictorial elements somehow serve as surrogates for seeing the real stimuli. It is a very peculiar ability, which relies upon us recognizing the game that is being played. It relies heavily on our adaptive skills in navigating in new environments and interacting with objects in relation to the comprehensive expectations that we have built up from previous experience. As far as painting is concerned, Hockney has invited us to participate in new visual games with a new rule-book.

Notes

1 Babington-Smith 1958. **2** Blake and Bulthoff 1990. **3** Watt and Bradshaw 2002. **4** Horn 1977. **5** Mamassian and Goutcher 2001, B1–B9. **6** Mamassian 2008, 2143–53. **7** Hershberger 1970, 407–11. 1970, 407–11. **8** Adams *et al*. 2004, 1057–58.

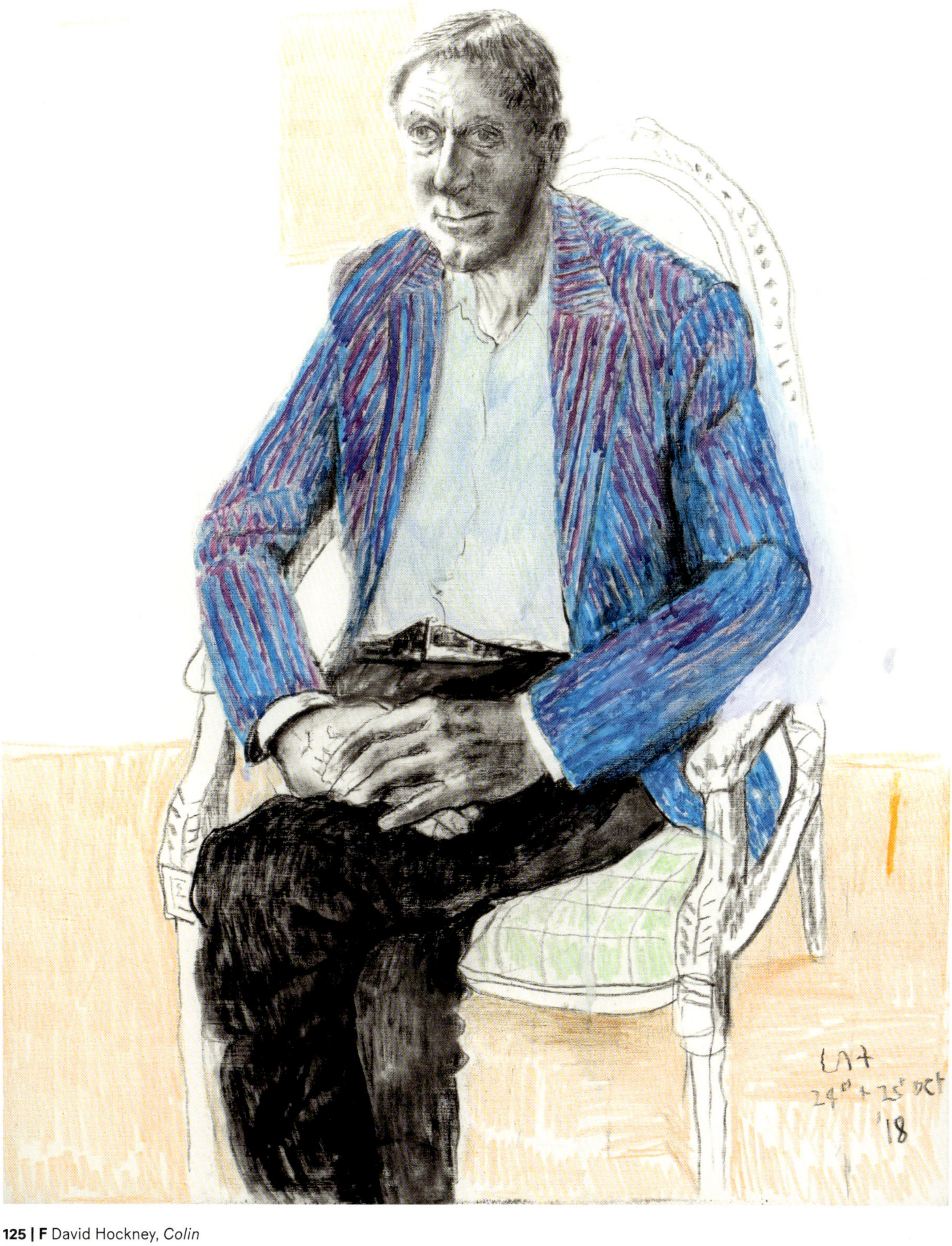

125 | F David Hockney, *Colin Blakemore*, 2018, charcoal and crayon on canvas, 122 x 91.5 cm. Private collection

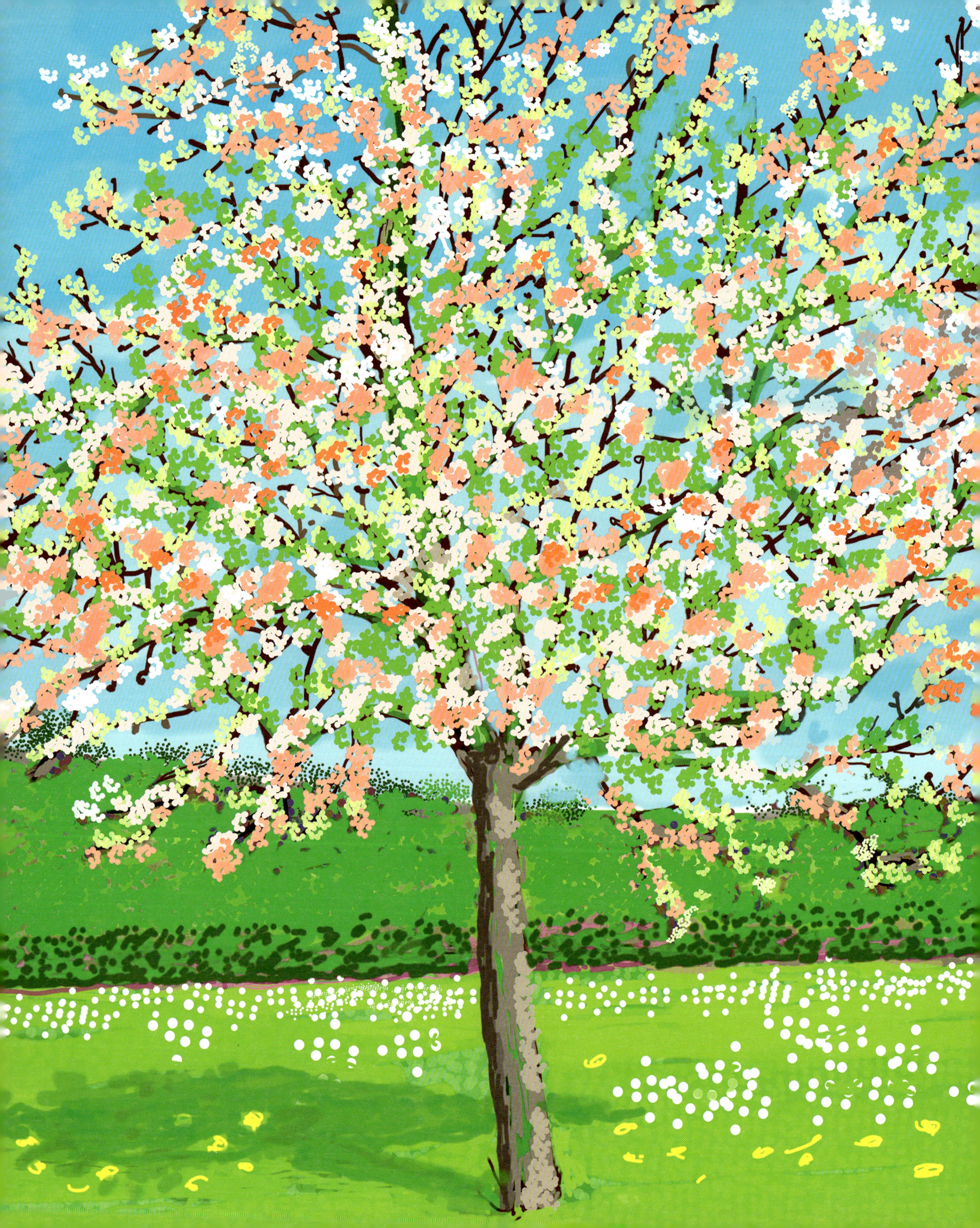

Anya Hurlbert

Colour in the mind of Hockney

David Hockney's 2021 show *The Arrival of Spring* at the Royal Academy might just as well have been called 'The Arrival of Green'. Green shouts, shoots and sprouts out from the walls. The effect is invigorating and provocative, both reaffirming and challenging the place of green in the natural world. And, as always from Hockney, there is a challenge to the way people see, and what seeing is all about. As art has done for centuries, Hockney's work embodies an implicit understanding of how human vision works, how the eye and brain transmute light from the real world into concepts, emotions and actions. His pictures distill from the retinal display the essential elements that arouse feeling, make meaning, and in turn drive behaviour. In his series 'The Arrival of Spring', Hockney captures the specialness of green, both in terms of its unique position in the science of colour vision and in its problematic history in art and symbolism.

There is also a trajectory in Hockney's relationship with light that naturally ends up in his iPad paintings, and parallels the evolution of the understanding, in science, of how light affects not only human perception but also mood and behaviour. In his earlier works, light is an incidental necessity; without it, there would be nothing to see, but it is only the things he sees that he paints, not the light itself. Then, as Hockney says of *The Room, Tarzana* (1967), "I realized the light in the room was a subject and for the first time it became an interesting thing for me, the light".[1] Now, even as neuroscience is discovering the importance of the brain's response to light itself, not just the surfaces it illuminates, Hockney is not only painting light on surfaces, but painting with light on tablets.

Getting the greens

In nature, green is a background colour. It is grass, or foliage, or moss, or algae, the colour of organic material that covers large areas, the colour of things in which the individual pieces – the blades, stalks or leaves – are less significant than the mass they make. The human visual system evolved its particular light-sensing equipment – its trichromatic retina – in order to distinguish better the fruits and flowers that are generally redder or yellower – and more edible – than their background greens.[2] Yet, in 'The Arrival of Spring', green is no mere backdrop. Green not only arrives, but refuses to surrender, going heartily into conflict. When pinks or purples intrude, as they do in the irises of *27th April 2020, No. 2*, the contrast is all the more shocking (fig. 126).

In painting, green is a challenging colour. Before the nineteenth century, pigments that produced pure greens were unstable (natural verdigris and copper resinate) or weak in effect (malachite) and mixtures that made green were complicated to control; later pigments were poisonous (copper arsenic and copper aceto-arsenite, the brilliant 'emerald green'); and it was not until the late nineteenth century that viridian (hydrated chromic oxide) gave the Impressionists a green to love.[3] Modern pigments offer more varied greens, yet also more varied toxicity warnings.

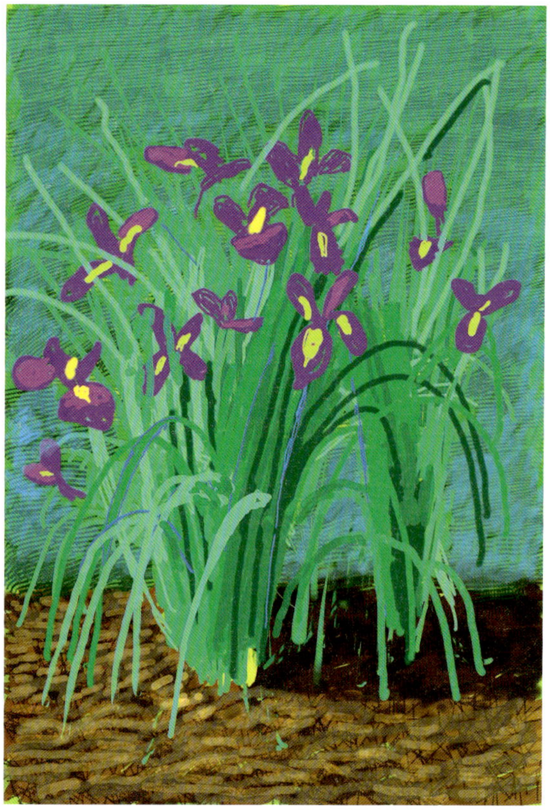

126 David Hockney, *27th April 2020, No. 2*, iPad painting. Collection of the artist

In using an iPad to paint green, Hockney goes beyond what can be done with pigments. His greens – and there are many – are made directly from light, emitted, not reflected; additive mixtures, not subtractive. And in generating a multiplicity of greens, he evokes its multiform meanings.

Hockney says of the preponderance of green in his show:

That's what I'm doing all the time, getting greens. I mean, the green of the spring is a luscious fresh green that's gone by about June really, but April and May have this very, very fresh green and need a few greens, you've got to use a few greens. It's a difficult colour but we can see more greens than any other colour.[4]

Seeing and feeling green

People have strong feelings about colour. These might arise in part from associations of colours with objects which directly arouse feelings: on average, people's preferences for colour parallel their preferences for similarly coloured objects, at least in Western societies.[5] This parallel makes sense because colour vision is tied to the perception of objects: colour vision evolved in humans to help them mark out boundaries of objects and assess their material properties. Yet most colours are associated with more than one object, and not all will arouse the same type of affective response. Deep red in a strawberry attracts; in a toadstool, it repels. Chocolate brown, or excrement? Blue sky, or mouldy bread? In industrialised societies, the tumult of manufactured colour – in clothing, packaging, furnishing, personal products, gadgets – has severed the natural connection between colour and object, but not the natural connection between colour and emotion. Instead, the proliferation of colour has amplified that connection, extending its reach across everyday activities.

A cross-cultural analysis of colour language suggests that people use warm colour names (reds, yellows, oranges, browns) more efficiently and precisely than cool colour names (blues, greens). Correspondingly, warm colour names go to objects, and cool colour names to backgrounds.[6] One might think that green, being a background colour against which objects stand out, would therefore also fade into emotional insignificance. Not so. Green arouses strong feelings too. The critic Mark Hudson writes a little peevishly about the "frigid, synthetic glow" of greens in Hockney's show *The Arrival of Spring*.[7] Their hues are "acidic, near-fluorescent" rather than "exhilarating, zinging" as they are in nature. Whether it is their unnatural foregrounding, atypical indoor context, or the basic colorimetric attributes of these greens that excite this individual, the point is that his feelings are aroused.

The fact that many of Hockney's greens do seem bright is a mark of his control and skill, as well as a demonstration of fundamental features of colour perception. To capture the luminosity of the greens in the real world, Hockney calls on colourfulness and contrast, with consummate painter's insight.

To reproduce the dynamic range of real-world light on a pigmented surface is a fundamental problem with which painters have long wrestled. Hockney's decision to make paintings on iPads – emissive displays – and then to print them

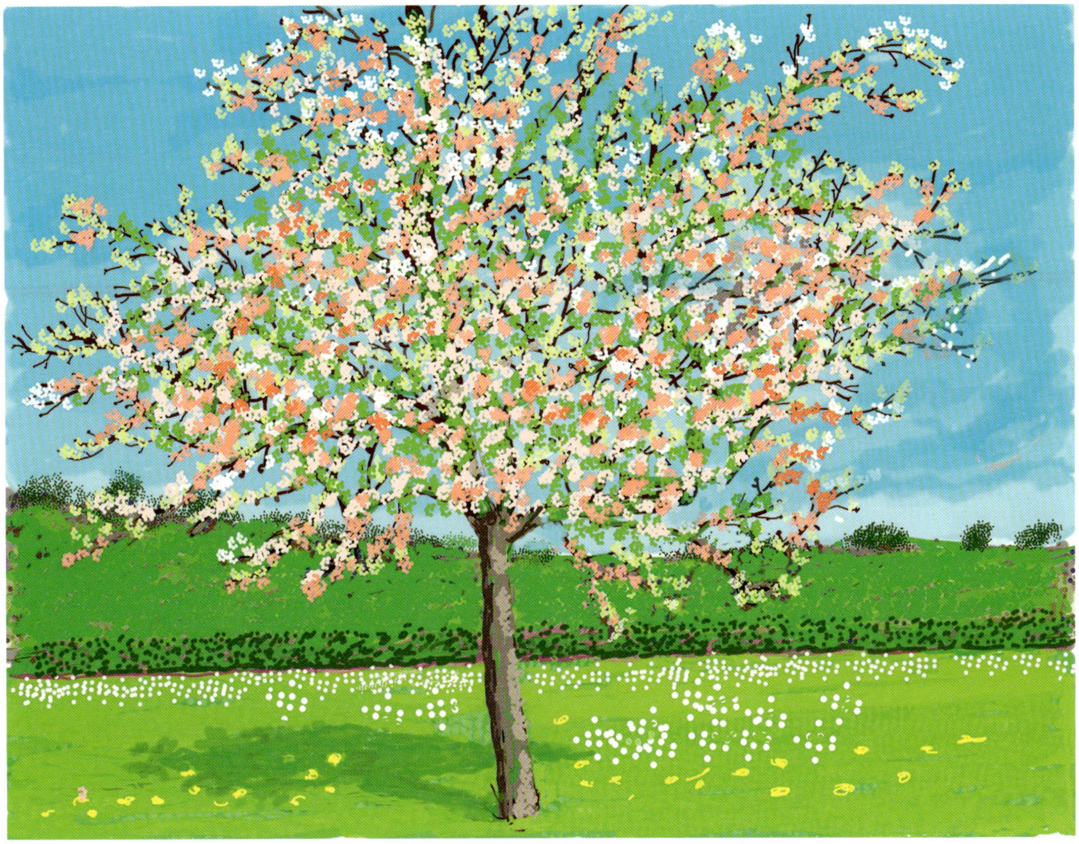

127 | F David Hockney, *20th April 2020, No. 1*, iPad painting. Collection of the artist

for permanent show reveals his fascination not only with light but also his thrill with a technical challenge. Light levels in a natural scene, with direct sunlight and shadow, might range over 10,000 levels, from darkest to brightest. A high-end tablet or computer screen can display only about 1000 levels. But, in print, that range drops by 10-fold again, to around 100:1. Yet even when printed, and now reflecting rather than emitting light, the iPad paintings retain a luminosity that put their surroundings in the shade.

As Hockney sat before the real scene, his eyes took in vast range of brightnesses, and he adapted – both conventionally, and unconventionally. Just as any human visual system would, his adapted to incoming light signals via hard-wired mechanisms that continually adjusted the sensitivity of his retinal photoreceptors to the incoming light levels. Visual adaptation translates absolute levels into relative levels, the contrasts between light and shade. Yet, through his perceptual and artistic skill, Hockney further adapts natural contrasts into painted contrasts that evoke the feeling of the absolute brilliance of the outdoors, despite the limitations of print. That he does so in a double conversion, from natural light to iPad light to print, requires both diligent oversight of the final printing process – which Hockney exercises – as well as foresight during the creation. The brightness ratio between the sunlit and shadowed areas of lawn in *20th April 2020, No. 1* is around 1.2–1.5 in print, not atypical of shadows outdoors (fig. 127).

Why, then, if the brightness contrasts are not unnatural, do the greens glow so in the show? Here is where Hockney draws on fundamental features of colour perception. The human visual system sometimes confounds colourfulness with brightness; the more chromatic a colour, the brighter it might seem. The extent of this effect (the Helmholtz-Kohlrausch effect) varies between hues, but its impact is often felt. Hockney's greens, in 'The Arrival of Spring', are often more chromatic than greens in nature. Their colourfulness enhances their salience, conferring an impact that might feel like luminescence. In our memories too, we oversaturate the colours

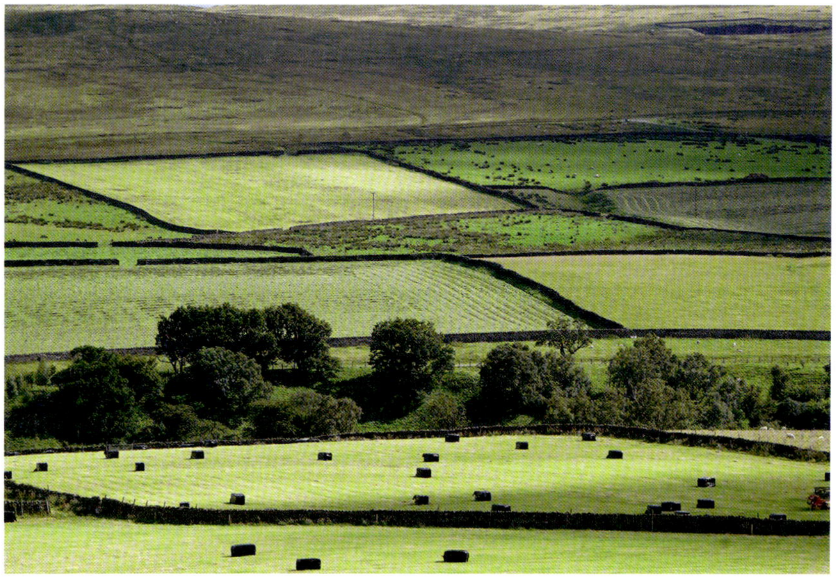

128 Greens in County Durham, July 2020

of familiar objects. For objects with diagnostic colours, such as bananas or strawberries, and even in other more abstract tests in the laboratory, it has been shown that people tend to remember colours as richer – more chromatic – than they actually are. Thus, although Hockney's greens might be more chromatic than in nature, they powerfully resonate with our memory of natural greens.

As Martin Gayford observes,[8] Hockney thinks about colour in terms of physical things, objects in nature. Hockney looks at things, sees their colours, and abstracts and transforms these into digital RGB values or pigment on paper. Averse to the naturalistic trap, or photographic reproduction, Hockney strives instead to recreate the psychological impact of what he perceives. Then he talks of the physical thing that is the artwork itself, which holds the colours that last:

You always have to print things out, I think. Things on a computer can be lost: if you print them out, they're solid things in this world.[9]

Printing the colours also fixes them precisely as physical objects, enabling real material again to generate psychological impact, as the original material did through Hockney's lens.

The size of green

Hockney's observation that there are many greens is typically astute. Vegetation covers a lot of ground in the natural world and the colour term 'green' covers a lot of vegetation. Put another way, green occupies a vast amount of physical space in nature, and a huge territory in mental space too. In the language of colour science, one would say that the category green occupies a huge volume in colour space (fig. 128). (Not all languages of all cultures refer to green in the same way, but that is another story, and here we talk about English.)

Colour spaces are geometrical constructions in which any discriminable colour can be pinpointed to a particular location; similar colours are located near each other; dissimilar colours are far apart.[10] Colour spaces are by definition perceptual, rather than physical; they map one realm into the other. Colour spaces are derived from colour-matching experiments in the laboratory, in which people adjust mixtures of three primary lights to match other chromatic lights, or from perceptual scaling experiments in which people judge the similarity of different mixtures in terms of prescribed attributes. For pigment mixtures, standard attributes are hue, value and chroma (or, in the terminology of art history, hue, tone and saturation). These attributes then define the dimensions of the colour space, with hue varying smoothly around a circle and chroma along the radius, and value varying from dark to bright in the third, orthogonal, dimension. The Munsell Color System orders pigment colours in this way.

Colour spaces are fundamentally three-dimensional because normal human colour vision is three-dimensional. The human eye filters incoming light into three channels, corresponding to segments of the spectrum collected by the short-, middle- and long-wavelength-sensitive cone types. Ultimately, all three-dimensional colour spaces – and there are many – find their origins in the three cone channel activations. Transformations between colour spaces are mathematicians' delights, and colour scientists' day jobs.

So-called 'perceptually uniform colour spaces' are contrived so that one unit of distance corresponds to the same perceived difference anywhere in the space. That is, if a pair of pinks are separated from each other by the same

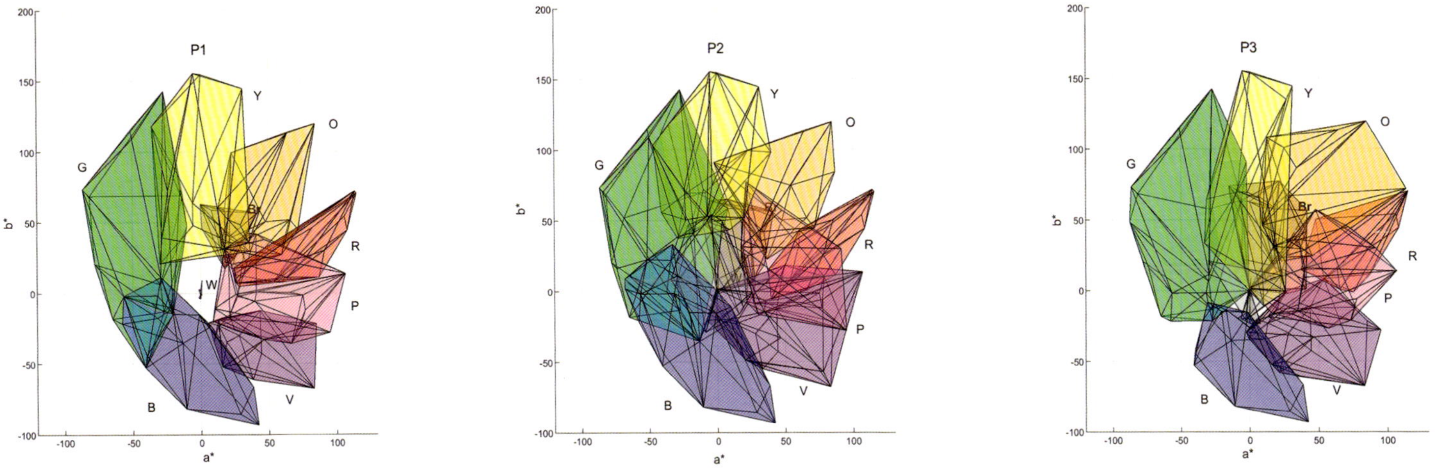

129 Colour spaces of 3 different normal trichromatic observers (P1, P2, P3), carved into their individual naming categories.

distance as a pair of blues, then the difference within each pair will look the same size. And it is in such a space, where distances correspond directly to differences, that green occupies the largest realm.

How does green stake its claim to this vast territory? Its boundaries are found by colour-naming experiments. In the classic paradigm, individual observers are presented with colour samples taken evenly from all parts of perceptually uniform colour space, and challenged to assign one colour to each sample from the set of eleven basic colour terms (black (K), white (W), red (R), green (G), yellow (Y), blue (B), brown (Br), pink (P), purple (V), grey (N)). Green is invariably the most frequently chosen colour term. It is the label people apply to the largest number of colours, out of all the colours that people are capable of distinguishing (fig. 129).

One reason the green category is so huge is that it spans a large range of lightnesses and saturations. Light green, dark green and pale green are all green, whereas other colours jump to different categories when they keep their hue but change lightness or saturation: yellow becomes brown, pink becomes red, orange becomes brown, and pale blue becomes white.[11] Indeed, to differentiate between the multitude of greens, people use qualifiers such as bright, light, dark or deep, but also words that point to green's origins in nature – apple, moss, meadow, forest, avocado, emerald and, of course, spring.

Nature gives another reason. As Hockney points out above, the physical properties of leaves change radically across the seasons. From spring, through summer, to autumn, they emerge, unfurl, thicken, ripen, develop and decay. Yet they still remain leaves, and people still see them as green, whether translucent, bright, dark or dull. If the category green is driven by the appearance of foliage, no wonder it is so huge.

The surprising fact about green is that although we see so much of it, and use the name so often, we do not see nearly as much of it in nature as we are capable of seeing. That is, there are far fewer greens occurring in the natural world than normal trichromatic humans are physiologically able to see. To fill the vast volume of greens in colour space, one must resort to artificial means, making and mixing lights or pigments, or to the rich expanse of memory. By painting with light on his iPad, Hockney reached far into colour space to get his greens.

These greens conjure up not only their physical origins, the things which gave rise to the perceptual category, but also the emotions that these things arouse, and their reverberations in memory. This direct reach of colour into the limbic areas of the brain is one that Hockney understands to the hilt. Colour gets to the emotional centres of the brain because of the meaning that it carries, and that meaning comes from the things that make colour. The human brain evolved to make seeing colours worthwhile. The glossy red of a ripe strawberry is the internal neural flag that sets the runners off down the track to the motor circuits, instructing the hands to pick the fruit, bite in, chew and extract nutritional goodness for better survival.

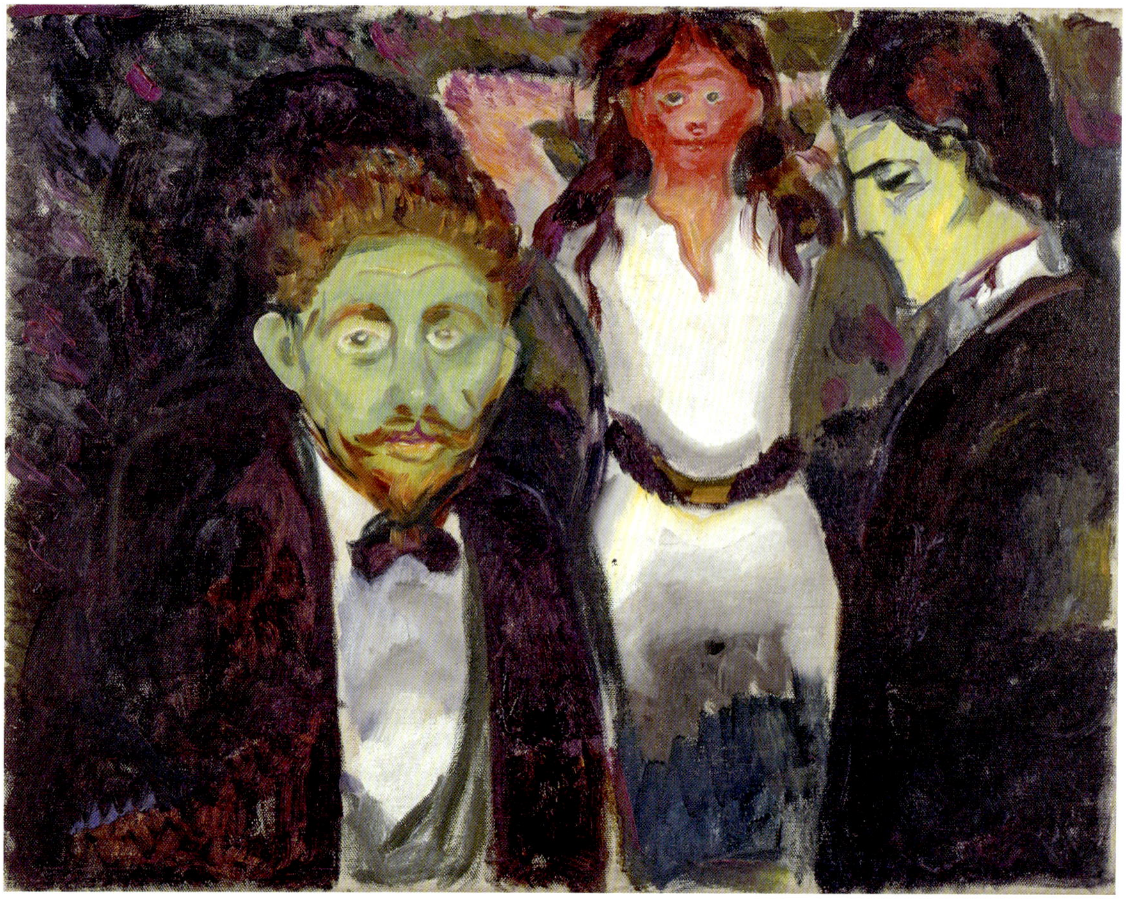

130 Edvard Munch, *Jealousy*, 1907, oil on canvas, 75 x 98 cm. The Munch Museum, Oslo, MM.M.00447

But the flag, instead of being tossed away once it has done its job, commandeers its own place in consciousness, laying itself out on a mental map.

By getting the greens, and putting them in front of our eyes, Hockney accesses that mental map in our brains and activates the neural circuits flagged by greens we have seen before. We respond viscerally to the visual stimulus.

The hugeness of green, and its emotional heft, also lends itself to symbolism. Pluck a green, and turn it into a sign for something else, a concept, a group, an attribute. Whether its meaning is positive or negative depends on its context. The emotional valence of green is unstable. Green may stand for growth, youth and vigour, or for jealousy, greed or illness. The greenness of the lover's face in Edvard Munch's *Jealousy* tells all (1907, fig. 130). Hockney definitively and deliberately anchors his greens to nature by placing them in representational contexts. In turn, the pictorial contexts anchor the viewer's emotions, while the fact that these are pictures allows the wider world in which the viewer exists to influence the response.

The unique non-uniqueness of green

Hockney's use of green in his iPad paintings is unique. And green itself is unique amongst the unique hues, for being highly variable. In colour science, the four unique hues red, green, yellow and blue are defined as hues which cannot be defined in terms of any other hues. In other words, unique red has no greenness, yellowness or blueness in it; unique yellow has no greenness, redness or blueness in it, and so forth. In painting, too, the idea of these four primary colours is fundamental.

In experiments, people are generally consistent in their unique hue settings. That is, when asked to adjust a mixture of lights or the RGB coordinates of a patch on the monitor, or to select a particular sample from a standard set, people tend to agree on the spectral stimulus that produces each unique hue.

There are caveats: the precise settings differ between experiments, and they vary between people more than they vary between repeated settings by the same person. Yet, even amongst this variability, unique green is unique in being the most variable. For any one person, there is only a very narrow set of colours that satisfies the call for 'unique yellow'. Partly, this is because yellow is uniquely bright. Darker yellows are brown, not yellow, whereas darker greens are still green.[12]

Again, Hockney's genius is in calling on this unique variability of green. While people may agree that he gets the greens, they may disagree on exactly which greens they are and, therefore, on what they mean. This makes Hockney's greens as fertile as can be, giving rise to different experiences in different viewers.

Light itself

Hockney gets not only the greens by painting with light on his iPad, but also the light itself. Colours of course need light, but light does more than make colours in people's minds. Without light, we would see nothing. We see because light interacts first with physical stuff in the real world – particles, surfaces, materials, volumes – and then with our eyes. Light sparks reactions in our eyes which ultimately create what we see – the perceptions that drive our behaviour. We see colours because of light, but we also see and feel light itself.

The human brain has a dual response to light. Dual pathways begin in the retina at the back of the eye: the visual pathway carries the signals which ultimately generate conscious perception; the non-visual pathway conveys information about light to brain areas that control circadian rhythms and influence mood, alertness and ultimately cognition. The non-visual pathway also governs the unconscious adjustment of pupil size in response to light levels. That these two pathways interact is certain, but the myriad ways in which they do are still unknown.[13] The creation of colours in our minds from the neural processing of light signals is a prime example of these mysterious interactions.

In the natural world, the spectrum of light changes continually, on different time scales. The sharp-eyed Hockney sees the "yellow going out of the light [late in the day], so that intensifies the blues"; "for a short moment the subtle cobalt violets and blues" that Monet used "became very intense while the sun was setting."

Daylight indeed has characteristic properties to which human brains have become attuned. Daylight is a mixture of directional sunlight and diffuse skylight; the varying combinations of these generate spectra that vary systematically from 'bluish' to 'yellowish', that is, from short- to middle-and-long-wavelength-dominated spectra. Daylight varies in brightness too, not only because of the elevation of the sun, but also because of clouds, fog, mist, rain and other atmospheric effects.

When the spectrum of light that shines on an object changes, the spectrum of light that the object reflects also changes. In seeing colour, the human brain discounts spectral variations in illumination in order to stabilize colours of objects; this is the perceptual phenomenon of colour constancy. A green apple stays green – in visual perception – whether lit by morning sun or in evening shade. Yet in feeling light, via the non-visual pathway, spectral variations in illumination are not discarded, but instead registered and followed. Changes in the environmental illumination guide the human brain and body, telling the time of day not only to synchronize biological rhythms but also to influence the actions and emotions that visual perceptions elicit. The green apple stays green, but you might feel differently about that green, in morning and evening.

Hockney says "early morning light is very special".[14] Yet the changes in light spectra are symmetric at either end of the day: in early morning, the illumination first becomes much 'bluer', then 'yellower' as its brightness increases; in late evening, the illumination becomes much 'bluer', then 'yellower', as brightness decreases. Given that the sun's low elevation is the same when it is setting or rising, the symmetry makes sense. Why then should early morning light differ from evening light? The answer may lie in the way light makes people feel. In the morning, light activates a cascade of hormones to waken the brain and body. People are therefore different creatures in the morning, cortisol coursing through their vessels. Early morning light feels special because we feel different, even if it might look the same as other times of day.

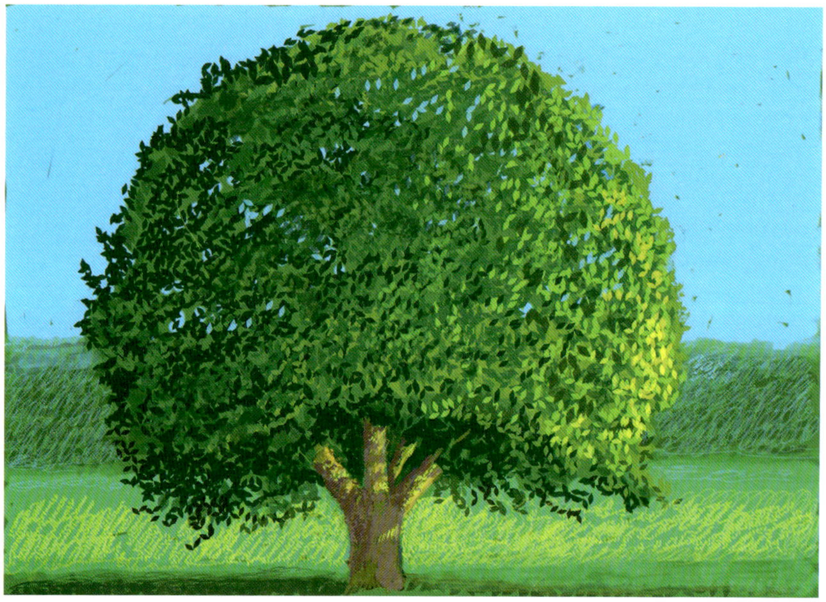

131 David Hockney, *7th June 2020*, iPad painting. Collection of the artist

132 Jean-Baptiste-Camille Corot, *Peasants under the Trees at Dawn*, 1840–45, oil on canvas, 27.3 x 38.8 cm. National Gallery, London, NG6439

How, then, does a visual artist capture these non-visual effects of light? Hockney grasps not only the spectral changes in daylight, but also its spatial complexities. Hockney talks about the movement of the sun through the landscape across the year; its directionality changes with the season. In paintings of familiar landscapes, the angle and placement of shadows, glints and highlights may reveal the time of both day and year. The glistening yellow on the right side of the leaves and trunk of the stolid, central tree in *No. 368* suggests a sun low in the sky; the full foliage with its saturated greens – graded from light to dark in accord with the rim of yellow – suggests the beginning of summer; and Hockney hints with the overall brightening effect that a sunny day is coming (fig. 131).

Painted shadows may also tell the time, but again, with ambiguity. As Gombrich observes of the sfumato in Jean-Baptiste-Camille Corot's *Peasants under the Trees at Dawn* (c. 1840–45, fig. 132), "Corot softens the shadow of the fallen tree and of the goose, thus convincingly suggest[ing] the mellow light of morning or evening".[15] In other words, despite the explicit clue

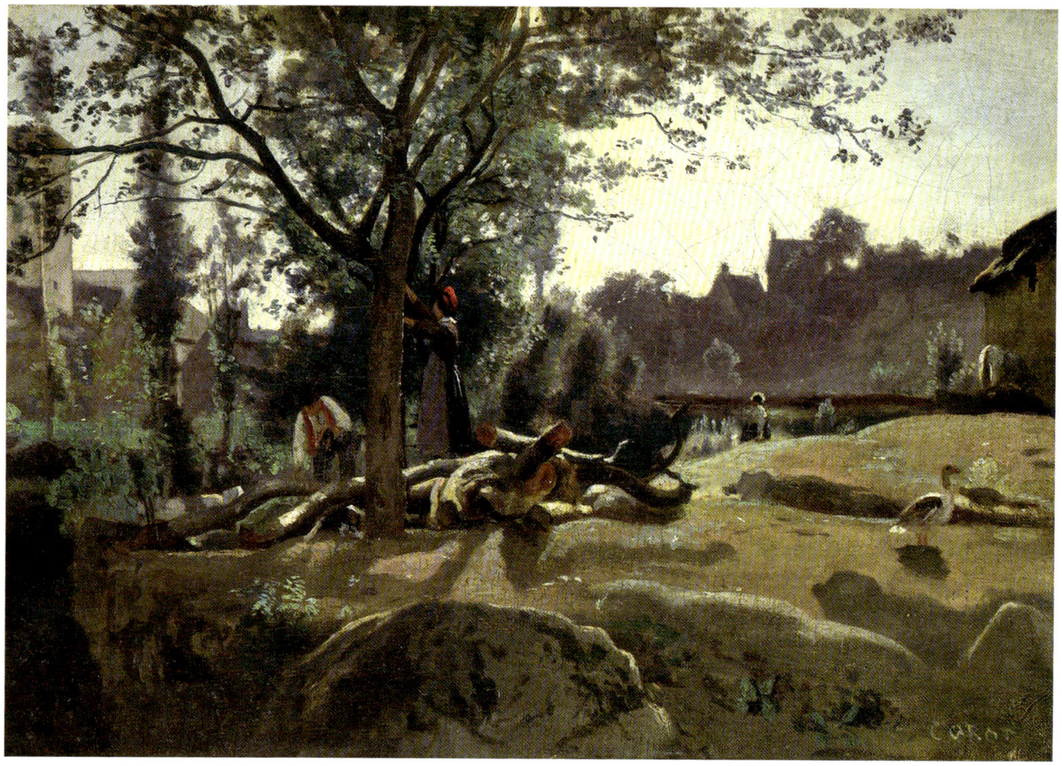

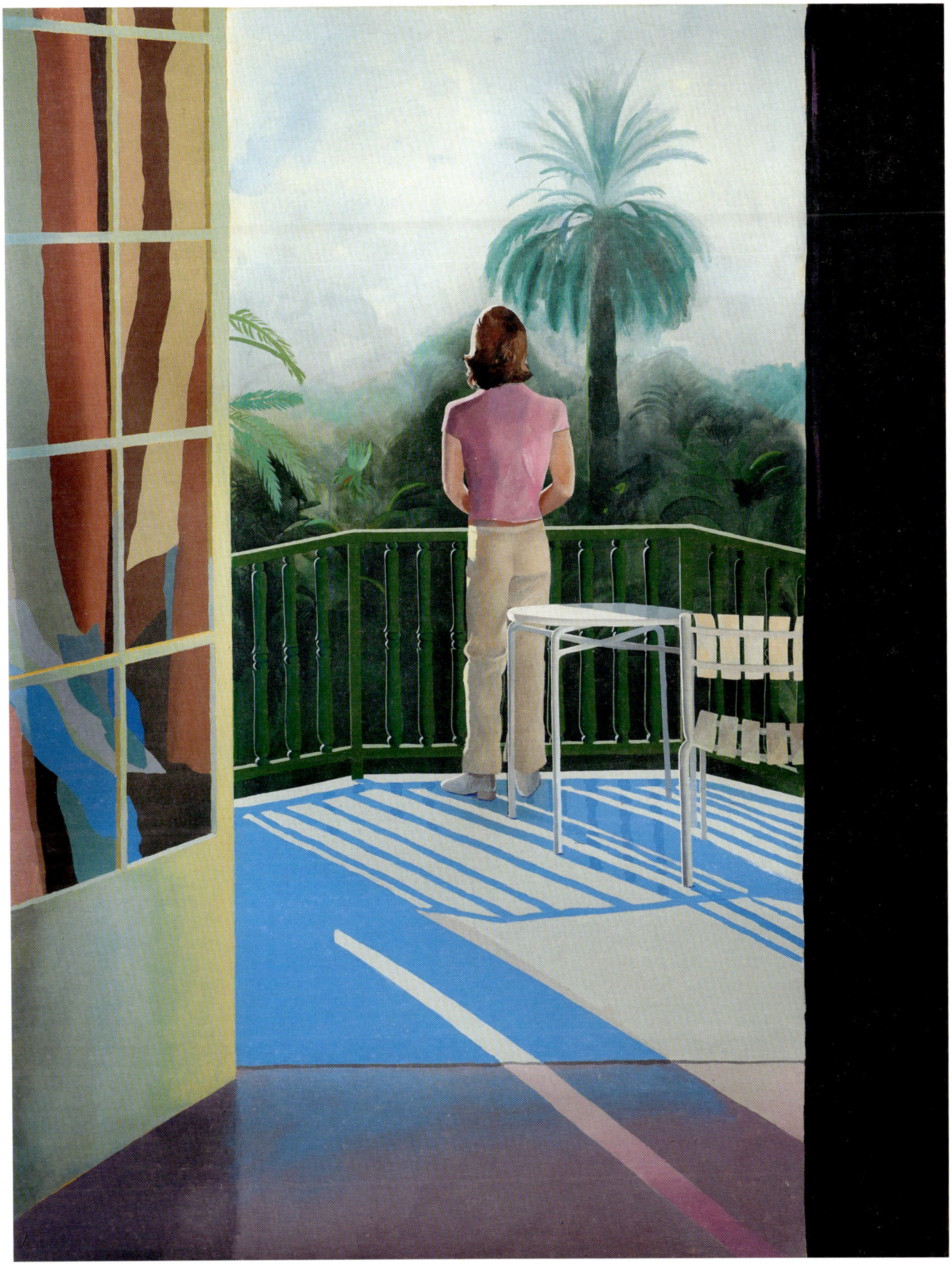

133 David Hockney,
Sur la Terrasse, 1971, acrylic
on canvas, 274 x 213.4 cm.
Private collection

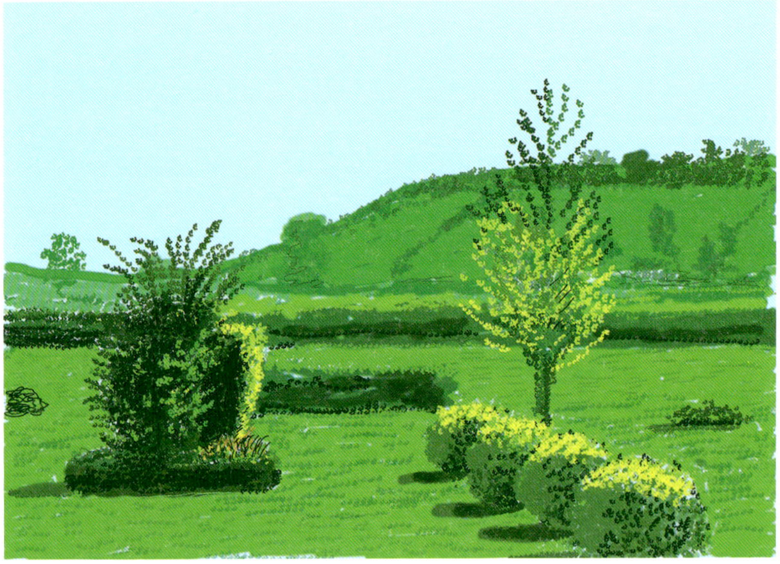

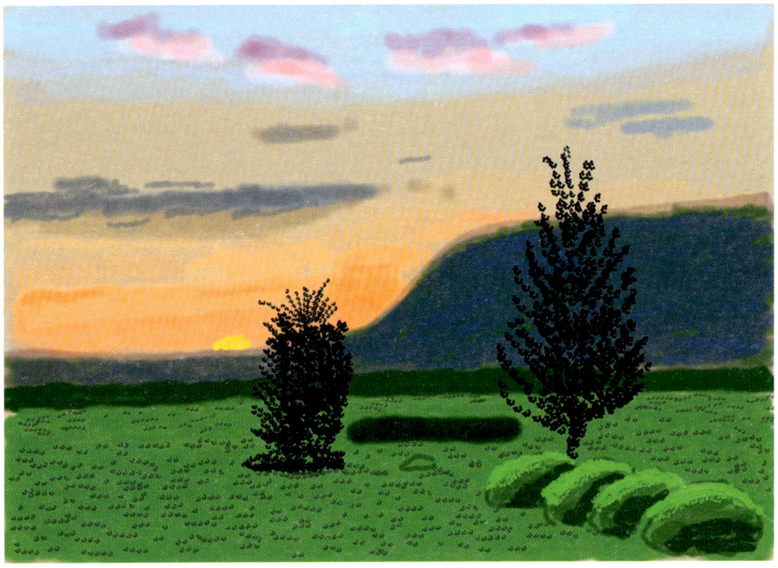

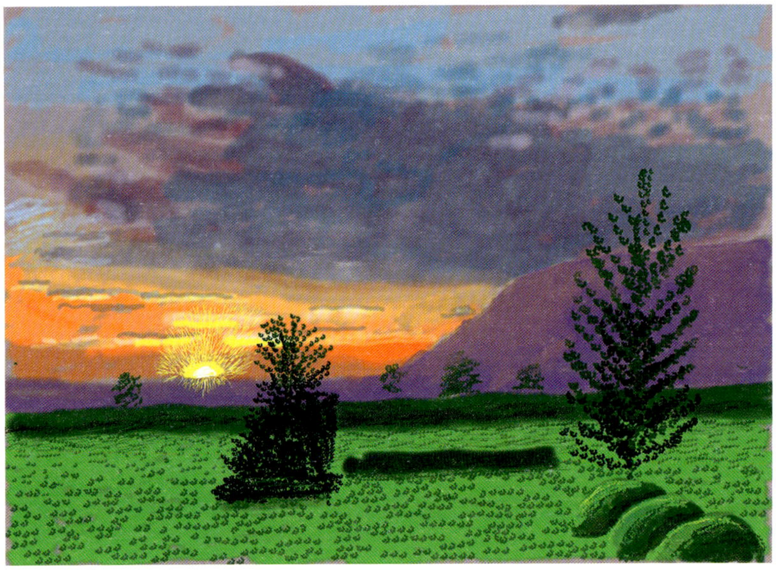

from the title, Gombrich allows for an inherent uncertainty in the depiction of grazing light.

In Hockney's *Sur la Terrasse* (1971, fig. 133), the evening light is all conveyed by shadows.[16] The inclination of the sun is told by the slant of the shadows cast by the railings. The downwelling light of evening is blue. Hence, the shadows formed when the grazing rays of direct sunshine are blocked are blue. Yet, in Hockey's painting, the shadows are bright blue, not dark as shadows should be. Their hue shimmers between cyan and cerulean blue, deepening from the balcony edge towards the interior door, where at the threshold it blends with a rose-pink floor, which in turns resonates with the shading on the central figure's pink t-shirt.

Although real shadows must obey the laws of physics, painted shadows do not. Artists have learned that painted shadows are just as effective when they satisfy a few crucial criteria as when they perfectly conform to physical constraints.[17] Hockney knows when to deploy these cues. In his earlier *A Bigger Splash* (1967), there are no shadows, apart from one long rectangle stretching beneath the overhang of the roof and a grey parallelogram under the deck chair. The sky is a uniform block of blue; the pool likewise, a more saturated, slightly greener blue. The intense saturation of the colours and minimal shadows suggest the sun is directly overhead in a cloudless sky.

134 David Hockney, *22nd April 2020, No. 3*, iPad painting. Collection of the artist

135 David Hockney, *26th April 2020, No. 1*, iPad painting. Collection of the artist

136 David Hockney, *27th April 2020, No. 1*, iPad painting. Collection of the artist

Colour constancy

Although colour constancy is hard-wired into human visual perception, artists know how to subvert the phenomenon when they so desire. Monet's series paintings, especially the 'Haystacks' and 'Rouen Cathedral' series, are prime examples. In these, Monet portrays changes in daylight spectra throughout the day of which a perfectly colour-constant viewer would be unaware. Monet thus paints the stone of Rouen Cathedral with dramatically different pigments at different times of day, from yellows to purples. In Hockney's *A Bigger Splash* not only are there no shadows, there is no hint of illumination colour. The sky and water are blue, in and of themselves, as if the light shining on them were perfectly neutral as well as bright and diffuse. Yet in a dramatic series in 'The Arrival of Spring', Hockney paints light as if it were a thing unto itself, an homage to Monet (figs. 134–36). In seven paintings, the same distant hill, beyond a tall tree and four spherical shrubs, goes from celadon to mauve to rose pink to forest green to deep cyan to grey to vivid green, as the atmosphere and elevation of the sun change, and consequently, the illumination too.

Colour constancy, even when not subverted, is not always perfect, but tends to be better under changes in daylight illumination, with which the human visual system became most familiar during its evolution. Many forms of artificial light spectra today stretch the capacity of the visual system to remain colour constant.

The capacity of illumination to change what we see has long fascinated Hockney. In his 1995–96 installation *Snails Space with Vari-Lites, 'Painting as Performance'*, he brought out different colours and shapes by varying the spectral and spatial properties of the light, in different parts of a vast painted landscape. In his stage sets, Hockney used lighting to bring about changes in colour both directly and indirectly, by altering the shapes that people see, the depth planes to which they belong, and their illumination frameworks. These are complicated interactions between illumination, shape, and surface properties, intensely explored in the study of human vision and implemented in machine vision systems, yet grasped in their entirety by Hockney, and transformed into art.

For the third act of his 1991 production of Puccini's *Turandot*, Hockney describes illuminating a brilliant red wall, first with blue lights, "which made it a deep purply shade", and then with red lights, increasing the red lights until "you think it can't get any redder, but it does, until the end when it just bursts".[18] That single wall is nothing like a constant surface with a single meaning. It is nothing like a natural surface whose material properties drive our emotional attachment to colour. Instead, it is an expression of pure colour, a glimpse into the mind of Hockney.

Notes

1 Sykes 2011, 192. **2** Regan et al. 2001. **3** Ball 2011. **4** Hockney and Devaney 2021. **5** Palmer and Schloss 2010 (https://doi:10.1073/pnas.0906172107). **6** Gibson et al. 2017 (https://doi.org/10.1073/pnas.1619666114). **7** *The Independent*, 15 May 2021 (https://www.independent.co.uk/arts-entertainment/art/features/david-hockney-review-ra-ipad-normandy-b1849499.html). **8** Gayford 2021a. **9** Hockney and Devaney 2021. **10** A colour space is defined as a "conjectural geometric space in which all possible human color experiences are arranged in some kind of rational order, forming a color solid": Kuehni and Schwarz 2008, 10. **11** Similarly, blue is a large category, although not as large as green. In English, light and dark blues all belong to same category, but in other languages – Russian and some Italian dialects, for example – they divide into different categories. **12** The quest to find the neural mechanisms underpinning unique hues and their variability is still unsolved: unique hues do not map to complementary colours in the traditional sense, i.e. unique red and unique green do not cancel each other when combined, nor does the colour tuning of the known colour-opponent neurons line up with unique hues. **13** Lucas et al. 2020 (https://doi.org/10.1146/annurev-vision-030320-041239). **14** Hockney and Gayford 2011, 2018, 218. **15** Gombrich (1995) 2014, 42. **16** Sykes 2011, 245, 250. **17** Casati and Cavanagh 2019. **18** Hockney and Gayford 2011, 228.

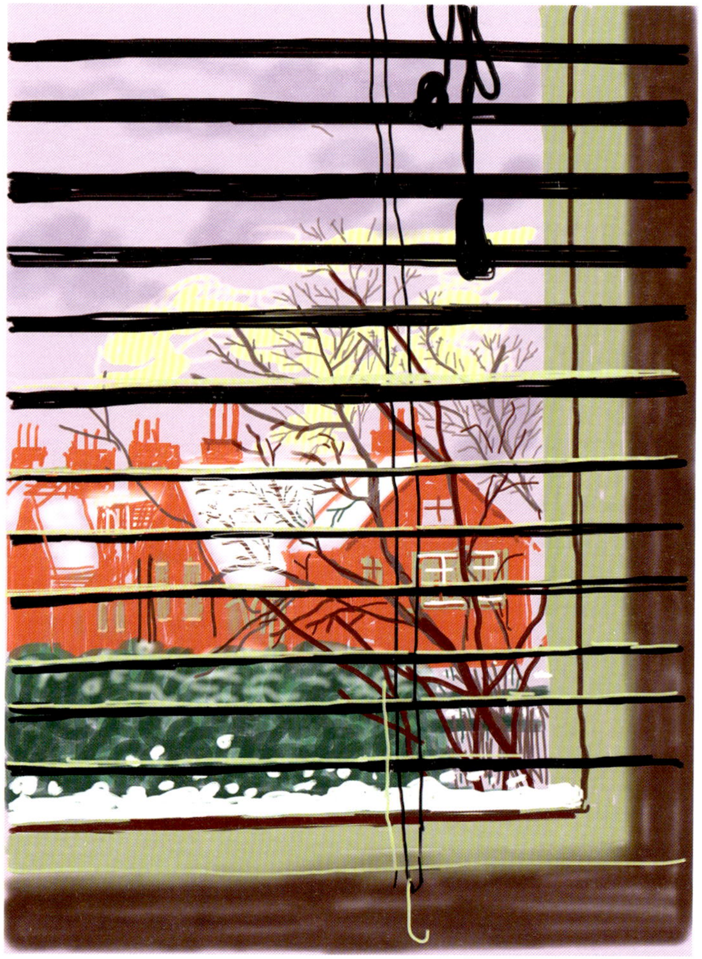

137 | F David Hockney, *28th November 2010*, iPad drawing. Collection of the artist

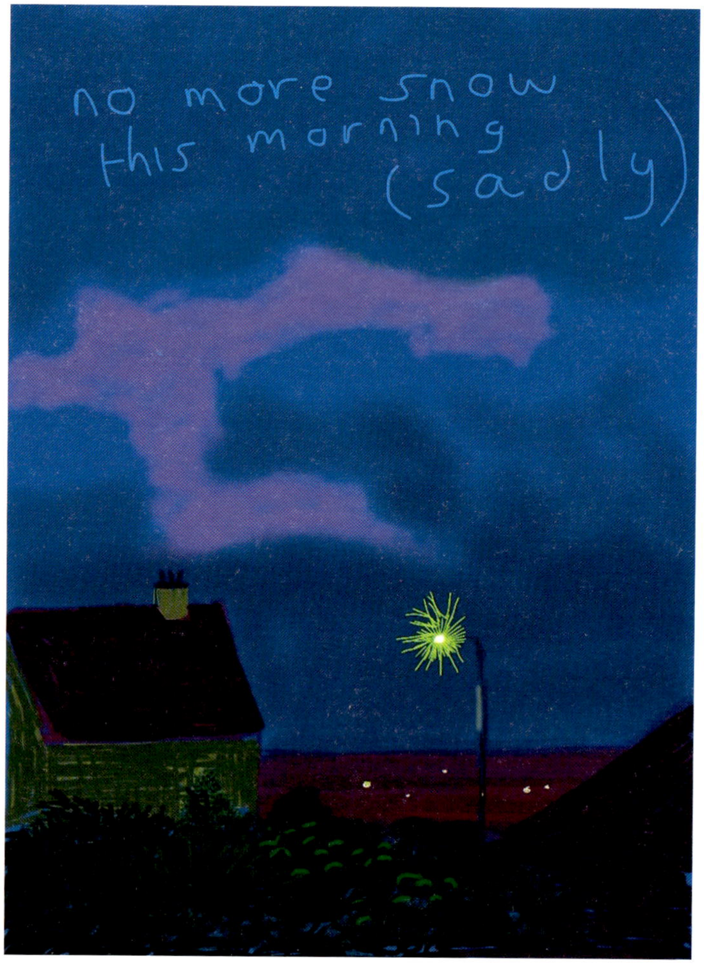

138 | F David Hockney, *30th November 2010*, iPad drawing. Collection of the artist

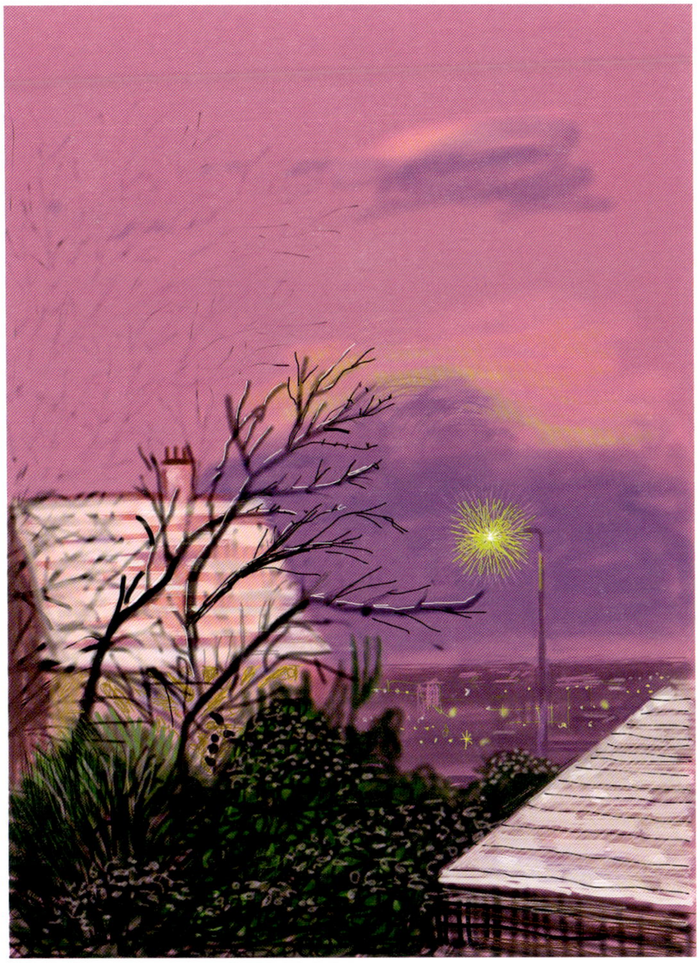

139 | F David Hockney, *6th December 2010*, iPad drawing. Collection of the artist

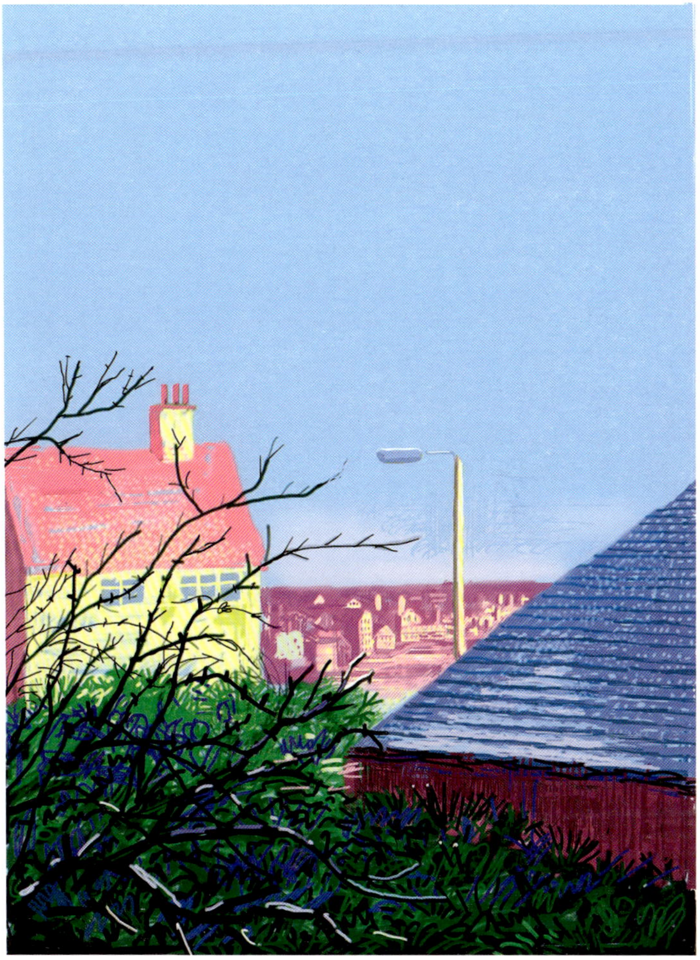

140 | F David Hockney, *7th December 2010*, iPad drawing. Collection of the artist

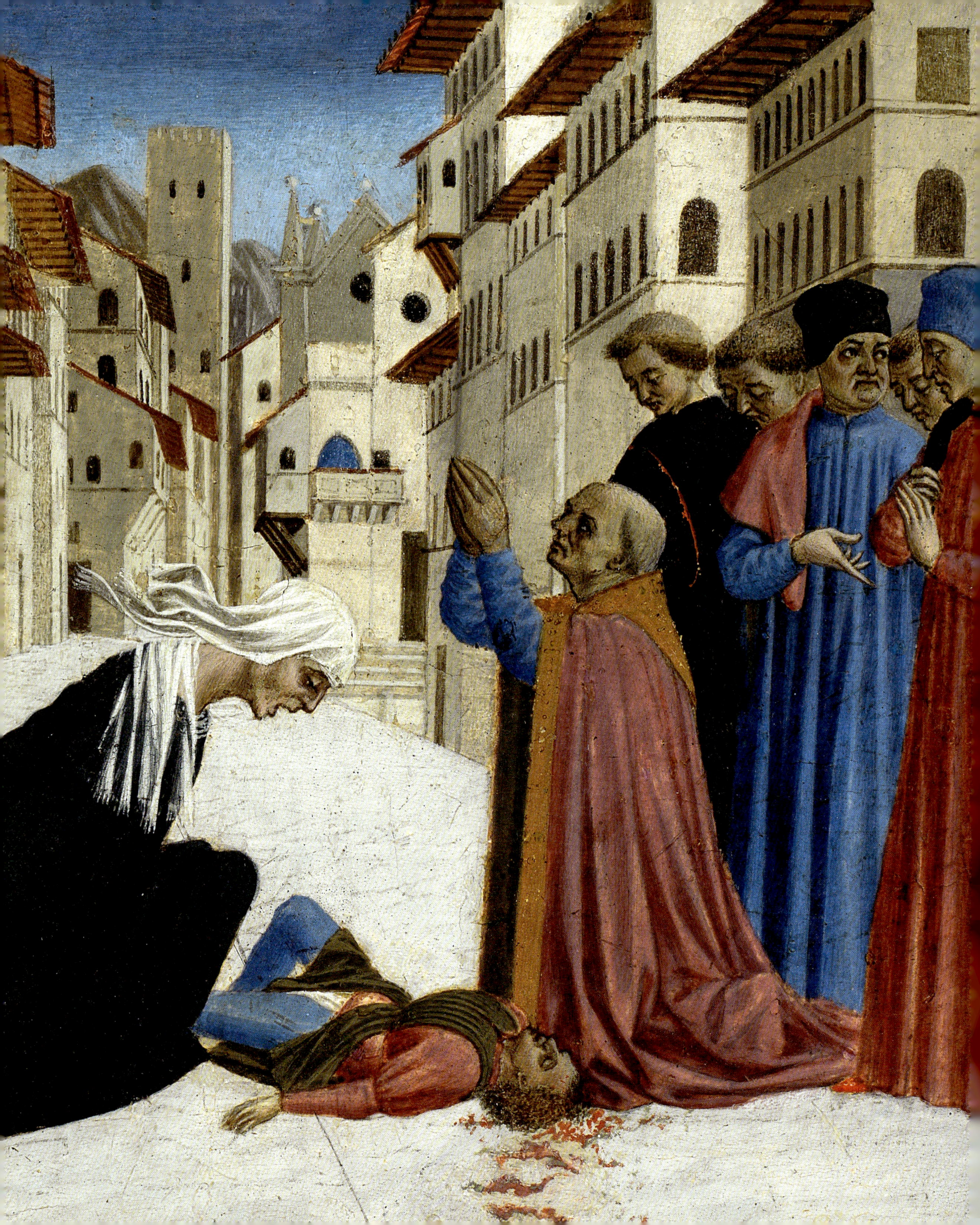

Donal Cooper, Francesca Aimi, Fabrizio Nevola and Luca Brunke

Escaping Alberti's prison

Space, narrative, and computer visualization in Domenico Veneziano's Fitzwilliam predella panels

David Hockney has often recalled that his first encounter with Renaissance perspective came in the form of a poster reproduction of Fra Angelico's San Marco *Annunciation* (fig. 141) in Bradford Grammar School. It is a theme that he has returned to repeatedly in his artworks and writings, famously characterizing the perspectival window of Leon Battista Alberti's treatise *On Painting* (1435/6) as "a prison really", before adding: "But I think that many painters have always known that there was something wrong with conventional, linear perspective; they realised that you could bend it".[1] Hockney's polygonal revision of Fra Angelico's *Annunciation* on display in the exhibition (fig. 142) is a visual exposition of his scepticism regarding the text-book account of Renaissance perspective and its adoption by artists of the time.

Fra Angelico's fresco remains on its wall at the top of the dormitory stairs in the Florentine convent of San Marco, but the Fitzwilliam is fortunate in being able to juxtapose Hockney's work with two small but seminal examples of Florentine perspectival painting from the 1440s: Domenico Veneziano's own version of the Annunciation (fig. 143) and the same artist's *Miracle of Saint Zenobius* (fig. 144), probably painted within a decade of Alberti's treatise and around 30 years after Brunelleschi is thought to have created his first perspectival illusions of Florence's Baptistery and main square. Precious little is known about Domenico: his name suggests Venetian origins but his training is unclear. By 1438 he was lobbying the Medici for commissions and the following year was painting frescoes in Florence alongside the young Piero della Francesca, whose later treatise on perspective would advance far beyond Alberti's in its sophistication and coherence. Only a handful of Domenico's works survive but they include several canonical stops in any history of Renaissance perspective. His acknowledged masterpiece is the Saint Lucy Altarpiece, of which the two Cambridge pictures are components.

Domenico's works have been scrutinized at length in the specialist historiography on perspective, but by using computer software to reverse-engineer their spatial projections it is possible to extract and visualize the varied ways in which Domenico deployed and manipulated perspective constructions, loosening the shackles of Alberti's 'prison' to bend linear perspective to his own ends. Martin Kemp and Antonio Criminisi pioneered this approach over fifteen years ago and since then off-the-shelf software applications have become widely available.[2] As Kemp and Criminisi observed, modern computer vision shares fundamental, monocular qualities with Albertian perspective. Applying software designed to derive spatial data from photographs to fifteenth-century paintings tests at face value the lineage often asserted between perspectival and photographic space. Arguably, the value of the exercise for our understanding of early perspectival practice lies in the discrepancies it reveals, anomalies which in turn offer points of departure for considering the artist's specific approach towards the agency of pictorial space.

Domenico painted his masterpiece for the main altar of a relatively modest Florentine parish

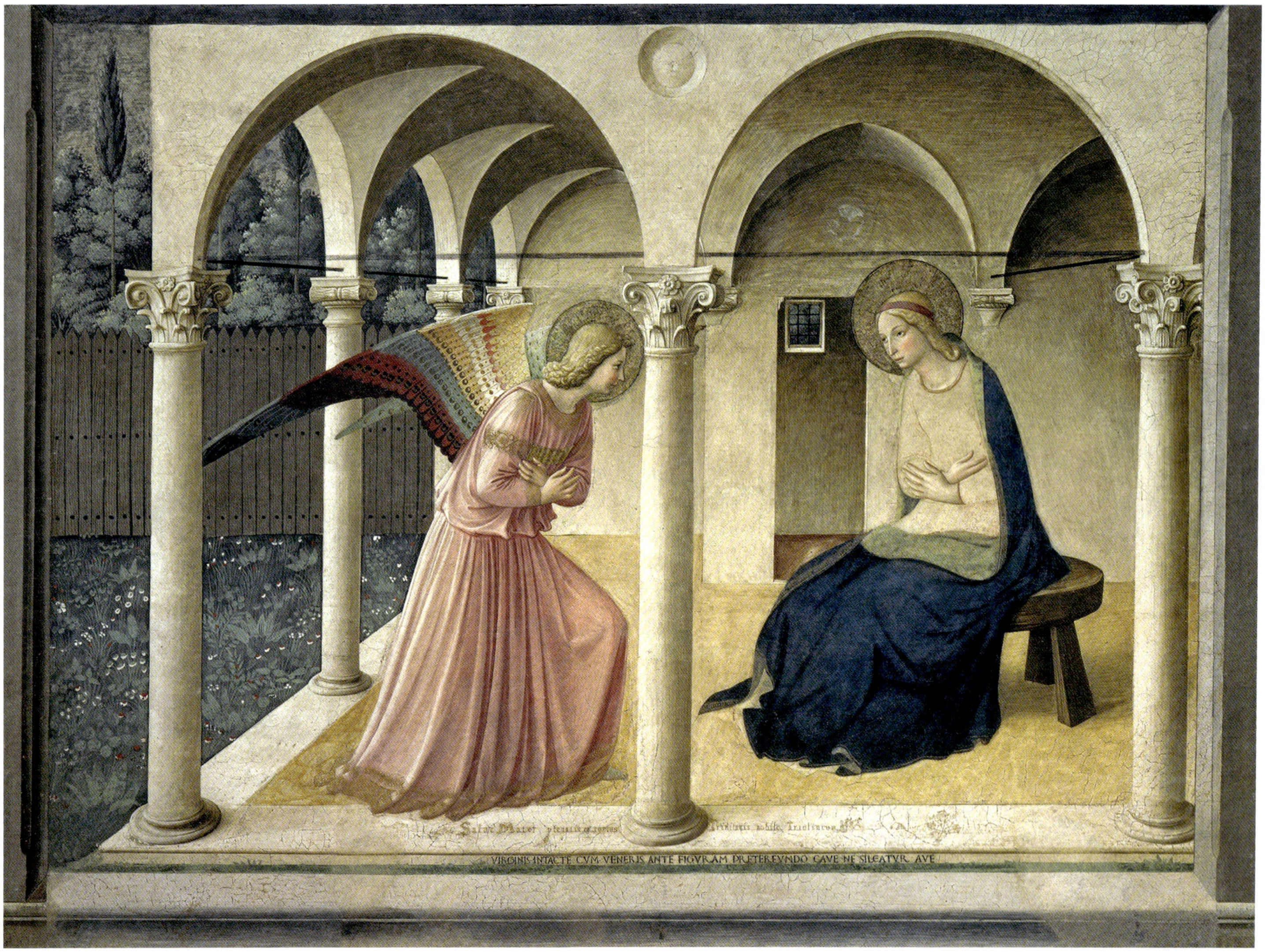

141 Fra Angelico, *The Annunciation*, c. 1440–45, fresco, 230 x 321 cm. Dormitory stairs, San Marco, Florence

church, Santa Lucia dei Magnoli, and it is now divided between different collections. Analysis has focused on the main panel, measuring 209 x 216 cm, which is now in the Uffizi (fig. 145). This offers a highly complex yet coherently realised perspectival projection to the viewer. Domenico's painted architecture is formed from a sequence of elements that can be plotted confidently on to a notional ground-plan of the pictorial space (fig. 146).[3] The Virgin and Child are enthroned on a dais that projects in front of an open loggia which combines classical columns with gothic vaults. Beyond the loggia, the architectural space is closed by a polygonal apse whose sides are filled with shell niches. The space is open to the sky, with trees visible over and above the cornice line. In the foreground, the four saints stand on a convincingly foreshortened geometric floor formed of stars and hexagons built up from a grid of equilateral triangles (fig. 147).[4] Domenico, however, moderates the visual impact of his spatial projection with surface conjunctions that seem to acknowledge contemporary expectations of altarpiece design. The arches at the top of the painting mimic the framing divisions of more traditional polyptychs; the arcade appears to rest on the painting's surface and it is only by following the columns to their bases that one locates the structure much deeper into the pictorial space.[5] Similarly, the Virgin and Child seem to be enthroned within the central shell niche (a frequent device in contemporary Marian

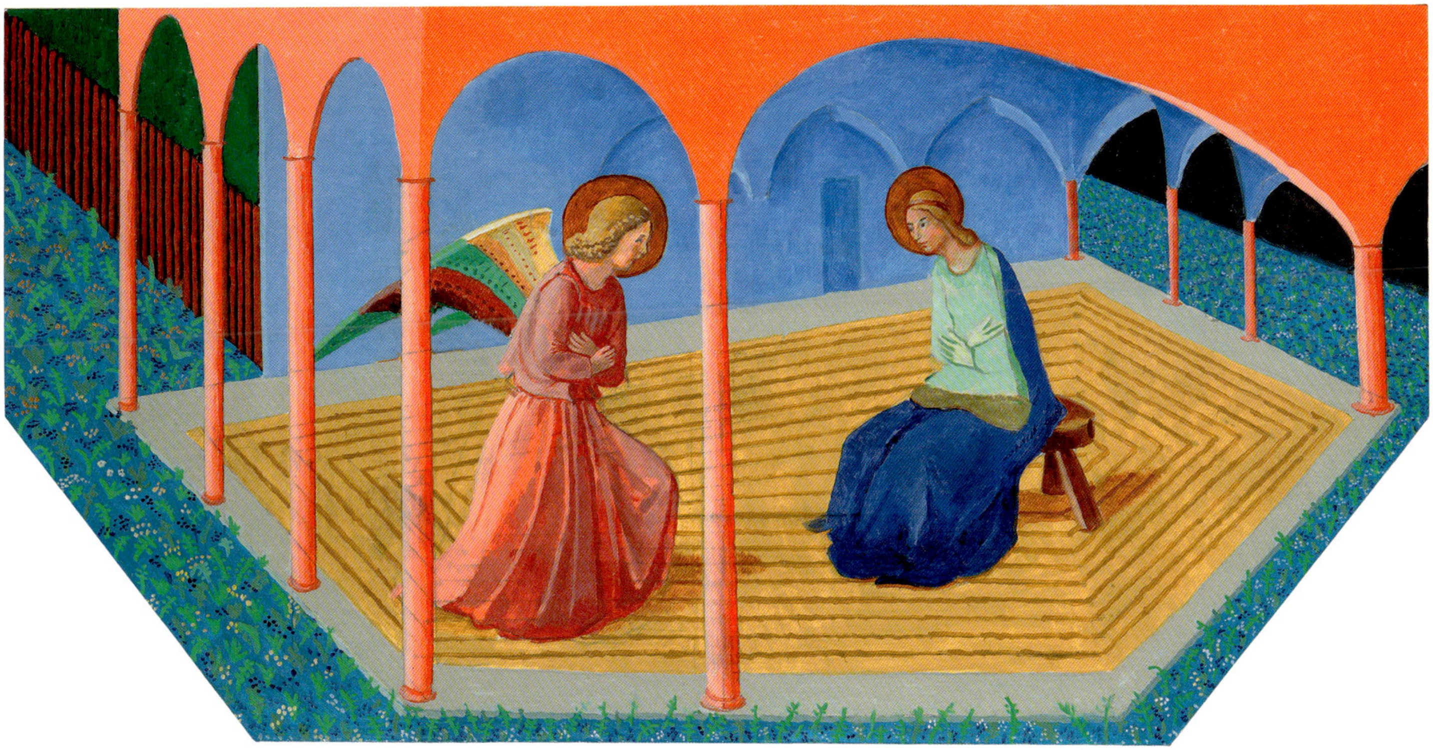

imagery, fig. 148), whereas there is a considerable distance between the two in terms of the depth of the perspectival projection.[6]

When assessing the main panel of the altarpiece it is important to remember its large scale and axial location within the church of Santa Lucia dei Magnoli. It would have been seen in conjunction with the overall interior, and the relatively low vanishing point (between the Virgin's knees) probably responds to the viewer's eye level, as the painting would have been set above the high altar, which was itself raised on a stepped platform.[7] By establishing a 'spatial continuum'[8] within and without the picture, Veneziano bestowed an architectural grandeur to the Virgin's surroundings that both responded to and yet also transcended the relatively modest interior of Santa Lucia. According to Kemp's convincing analysis of the perspectival construction, the ideal viewing distance would have been four metres from the painting (the church itself is only some 24 metres in length).[9] It is likely that on entering the church from the street the viewer would have seen the main panel framed within the doorway of a choir screen, a dividing structure situated half-way up the nave.[10] At the same time, the screen would have occluded the apse and immediate surroundings of the high altar at the far end of the church, further heightening the illusionistic power of the main panel.

Domenico's altarpiece was completed by a frieze of five smaller scale scenes at its base, painted on the front face of a step-like box structure termed a *predella* that raised the main panel above the altar table. The *predella*, originally a continuous wooden support, had been cut up by 1815 to create independent paintings that are now dispersed in different collections. In addition to the Cambridge pair, two scenes are in the National Gallery of Art in Washington and one is in the Gemäldegalerie in Berlin. Both the Fitzwilliam scenes deploy perspective but in different ways and to different ends than the main panel. When assessing these predella images, it is important to bear in mind that they would have been viewed at close quarters and not from afar, nor in relation to the physical architecture of the church: here there was no call for a 'spatial continuum' with the viewer's space. They were also narrative images, and perspectival 'rules' were tailored

142 | F David Hockney, *Annunciation II, after Fra Angelico,* from *The Brass Tacks Triptych*, 2017, acrylic on canvas, 121.9 x 243.8 cm (hexagonal). Collection of the artist

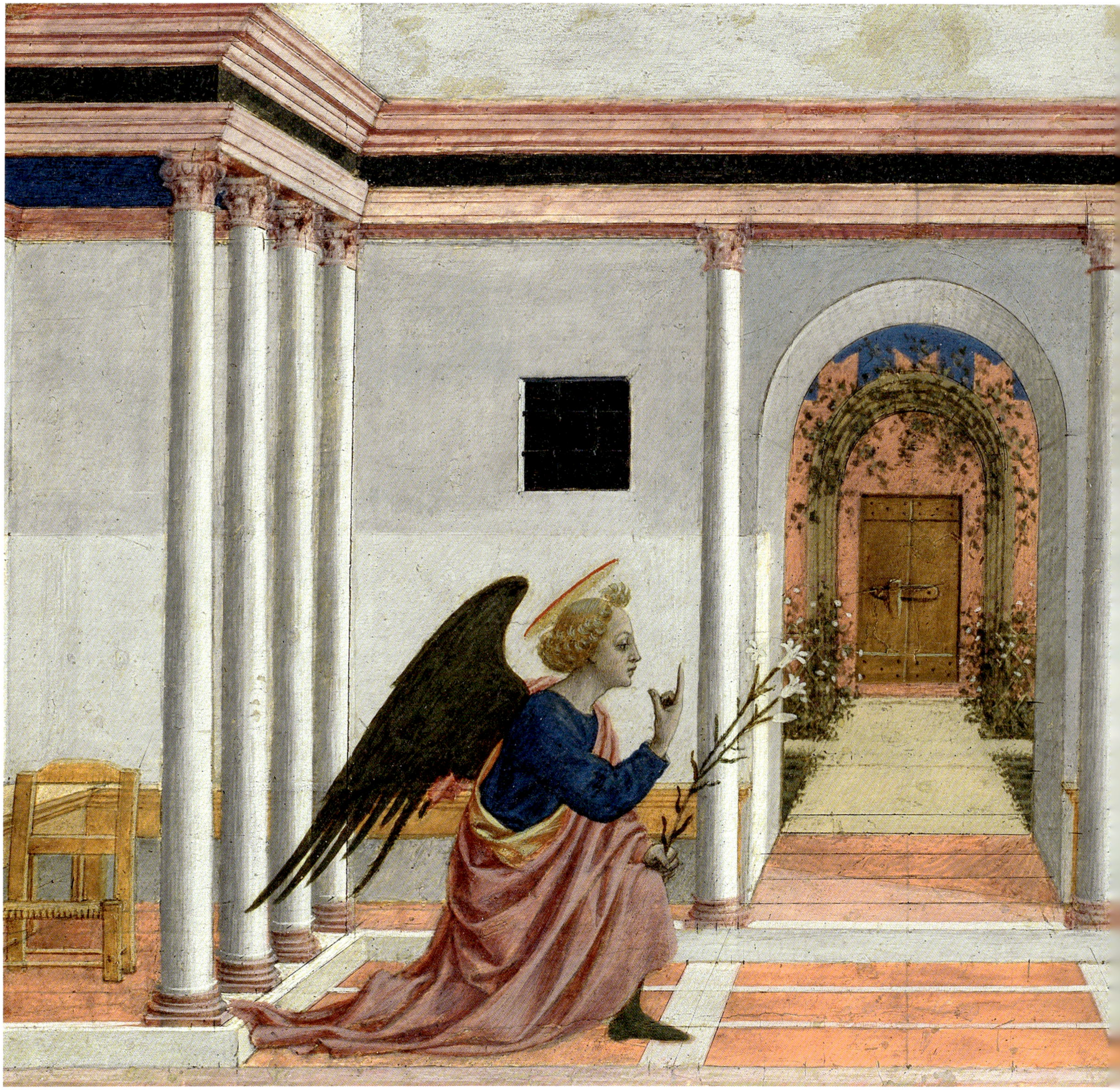

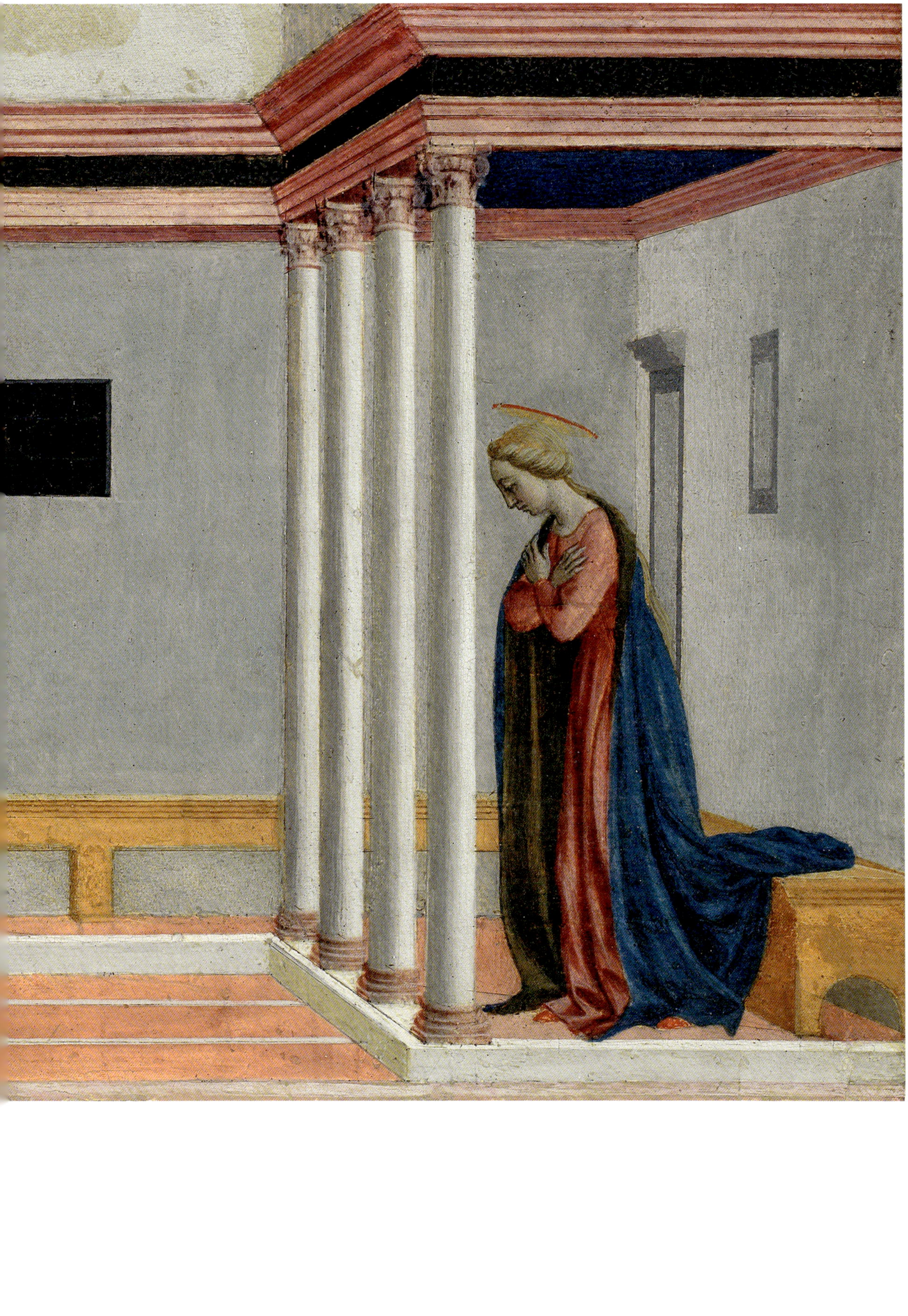

143 | F Domenico Veneziano (Domenico di Bartolomeo da Venezia), *The Annunciation*, c. 1444–47, tempera on panel, 27.3 x 54 cm. Fitzwilliam Museum, Bequeathed by Frederick Fuller, 1923, No. 1106

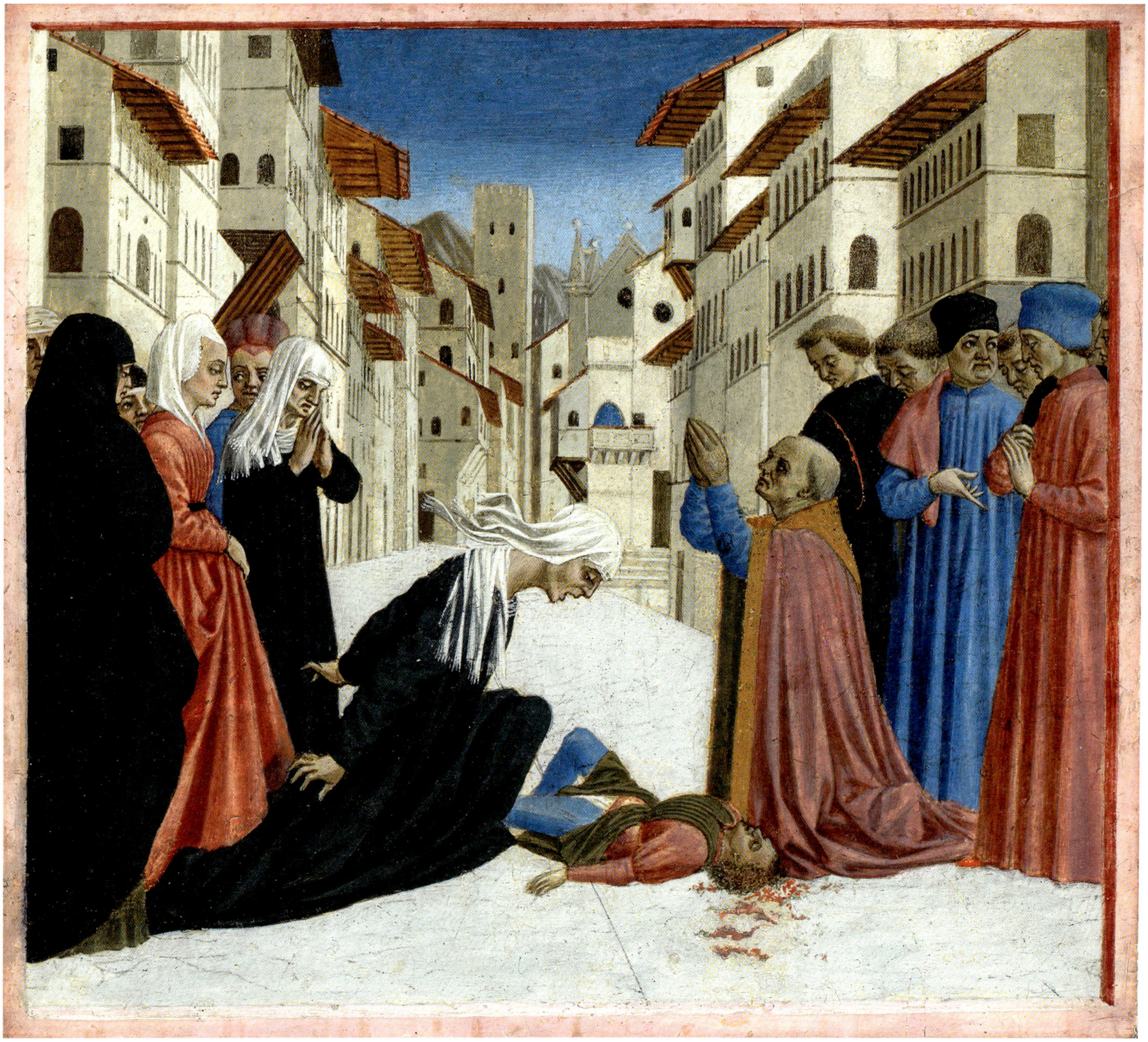

144 Domenico Veneziano (Domenico di Bartolomeo da Venezia), *A Miracle of Saint Zenobius*, c. 1445–47, tempera on panel, 28.6 x 32.5 cm. Fitzwilliam Museum, No. 1107

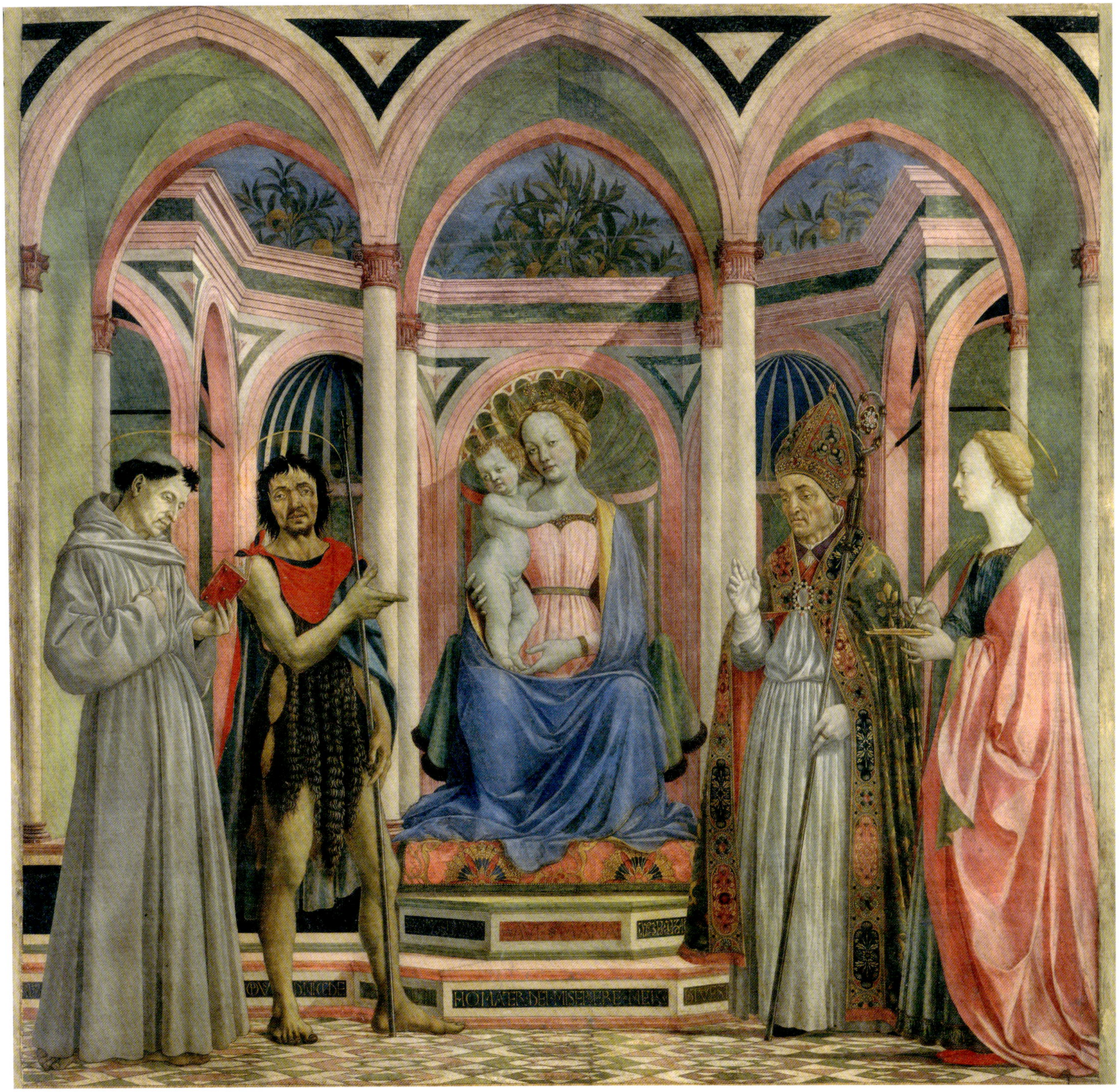

145 Domenico Veneziano (Domenico di Bartolomeo da Venezia), The Saint Lucy Altarpiece (main panel), c. 1445–47, tempera on panel, 209 x 216 cm. Galleria degli Uffizi, Florence, 1890: 884

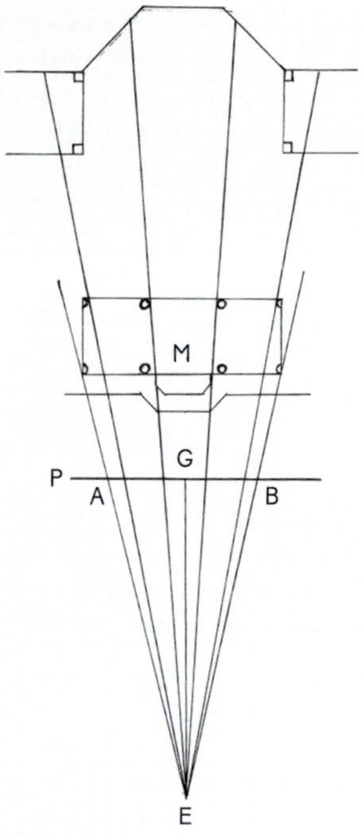

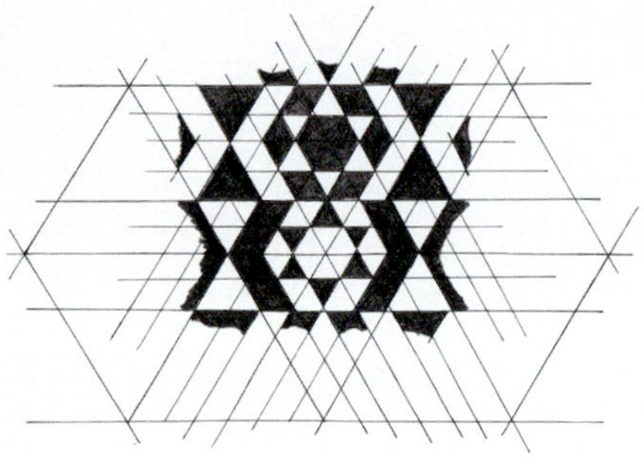

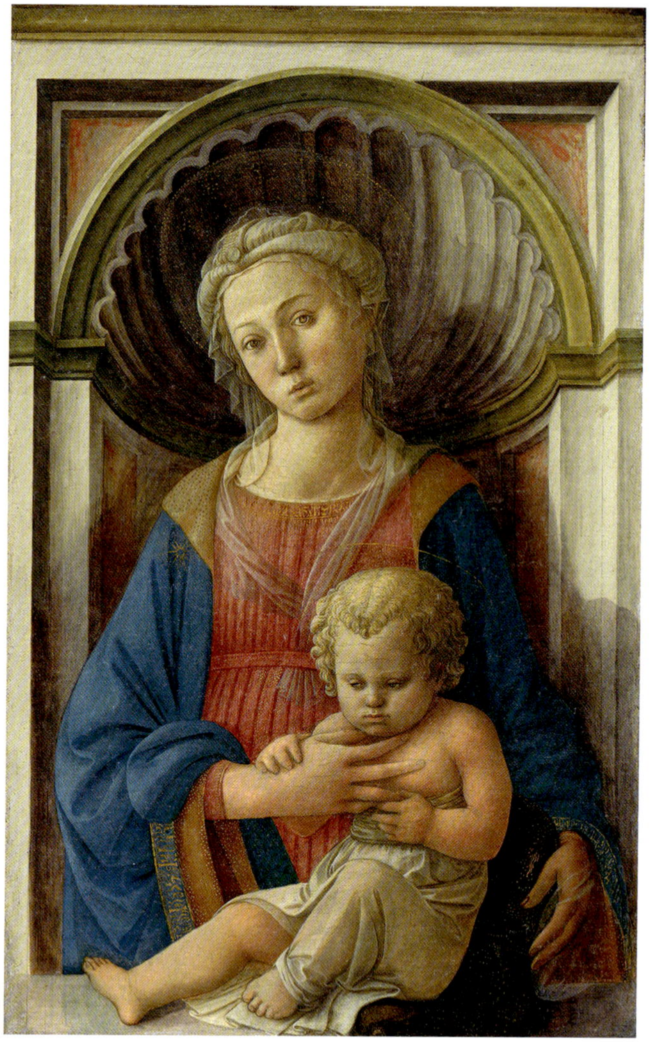

148 Filippo Lippi, *The Virgin and Child*, c. 1440, tempera on panel, 79 x 51.1 cm, National Gallery of Art, Washington, 1939.1.290

146 Projection of groundplan of fig. 145 (Martin Kemp, *The Science of Art*, 1990, fig. 55)

E: observer; M: position of Madonna under loggia; AB: width of picture; P: picture plane; EG: viewing distance

147 Reconstruction of tile pattern in fig. 145 (Martin Kemp, *The Science of Art*, 1990, fig. 52)

to meet the bespoke story-telling needs of the dramas depicted. Figures had to be legible and foregrounded, allowing the viewer to read across the scenes in coherent fashion.[11] In the Zenobius panel, this helps to explain Domenico's strategy of crowding the action close to the picture plane. By separating his figures from the cityscape beyond so sharply, he ensured that they were not lost within it.

With the two Fitzwilliam predella scenes one cannot plot pictorial space in the tidy fashion one can for the main panel without swiftly encountering geometric inconsistencies and spatial contradictions. These defy representation in traditional diagrammatic form but show up clearly when the pictures are analysed in camera matching software. In the case of *A Miracle of Saint Zenobius*, Domenico has used overlapping perspectival constructions and more than one vanishing point. Most of the buildings recede towards one of two dominant vanishing points (fig. 149), while others follow their own logic.

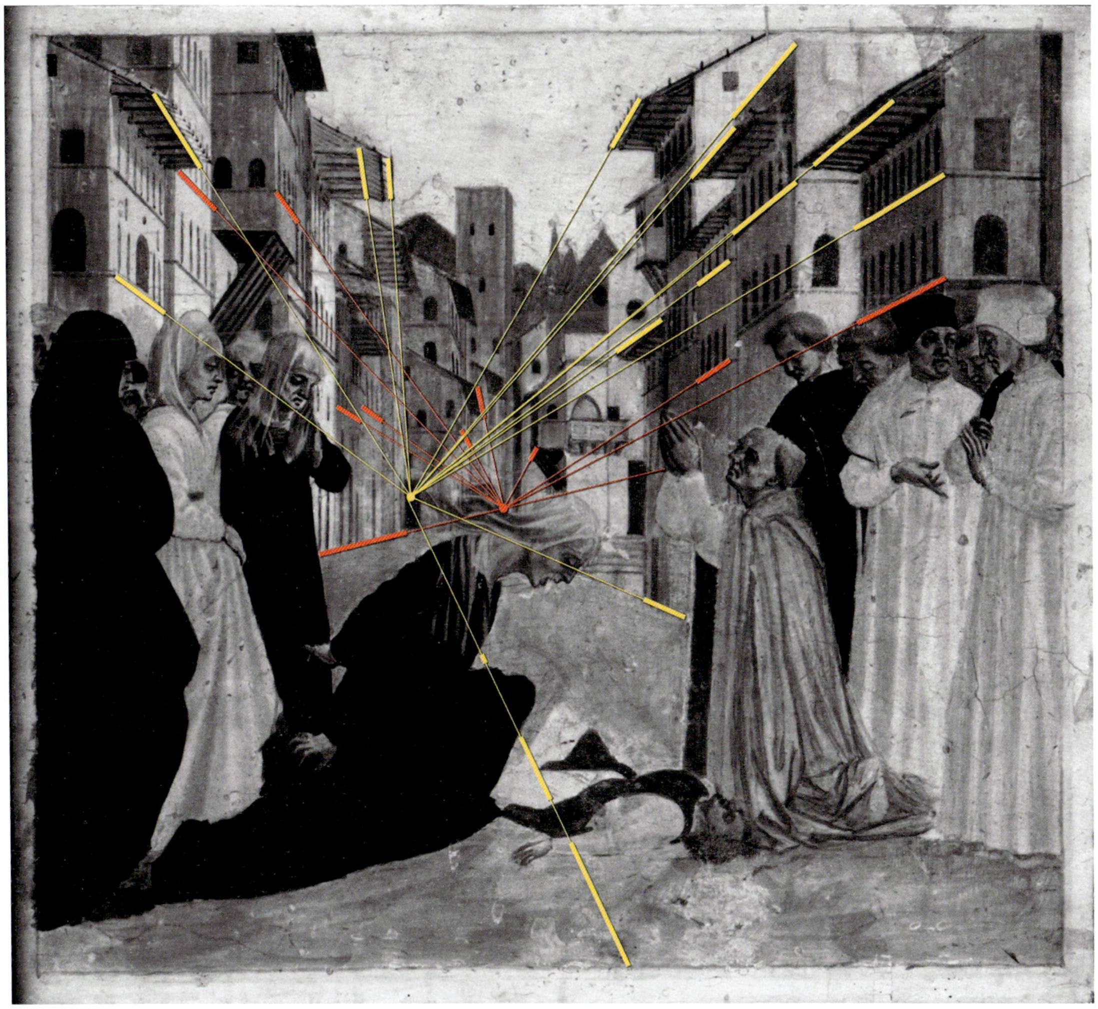

149 Infrared reflectogram of fig. 144 with alternative vanishing points plotted in red and yellow

Domenico seems to be using perspectival space as an armature around which he weaves a whole variety of angled recessions, a conscious strategy to capture the irregularities of the Florentine built environment.[12] This fluid approach also allows the artist to 'splay' the view, widening the street relative to the height of the buildings, and showing the individual palaces and houses at a less extreme – but still impressively oblique – angle.[13] This accentuates the sense in which the buildings surround the scene, and also pushes the drama towards the viewer.

The miracle depicted had a specific Florentine topography, with a stone marker in the street of Borgo Albizi identifying the spot on which a boy had been miraculously revived by the city's first bishop. It was important that Domenico place his scene in a setting that was easily recognizable to his audience as opposed to rigorously accurate in topographical terms. Offering a clearer view of an important landmark like the church of San Pier Maggiore served this purpose well.[14] Nonetheless, software modelling of the vanishing points for Domenico's street vista scaled for the figures in the foreground suggests significant distortions (fig. 150), and a substantial reduction of the 150 metres that separated the miracle marker and the church (down to 33 metres using the 'red' vanishing point reconstructed here).[15] Domenico's approach is fundamentally akin to creating scenery for a stage set, fashioning a spatial illusion which coheres for a specific audience but which is fundamentally dictated by the dramatic demands of the foreground action.

The *Annunciation* has a more coherently realised perspectival space with a single vanishing point, but here too we can see a good deal of Domenico's working procedure on the

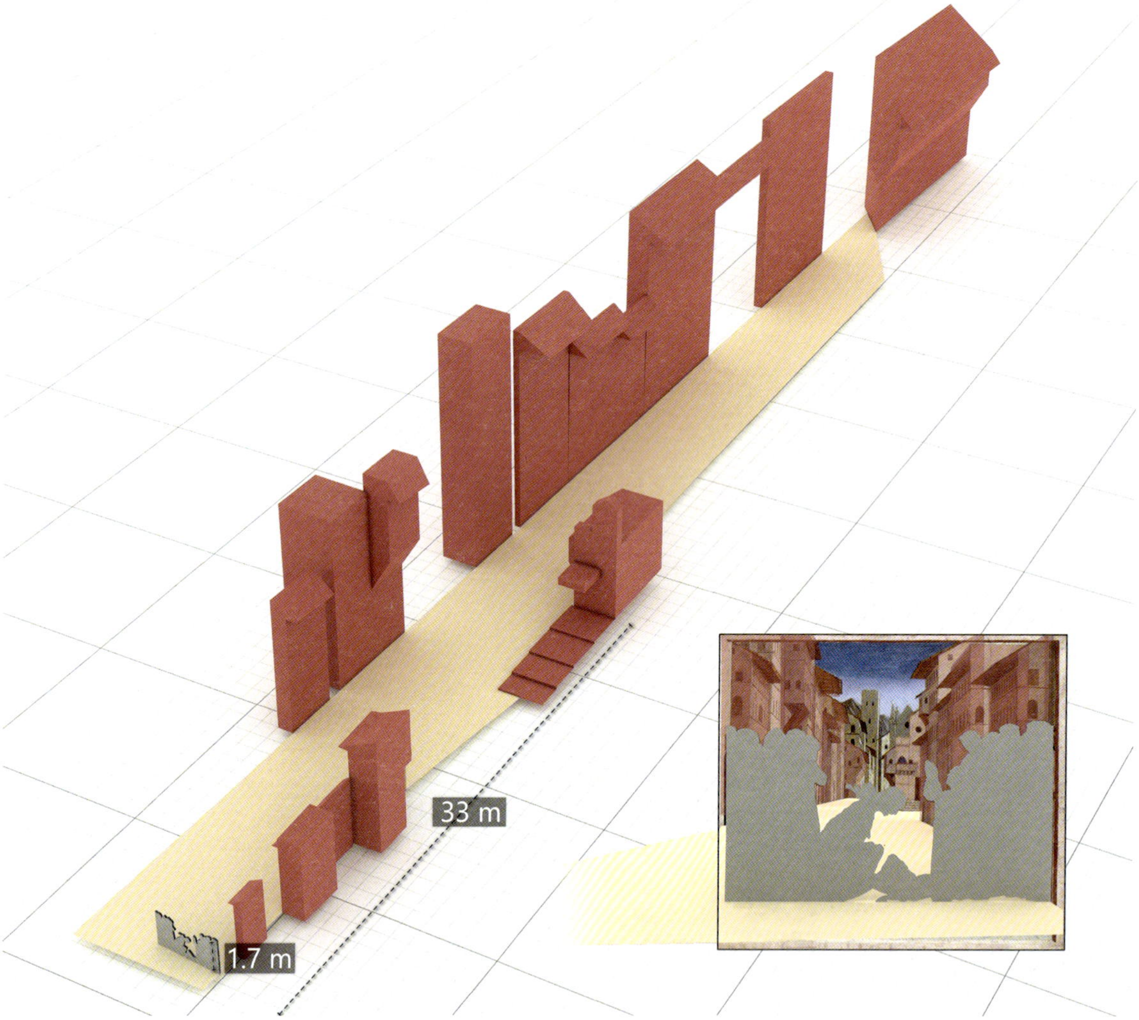

150 Projection of perspectival space ('red' vanishing point) in fig. 144 using camera matching software

surface of the panel. The scene was originally the central section of the predella, directly below the Virgin and Child in the main panel. The Fitzwilliam picture has been cut down on the left-hand side by around 6.3 cm, perhaps to provide a more symmetrical compositional balance between the Virgin and Gabriel when the panel was prepared for sale in the early 1800s. The vanishing point is set on the distant wooden door (and more specifically on the join with the door's upper reinforcing bar) that closes the vista through the garden. This gives a more conventional horizon line broadly aligned with the Virgin's head: there was no need for a low viewpoint here as there was for the main panel (fig. 151). Two receding orthogonals incised in the pavement grid indicate that Domenico originally anticipated a slightly higher vanishing point, which would have been more precisely in line with the Virgin's head, as recommended by Alberti. These initial lines (marked as red in fig. 151), which were probably some of the first incised on the panel, also relate to a series of evenly spaced marks along the bottom border, made as Domenico began to plot his perspectival grid. Having opted for a marginally lower vanishing point for his final perspectival construction, Domenico suggested a lower one still when adding the finishing touches to the painting by allowing the encroaching foliage to taper the pathway beyond the incised orthogonals.[16]

Incised lines visible in raking light also show that Domenico had originally intended the arch framing our view of the garden to be larger, or at least higher (fig. 152). In terms of their arrangement on the picture surface, the arch

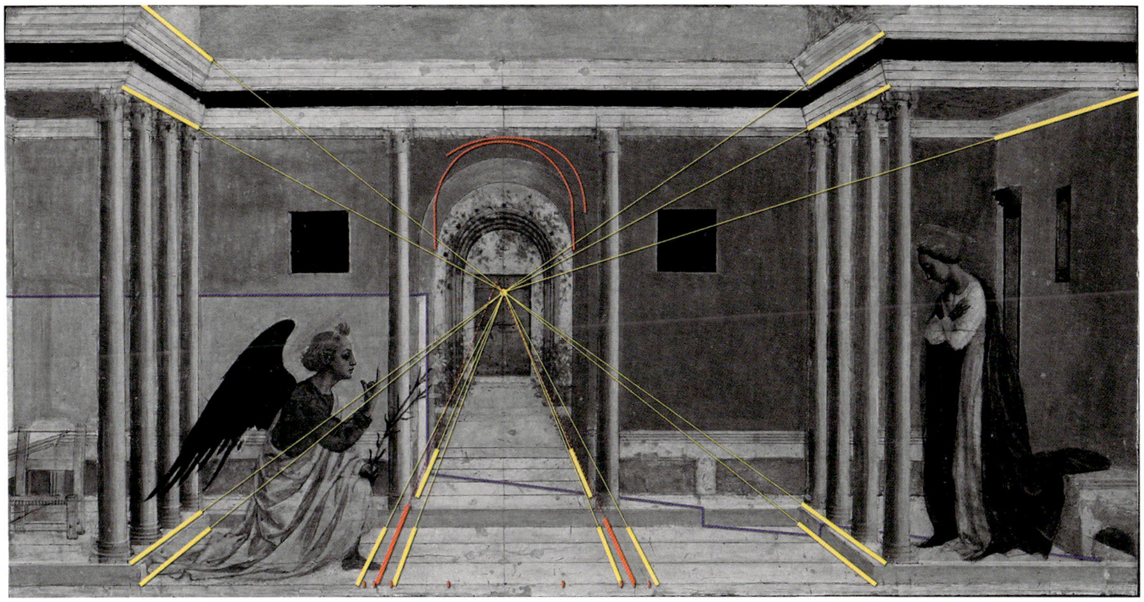

151 Infrared reflectogram of fig. 143 showing initial compositional incised lines and marks (red), main perspectival construction and vanishing point (yellow) and line of cast shadow across the courtyard (blue)

and door beyond would have recalled the small tabernacles to hold the consecrated Host (the literal body of Christ in Catholic doctrine) with hinged doors that were often integrated at the centre of altarpiece predellas in this era: another example of Domenico weaving conventions of altarpiece design into his perspectival practice. The Eucharistic associations of the central vista would have been easily recognized by viewers attuned to pick up symbolic details in Annunciation iconography. Domenico's scene reprises several of the most common tropes of contemporary Annunciation imagery. The garden refers to the Virgin as the 'closed garden' (*hortus conclusus*) and terminates in the 'closed door' (*porta clausa*), another allusion to her virginity and the miraculous nature of the Incarnation. The Virgin herself rises from her seat before another door leading off the right-hand side of the *cortile*, signifying her role as the 'gate of heaven' (*porta coeli*). The open vista afforded of the garden is contrasted with the barred windows to either side, their dark voids sitting like black squares on the picture surface.

Given the single vanishing point (marked in yellow in fig. 151), the spatial quirks of the *Annunciation* are not as obvious as those in the *Miracle of Saint Zenobius*, but they do emerge when one tries to model the space (fig. 153). One unexpected anomaly is the way in which the floor of the far side of the *cortile* slopes down to the

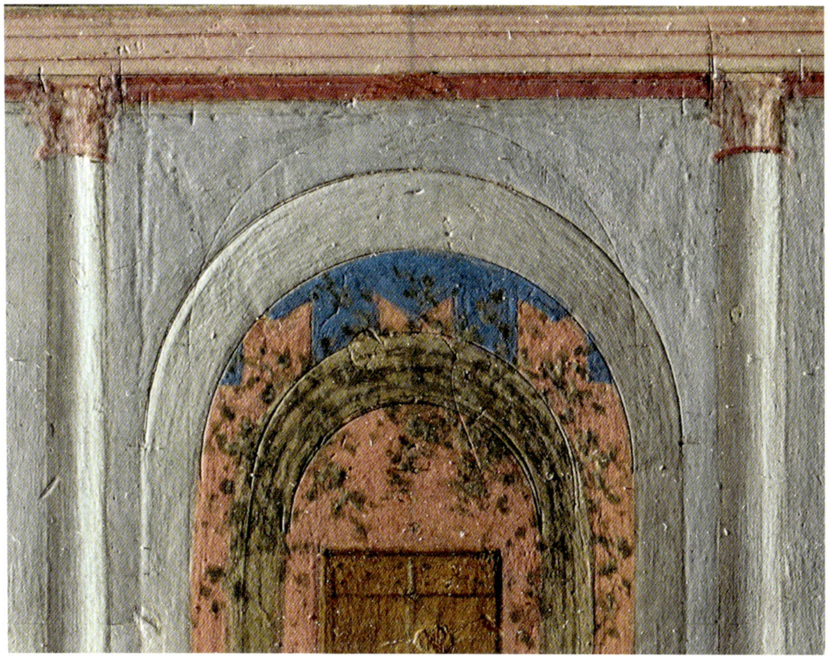

152 Detail of incised archway in fig. 143 seen in raking light

153 Projection of perspectival space in fig. 143 using camera matching software

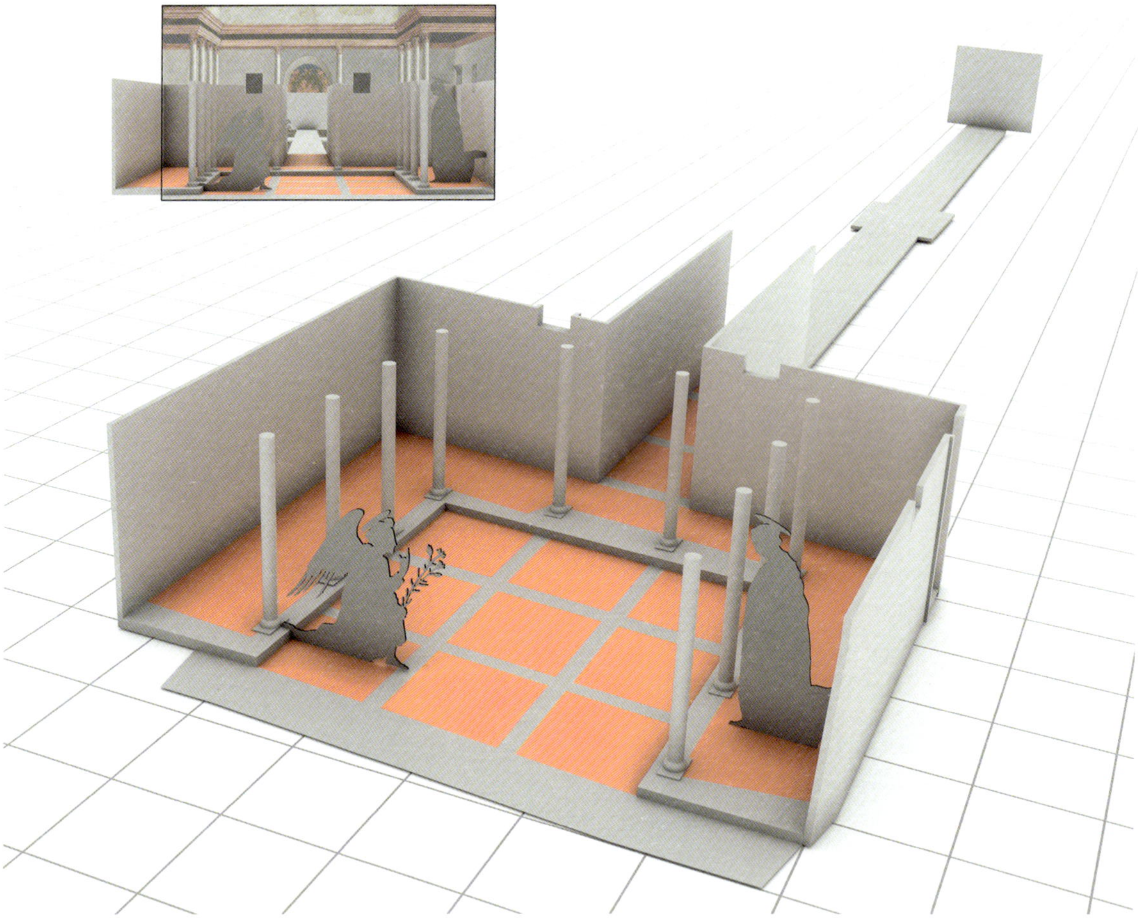

left. Whatever the iconographic significance of the simple chair in the left-hand corner, it also allowed Domenico to fudge what was turning out to be an awkward corner behind. The figure of Gabriel also masks a misalignment in the front step of the portico behind him, caused by the same gradual slope, which shows up as a marked discontinuity in the reconstruction. Much depends on whether one assumes that the grid of the pavement is in fact formed of squares, a common enough expectation when analysing perspectivally conceived floors which receives additional reinforcement here from the fact that the grid matches the spacing of the columns, which would normally be equal on all sides of the *cortile*.[17] The software produces a significantly more shallow space when it is left to calculate the space without this precondition. But in either case, the arched passage opening into the garden proves to be much deeper than a casual glance suggests, allowing for the presence of two rooms behind the barred windows between the *cortile* and the garden.

While the perspectival constructions in the main panel and predella scene are organized independently from one another, Domenico sought to unify the different elements of the altarpiece by another means – the deployment of lighting and cast shadows.[18] The chromatic and tonal qualities of the main panel suffered greatly from an over-zealous cleaning in 1862, but the viewer is still struck by the strong cast shadow falling diagonally across the architecture behind the Virgin and Child, signalling that the scene is lit from the upper right and slightly in front of the picture plane. Other shadows cast by the standing saints and the steps of the Virgin's dais confirm the same illumination, which would equate with morning sunshine from the south-east in terms of the orientation of the church. The same illumination is carried over into the Annunciation scene where the roof of the cortile casts a shadow against the back wall of the courtyard. The shadow line, incised in the gesso priming, falls diagonally across the pavement grid, accommodating the step and the recession into the open passage of the arch (marked in blue in fig. 151). To the left, the lower section of the back wall remains in sunlight, serving to frame and silhouette the kneeling Archangel. Software modelling can generate a good approximation of Domenico's cast shadows within a 3D visualization of the courtyard, while also confirming a number of understandable simplifications (notably, the shadows that would be cast by the colonnade are omitted). The lighting in the other predella scenes is less ambitious. In the *Miracle of Saint Zenobius* the prevailing sunlight is from the right but the figures cast no shadows and the buildings are lit inconsistently, especially their front faces parallel with the picture plane. In *The Martyrdom of Saint Lucy* (Berlin, Gemäldegalerie), the main figures cast shadows that follow the standard light source, but the system is not extended to the architecture. Probably the more coherent spatial projections of the main panel and the *Annunciation* facilitated this virtuoso display of sunlight and shadow within fictive architecture. The five predella scenes were, however, unified by their fictive pink frames (still preserved on all sides of the *Zenobius* panel and just visible along the bottom edge of the *Annunciation*), which reprised the lighting of the main panel.

Domenico's Fitzwilliam pictures and the larger altarpiece of which they were originally part document a varied approach to linear perspective. The artist's mastery of the principles is not in doubt and the main panel provides a virtuoso demonstration, but for Domenico it was one technique amongst several rather than a consistently applied approach, and in the *predella* images he sometimes subordinated it to other compositional and narrative needs.[19] Perspective could also be deployed in discrete projections, which could co-exist within the same image for dynamic effect. In Veneziano's hands, linear perspective was a fluid and creative practice rather than a prescriptive set of rules, or a 'prison' of Alberti's making. While the main panel must have required cartoons and calculations, the predella panels reveal a much more immediate procedure, with Domenico correcting his spatial construction on the panel. In the *Annunciation*, the architecture took precedence over the figures, which were drawn at a later stage, something visible in the lines crossing Gabriel's body and wings. In the *Miracle of Saint Zenobius*, however, the city scape in the background seems to have been worked out after the figures, suggesting a rather different compositional procedure. For an experienced draughtsman and painter like Domenico, relying on the judgement of the naked eye must often have been the most time-efficient solution, especially when working on a small scale.

Domenico was not an isolated case: similar slippages, manipulations and shortcuts can be seen in the perspectival practice of other artists. Returning to Fra Angelico's San Marco *Annunciation*, the ceiling and the floorplan follow two very different perspectival projections, albeit from the same vanishing point. Any attempt to integrate them leads to severe distortions in the arches and bays. Fra Angelico had his own reasons for this dual projection, doubtless intended to respond to the viewer approaching the fresco from below, up the dormitory staircase. Even as early as the 1440s, perspective was more often a practical technique for selected application rather than a systematic theory applied rigidly to image-making. It was deployed by skilled craftsmen who often trusted their own judgment more than rules, and who could rely on a public that was already sufficiently familiar with this way of conceiving space that it was able both to recognize the convention and appreciate its creative application.

Notes

1 Hockney and Gayford 2016, 107. Our understanding of Domenico's perspectival practice has benefited greatly from discussions with Martin Kemp, Martin Gayford, Jane Munro, Andrea De Marchi and Neville Rowley. Research and visualization work for this essay was undertaken as part of the Florence4D project (www.florence4d.org), funded by the Getty Foundation, AHRC, and the Universities of Exeter and Cambridge. **2** For a pioneering application of this approach to Masaccio's *Trinity*, see Martin Kemp and Antonio Criminisi, 'Computer vision and painters' visions in Italian and Netherlandish art of the fifteenth century', in Carpo and Lemerle 2007, 31–46. Camera matching software is designed to convert photographs of built environments into 3D models by extracting their perspectival qualities. The software used on this occasion is fSpy, an open-source application. **3** The most precise diagrammatic analysis is provided in Kemp 1990, 36; but see also Elkins 1994, 243, who notes that, while the painting's foreground is measurable, its background – beyond the colonnade – is "effectively immeasurable (for Renaissance theorists, at any rate"). **4** For the pavement geometry, see Kemp 1990, 35. **5** An ambiguity first noted by White 1957, 188, n. 16. **6** White 1957, 188, n. 16; Kemp 1990, 36. **7** The relatively low horizon line in the altarpiece, and its departure from Alberti's recommendation that the 'centric line' should determine the level of heads within the image, has been frequently noted: see Edgerton 1975, 58; Wohl 1980, 41. Iconographic significance is attributed to the location of the vanishing point between the Virgin's knees in Moffitt 1997. The connection between the vanishing point, the raised altar and the viewer's eye level was made by Miller 1983, 213–15; repeated by Luciano Bellosi, 'Sulla formazione fiorentina di Piero della Francesca', in Bellosi 1992, 19. **8** The phrase is used by Keith Christiansen in his catalogue entry (no. 22), in Christiansen 2005, 190. **9** Kemp 1990, 36. **10** The allusion to the screen was suggested by De Marchi 1994, 36; the interior furniture of the church will be discussed by Francesca Aimi in future publications. **11** The reconstruction of the altarpiece makes it clear that the individual scenes must originally have been divided by simple mouldings of no more than 5 cm, with no space for more elaborate relief elements in gesso or pastiglia: see De Marchi 1994, 37. For the identification and attribution of the predella scenes, see Rowley 2017 **12** Domenico seems to have been the first to attempt to mix perspective with the irregularity of a townscape, although there are important precedents in the earlier cityscapes of Ambrogio Lorenzetti. **13** In addition, Domenico has radically simplified the streetscape by reducing the number of façades depicted to avoid a crowded concertina-like effect of recession into depth. **14** The exaggerated size of the church in Veneziano's painting is noted by Wohl 1980, 48. Elements of the depiction of the façade and northern transept (or more properly the *cappellone* extension added in the early 1400s) beyond are remarkably accurate: for the reconstruction of San Pier Maggiore, see Cooper, 'Firenze scomparsa: le chiese di Santa Chiara e San Pier Maggiore e la loro ricostruzione digitale presso i musei di Londra', in Vitolo 2018, 67–80. **15** In this sense, Domenico's approach to the streetscape departs from the likely roots of perspectival space in contemporary surveying techniques, for which see Kemp 1978, 134–61. **16** The manner in which Veneziano seems to be working out and progressively adjusting his perspectival system as he prepared the *Annunciation* panel underline doubts regarding the over-simplistic and diagrammatic application of surface geometry in art historical analysis: see Elkins 1991. **17** The point is made by Welliver 1973, 16. **18** The fullest account of Veneziano's '*prospettiva di luce*' in the altarpiece is De Marchi 1992, 37–38. For broader discussion and the potential association of this trend with Medici patronage, see Rowley 2010. **19** As noted by Christiansen in Christiansen 2005, 191, Domenico's subordination of perspective to narrative drama owed much to Donatello, and can be contrasted with Piero's later works.

Checklist of exhibited works

List of objects displayed in *Hockney's Eye: The Art and Technology of Depiction*. All works belong to the Fitzwilliam Museum unless otherwise stated. Dimensions given are height, width, and depth where applicable. Dimensions for 2D works are given unframed unless otherwise stated. Dimensions for works on paper are for the whole sheet (with plate size for prints, where applicable); dimensions for books or albums refer to the size of a single leaf.

F | Works exhibited at the Fitzwilliam Museum

H | Works exhibited at the Heong Gallery

Introduction

F | David Hockney, *Self-Portrait III, 20th March 2012,* iPad drawing. Collection of the artist

F | David Hockney, *Self Portrait, 9th March 2012,* iPad drawing. Collection of the artist

F | David Hockney, *Self Portrait, 10th March 2012,* iPad drawing. Collection of the artist

F | David Hockney, *Self Portrait I, 13th March 2012,* iPad drawing. Collection of the artist

F | David Hockney, *Self Portrait II, 14th March 2,* iPad drawing. Collection of the artist

F | David Hockney, *Self Portrait I, 25th March 2012,* iPad drawing. Collection of the artist

F | David Hockney, *Self Portrait IV, 25th March 2012,* iPad drawing. Collection of the artist

F | David Hockney, *Self Portrait, 19th April 2012,* iPad drawing. Collection of the artist

F | David Hockney, *Self Portrait I, 16th March 2012,* iPad drawing. Collection of the artist

F | *Self Portrait, 22nd November 2021,* acrylic on canvas, 91.4 x 76.2 cm. Collection of the artist

David Hockney: space explorer

H | David Hockney, *Arizona*, 1964, acrylic on canvas, 153 x 153 cm. Private collection

H | David Hockney, *Skeleton, Study II, Royal College of Art*, 1959, pencil on paper, 104 x 71 cm. Private collection

F | David Hockney, *Tyger*, c. 1960, oil and pencil on board, 76.2 x 50.8 cm. Private collection

F | David Hockney, *Tyger Painting No. 2*, 1960, oil on board, 102 x 63.5 cm. Private collection

F | David Hockney, *Shame*, 1960, oil on board, 127 x 102 cm. Private collection

F | David Hockney, *A Man Thinking*, 1962–63, oil on canvas, 91 x 63 cm. Private collection

H | David Hockney, *Portrait Surrounded by Artistic Devices*, 1965, acrylic on canvas, 152.4 x 182.9 cm. Arts Council Collection, Southbank Centre, London, AC 823

H | David Hockney, *24th February 2011,* iPad drawing, Collection of the artist

F | David Hockney, *Beach Umbrella*, 1971, acrylic on canvas, 121.9 cm x 90.8 cm. Private collection

F | David Hockney, *Le Parc des Sources, Vichy*, 1970, acrylic on canvas, 213.8 x 306.8 cm. Private collection

H | David Hockney, *Walking in the Zen Garden at the Ryoanji Temple, Kyoto, February 1983*, photographic collage, edition 15 of 20, 101.6 x 158.8 cm. Collection of the artist

H | David Hockney, *The Scrabble Game, January 1st 1983,* photographic collage, edition 10 of 20, 99 x 147.3 cm. Collection of the artist

H | David Hockney, *Matelot Kevin Druez 1*, 2009, inkjet printed computer drawing on paper, edition 20 of 30, 124.5 x 85 cm. Private collection

F | David Hockney, *Woldgate Woods, Winter 2010*, 2010–11, 9 digital videos synchronized and presented on 9 monitors to comprise a single artwork, duration: 49:00. Collection of the artist

Seeing through perspective

F | David Hockney, *The Ballroom, Santa Cruz*, 1966, pen and ink on paper, 25 x 31.1 cm. Private collection

F | David Hockney (b. 1937), *California Bank*, 1964, acrylic on canvas, 76.2 x 63.5 cm. Private collection

H | David Hockney, *Rubber Ring Floating in a Swimming Pool*, 1971, acrylic on canvas, 91.4 x 122 cm. Private collection

H | David Hockney, *10th August 2010*, iPad drawing, Collection of the artist

F | David Hockney, *Annunciation II, after Fra Angelico* from *The Brass Tacks Triptych*, 2017, acrylic on canvas, 121.9 x 243.8 cm (hexagonal). Collection of the artist

H | David Hockney, *Viewers Looking at a Ready-made with Skull and Mirrors*, 2018, photographic drawing printed on four sheets of paper, mounted on four sheets of Dibond, paper sheets 222.3 x 92.7 cm, 222.3 x 370.8 cm overall, assisted by Jonathan Wilkinson. Collection of the artist

Appendix: where is the evidence

F | Thomas Girtin, *View of the Louvre and the Pont des Tuileries from the Pont Neuf, from A Selection of Twenty of the Most Picturesque Views in Paris and its Environs*, 1801, soft-ground etching, pencil and watercolour on paper, 17.5 x 44.9 cm. Bought from the Biffen Fund, with a contribution from the Victoria and Albert Museum Grant-in-Aid, PD.5-1983

Hobbema's *Avenue* and the ordering of nature: arboreal and optical

F | David Hockney, *After Hobbema (Useful Knowledge)*, 2017, acrylic on 6 canvases, framed: 2 canvases: 61 x 61 cm; 4 joined hexagonal canvases: 113 x 277.5 cm. Collection of the artist

F | Meindert Hobbema, *The Avenue at Middelharnis*, 1689, oil on canvas, 103.5 x 141 cm. The National Gallery, London, Bough, 1871, NG830

F | David Hockney, *Huggate, St Mary's Church Spire*, August 2005, oil on canvas, 60.9 x 91.4 cm. On loan from the Estate of the late Mrs Elizabeth Corob

All kinds of objects

F | Thomas Sandby, *Windsor Castle from the Goswells drawn in a camera*, c. 1760–70, pencil, pen and ink and watercolour on paper, 12.4 x 57.8 cm. Royal Collection Trust, RCIN914602

F | John Varley, *Portrait of William Havell*, c. 1810–11, pencil on paper, 21.3 x 15.4 cm. The Wordsworth Trust, Dove Cottage, Grasmere, 1997.2.2

F | Cornelius Varley, Portrait of *William J. Booth, head in profile*, 1811, pencil on paper, 37.8 x 27.7 cm, Sir Ivor and Lady Batchelor Bequest, PD.178-2015

F | Cornelius Varley, *Study of a Masted Boat*, c. 1823, pencil and watercolour on paper, 47.8 x 32.5 cm. Purchased from the Biffen Fund, 1993, PD.42–1993

F | Thomas Girtin, *View of Lancaster*, c. 1797, pencil on paper, 14.3 x 21.8 cm. Tate, Accepted by the nation as part of the Turner Bequest, 1856, D 36575

F | J.M.W. Turner, *Holy Island, Northumberland* – a page from the 'North of England' sketchbook, 1797, pencil on paper, 21.0 x 27.0 cm. Tate, Accepted by the nation as part of the Turner Bequest, 1856, D 00959 / TB XXXIV 51

F | Cornelius Varley, *Vale of the Exe from Tiverton*, 1824, pencil on paper, 38.5 x 54.8 cm. Sir Ivor and Lady Batchelor Bequest, 2015, PD.179–2015

The camera lucida and technologies of imitation

F | *Camera lucida*, 1850, metal (brass), glass, 19.1 x 5.5. x 4.9 cm. Whipple Museum of the History of Science, University of Cambridge, 0093

F | *Camera lucida*, owned by the Herschel family, 19th century, glass; brass, 3.7 x 6.0 x 5.2 cm. National Maritime Museum, Greenwich, London, Herschel Collection, AST0794

F | Cornelius Varley, *Patent Graphic Telescope*, c. 1840, metal (brass), bronze, copper, glass, telescope 31.0 cm; max. diameter 6.3 cm; tripod 43.5 x 13.0 x 6.0 cm; eyepiece 1: 8.6 cm; max. diameter 5.7 cm; eyepiece 2: 8.2 cm; max. diameter 5.7 cm eyepiece 3: 8.4 cm; max. diameter 5.7 cm. Whipple Museum of the History of Science, University of Cambridge, 0069

F | Box camera obscura, 19th century, wood, metal, glass, 8.7 x 26.8–19.0 x 14.4 cm. Whipple Museum of the History of Science, Cambridge, 6492

F | Reflex camera obscura, c. 1820, wood, glass, paper, 37.5 x 19.8 x 21.5 cm. History of Science Museum, University of Oxford, 78618

F | Model of the human eye in the form of a camera obscura, mid-19th century, metal (brass and lead alloy), glass, enamel, 23 x 7.7 x 11.4–12 cm. Whipple Museum of the History of Science, University of Cambridge, 5984

F | William Henry Fox Talbot, *Villa Melzi*, 5 October 1833, pencil on paper, 14.2 x 21.8 cm. Science Museum Group, 1937-2537/06

F | Caroline Augusta Fielding, *Casaccia a Bellagio, Lago di Como*, n.d., pencil on paper, 27.3 x 37.6 cm. The Bodleian Libraries, University of Oxford, MS. WHF Talbot 89, fol. 14

F | Caroline Augusta Fielding, *Lago Maggiore from the Theatre in the Isola Madre*, n.d., pencil on paper, 27.5 x 38.5 cm. The Bodleian Libraries, University of Oxford, MS. WHF Talbot 74, fol. 25

F | Constance Fox Talbot, *Villa Melzi lago di Como*, 1833, pencil and watercolour on paper, 19 x 27.6 cm. The Bodleian Libraries, University of Oxford, MS. WHF Talbot 98, fol. 9

Ingres and Hockney: art, science and uniformity

F | David Hockney, *Ian McKellen. London, 27th May 1999,* pencil and coloured pencil on paper using a camera lucida, 38.1 x 28.5 cm. Collection of the David Hockney Foundation

F | David Hockney, *Alan Bennett. London, 25th May 1999,* pencil on paper using a camera lucida, 38.1 x 23.5 cm. Collection of the David Hockney Foundation

F | David Hockney, *Colin St John Wilson. 3rd June 1999,* pencil and coloured pencil on paper using a camera lucida, 38.1 x 48.5 cm. Collection of the David Hockney Foundation

F | David Hockney, *Martin Kemp. London. 22nd June 1999,* pencil and coloured pencil on paper using, a camera lucida, 38.1 x 36.8 cm. Collection of the David Hockney Foundation

F | David Hockney, *Damien Hirst. London, 18th June 1999,* pencil on paper using a camera lucida, 38.1 x 43.5 cm. Collection of the David Hockney Foundation

F | David Hockney, *Margaret Hockney. Bridlington, 16th May 1999,* pencil on paper using a camera lucida, 29.8 x 20 cm. Collection of the David Hockney Foundation

F | Jean-Auguste-Dominique Ingres, *Portrait of Maréchale Kutusov*, 1815, pencil on paper, 13.2 x 8.7 cm. Accepted by H.M. Government in lieu of Inheritance Tax and allocated to the Fitzwilliam Museum, 2010, PD.40-2010

F | Charles Joseph Hullmandel, after Jean-Auguste-Dominique Ingres, *Katherine Anne (North) Lady Glenbervie*, c. 1815–23, lithograph on paper, 31.3 x 22.4 cm. Given by John Charrington, 1933, P.14248-R

F | Charles Joseph Hullmandel, after Jean-Auguste-Dominique Ingres, *Sylvester (Douglas) Baron Glenbervie*, c. 1815–23, lithograph on paper, 31.3 x 21.5 cm. Given by John Charrington, 1933, P.14249-R

F | Charles Joseph Hullmandel, after Jean-Auguste-Dominique Ingres, *The Hon Frederic Sylvester Douglas*, c. 1815–23, lithograph on paper, 30.1 x 22.1 cm. Given by John Charrington, 1933, P.14250-R

F | Charles Joseph Hullmandel, after Jean-Auguste-Dominique Ingres, *Frederick (North) Earl of Guilford*, c. 1815–23, lithograph on paper, 30.5 x 22.1 cm. Given by John Charrington, 1933, P.14251-R

F | Jean-Auguste-Dominique Ingres, *Portrait of Mrs John Mackie*, 1816, pencil on paper, 27.7 x 22.7 cm. Victoria and Albert Museum, Gift of Miss Winifred M. Giles through the Art Fund, E.230–1946

F | Jean-Auguste-Dominique Ingres, *Mr and Mrs Joseph Woodhead and Mr Henry Comber in Rome*, 1816, pencll on paper, 30.4 x 22.4 cm. Given by the National Art-Collections Fund, 1947, PD.52–1947

F | David Hockney, *William Hardie, March 11 1994*, pencil and crayon on paper, 57 x 76 cm. Private collection

F | David Hockney, *12 Portraits After Ingres in a Uniform Style; Devlin Crow, London, 11th January 2000,* pencil and coloured pencil and gouache on paper, 56.2 cm x 38.1 cm. Private collection

F | David Hockney, *12 Portraits After Ingres in a Uniform Style; Pravin Patel, London, 5th January 2000*, pencil and coloured pencil and gouache on paper, 56.2 cm x 38.1 cm. Private collection

F | David Hockney, *12 Portraits After Ingres in a Uniform Style; Katherine Dooley, London, 6th January 2000*, pencil and coloured pencil and gouache on paper, 56.2 cm x 38.1 cm. Private collection

F | David Hockney, *12 Portraits After Ingres in a Uniform Style; Graham Eve, London, 7th January 2000,* pencil and coloured pencil and gouache on paper, 56.2 cm x 38.1 cm. Private collection

F | David Hockney, *12 Portraits After Ingres in a Uniform Style; Brian Wedlake, London, 10th January 2000,* pencil and coloured pencil and gouache on paper, 56.2 cm x 38.1 cm. Private collection

F | David Hockney, *12 Portraits After Ingres in a Uniform Style; Lena James, London, 3rd January 2000*, pencil and coloured pencil and gouache on paper, 56.2 cm x 38.1 cm. Private collection

F | David Hockney, *12 Portraits After Ingres in a Uniform Style; Ron Lillywhite, London, 17th December 1999,* pencil and coloured pencil and gouache on paper, 56.2 cm x 38.1 cm. Private collection

F | David Hockney, *12 Portraits After Ingres in a Uniform Style; Maria Vasquez, London, 21st December 1999,* pencil and coloured pencil and gouache on paper, 56.2 cm x 38.1 cm. Private collection

F | David Hockney, *12 Portraits After Ingres in a Uniform Style; Ken Bradford, London, 20th December 1999,* pencil and coloured pencil and gouache on paper, 56.2 cm x 38.1 cm. Private collection

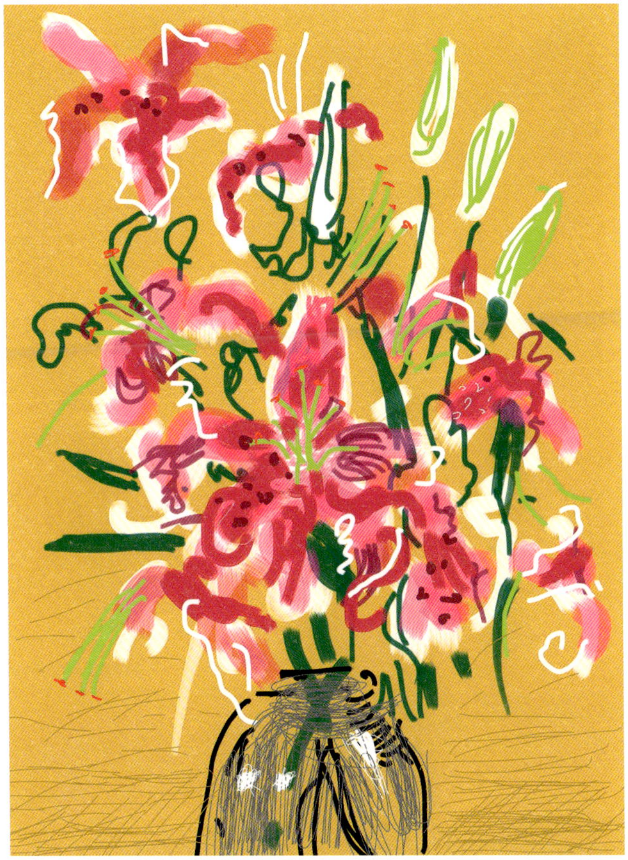
154

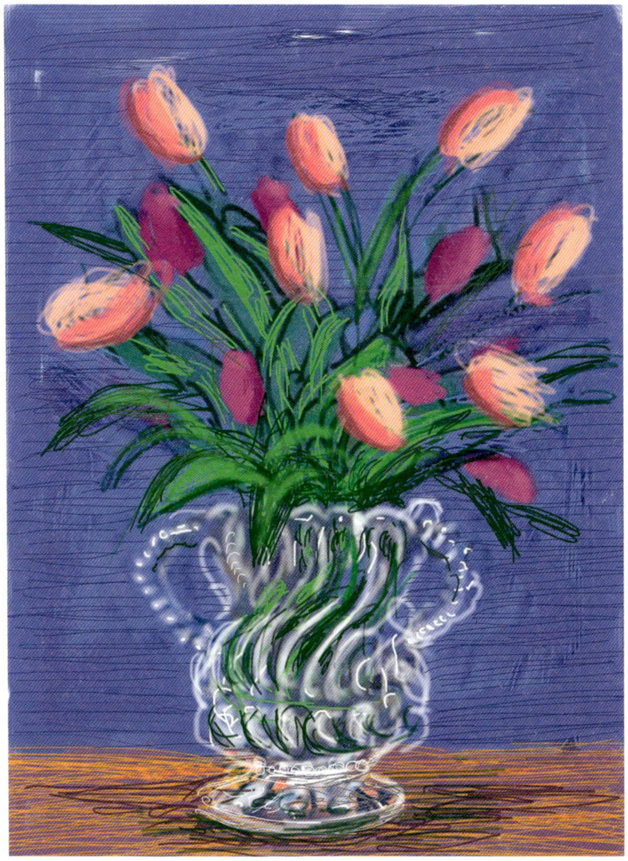
155

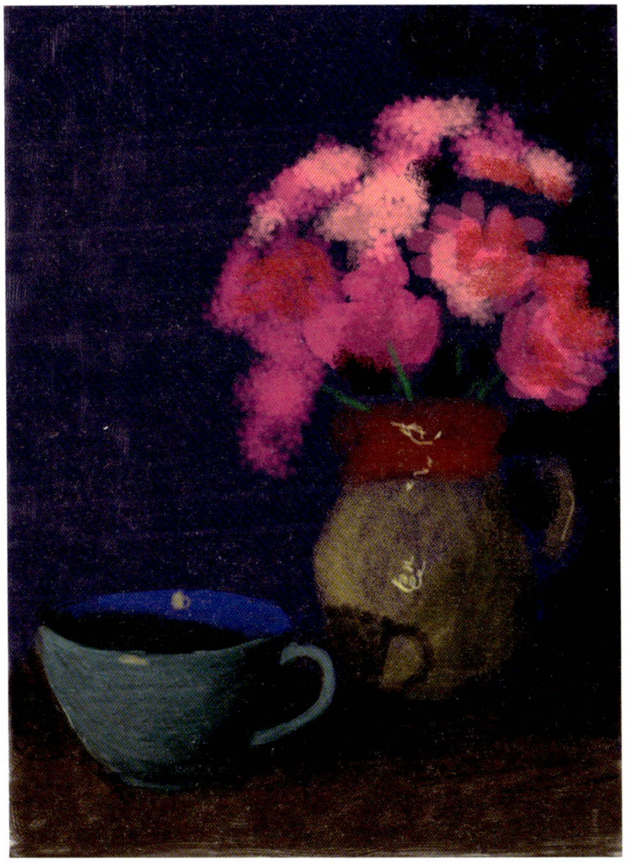
156

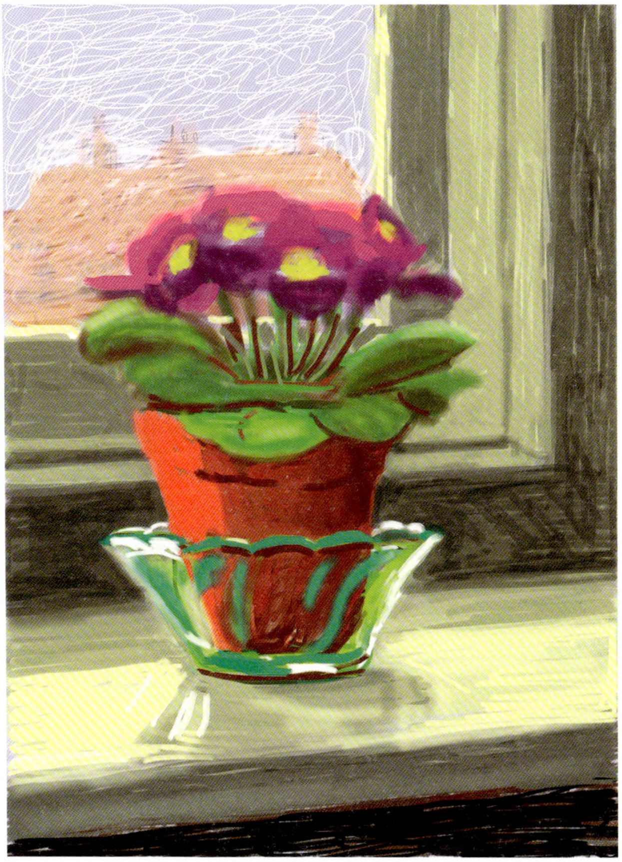
157

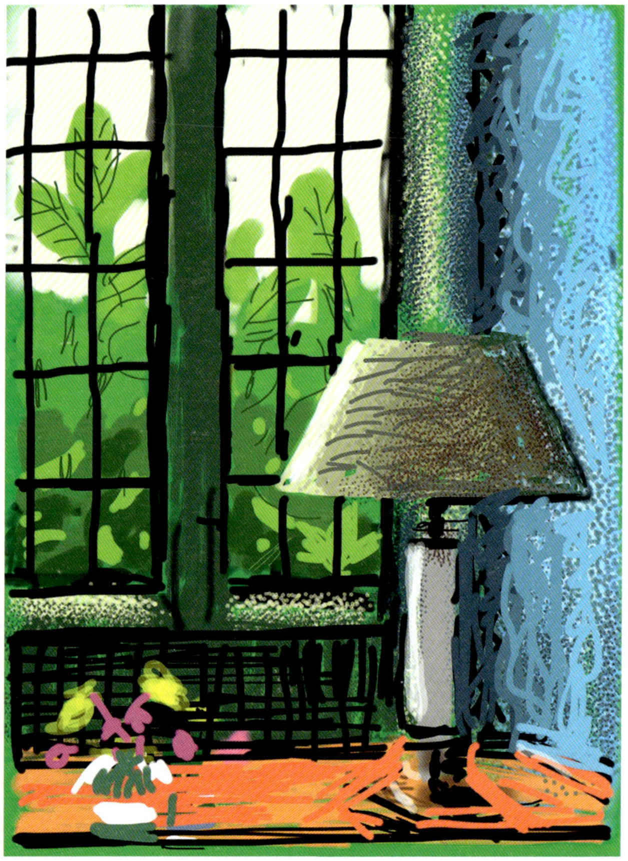

158

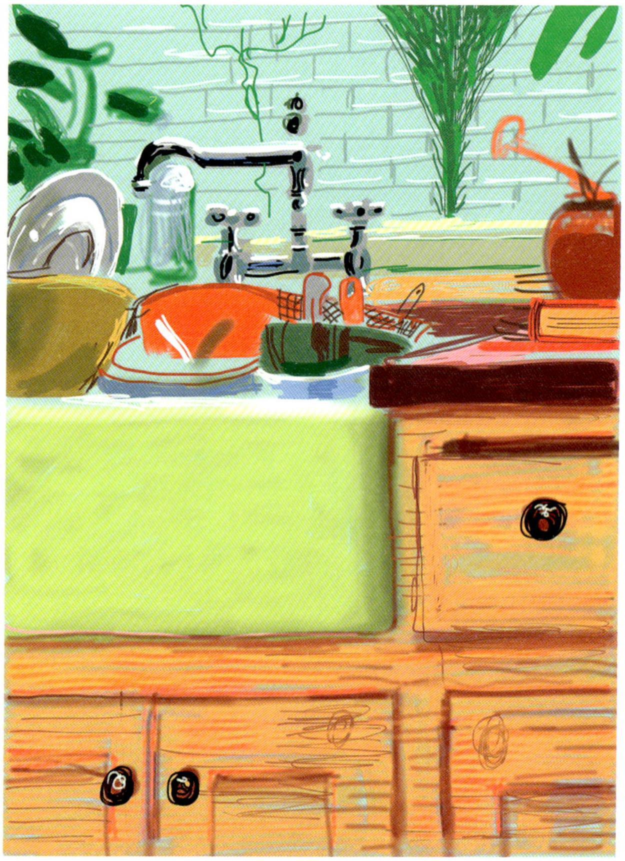

159

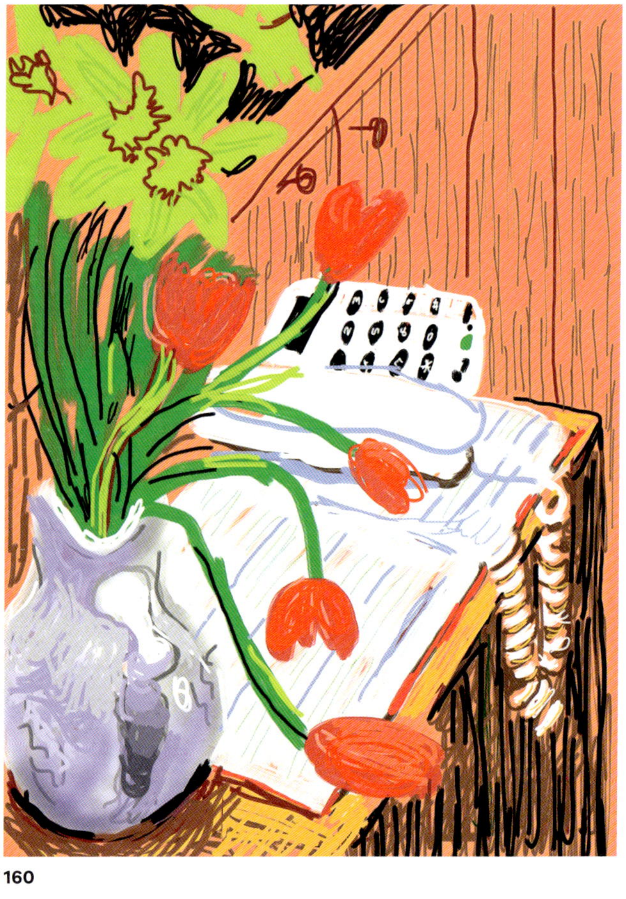

160

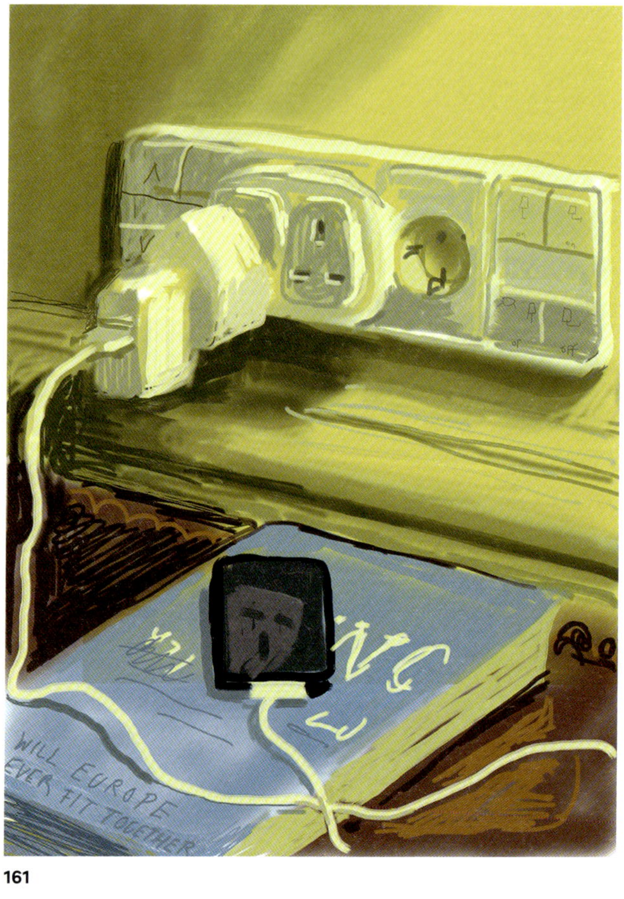

161

F | David Hockney, *12 Portraits After Ingres in a Uniform Style; Jack Kettlewell, London, 13th December 1999, pencil and* coloured pencil and gouache on paper, 56.2 cm x 38.1 cm. Private collection

F | David Hockney, *12 Portraits After Ingres in a Uniform Style; Fazila Jhungoor, London, 18th December 1999,* pencil and coloured pencil and gouache on paper, 56.2 cm x 38.1 cm. Private collection

F | David Hockney, *12 Portraits After Ingres in a Uniform Style; Vincent Simon, London, 16th December 1999*, pencil and coloured pencil and gouache on paper, 56.2 cm x 38.1 cm. Private collection

F | David Hockney, *Martin Gayford, 4th, 5th, 6th December 2013*, from *82 Portraits and 1 Still Life*, acrylic on canvas (one of an 82-part work), 121.9 x 91.4 cm. Collection of the artist

Hockney through the mind's eye

F | David Hockney, *Portrait of Sir David Webster*, 1971, acrylic on canvas, 144.8 x 182.9 cm. Ross Foundation

H | David Hockney, *Grand Canyon I*, 2017, acrylic on canvas, 121.9 x 243.8 cm (hexagonal). Collection of the artist

H | David Hockney, *Grand Canyon Arizona with my Shadow, October 1982,* photographic collage, edition 13 of 15, 96.5 x 158.8 cm. Collection of the artist

F | David Hockney, *Colin Blakemore*, 2018, charcoal and crayon on canvas, 122 x 91.5 cm. Private collection

H | David Hockney, *12th November 2010*, iPad drawing. Collection of the artist

F | David Hockney, *14th July 2010*, iPad drawing. Collection of the artist

Colour in the mind of Hockney

F | David Hockney, *20th April 2020, No. 1*, iPad painting. Collection of the artist

F | David Hockney, *28th November 2010*, iPad drawing. Collection of the artist

F | David Hockney, *6th December 2010*, iPad drawing. Collection of the artist

F | David Hockney, *7th December 2010*, iPad drawing. Collection of the artist

F | David Hockney, *30th November 2010*, iPad drawing. Collection of the artist

Escaping Alberti's prison

F | Domenico Veneziano (Domenico di Bartolomeo da Venezia), *The Annunciation*, c. 1445–47, tempera on panel, 27.3 x 54 cm. Bequeathed by Frederick Fuller, 1923, No. 1106

Checklist of exhibited works

F | David Hockney, *6th July 2010*, iPad drawing. Collection of the artist

F | David Hockney, *21st August 2010*, iPad drawing. Collection of the artist

F | David Hockney, *9th January 2011*, iPad drawing. Collection of the artist

F | David Hockney, *16th June 2011*, iPad drawing. Collection of the artist

H | David Hockney, *20th February 2011*, iPad drawing. Collection of the artist

H | David Hockney, *6th August 2010*, iPad drawing. Collection of the artist

F | David Hockney, *6th January 2011*, iPad drawing. Collection of the artist

H | David Hockney, *22nd January 2011*, iPad drawing. Collection of the artist

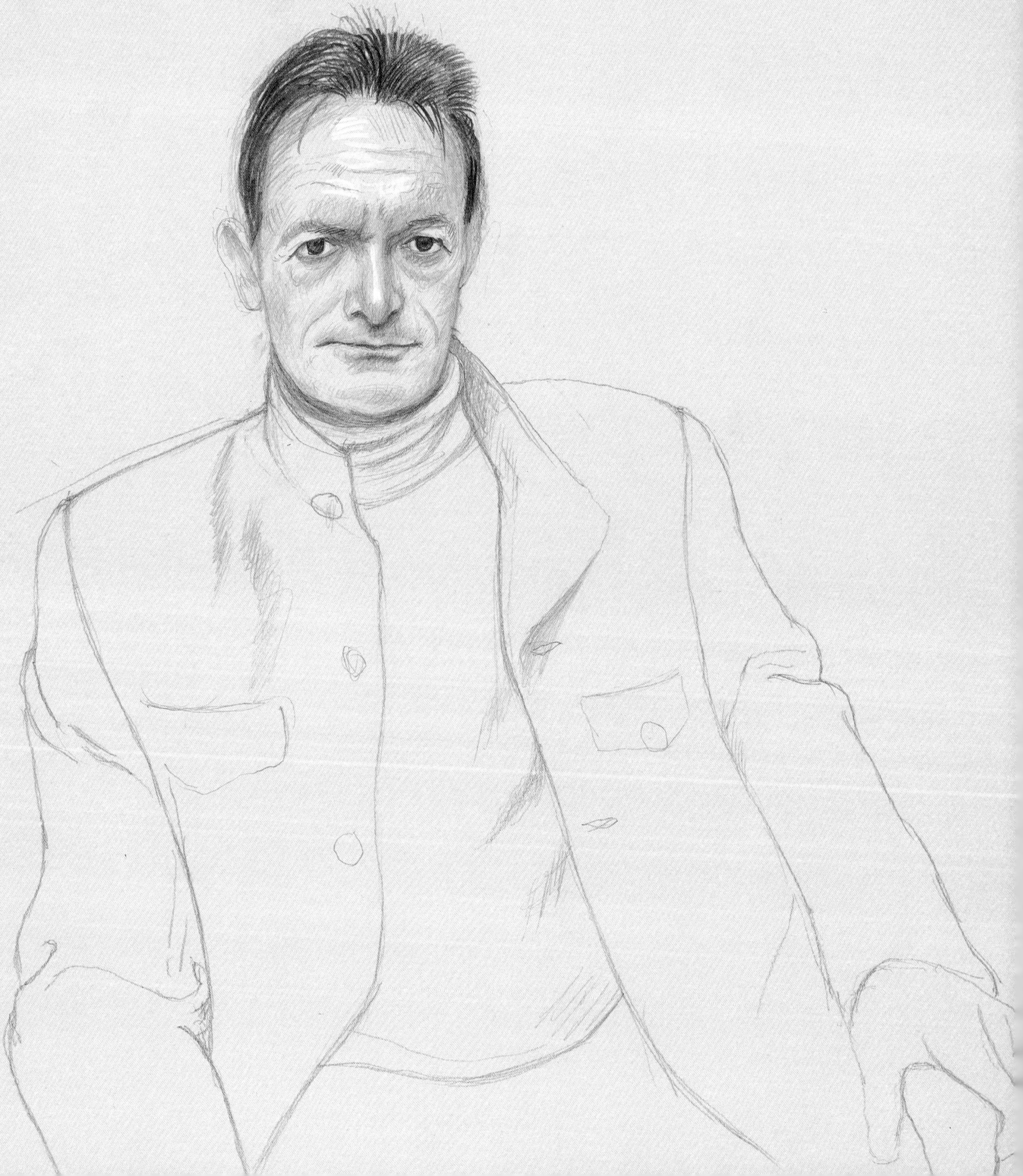

Bibliography

Adams *et al.* 2004
Wendy J. Adams, Erich W. Graf and Marc O. Ernst, 'Experience can change the "light from above" prior', *Nature Neuroscience*, vol. 10, 1057–58

Alpers 1984
Svetlana Alpers, *The Art of Describing. Dutch Art in the Seventeenth Century*, Chicago 1984

Andersen 2007
Kirsti Andersen, *The Geometry of Art*, New York 2007

Anonymous 1840
Anonymous, 'Wollaston's Camera Lucida, Amici's Ditto, and Alexander's Graphic Mirror', *The Magazine of Science, and School of Arts,* vol. I/XLIII, 1840, 338–39

Antonova 2016
Clemena Antonova, *Space, Time, and Presence in the Icon: Seeing the World with the Eyes of God*, London 2016

Babington-Smith 1958
Constance Babington Smith, *Evidence in Camera: The Story of Photographic Intelligence in World War II*, London 1958

Baetjer and Links 1989
Katherine Baetjer and J.G. Links (eds), *Canaletto*, exh. cat., Metropolitan Museum of Art, New York, 1989

Ball 2011
Philip Ball, *Bright Earth: The Invention of Colour,* London 2011

Balze 1880
Raymond Balze, *Ingres, son école, son enseignement du dessin par un des ses élèves*, Paris 1880

Bellosi 1992
Luciano Bellosi, ed., *Una scuola per Piero: luce, colore e prospettiva nella formazione fiorentina di Piero della Francesca*, exh. cat. Galleria degli Uffizi, Florence, 1992

Blake and Bulthoff 1990
Andrew Blake and Heinrich Bülthoff, 'Does the Brain know the Physics of Specular Reflection?', *Nature*, Nature, vol. 343, 1990, 165–168

Blanc 1861
Charles Blanc, 'Le Salon des Arts-Unis', *Gazette des Beaux-Arts*, vol. 9, 1 February 1861, 189–92

Blanc 1870
Charles Blanc, *Ingres sa vie et ses ouvrages,* Paris 1870

Boyer d'Agen 1909
Augustin Boyer d'Agen, *Ingres d'après une correspondance inédite*, Paris 1909

Butlin 1969
Martin Butlin*, The Blake-Varley Sketchbook of 1819*, London 1969

Butlin 1978
Martin Butlin, *William Blake*, exh. cat., Tate Gallery, London 1978

Butlin 1990
Martin Butlin, *William Blake, 1757–1827: Tate Gallery Collections Volume Five*, London 1990

Cantor 1975
Geoffrey Cantor, 'The Reception of the Wave Theory of Light in Britain: A Case Study Illustrating the Role of Methodology in Scientific Debate', *Historical Studies in the Physical Sciences*, 1975, vol. 6, 109–32

Carpo and Lemerle 2007
Mario Carpo and Frédérique Lemerle, eds., *Perspective, Projections and Design. Technologies of Architectural Representation,* London and New York 2007

Casati and Cavanagh 2019
Roberto Casati and Patrick Cavanagh, *The Visual World of Shadows*, Cambridge, Mass., 2019

Castel, Leith and Riley 1994
B. Castel, J. Leith and A. Riley (eds.), *Muse and Reason: The Relation of Arts and Sciences 1650–1850* (Queen's Quarterly for the Royal Society of Canada), Kingston, Ontario, 1994

Chen 2000
Xiang Chen, *Instrumental Traditions and Theories of Light. The Uses of Instruments in the Optical Revolution*, Dordrecht 2000

Chevalier 1834
Vincent Chevalier, *Notice sur l'usage de la chambre claire selon Amici perfectionnée par Vincent Chevalier Ingénieur-Opticien*, Paris 1834

Christiansen 2005
Keith Christiansen, ed. *From Filippo Lippi to Piero della Francesca: Fra Carnevale and the making of a Renaissance master*, exh. cat. Metropolitan Museum of Art, New York, 2005

Cogniet 1947
Raymond Cogniet (ed.), *Ingres, écrits sur l'art*, Paris 1947

Conisbee 1999
Philip Conisbee, 'Rome , 1806–1820' in Tinterow and Conisbee 1999–2000, 97–115

Corboz 1985
André Corboz, *Canaletto: Una Venezia Immaginaria*, 2 vols, Milan 1985

Crouan 1982
Katharine Crouan, *John Linnell: A Centennial Exhibition*, exh. cat., Fitzwilliam Museum, Cambridge, and Yale Center for British Art, New Haven 1982

Daston and Galison 2010
Lorraine Daston and Peter Galison, *Objectivity*, New York 2010

Davies 1992
Maurice Davies, *Turner as Professor: the Artist and Linear Perspective*, exh. cat., Tate Gallery, London 1992

Delaborde 1861
Henri Delaborde, 'Les dessins de M. Ingres au Salon des Arts-Unis', *Gazette des Beaux-Arts*, vol. 9, 1 March 1861, 257–69

Delaborde 1870
Henri Delaborde, *Ingres, sa vie, ses travaux, sa doctrine d'après les notes manuscrites et les lettres du maître*, Paris, 1870

della Francesca 1470
Piero della Francesca, *De Prospectiva Pingendi*, c. 1470 (known in 7 MSS versions)

De Marchi 1994
Andrea De Marchi, 'Domenico Veneziano alla mostra degli Uffizi: Appunti e verifiche', *Kermes* 7, no. 20, May-August 1994, 30–40

De Montrond 1868
Maxime Fourcheux de Montrond, *Ingres: étude biographique et historique*, Paris and Lille 1868

Dethloff, Murdoch, Sloan and Elam 2015
Diana Dethloff, Tessa Murdoch, Kim Sloan and Caroline Elam (eds.), *Burning Bright: Essays in Honour of David Bindman*, London 2015

Dollond 1830
Description of the camera lucida, an instrument for drawing in true perspective, and for copying, reducing, or enlarging other drawings : to which is added ... A letter on the use of the camera by Capt. Basil Hall ..., London 1830

Dubrueil 1665
Jean Dubrueil, *L'Art universel des fortifications*, Paris 1665

Jean Dubreuil, *La Perspective Pratique*, 2nd edn, 3 vols., Paris 1679 (English trans. *Perspective Practical. Or, A Plain and Easie Method of True and Lively Representing all Things to the Eye at a Distance, by the Exact Rules of Art*, London 1691)

Edgerton 1975
Samuel Y. Edgerton, *The Renaissance Rediscovery of Linear Perspective*, New York 1975

Elkins 1991
James Elkins, 'The Case Against Surface Geometry', *Art History* 14, 1991, 143–74

Elkins 1994
James Elkins, *The Poetics of Perspective*, Ithaca 1994

Fiorentini 2006
Erna Fiorentini, 'Camera Obscura vs Camera Lucida – Distinguishing early nineteenth century modes of seeing', *Max-Planck-Institut für Wissenschaftsgeschichte*, vol. 307, 2006, 1–38

Fiorentini 2021
Erna Fiorentini, *Genealogy of Popular Science: From Ancient Ecphrasis to Virtual Reality*, New York 2021, 367–90

Fleming-Williams 1990
Ian Fleming-Williams, *Constable and his Drawings*, London 1990

Florensky 2002
Pavel Florensky, 'Reverse Perspective' (1919), in *Beyond Vision: Essays on the Perception of Art,* ed. Nicoletta Misler, trans. Wendy Salmond, London 2002, 197–272

Ford 1939
Brinsley Ford, 'Ingres's Portrait Drawings of English People at Rome, 1806–1820', *The Burlington Magazine,* no. 436, vol. 75, July 1939, 3–13

Galichon 1861a
E. Galichon, 'Description des dessins de M. Ingres exposés au Salon des Arts-Unis', *Gazette des Beaux-Arts*, vol. 9, 1861, 343–82

Galichon 1861b
E. Galichon 'Dessins de M. Ingres', *Gazette des Beaux-Arts*, vol. 11, 1861, 38–48

Galichon 1861c
Emile Galichon, *Catalogue de dessins tirés de collections d'amateurs et exposés dans les Salons des arts-unis*, Paris 1861

Gayford 2021
Martin Gayford, *Spring Cannot be Cancelled*, London 2021

Gay-Lussac and Arago 1823
Joseph-Louis Gay-Lussac and François Arago, 'Sur la chambre claire (camera lucida). Par le Professeur J.B. Amici, de Modène. Traduit de l'italien,' *Annales de Chimie et Physique*, vol. 22, 1823, 137–55

Gibson et al. 2017
E. Gibson, R. Futrell, J. Jara-Ettinger, K. Mahowald, L. Bergen, S. Ratnasingam, M. Gibson, S.T. Piantadosi and B.R. Conway, 'Color Naming Across Language Reflects Color Use', *Proceedings of the National Academy of Sciences*, vol. 114 (40), 2017, 10785–90

Gioseffi 1959
Decio Gioseffi, *Canaletto: il Quaderno della Galleria Veneziane e l'Impiego della Camera Ottica* (Istituto di Storia dell'Arte Antica e Moderna, no. 9), Trieste 1959

Gombrich (1995) 2014
E.H. Gombrich, *Shadows: The Depiction of Cast Shadows in Western Art*, New Haven and London 2014

Gounod 1896
Charles Gounod, *Mémoires d'un artiste*, Paris 1896

Gowing 1952
Lawrence Gowing, *Vermeer*, London 1952

's Gravesande 1711
G.J. 's Gravesande, *Essai de Perspective*, The Hague 1711

Guérin 1995
Marcel Guérin, *Lettres de Degas*, Paris (1945), 2nd edn 1995

Hammond and Austin 1987
John H. Hammond and Jill Austin, *The Camera Lucida in Art and* Science, Bristol 1987

Hockney 1977
David Hockney, *David Hockney by David Hockney*, London 1977

Hockney (2001) 2006
David Hockney, *Secret Knowledge. Rediscovering the Lost Techniques of the Old Masters*, London (2001), edn 2006

Hockney 2018
David Hockney, *Something New in Painting (and Photography) [and even Printing]*, with an essay by Laurence Weschler, New York 2018

Hockney and Devaney 2021
David Hockney in conversation with Edith Devaney, in *David Hockney: The Arrival of Spring, Normandy, 2020*, exh. cat., Royal Academy of Arts, London, 2021

Hockney and Gayford 2011
David Hockney and Martin Gayford, *A Bigger Message. Conversations with David Hockney*, London 2011

Hockney and Gayford 2016
David Hockney and Martin Gayford, *A History of Pictures, From the Cave to the Computer Screen*, London and New York 2016

Horn 1977
B.K.P. Horn, 'Understanding Image Intensities (sic),' *Artificial Intelligence*, vol. 8, no. 2, 1977, 201–31

Jardine 2020
Boris Jardine, 'Wollaston's Experimental Camera Lucida at the Whipple Museum, c. 1806', *Bulletin of the Scientific Instrument Society*, vol. 144, 2020, 41–43

Jelley 2017
Jane Jelley, *Traces of Vermeer*, Oxford 2017

Jones and Galison 2013
Caroline A. Jones and Peter Galison, eds., *Picturing Science, Producing Art*, London and New York: Routledge (1998) edn 2013

Kahn 1907
Gustave Kahn, 'Louis Legrand et son oeuvre', *L'Art et Le Beau*, no. 5, 1907, 1–36

Kauffmann 1984
C.M. Kauffmann, *John Varley 1778–1842*, London 1984

Keele and Pedretti 1997–80
Kenneth Keele and Carlo Pedretti, *Leonardo da Vinci. A Corpus of Anatomical Drawings at Windsor Castle*, 3 vols., London and New York 1997–80

Kemp 1978
Martin Kemp, 'Science, non-science and nonsense: The interpretation of Brunelleschi's perspective', *Art History* 1, 1978, 134–61

Kemp 1990
Martin Kemp, *The Science of Art. Optical Themes in Western Art from Brunelleschi to Seurat,* London and New Haven 1990

Kemp 2007
Martin Kemp, 'Imitation, Optics and Photography: Some Gross Hypotheses', in *Inside the Camera Obscura – Optics and Art under the Spell of the Projected Image*, ed. Wolfgang Lefrevre, Berlin 2007, 243–64

Kemp, Criminisi and Kang 2004
Martin Kemp, Antonio Criminisi and Sing Bing Kang, 'Reflections of Reality in Jan van Eyck and Roger Campin', *Historical Methods*, vol. III, 2004, 109–21

Kemp and Criminisi 2005
Martin Kemp and Antonio Criminisi, 'Paolo Uccello's "Rout of San Romano": Order from Chaos', *New*, vol. I, 2005, 84–89

Klonk 1996
Charlotte Klonk, *Science and the Perception of Nature*, New Haven and London 1996

Kuehni and Schwarz 2008
Rolf. G. Kuehni and Andreas Schwarz, *Color Ordered: A Survey of Color Order Systems from Antiquity to the Present*, Oxford and New York 2008

Lami 1882
Eugène-Oscar Lami, *Dictionnaire encyclopédique et biographique de l'industrie et des arts industriels*, vol. 2, Paris 1882

Lapauze 1901
Henry Lapauze, *Les dessins de J.-A. Ingres du Musée de Montauban,* Paris 1901

Lefrevre 2007
Wolfgang Lefrevre, ed., *Inside the Camera Obscura – Optics and Art under the Spell of the Projected Image*, Berlin 2007

Levey 1989a
Michael Levey, *The National Gallery Collection*, London, 1989

Levey 1989b
Michael Levey, 'Canaletto as artist of the urban scene', in Katherine Baetjer and J.G. Links (eds), *Canaletto*, exh. cat., Metropolitan Museum of Art, New York, 1989, 17–29

Libson 2005
Cornelius Varley: The Art of Observation, exh. cat. Lowell Libson, with contributions from Timothy Wilcox, Michael Pidgley, Huon Mallalieu and Peter Bower, Lowell Libson, London 2005

Links 1977
J.G. Links, *Canaletto and His Patrons*, London 1977

Lucas et al. 2020
R.J. Lucas, A.E. Allen, N. Milosavljevic, R. Storchi and T. Woelders, 'Can We See with Melanopsin?', *Annual Review of Vision Science*, 6:15.1–15.16, 2020

McLaren and Brown 1991
Neil McLaren revised by Christopher Brown, *The Dutch School, 1600–1900*, 2 vols., National Gallery London, 1991

Mamassian and Goutcher 2001,
Pascal Mamassian and Ross Goutcher, 'Prior knowledge on the illumination position', *Cognition*, vol. 81(1), B1–B9

Mamassian 2008
Pascal Mamassian, 'Ambiguities and conventions in the perception of visual art', *Vision Research*, vol. 48, no. 20, 2143–53,

Miller 1983
Julia Isabel Miller, 'Major Florentine altarpieces from 1430 to 1450', unpublished PhD dissertation, Columbia University, New York, 1983

Moffitt 1997
John F. Moffitt, 'Domenico Veneziano's "Saint Lucy" Altarpiece: The case for "uterine perspective"', *Source: Notes in the History of Art* 16, no. 4, Summer 1997, 14–24

Morrison-Low and Christie 1984
A.D. Morrison-Low and J.R.R. Christie, eds., *'Martyr of Science': Sir David Brewster 1781–1868*, Edinburgh 1984

Munro 1996
Jane Munro, *John Downman 1750–1824. Landscapes, figures studies and portraits of 'Distinguished persons'*, Cambridge 1996

Munro 2014
Jane Munro, *Silent Partners. Artist and Mannequin from Function to Fetish*, London and New Haven 2014

Naef 1977
Hans Naef, *Die Bildniszeichnungen von J.-A.-D. Ingres*, Bern, vol. I, 1977

Naef 1978
Hans Naef, *Die Bildniszeichnungen von J.-A.-D. Ingres*, Bern, vol. II, 1978

Olby, Cantor, Christie and Hodge
R.C. Olby, G.N. Cantor, J.R.R. Christie and M. Hodge, eds., *Companion to the History of Modern Science,* London and New York 1990

Paley and Phillips 1973
Morton D. Paley and Michael Phillips (eds.), *William Blake: Essays in honour of Sir Geoffrey Keynes*, Oxford 1973, 294–304

Palmer and Schloss 2010
S.E. Palmer and K.B. Schloss, 'An ecological valence theory of human color preference', *Proceedings of the National Academy of Sciences*, vol. 107 (19), 8877–82

Parker 1948
K.T. Parker, *The Drawings of Antonio Canaletto in the Collection of His Majesty the King at Windsor Castle*, Oxford and London 1948

Payne 1982
Christiana Payne, 'John Linnell and Samuel Palmer in the 1820s', *The Burlington Magazine*, March, vol. 124, no. 948, 1982, 131–36

Pickering 1995
Andrew Pickering, *The Mangle of Practice: Time, Agency, and Science*, Chicago and London 1995

Pidgely 1972
Michael Pidgely, 'Cornelius Varley, Cotman and the Graphic Telescope', *The Burlington Magazine*, November 1972, vol. 114, 781–86

Pignatti 1958
Terisio Pignatti, *Il Quaderno di Disegni del Canaletto alle Gallerie di Venezia*, 2 vols., Milan 1958

Prieur 2012
Jérôme Prieur, *Ingres en miroir*, Paris and New York 2012

Razzall and Whitaker 2017
Rosie Razzall and Lucy Whitaker, eds., *Canaletto and the Art of Venice*, exh. cat., The Queen's Gallery, Buckingham Palace, Royal Collection Trust 2017

Regan et al. 2001
B.C. Regan, C. Julliot, B. Simmen, F. Viénot, P. Charles-Dominique, and J.D. Mollon, 'Fruits, Foliage and the Evolution of Primate Colour Vision', *Philosophical Transactions of the Royal Society London,* B:356, 2001, 229–83

Reverdy 1997
Georges Reverdy, *L'histoire des routes de France. Du Moyen-Âge à la Révolution*, Paris 1997

Richter 1970
The Literary Works of Leonardo da Vinci, ed. J.P. Richter, 2 vols., 3rd edn, Oxford 1970

Rowley 2010
Neville Rowley, 'Pittura di luce: la manière claire dans la peinture du Quattrocento', PhD dissertation, Université Paris-Sorbonne, 2010

Rowley 2017
Neville Rowley, 'Domenico Veneziano 1925: una predella ricomposta', in *Il mestiere del conoscitore: Roberto Longhi*, eds. Anna Maria Ambrosini Massari, Andrea Bacchi, Daniele Benati, Aldo Galli, Bologna 2017, 103–121

Ruurs 1983
Rob Ruurs, '"Even If It Is Not Architecture": Perspective Drawings by Simon de Vlieger and Willem van de Velde the Younger', *Simiolus: Netherlands Quarterly for the History of Art*, vol. XIII, 1983, 189-200

Ryskamp 1990
Charles Ryskamp, 'A Cornelius Varley sketchbook in the Morgan Library', *Master Drawings*, Autumn 1990, vol. 28, no. 3, 344–59

Seddon 1945
R. Seddon, 'Turner and Cotman: two Portraits by Cornelius Varley', *The Burlington Magazine*, August 1945, vol. 87, no. 509, 202–05

Smith 2002
Greg Smith, *Thomas Girtin: the Art of Watercolour*, exh. cat., Tate Britian, London 2002

Steadman 2002
Philip Steadman, *Vermeer's Camera: Uncovering the Truth Behind the Masterpieces*, Oxford 2002

Sykes 2011
Christopher Simon Sykes, *Hockney: The Biography. Volume 1 (1937–1975)*, London 2011

Tinterow and Conisbee 1999–2000
Garry Tinterow and Philip Conisbee, eds., *Portraits by Ingres. Image of an Epoch*, exh. cat., The National Gallery, London, The National Gallery of Art, Washington DC, and The Metropolitan Museum of Art, New York, 1999–2000

Torrini 2012
Annalisa Perissa Torrini, *Canaletto: Il Quaderno Veneziano*, Venice 2012

Usselman 2015
Melvyn C. Usselman, *Pure Intelligence: The Life of William Hyde Wollaston*, Chicago and London 2015

Varley 1845
Cornelius Varley, *A Treatise on Optical Drawing Instruments,* London 1845

Varley Jeffery 1997–98
John Varley Jeffery, 'Cornelius Varley: artist and scientist', *RSA History Study Group*, 1997–98, n.p.

Vitolo 2018
Paola Vitolo, ed., *Progetti digitali per la storia dell'arte medievale (Archeologia e calcolatori,* supplemento 10) 2018

Watt and Bradshaw 2002
Simon J. Watt, Mark F. Bradshaw, 'Binocular information in the control of prehensile movements in multiple-object scenes', *Spat. Vis.*, vol. 15(2), 2002, 141–55

Welliver 1973
Warman Welliver, 'The Symbolic Architecture of Domenico Veneziano and Piero della Francesca', *The Art Quarterly* 36, 1973, 1–30

Wheelock 1977
Arthur Wheelock, *Perspective, Optics and Delft Artists around 1650*, London and New York 1977

White 1957
John White, *The Birth and Rebirth of Pictorial Space*, London 1957

Wohl 1980
Hellmut Wohl, *The Paintings of Domenico Veneziano, ca. 1410–1461: A Study in Florentine Art of the Early Renaissance,* New York 1980

Young 1804
Thomas Young, 'The Bakerian Lecture. Experiments and Calculations Relative to Physical Optics', *Philosophical Transactions of the Royal Society of London* 1804, 1–16

Zanetti 1771
Antonio Zanetti, *Della Pittura Veneziana e delle Opere Pubbliche de' Veneziani Maestri*, Giambatista Albrizzi, Venice 1771

Index

Author biographies

Francesca Aimi is a PhD candidate in the Department of History of Art at the University of Cambridge. Her research explores the role of Domenico Veneziano in mid-15th-century Florence by studying his key works in their specific contexts.

Luca Brunke is an AHRC-funded PhD student, working on a collaborative doctoral project 'Research-based 3D modelling of Renaissance built environments', jointly supervised by the University of Exeter and the National Gallery, London. He has previously worked as a researcher on the Florence4D project.

Donal Cooper is Associate Professor in Italian Renaissance Art at the University of Cambridge. He has published widely on the ecclesiastical art and architecture of late medieval and Renaissance Italy; his co-authored book *The Making of Assisi* (2013) won the 2014 Art Book prize. He has extended his work on sacred space through digital humanities, most recently as Co-Investigator on the Florence4D project.

Martin Gayford is art critic of the *Spectator* and the author of studies of Michelangelo, John Constable, Lucian Freud and Vincent van Gogh. He wrote *A History of Pictures* (2016) and *Spring Cannot be Cancelled* (2021) in collaboration with David Hockney and also published *A Bigger Message* (2012), a volume of conversations with Hockney.

Gabriel Hemery is an award-winning author, tree photographer, and forest scientist. He is the author of four books (fiction and nonfiction) including *The New Sylva* (2014), and is currently writing a guide to Scotland's forests. He co-founded and is Chief Executive of Sylva Foundation.

Anya Hurlbert is Professor of Visual Neuroscience at Newcastle University and former Scientific Trustee of the National Gallery. She specializes in the perception of colour and light. In addition to original scientific papers, her publications include 'Colour and Vision' (in *Vision*, 2021), 'Understanding Colour Perception and Preference' (in *Colour Design: Theories and Applications*, 2017) and 'The Perceptual Quality of Colour' (*Handbook of Experimental Phenomenology*, 2013).

Boris Jardine works on the history of scientific instrumentation, with a particular focus on the instrument trade in Britain, 1550–1700. He has also written extensively about the history of optical instruments. He is currently Co-Investigator on the AHRC-funded project 'Tools of Knowledge: Modelling the Creative Communities of the Scientific Instrument Trade, 1550–1914', at the Whipple Museum of the History of Science, University of Cambridge.

Martin Kemp is Emeritus Professor of the History of Art at the University of Oxford. He specializes in the relationship of images in art and science. Relevant publications include *The Science of Art. Optical Themes in Western Art from Brunelleschi to Seurat* (1990), *Seen and Unseen. Art, Science, and Intuition from Leonardo to the Hubble Telescope* (2006), and *Structural Intuitions. Seeing Shapes in Art and Science* (2016).

Zoe Kourtzi is Professor of Experimental Psychology and Cognitive Computational Neuroscience at the University of Cambridge and the Angharad Dodds John Fellow at Downing College. Her work focuses on understanding the role of lifelong learning and brain plasticity in enabling humans of all ages to translate sensory experience into adaptive behaviours. Her publications include reviews in *Annual Review of Neuroscience, Current Opinion in Neurobiology, Visual Neuroscience*, as well as 'Neural Codes for Shape Perception' (in *Brain Mapping: An Encyclopedic Reference*, Academic Press), 'Visual learning for optimal decisions in the human brain' (in *Object Categorization: Computer and Human Vision Perspectives*).

Anne Lyles is an independent art historian specializing in late 18th- and early 19th-century British landscape painting. She worked at Tate Britain for 25 years, and has written widely on the art of J.M.W.Turner, John Constable and British watercolours. Recent publications include essays in *Turner and Constable: Sketching from Nature* (2013) and *Late Constable* (2021).

Jane Munro is Keeper of Paintings, Drawings and Prints at the Fitzwilliam Museum, Cambridge. She specializes in European painting and drawing of the 19th and early 20th centuries, and has curated numerous exhibitions, many with an interdisciplinary emphasis.

Fabrizio Nevola is Professor of Art History and Visual Culture at the University of Exeter. He works on the urban and architectural history of Early Modern cities, with a particular focus on public space, most recently adopting digital art history approaches in collaborative research, as with the Florence4D project. He is the author of *Siena: Constructing the Renaissance City* (2007) and *Street Life in Renaissance Italy* (2020).

Philip Steadman is Emeritus Professor of Urban and Built Form Studies at University College London. He currently has a Fellowship from the Leverhulme Trust for a project on 'Canaletto's Camera'. He is the author of *Vermeer's Camera* (2001) and *Renaissance Fun* (2021).

Andrew Welchman is a neuroscientist and entrepreneur. He is Executive Vice President for Impact at Ieso digital health, and formerly Head of Neuroscience and Mental Health at the Wellcome Trust and Professor of Neural Intelligence at the University of Cambridge. His expertise is in human brain imaging, behavioural science, mental health science, and the application of machine learning to solve biological problems. In addition to original scientific papers, he has published reviews in *Annual Review of Vision Science* and *Current Opinion in Neurobiology.*

Photographic credits

All works by David Hockney © The David Hockney Foundation unless otherwise stated

© 2021. Photo Scala, Florence - courtesy of the Ministero Beni e Att. Culturali e del Turismo: fig. 145

© The American Philosophical Society: fig. 71

© Anya Hurllbert: figs. 128, 129

Arts Council Collection, Southbank Centre, London. Photo: Richard Schmidt: fig. 19

© Ashmolean Museum, University of Oxford, WA1850.31: fig. 24

Bibliothèque nationale de France: fig. 112

© The Board of Trustees of the Science Museum, London/Science & Society Picture Library. All rights reserved: fig. 84

Bodleian Libraries, University of Oxford: figs. 85–87

© The David Hockney Foundation. Photo: Christie's: fig. 21

© The David Hockney Foundation. Photo: Fabrice Gibert: figs. 13, 26

© The David Hockney Foundation. Photo: Michelle Wilson: figs. 15–17

© The David Hockney Foundation. Photo: Parker Kay: figs. 18, 34, 114, 115a–l, 125

© The David Hockney Foundation. Photo: Prudence Cuming Associates Ltd.: fig. 121

© The David Hockney Foundation. Photo: Richard Schmidt figs. 25, 27, 41–43, 48, 56, 97–102, 116, 118–20

© Detroit Institute of Arts / Gift of W. R. Valentiner / Bridgeman Images: fig. 94

© Fine Art Images / Bridgeman Images: figs. 96a,b

© The Fitzwilliam Museum, Cambridge figs. 33, 45, 47, 56–58, 62–63, 66–67, 69, 70, 103–07, 109–10, 113, 143–45

Gallerie dell' Accademia di Venezia / su concessione del Ministerio della Cultura: fig. 88

Getty Research Institute: figs. 30, 54–55

© George Lawson: fig. 23

Hamilton Kerr Institute: fig. 151

© History of Science Museum, University of Oxford: fig. 82

The J. Paul Getty Museum, Los Angeles: fig. 26

Luca Brunke/Donal Cooper: figs. 149–50, 152

Luisa Ricciarini / Bridgeman Images: fig. 130

© Museum Prinsenhof Delft. Loan Cultural Heritage Agency of the Netherlands (photo Tom Haartsen): fig. 31

© The National Gallery, London: figs. 49–52

Courtesy National Gallery of Art, Washington: fig. 148

National Maritime Museum, Greenwich, London, Herschel Collection: fig. 78

© Nationalmuseum/ Erik Cornelius: fig. 111

© Philip Tabor and Philip Steadman: figs. 90, 92

Reproduced courtesy of Thames & Hudson, London: figs 1 and 37

Royal Collection Trust / © Her Majesty Queen Elizabeth II 2021: figs. 59, 93

Scala, Florence - courtesy of the Ministero Beni e Att. Culturali e del Turismo: fig. 32

Scala, Florence. Photo © Raffaello Bencini: fig. 141

Courtesy Seyla Martayan: fig. 89

© Siân Lewis: fig. 45

Sotheby's: fig. 95

© Tate Images: figs. 64–65, 79–81, 83

Tretyakov Gallery, Moscow, Russia/Bridgeman Images: fig. 40

© The Trustees of the British Museum: figs. 53, 68

© Victoria and Albert Museum, London: fig. 108

Whipple Museum of the History of Science, University of Cambridge: figs. 74–76

© The Whitworth, The University of Manchester. Photography by Michael Pollard: fig. 60

From the Woburn Abbey Collection: fig. 91

© The Wordsworth Trust, Dove Cottage, Grasmere: fig. 61

Yale University Library (CC BY 4.0): fig. 72

Courtesy Yale Representation Limited: figs. 146–47